grammar = teaches us to speak well.   49

phoneme defined, p.152

alternations ≠ transformati

    Saussure likewise: p.26

exceptions = harbingers of future, 52

Automatic alternation? 23

A

Baudouin de Courtenay

ANTHOLOGY

Indiana University Studies

in the

History and Theory of Linguistics

A

Baudouin de Courtenay

A N T H O L O G Y

The Beginnings of Structural
Linguistics

By Jan Baudouin de Courtenay
Translated and edited with an introduction by

Edward Stankiewicz

Indiana University Press

BLOOMINGTON / LONDON

Published in Canada by Fitzhenry & Whiteside Limited, Don Mills, Ontario

Library of Congress catalog card number: 78–135012

ISBN: 253–31120–9

Manufactured in the United States of America

CONTENTS

A

Baudouin de Courtenay

ANTHOLOGY

Baudouin de Courtenay:

His Life and Work

1. The rise of structural linguistics in the twentieth century has been associated in the West with the seminal book of Ferdinand de Saussure, *Cours de linguistique générale*, which was published posthumously (in 1916) by his students A. Sechehaye and Ch. Bally on the basis of his lectures at the University of Geneva. During his lifetime de Saussure had published (at the age of 19) only one book, the *Mémoire sur le système primitif des voyelles dans les langues indo-européennes* (1878), which was perhaps as important for the further development of linguistics as the *Cours*, although it was primarily a diachronic study, while the *Cours* tried to formulate the "general," synchronic principles of language. The implications of the *Mémoire* were stated succinctly by A. Meillet: "le *Mémoire*," he writes, "apportait, par une innovation, un système cohérent qui embrassait tout les faits, mettait à leur place les faits connus. . . . Des hors il n'était plus permis d'ignorer à propos d'aucune question, que chaque langue forme un système où tout se tient."[1]

De Saussure's monograph was highly evaluated also by Baudouin de Courtenay, who was at the time of its publication professor at the University of Kazan': "De Saussure's discovery of the vowel alternations is crucial for the understanding of Indo-European morphology. . . . It is the great merit of de Saussure to have emphasized the role of phonetic relations within the morphological structure of words," a phenomenon which Baudouin preferred to call, in the terminology of the Kazan' school, "morphologization of phonetic differences" (1909 (2), 219).*

* For the references to Baudouin's works see p. 48.

While Baudouin de Courtenay was in Kazan' working out his theory of "semasiologization and morphologization of phonetic differences," i.e., of the function of sounds in the lexical and grammatical system of a language, de Saussure was occupied with the formulation of his "phonétique sémiologique," a discipline he defined as dealing with "des sons dans chaque idiome en tant qu'ayant une valeur pour l'idée."[2] De Saussure did not, however, publish his findings, for he was ridden with doubts about the validity of his new method and was deeply troubled about the consistency and cohesion of his new, synchronic approach to language.[3]

Unlike de Saussure, who lived in the hub of linguistic activity, which was at that time dominated by a genetic approach to language, Baudouin de Courtenay moved boldly ahead with a small following of students to elaborate and to publish his findings, for in the remote Russian city of Kazan' he was more or less immune to the criticisms and attacks of his Western and Russian colleagues.

Both men were thus essentially set on the same course of inquiry, which amounted to no more nor less than a complete overhaul of contemporary linguistics. Their principal goal was a description of language as it is, and not as it was, or how it came about—a goal that, in the words of Baudouin de Courtenay, could only be accomplished through "a radical revision of [linguistic] principles and methods" that would be predicated in the first place on the coining of a "completely new terminology" and, in the second place, on a "reformulation of the relations of linguistic elements" (1909, 261). De Saussure echoes these statements: "En matière de la langue on s'est toujours contenté d'opérer sur des unités mal définies," and "la linguistique travaille sans cesse sur de concepts forgés par les grammairiens, et dont on ne sait s'ils correspondent réellement a des facteurs constitutifs du système de la langue."[4]

The striking similarities of formulation and outlook between the Polish and French scholars were not the result of mere convergence of ideas. Baudouin de Courtenay followed the linguistic literature of his time closely (as attested by the long biographical lists attached to his programs of lectures and books) and, as we have seen, he regarded de Saussure as a true innovator in linguistic theory, whereas de Saussure's writings reveal an intimate familiarity with Baudouin's thought, to the extent that some passages of the *Cours* echo almost verbatim Baudouin's formulations. Baudouin and his pupil, Kruszewski, were also singled out by de Saussure as

4

the only European scholars who truly contributed to linguistic theory: "Baudouin de Courtenay et Kruszewski ont été plus près que personne d'une vue théorique de langue; cela sans sortir de considérations linguistiques pures; ils sont d'ailleurs ignorés de la généralité de savants occidentaux."[5] The intellectual affinity between Baudouin de Courtenay and de Saussure was recognized by other linguists, for example by de Saussure's disciple, Meillet, who wrote that between the Russian and French schools of linguistics "on ne constate du reste . . . aucune différence essentielle de principes et de méthodes,"[6] whereas some of Baudouin's disciples are known to have claimed that de Saussure's *Cours* contained nothing that they had not already learned from Baudouin.[7] Neither of these claims were quite accurate, for although Baudouin and de Saussure were guided by a common objective and principles, they differed in their emphasis on and the solutions given to various linguistic problems.

It would, however, be an oversimplification to credit only Baudouin de Courtenay and de Saussure with the revival of general linguistics and the broadening of its scientific horizon. As early as in the seventies and eighties of the last century, i.e., at the very height of the Neogrammarian movement, a reaction to the one-sided historicism and blunt empiricism of the "comparativists" had already set in. This reaction started mostly outside of Germany, since the Leipzig school of linguists had, according to H. Schuchardt, succeeded in silencing all other linguists in Germany.[8] Some of these linguistic reformers propounded ideas which were clearly at variance with Neogrammarian dogma; thus the American W. D. Whitney emphasized, like de Saussure, the social character of language and its importance as a system of signs; in France, M. Bréal and A. Meillet were raising the questions of meaning and of semantic change; G. I. Ascoli and H. Schuchardt (of Graz), like Baudouin de Courtenay, undermined the notion of linear development of languages through the study of linguistic geography and language mixture. Schuchardt stressed, like Baudouin de Courtenay, the creative role of the speaker in linguistic change; G. von der Gabelentz, like de Saussure and Baudouin de Courtenay, focused attention on the general and synchronic aspects of language; the Swiss J. Winteler, the Englishman H. Sweet and the Russian Caucasianist P. Uslar were about to arrive, independently of Baudouin de Courtenay, at the concept of the phoneme. This ferment in European and American linguistics did not, however, procede in a straight line, but, like all novel intellectual currents, followed a somewhat meandering course. The boldest and most systematic among these innovators, de Saussure, Baudouin de Courtenay, and Kruszewski, were not themselves consistent in their views and shared, in fact, many tenets of the Neogrammarians, together with the scientific preconceptions of their time. Thus de Saussure believed for some time that a diachronic approach must precede the synchronic study of language, and that historical change is not subject to systematization, whereas Kruszewski and Baudouin were convinced that one of their main achievements was the discovery of the laws of analogy, in which they merely preceded the Neogrammarians. Baudouin shared with the latter, furthermore, a dualistic conception of language as a complex of physiological and psychological phenomena, and especially in his early writings he showed faith in the strict laws of causality and in the march of progress, leading to the greater "humanization" of language and to its greater simplicity determined by the principle of least effort. These positivistic and mechanistic elements that are ingrained in the thought of the Swiss and Polish linguists do not, however, diminish the novelty of their ideas, which formed the foundation of modern linguistics.

It may be pointless and unrewarding to compare the respective merits of Baudouin and de Saussure for the subsequent direction and development of twentieth-century linguistics. Neither of them produced a unified system or a mature work which would weave the various strands of their thought into one fabric. The impact of the *Cours* (whose elliptical and inconsistent statements can only in part be blamed on the notes of de Saussure's students) on twentieth-century linguistics is well known, and it has remained until now the most programmatic and most cited work of that linguistic trend which has become known in Europe and America as "structural linguistics" (a term that was actually coined by R. Jakobson). The work of Baudouin, on the other hand, has remained virtually unknown in the West, first because most of it was written in languages that are inaccessible to Western scholars (Polish and Russian), and second because it is scattered in journals and publications that are not readily available even in Eastern Europe (the 1963 Soviet edition of Baudouin's writings has now made most of them accessible in Russian). And yet it now seems possible to assert that the ideas of Baudouin have been more seminal and have withstood the test of time better than the structuralist ideas advanced by Ferdinand de Saussure. It will be remembered that the linguistic conception of de Saussure is organized around a set of dichotomies, or rather irreconcilable antinomies, which were apparently designed to overcome the blunt empiricism and mechanism of late nineteenth-century linguistics, and which include such well-known terms as *synchrony/diachrony, langue/parole, social/individual, paradigmatic/syntagmatic, external/internal* (approaches to language). Some of these terms and concepts were first formulated by the Kazan' linguists, who, as Baudouin tells us, developed at one time a veritable "mania" for coining new linguistic terminology (1895 [150]; 1903, 54ff.). To Baudouin and his followers we owe in addition such technical terms as "phoneme," "morpheme," "grapheme," "syntagm," "distinctive feature," "alternation," which have become the stock-in-trade of any practicing linguist. The polarities established by Baudouin were, on the other hand, less extreme than those introduced by de Saussure, and in consequence more realistic and fruitful. In place of an ordered synchrony, which is opposed to a disordered diachrony, Baudouin speaks of the laws of statics and dynamics that apply to history and to synchrony; and in place of a collective *langue* that is opposed to an individual *parole*, Baudouin recognizes the role of the speaker and the interaction between the conservative social norm and the creative, innovative power of the speaker in the speech act. For de Saussure language is only "form, not substance," whereas for Baudouin it is both form and substance. That is why for de Saussure "dans la langue il n'y a que des différences sans termes positifs,"[9] and why de Saussure defines the phonemes as having "une valeur purement oppositive, rélative, négative,"[10] while for Baudouin the phonemes are oppositional and relative, but at the same time consist of positive, phonetically definable properties. For de Saussure language is, like a game of chess, a tightly ordered, "algebraic" system of relations, whereas Baudouin admits fluctuations and free choice, as well as the constant interference of social, spatial, and temporal factors. De Saussure's *Cours* has, furthermore, remained a theoretical program, a guidepost for modern linguistics, whereas Baudouin's work has from the beginning had a more pragmatic orientation and has pointed the way to concrete, empirical investigations. Thus there is hardly a topic in modern linguistic research that has not in one way or another been inspired by Baudouin and for which he has not himself done the spadework. This is of course partly due to Baudouin's long and productive life, and partly to the fascination he holds for generations of linguists, beginning with his Kazan' disciples and continuing with his students in Europe and in America. The vitality of his thought, however, is mostly due to the activity of those linguists who were directly or indirectly associated with the Linguistic Circle of Prague, who have consciously continued in the course he set and who have more than any single "structuralist" group or school defined the landscape of modern linguistics. R. Jakobson's work on phonology and distinctive features; N. Trubetzkoy's research in Russian morphophonemics; L. Ščerba's, R. Jakobson's, and U. Weinreich's studies of "mixed languages" and areal diffusion; Jakovlev's and J. Vachek's contributions to graphemics; E. Polivanov's and L. Ščerba's work on the various levels of language and types of scientific notation; A. Martinet's and R. Jakobson's investigations in diachronic phonology; R. Jakobson's analysis of child-language—all are, in one way or another, the outgrowth and further elaboration of Baudouin's ideas and program. And what is even more striking is that Baudouin himself has clearly delineated (and indicated as the impending tasks of twentieth-century linguistics) a number of linguistic areas such as typology, language universals, sociology of language, and the relation of linguistics to other sciences, which are only now beginning to move into the forefront of linguistic research.

2. Jan Baudouin de Courtenay (whose full Christian name was actually Jan Ignacy Niecisław) was born on the first of March 1845 in Radzymin near Warsaw.

After the completion of high school (where his chief interest was mathematics), Baudouin entered the historical-philological faculty of the short-lived Polish University (Szkoła Główna) in Warsaw, where he received his master's degree in 1866. By ancestry a Frenchman and nominally a Catholic, he considered himself a Pole and an atheist. But having lived and taught most of his life in Russia, Austria, Latvia, and Poland, he was, in effect, a cosmopolitan who, in the words of Meillet, "a eu le maleur de n'appartenir tout à fait à aucun pays."[11] He could trace his origin to a long line of French aristocrats that included Baldwin, count of Flanders, the founder of the Latin Empire in Constantinople in the thirteenth century. His impoverished great-grandfather migrated to Poland, where he became colonel of artillery and head of the court-guard of the Polish king, August II. His grandfather was *Kammerherr* (Chamberlain) of the last king of Poland, Stanisław August Poniatowski, a man of letters, who translated Molière and wrote several books on mesmerism.

Baudouin continued his studies in comparative Indo-European, in Sanskrit, and in Slavic philology in Prague (under Schleicher), in Berlin (under Weber), in Jena, Leipzig, and St. Petersburg. He received a doctorate in Leipzig (in 1870) for previously published linguistic work, and a master's degree in St. Petersburg (where his Polish degree was not recognized) for his study on the Old Polish language before the fourteenth century.

An independent and searching spirit, he had respect neither for his Neogrammarian mentors in Leipzig (Leskien, Brugmann, Delbrück) nor for his Russian supervisor, I. I. Sreznevskij, whom he considered a dry and narrow-minded philologist. All his life he claimed to be self-taught, though he was obviously concerned (certainly in his early work) with similar problems as the former, and owed some of his interests (especially the one in Slovenian dialectology) to the latter. To Sreznevskij he was also indebted for his first position as docent (assistant professor) of comparative grammer at St. Petersburg University. In 1872 he was sent by the Russian Academy on a field trip to Southwestern Austria and Northern Italy to investigate the local Slovenian dialects. The main result of this field trip was his *Opyt fonetiki rez'janskix govorov (Phonetic Outline of the Rezija Dialects)* for which he was awarded the Russian doctorate in comparative Indo-European grammer. In conjunction with his Slovenian fieldwork, he came into personal contact with Ascoli, whose lectures he attended in Milan and who must have influenced his view on dialectology and on the mixed character of languages.

In the fall of 1875 Baudouin moved to Kazan', first as assistant professor, and, a year later, as full professor of comparative Indo-European linguistics and Sanskrit. The nine years spent in Kazan' mark the "Sturm and Drang" period of Baudouin's scholarly and pedagogical career. Although he tried his best to get out of this provincial, frontierlike Russian-Tartar city (as evidenced by his letters and pleas to Jagić), he found there a lively and exciting scholarly community, a group of brilliant disciples and followers (including

9

N. Kruszewski, V. Bogorodickij, S. Bulič, and the Turcologist V. Radloff), and immediate publication opportunities (in the *Zapiski* of Kazan' University). Baudouin's linguistic program subsequently became known as the teachings of the "Kazan' school," whose primary aim was—according to the testimony of one of his students— "the application of a strict scientific method to linguistics and the study of the modern [linguistic] ideas of European scholarship."[12]

In 1883 Baudouin de Courtenay moved to Dorpat (Tartu) to occupy the newly founded Chair in Comparative Slavic Grammar. In addition to Slavic linguistics, he continued to study and teach general linguistics, Baltic dialectology, and Lithuanian texts (Donelaitis). From Dorpat he transferred in 1893 to Cracow as professor of comparative linguistics and Sanskrit. His delight in being finally at a Polish university and in the company of an eminent colleague, J. Rozwadowski (a general linguist and Indo-Europeanist), and within the fold of the Polish Academy of Sciences was, however, short-lived. As a result of his attacks against the bureaucratic and nationalistic Austro-Hungarian administration, his five-year contract was not renewed, upon which Baudouin returned to Russia, to St. Petersburg, where he remained until the end of World War I. He again attracted and raised a new generation of outstanding linguists and Slavists (E. Polivanov, L. Ščerba, L. Jakubinskij, S. I. Bernštejn, M. Vasmer). But his commitment to social and political causes got him into personal difficulties there too. Because of a brochure in which he attacked the Czarist political suppression of national minorities (entitled "The Territorial and National Mark in Autonomy" and dedicated to "all patriots"), he received a two-year prison sentence (in 1913), which forced him to suspend his teaching and to spend several months in jail.

He was actually freed by the outbreak of World War I and he resumed for a brief period his teaching at St. Petersburg University. With the formation of an independent Polish state, he was invited to the Chair of Indo-European Linguistics at the University of Warsaw. He died November 3, 1929, at the age of 85.

Baudouin de Courtenay combined a profound belief and passion for science with an equally strong faith in the rights of man and social justice. He would make no compromise for reigning fashions, and he chided some of his compatriots for their obsequiousness to German scholarship ("a Russian or Pole," he said, "may also have original ideas" (1901 [217]). He had little patience with "nihilism" and "apathy" in science, with philological plodders and collectors of data. At the same time he believed that ideas are not the exclusive monopoly of "specialists," and he viewed his teaching as a venture to be shared with his students. He defended his students from unfair attacks and credited them with their discoveries and terminological inventions. "Kruszewski," he wrote on more than one occasion, "enlivened the intellectual atmosphere of Kazan'," "has taught me many things," and has been able "to develop the 'theory' of alternations more 'philosophically,' more comprehensively and more precisely than I myself have done, thanks mainly to his strict application of the analytic method" (1895 [150]).

His attitude toward Kruszewski was not, however, free of ambiguity and jealousy, as evidenced by the petty and ungenerous Necrology (1888) which he wrote upon the death, at the age of 37, of this brilliant Polish linguist.

Baudouin dedicated all of his long and active life to the study and understanding of language and languages. He embraced the nineteenth-century belief in "generalizations" and "laws," though he conceived them in a spirit quite different from that of his Western colleagues. He could speak and write a large number of languages (Polish, Russian, Slovenian, Czech, German, French, Italian, Lithuanian, Yiddish) and was a specialist in various Indo-European and other languages (Sanskrit, Latin, Slavic, Baltic; Turkic, Finno-Ugric; Ido, Esperanto).

During his life he was honored by many societies and universities, mostly for his work in historical linguistics. His more important work in general linguistics found almost no echo outside the circle of his immediate students and followers. Meillet himself, who paid him otherwise high tribute, considered him "le dernier survivant du grand renouvellement de la linguistique, et en particulier de la linguistique historique."[13] It is for this reason, and because of his deep modesty, that Baudouin could not divest himself of doubts concerning the value of his lifetime work or of the importance of his school. "Any mention of the so-called Kazan' school," he wrote, "is bound to evoke an ironic smile," "a playful operatic mood," if not "downright hostility. . . . The Moscow linguistic school [of Fortunatov] is quite a different matter; its founder is a scholar of great knowledge and has the ability to concentrate on a few problems; Moscow is a great city, and the Moscow school can boast of many disciples" (1903, 48).

He looked back with "bitterness" at the "fragments" and "pieces" in which he advanced his pioneering ideas, and he blamed his lack of training, his inability to concentrate, and his personal hardships for his failure to leave any "major unifying works." Like the other bold innovators in linguistic theory at the turn of the century, he was acutely aware of the incompleteness of his results and of being out of step with his own generation. This feeling must have been particularly poignant toward the end of his life, for in his native Poland he had almost no followers. In a late letter to Ułaszyn, one of his few Polish disciples, he wrote: "At every step I have met only blows and disappointments. . . . Laisse nous oublier que nous avons vécu."[14] It was the task of the following generations to vindicate his name and outstanding achievements.

3. It is generally agreed that the emergence of a structural approach to language is intimately connected with the formulation of the two interrelated concepts of system ("où tout se tient") and of invariant (with the corollary notion of variant) which modern linguistics has come to share with other sciences.[15] It must not, however, be forgotten that these concepts were first advanced in early nineteenth-century linguistics, though they were then given a somewhat different interpretation.

The idea of an "organic" whole (which determines the function and properties of the parts) as opposed to a "mechanical" system (in which the whole is a sum of its parts) was the credo of the Romantic philosophers of language, and it was clearly stated by W. v. Humboldt: "Es gibt nichts Einzelnes in der Sprache; jedes ihrer Elemente kündigt sich nur als Teil eines Ganzen an . . . [die Sprache] muss in jedem Augenblicke ihres Daseins dasjenige besitzen, was sie zu einem Ganzen macht."[16] But, since the sign cannot, according to Humboldt, be separated from what it designates (for it is neither the product of reason nor of social agreement), it follows that the study of language would remain a chimerical enterprise if it were to ignore "the dry mechanical analysis of its physical aspect." The analysis of language must recognize the mutual dependence of its external and "internal form": "Die Verbindung der Lautform mit den inneren Sprachgesetzen bildet die Vollendung der Sprachen, und der höchste Punkt dieser ihrer Vollendung beruht darauf, dass diese Verbindung . . . zu wahren und reinen Durchdringung werde."[17] The degree of "per-

fection" and "interpenetration," or of the "synthesis" of phonetic
matter with grammatical form, was, however, soon to be measured
(especially through the works of Schlegel and Steinthal) in terms of
"internal flexion" (i.e. the vowel alternations within the stem),
which was supposed to lend proof to the superiority of the "synthetic" languages over other types of linguistic structure.

Despite its reputed "atomism," nineteenth-century linguistics
also had a fairly clear conception of "invariance" which it applied
historically and not synchronically, for the actual aim of the comparative method was to reduce the *variant forms* of the Indo-
European languages to a common prototype, i.e. to original *in-
variants*.[18] But the subsequent refinement of this method led to a
stronger interest in the "formulas of correspondence" and in the
processes of phonetic change than in the reconstruction of the
proto-language. The success of the physical and biological sciences
inspired, further, the belief that language develops according to
natural and immutable laws that are independent of man and
society. Imbued with the notion that causality and determinism
are the only valid principles of science, linguists were no longer
content with "predicting" the past on the basis of the present, but
attempted to establish laws of change valid for all time. To admit
any exceptions to the "blind" and "necessary" forces of phonetic
change was, according to Leskien, to deny the scientific character
of our discipline, and the first thesis of the Neogrammarian program enunciated by H. Osthoff and K. Brugmann reads: "All
sound changes follow laws that are without exception [aus-
nahmslos] . . . for all speakers of a given speech community and for
all words in which the given sound occurs."[19] But when Osthoff
elaborated on these "laws" he felt it necessary to specify that the
boundary of any given dialect must be defined "as narrowly as
possible" ["so eng als möglich"],[20] while the second thesis of the
above-mentioned program had already made allowance for forms
that result from analogical levelling and thereby elude the effect
of the "phonetic laws." In the words of Baudouin, the vaunted
"phonetic laws" turned out to have a predictive power similar to
that of "meteorological" forecasts (1910 [276]). The concept of
phonetic laws thus underwent, toward the end of the nineteenth
century, the same transformations as the general concept of natural
law: From a universally valid principle applicable to all cases, it has
been demoted to a rule of uniformity and statistical regularity that

is not exempt from the workings of chance.[21] On a theoretical plane the new scientific mood is most clearly reflected in H. Paul's *Prinzipien der Sprachgeschichte* (1886). Linguistics, declares Paul, is not, like the natural sciences, a "science of laws," but a "historical science" that deals with unique, nonrepeatable events, and its hero is not abstract society, nor the no less abstract "Völkerpsychologie," but man and the individual speech-act (*Sprachtätigkeit*). "For between abstractions there can be no causal relations; these obtain only between real objects and [concrete] facts."[22] This attitude, in turn, prompted him to question the possibility of scientific hypotheses and generalizations about language and to deny the very existence of language as a social norm: "In reality we have to recognize as many languages as there are individuals."[23] The presumed aversion to theory and the call for plain fact gathering are also proclaimed by Osthoff and Brugmann, who urged the linguist "to leave the murky circle of his workshop, which is beclouded with hypotheses, and to step out into the clear air of palpable reality."[24] And since linguistic reality is made up in its entirety of "speaking individuals," the linguist deals, in effect, with only two types of phenomena: the physiological production of speech-sounds which are subject to mechanical change, and the psychological processes of association which generate new linguistic forms. This methodological dualism did not, however, seem to involve any contradiction, for in the final analysis both types of phenomena could be reduced to a common psychophysical or physiological base. "The constant interaction of phonetic laws and analogy formation," wrote Wundt, "becomes more comprehensible when we consider them not as disparate and opposing forces, but as conditions both of which are in some way ultimately rooted in the unitary psychophysical organization of man."[25] The *fin de siècle* was thus in linguistics (as in other sciences) a period of intellectual disarray in which its practitioners not only gave up faith in the integrating and explanatory function of science, but lost hold of the very object of their study, language. Having renounced the great explanatory schemes of history propounded by their predecessors, they clung to the positivistic belief in the "bare fact" which finds its explanation in a preceding fact, and to the psycho-physiological view of language as an activity that is shared by a given speech community by virtue of repetition and imitation. It was this mechanistic and atomistic conception of language that Baudouin de Courtenay set out to correct, even though he did not always succeed in shaking off its influence.

Baudouin de Courtenay has on various occasions summarized the main tenets of his "school," but none of his "statements of linguistic principles" (including the one reprinted on p. 213) can serve as an accurate measure of his theory of language, for they mix polemic and topical pronouncements with statements of a more general and lasting import. As a true "philosopher of language," Baudouin was always deeply absorbed in general linguistic questions, and utterances on these questions are scattered in all his books, articles, and even insignificant reviews. Baudouin saw the first and indispensable step toward a renewal of linguistics in its emancipation from the "philological and archeological approach" that had dominated it throughout the nineteenth century (1909, 237), and in its return to a synchronic analysis of language. "The study of living languages," he wrote, "must precede the study of extinct languages," as the study of any subject must proceed from the known to the unknown and not vice versa (1897 [215]). "When one is too absorbed in things that happened in the past," he quoted Descartes as saying, "one remains quite ignorant of things that happen in the present" (1909, 254). He proposed that each subject be first of all treated in terms of its own, intrinsic properties "without forcing upon it alien categories" (1897 [214]), for only thus can one gain an understanding of the "static laws and forces which act in the synchronic state of a language" (1876/77 [107]) as opposed to the dynamic laws and forces which condition the development of a language. What he held most against so-called comparative grammar was that it "works only with several dozens of roots" and does not attempt to "cover entire languages" with "fragments" but to provide "an insight into the entire structure of a given language" (1901 [216]). From this, he said, stem the "perverted methods of investigation" which characterize "philological linguistics" (1889 (2) [127]). Although Baudouin distinguished and emphasized the two dimensions of synchrony and diachrony and the two types of "laws and forces" that govern their difference, he was never tempted to exaggerate the importance of one at the expense of the other, nor to say with de Saussure that "tout dans la langue est histoire, . . . qu'elle se compose de faits, et non de lois," or that "tout ce qui semble organique dans la langue est en réalité contingent et complètement accidental."[26] On the contrary, even in his early Programs he pointed out the complementary aspects of permanence and change (1871 [71]; 1876/77 [93]), while in his later works he explores in detail the interplay of statics and dynamics and the presence of synchrony (i.e. of stability) in diachrony, and the penetration of diachrony (through the accumulation of historical layers) into synchrony.

Baudouin's conception of the tasks of linguistics differed in most other respects from that of his positivistic colleagues, whose scientific credo was "zuerst sammeln, dann erklären." "The goal of all science," he wrote, "is explanation," because "reality [is not] a heap of incoherent and disconnected phenomena" (1871 [72]). Observation and interpretation must go hand in hand, and though it is an empirical science, linguistics must not be content with pure induction but must make "the broadest possible use of the deductive method" (1871 [64]. He rejected as arbitrary the division between natural science as a science of "laws" and historical science (including linguistics) as a science of "facts." "All sciences dealing with comparison and generalization of details," he wrote, "are 'natural sciences' if they reveal the organization and regularity hidden in the phenomena, whereas they become 'historical sciences' if they dwell only on accidents and exceptions" (1881 (2)). The linguist must not be content with the registration of haphazard and sporadic facts (1877/78 [118]) but must attempt at each step to discover "the genuinely distinctive properties of language" and "the laws [which] are hidden in the depth, in the intricate combination of various elements" (1910 [276]).

The historical-comparative method, he insisted, is not the sole approach to language but constitutes only "a single moment in the history of our science," since "comparison is not an end but only a means" and "cannot be considered the monopoly of one or a few sciences" (1871 [56ff.]). The so-called phonetic laws which aspire to the status of "natural laws" are, in effect, no more than "observations" about the uniformity of phonetic correspondences (1910 [275]). Although Baudouin himself appears to have been a believer in strict historical determinism—"given the knowledge of the past," he wrote, we can "predict the further internal development of a language" (1876/77 [108])—he later abandoned this optimistic nineteenth-century viewpoint: "The assumption of 'sound laws' operating 'without exceptions,' of gradual, purely physiological change in a definite direction," he wrote, "is not confirmed by the actual facts of language and is in contradiction with its socio-psychological character" (1927 [283]). And when he contemplated the direction of morphological change, he formulated for himself —as he tells us—a theory which he labelled "evolutiones linguarum terrestrium." According to this theory the formal expression of some grammatical categories keeps alternating cyclically, "like a 'perpetuum mobile,' between suffixation and prefixation." "The result [of this change] is constant oscillation, vibration and eternal evolution which is reminiscent of the ebb and flow of the tides" (1930 [307]).

In opposing the reigning concern with historical change, Baudouin pointed out that "in spite of all the fluctuations and variations, we must note the presence of 'conservatism'" (1910 [269]) and that the concept of "statics" is applicable not only to synchrony but also to diachrony. The "laws of development in time should therefore be viewed as a counterpart to the laws of resistance to historical change," i.e. the laws of "dynamic stability" (1877/78 [116]); certain features are exempt from change, for "there is a limit to the changeability of sounds" (1876/77 [94]). The formula that "something is constantly being changed" should therefore be complemented by the formula that "something is constantly being preserved, something remains stable" (1910 [269]). The mere registration of phonetic, lexical, and formal differences between languages does not explain the direction of historical change. In describing the development of a given language, the linguist should rather attempt to identify "the general tendencies" which constitute "characteristic and invariant properties" (1871 [65]) and enable us to identify languages or entire groups of languages.

The theory of gradual, uninterrupted, and unidirectional change found, in Baudouin's opinion, a striking refutation in the phenomenon of language mixture which he had occasion to observe *in vivo* during his field work in Slovenia. Linguistic diffusion, he noted, took place both on the axis of spatial contiguity (between speakers of different languages and dialects living in adjacent areas), and on the axis of temporal succession (between speakers of different generations), though he did not fail to notice that it also operates at a "distance" (among nomads and migrants and between old and modern languages). Distrustful of genealogical reconstructions and bent on refuting the concept of linear development, Baudouin exaggerated the importance of language mixture (though probably no more than his contemporary, Schuchardt). Thus, he ascribed the phenomenon of "mazurzenie" in Polish dialects and the loss of free stress in West Slavic to the influence of a Finno-Ugric substratum, and the formation of Armenian to the mixture of the Indo-European with a Japhetic language (1901 [219ff.]). At the same time he made some truly cogent observations, such as that in linguistic diffusion the victory generally goes to those forms that are grammatically simpler. In addition to explaining the history of certain linguistic facts, the problem of languages in contact was for Baudouin connected with the synchronic issues of coexisting systems and the speaker's ability for code switching. In recognizing the coexistence of languages serving special social and expressive functions (e.g., argots, secret languages, languages of traders, and different styles of speech, such as slovenly, rapid, or solemn speech) he rejected the myth, so dear to the Neogrammarians, of a homogeneous society and an "average national language" (1871 [79]; 1910 [269]). He defended the usefulness of international artificial languages (against the attacks of Brugmann, Delbrück, and Leskien), arguing that "artificiality in language" or man's conscious participation in the fate of a language is only a matter of degree (1871 [52]; 1907 [256ff.]).

Baudouin's position also differed from that of most of his contemporaries with regard to the status of territorial dialects. The "phonetic laws" were, according to prevailing opinion, most tangibly at work in dialectal speech, which was allegedly least affected by foreign or cultural influences. Dialects were consequently regarded as the most reliable source for the reconstruction of an original language. "Only in the veins of dialect speech," wrote Osthoff, "flows pure, unadultered blood of millennia."[27] The belief that language varies from individual to individual led, on the other hand, to the conclusion (shared by such men as H. Paul, G. Paris, and J. Gilliéron) that dialect boundaries do not exist and are only an invention of the linguist.[28] Similar considerations weakened the faith in the accepted divisions of Indo-European languages, a faith some linguists (e.g., Brugmann and Förstermann) tried to salvage by comparing the largest possible number of diverse features. "One must view with utmost scepticism," wrote Delbrück, "all classifications of the Indo-European languages except the Asiatic group," whereas Meillet was of the opinion that the only valid criterion for defining a linguistic unity was "le sentiment des sujets parlants."[29] Baudouin, on the other hand, who was an experienced dialectologist and who came into contact with "mixed" German-Slovenian and Italo-Slovenian dialects, recognized that dialects could be described as independent linguistic entities, or what he called "linguistic individuals" (1875, IV). With respect to the Indo-European languages Baudouin also questioned the established classificatory schemes, quipping that "A. Schleicher built his classification (the "tree theory") on wood, whereas J. Schmidt built his (the "wave theory") on water (1909, 227), and arguing that "the genealogy of languages is not as simple as the pedigrees of nobility (1884 [312]). Genealogical classification was for him only one of the possible, and by no means the most important, way of grouping languages. "At the present state of our science . . . ," he wrote, "one cannot speak (in most cases) of a genetic classification in the strict sense of the word, but only of a scientific characterization of various groups of languages and dialects" (1877/78 [118]), for "what is important is to identify characteristic traits that are of general significance that pervade the phonetic and morphological structure of language and not disparate details of a secondary nature, or facts which are mere surrogates of the general features" (1884 [312]; 1871 [64]). He implemented this program by providing the first typological description of the Slavic phonemic systems and a brilliant outline of the phonological history of a Slavic language (Polish). What he tried to emphasize in his diachronic studies was not so much the phenomena of change as the phenomenon of "dynamic stability," and the "common tendencies" which define the limits of historical change and "determine the unique structure or composition of a given language" or group of languages (1877/78 [118]).

Just as he opposed the reduction of language to an aggregate of disparate facts, he resisted the efforts to treat the language of a community as a sum of individual speech-acts. "Language as a complex of constituent parts and categories," he wrote, "exists only *in potentia*" (1871 [68, 78]; 1889 (2) [134]), and must be distinguished from the "continuously recurrent process of social communication" and "knowledge and understanding of languages differ from [their] command more or less as knowledge of physiological processes differs from their performance" (1870 [70]). But the distinction *langue/parole* was not, in his opinion, reducible to the opposition "social product" vs. "individual activity," for he recognized that the speech-act itself is a social act, and that language opens to the speakers possibilities of choice which presume an active and creative process. "Language," he said, "is throughout a psycho-logical-social phenomenon" (1889 (1) [200]; 1889 (2) [139]; it is both "a tool and an activity," (1907 [256]) because "thinking and membership in society are the two basic conditions for language in the proper sense of the word" (1889 (2) [134]). The opposition between the individual and the collective "will be overcome if we adopt the concept of *collective individuality*" (1910 [275]). "The feeling for language is not merely a clever formula or will-o'-the-wisp but a real and objective phenomenon of language" (1902 [313]). Thus he returned to Humboldt's conception of language as a dialectical unity in which the "I" and the "Thou," the individual and the social, the inherited and the acquired constantly define and presuppose each other.

"Even the most ordinary and least scientifically trained mind performs tentative, unconscious, and partly conscious [linguistic] operations," Baudouin wrote in 1889; "the science of linguistics introduces nothing new in this respect; it only perfects and refines our thinking [about these processes], frees it from the accidents of chance, and substitutes a chain of conscious and clearly defined concepts for a mass of vague and diffuse ideas" ([128]). Linguistic activity is not, in other words, mere "repetition" and "imitation" but a process of "integration and systematization," of "uninterrupted semantization and classification" in which every word (be it even a nonsense word) is interpreted in terms of its phonetic and "structural" (i.e., morphological) affinity to other words. The phenomena of folk etymology and analogical levelling (which Baudouin called "morphological assimilation"), the grammatical mistakes made by children and the reinterpretation of foreign words are not, therefore, to be treated as a sign of "linguistic pathology," but rather as "a sign of the creative ability" of the speaker to "group isolated words into semantically well-defined patterns" (1915, 188ff.). This grouping, according to Baudouin, involves two principles of association that were first formulated by Kruszewski (who adopted them, in turn, from the English philosophers): association by similarity and association by contiguity. These two laws of association make the mass of words into a harmonious whole of coordinate systems (or nests) and ordered series (or rows)" (1889 (1), 184ff.). But unlike Kruszewski, who applied these principles only to morphology, Baudouin recognized their validity for phonology as well, because, as he pointed out, the laws of "grouping" and "equilibrium" apply to all the elements and levels of a language (1889 (1) 185).

4. Baudouin de Courtenay's principal contribution to modern linguistics is his elaboration of a theory of phonology and morphophonemics which has served as a point of departure for all subsequent research in these twin branches of linguistics. His work on the role of sounds in the structure of language was, however, a direct outgrowth of the nineteenth-century development of phonetics and the phonetic orientation of comparative grammar, which in the seventies had become bogged down in practical difficulties and internal contradictions.

The phoneticians of that time (mostly students of the physiological and physical aspects of speech) were inspired by a quest for maximal accuracy and objectivity, which could be reached, they believed, by recording and classifying the minutest, "microscopic" nuances of the speech-sounds and by analyzing them into ultimate articulatory activities. "Like the chemist," writes Techmer, "who decomposes cells into molecules and atoms, the phonetician is interested in the simplest physical properties of sound matter,"[30] whereas Osthoff exhorted the linguist "to catch the smallest nuances of live language with photographic faithfulness and precision . . . and to put into fetters the fleeting, changing sound [den beweglichen, lebendigen Sprachlaut in Fesseln zu schlagen],"[31] a program which is reminiscent of the impressionist ideal of the time to capture on canvas all the transient visual impressions with an innocent eye ("Monet," wrote Cézanne, "n'est qu'un oeil, mais quel oeil").

The realization of this ideal turned out to be elusive when the phonetician was confronted with the practical task of describing previously unanalyzed dialects or "primitive" languages, which imposed the need for a unified system of notation and which prompted research on international, "rational" alphabets that would employ a manageable number of distinctive signs. This dilemma between theory and practice was clearly stated by Ascoli: "In describing dialects [the linguist faces] only two real difficulties: to reconcile the requirements of physical precision which are by nature [le quali sono di lor natura] infinite with the needs of history and practice, to eliminate the uncertainty of acoustic perceptions."[32] Skepticism in the value of physical measurements was also expressed by Sievers: "Even the most subtle acoustic investigations will not yield to the linguist any more useful material than the simple subjective evaluation by ear."[33] Because of the constant fluctuation of the sound, the researcher, he concluded, "must select only that nuance of sound which is its typical representative."[34] The isolation of the "typical representative" of a sound, the distinction between its "essential" and "accidental" properties (Winteler) or, finally, the quest for sounds which are in "gegensätzlicher Verwendung" (Sievers) or "independently significant" (Sweet) imposed itself in the seventies of the last century as an inescapable problem that demanded theoretical solution, and prepared the ground for Baudouin's phonological theory.

The more immediate impulses for this theory came, however, from the contemporary debate concerning the role of "analogy" in phonetic change, or more generally, the interrelation of the "psychological" (i.e., morphological) and "physiological" (i.e., phonetic) aspects of language. The purely historical and physical approach of the "comparativists" to phonetic change was first most seriously challenged by de Saussure's monograph, in that it (1) treated proto-Indo-European as a synchronic system; (2) discussed the vowel changes in terms of morphological alternations; and (3) posited the existence of purely relational, unspecified phonetic units. After the appearance of de Saussure's monograph, it was no longer possible to treat "phonetic change" apart from morphology, or to claim that analogy is an exception to the regularity of phonetic laws. The opposite seemed now rather to be the case, namely, that phonetic change disturbs the regular relations of the grammatical forms, while analogical levelling counteracts the "blind" force of phonetic change or, as de Saussure put it:

> Le phénomène phonètique est un facteur de trouble. Partout où il ne crée pas des alternances, il contribue à relâcher les liens grammaticaux qui unissent les mots entre eux . . . le mécanisme linguistique s'obscurcit et se complique dans la mesure où les irrégularités nées du changement phonétique l'emportent sur les formes groupées sous des types généraux.[35]

De Saussure's ideas fell on fertile ground in Kazan', for they converged on many points with those of Baudouin and Kruszewski (the latter wrote an enthusiastic review of de Saussure's work in 1880). Kruszewski's study, *Über die Lautabwechslung* (Kazan',

1881),[36] provides the most lucid summary of Baudouin's and Kruszewski's solution to the question of analogy and phonetic change and of the phonological theory to which it gave rise.

In the synchronic state of a language, Kruszewski argues, there are two types of "sound-changes," or to be more precise, of alternations of sounds. The first type (which Kruszewski calls "divergents") involves imperceptible, "microscopic" variations of one and the same sound and is due to different "anthropophonetic" (i.e., purely physical) conditions, whereas alternations of the second type (the so-called correlatives) involve phonetically different sounds and are due to different morphological conditions. An example of the first type is the "change" of *s* to *z* in intervocalic position in the German *Haus: Häuser* (where *s* is the "primary" and *z* the "secondary" divergent), and an example of the second type the alternation of *s* with *r* in such German forms as *gewesen: war* (where *s* is the "primary" and *r* the "secondary" correlative). The mistake of the historical linguist lies, according to Kruszewski, in that he applies the criteria of gradual phonetic change, which concern the alternations of the first type, to those which belong to the "psychological sphere" and are phonetically dissimilar and discontinuous. The correlatives are neither exceptions to the "regular" (or "pure") phonetic laws, as argued by the Neogrammarians, nor are these laws less regular at the present than they were in the remote past, as claimed by Curtius. Both types must be viewed as being equally regular and "without exceptions," their difference consisting only in that the variations of the first type are conditioned (or as we would say now, "predictable") phonetically, whereas the modifications of the second type are conditioned morphologically and are thus associated with different grammatical functions. Between the alternations of the first and second type there is, indeed, a necessary relationship of a historical order, for "a spontaneous process of degeneration" inevitably transforms the variations of the first type into alternations of the second type. Kruszewski subdivides the latter alternations further into "correlatives" which express "minor internal differences" (i.e., different lexical items), and into "correlatives" which render "broader internal differences," or those between "entire families of words." Kruszewski thus draws a sharp distinction between the "combinatorial," contextual variants which are incapable of carrying grammatical functions and "independent phonemes" which are associated with grammatical distinctions. "Without the concept of the phoneme," he concludes, "it is impossible to study either phonetics or morphology" (45).

It is through the study of alternations that the perennial question of the relationship of sound and meaning, the *signans* and the *signatum*, was thus again brought into sharp focus, serving as a point of departure for a deeper and many-sided functional interpretation of the role of the sounds in language. Baudouin was the first in modern linguistics to recognize that "sounds and their combinations, or the sensory, external, peripheral aspect of language, means nothing by itself" (1889 (2) [139]), and that "languages are neither phonetic nor acoustic in their nature" (1910 [262]), but that the proper function of sound is to serve the "central, psychological" level of language, i.e. that distinctions of sounds are connected with distinctions of meaning. According to Baudouin the semiotic function of sound was first understood by the Hindu grammarians, who "by means of analysis (*vyākaraṇa*) and abstraction tried to establish the sounds and sound complexes that serve to modify meanings," and who "to a large extent surpassed all that was accomplished after so many centuries by European scholars" (1909, 111). The "role of sound in the mechanism of language" (1871 [61]), and the interrelation of the meaningful and meaning-differentiating elements of languages was to absorb Baudouin's attention during his entire life, starting with his first paper on consonantal alternations in Polish (in 1869) up to his late inquiries on the "morphologization and semasiologization of phonological elements" on the one hand, and the "phonologization of morphological elements" on the other (1915, 177–78).

In the same year, 1881, Baudouin published his lectures on the comparative grammar of the Slavic languages (*Nekotorye otdely . . .*), in which the interpretation of the alternations resembles closely the one offered by Kruszewski. The alternants (or "comparents") are still treated from both a comparative and intralingual viewpoint with an equation established between the etymological "correspondences" and the alternating "correlatives" of homogeneous morphemes. The phoneme is still defined here as a "mobile component of a morpheme and a marker of a given morphological category." However, the same study also makes an attempt to broaden the definition of the phoneme beyond its purely morphophonemic framework. Baudouin proposes here to limit the use of the term "sound" only to "conditions of anthropophonetic dependence." The linguistically autonomous sound, or the phoneme, can on the other hand be arrived at only by "purging it of the accidence of divergence" which splits the unified sound into its anthropophonetic varieties. This unified, discrete sound is the result of "abstraction" and of "phonetic generalization," or "the sum of generalized anthropophonic properties." As such it must be distinguished from that other notion of the phoneme which treats it as "an alternating component of a morpheme." In the future, Baudouin concludes, it will be necessary to have different terms and a different notation for these "two aspects of the concept of the phoneme" (1881(2), 122).

The theory of alternations received the fullest treatment in Baudouin's *An Attempt at a Theory of Phonetic Alternations* (1895), through which he, no doubt, also tried to assert his claim to the authorship of the theory vis-à-vis Kruszewski. The principal emphasis of the essay is on the interdependence of the diachronic and synchronic aspects of alternations, for, as the author tells us in the Introduction, the former aspect had been ignored by the Hindu grammarians (who "lacked a feeling for history and chronology"), while the latter had been ignored by contemporary European grammarians. What Baudouin specifically examines is how the phenomena belonging to the axis of succession (*Nacheinander*) acquire different functions and coexist on the axis of simultaneity (*Nebeneinander*). For "the periods of development," he had written in another context, "do not replace each other, as one sentry replaces another, but each period creates something new, which in the imperceptible transition from one stage to another prepares the basis for subsequent development" (1871 [63]). The synchronic state of a language is the result of a historical process in which the same means are used for different ends (1871 [76]) and in which, as in a geological cross-section, layers of different historical periods exist side by side as mobile and productive formations and as unproductive, inert residues that resemble "extinct volcanoes."

According to Baudouin there is an unceasing tendency to endow sound matter with "semasiological and morphological" functions so that the "divergents" become in time converted into "traditional alternations," and the latter into "mobile correlatives." The correlatives themselves may eventually replace each other, as when the Sanskrit *guṇa* is replaced by *vṛddhi*, or when the Slavic *k~č*,

$k \sim c$ alternation is replaced in Russian verbs by the more general $k \sim k'$ alternation (by analogy to verbs which employ the alternation of hard and soft consonants). A peculiar place is in Baudouin's triadic scheme assigned to the "traditional alternations" (i.e., alternations which are maintained only by force of tradition), which hover between the anthropophonic divergents and the psychophonetic correlatives as an unmotivated "irrational" type that has no clear-cut morphological function and is doomed to be either eliminated or converted into productive "correlatives." Intent on drawing a sharp demarcation line between the phonetically conditioned and morphologically motivated types, Baudouin failed to examine in any detail the complex, systematic relations between the various types of alternations and to discover that, like other elements of language, the alternations form a dynamic, hierarchical system which is correlated with the stratification of grammatical categories. A more serious methodological shortcoming is Baudouin's tendency to list the alternants but to omit rules that would correlate and derive one set of alternants from another, more basic set. "If it is claimed," Baudouin writes, "that the *č* in *pieczę*, *rączka* is derived from *k*, then one could with equal right insist that, on the contrary, the *k* of *piekę*, *ręka* is derived from *č*. . . . It would be a sign of poor thinking, and a historical error, to claim that the *c* in *ciec*, *móc* is based on *kć* (or *gć*)" (1895 [160]). In a synchronic description, he insisted, we must operate with "purely phonetic difference between etymologically related morphemes," and not with "change." Note that a similar approach to the alternations is taken by de Saussure: "Il est très incorrect de dire, comme on le fait volontiers, que la *a* de *Nacht* se change en *ä* dans le pluriel *Nächte*: cela donne l'illusion que de l'un a l'autre terme il intervient une transformation. . . . En réalité nous avons affaire à une simple opposition de formes."[37] It is only in his later work that Baudouin came to posit the question of the "irreversibility of alternating relations" and to emphasize that the Polish *u* or *š* can be "predicted" from *o* and *x* (as in the forms *koza/kózka*, *mucha/muszka*) but not vice versa. Baudouin's reluctance to operate with base forms and rules is understandable if we keep in mind the novelty of his theory and his apprehension that any reference to "change" or to prior and "derived" forms might be misinterpreted as meaning historical phonetic change (which happened anyway). Another reason why Baudouin might have rejected an approach that operates with "primary" and "secondary" alternants was that he found it wanting also with respect to "primary" and "secondary" divergents which were posited by Kruszewski and which, Baudouin must have felt, could not lead to a correct interpretation of the phoneme. That this was indeed the case is apparent from Baudouin's critical review of Kruszewski's work written in 1889, which marks in many ways a new phase in the development of Baudouin's phonological theory. In this review Baudouin takes exception to Kruszewski's one-sided approach to the phoneme as a member of alternations, and to the putative distinction set up between sounds as purely physical phenomena and sounds that possess, because of their morphological function, a psychological reality. "Linguistics," he argues, "is throughout a socio-psychological science." Kruszewski's "anthropophonetic" bias prevents him from recognizing the linguistic status of both the phonemes and the divergents. He makes "an unjustified and illogical jump" and "switches from the central, psychological aspect of language to its periphery" when he divides the morphemes into "plain, bare sounds" in the way he divides sentences into words, and words into morphemes (182;183). It is, perhaps, only in the language of a talking machine or phonograph that morphemes, words, and sentences are made up of complexes of "physical, semantically irrelevant sounds." Kruszewski's "acoustic" approach causes him also to treat speech-sounds as ultimate indivisible units, whereas "in the language of physiology and analysis, the sound is a "complex of heterogeneous, but coordinated activities," which must, in turn, be reduced like all elements in language to "the common denominator of their meaningful associations" (184). Kruszewski "precludes the possibility of precise analysis" when he treats the phonemes of language as if they were "species of animals and plants." Phonetic change is not the result of natural laws, but of the different complexity or clarity (*określoność*) of the sounds themselves. Equally misleading is Kruszewski's attempt to group the phonetic divergents into a single unit on the basis of their phonetic similarity or "anthropophonetic affinity." This criterion, according to Baudouin, is "completely false and without any foundation," and is ultimately based on the "subjective opinion of the investigator." Kruszewski himself indicates the inadequacy of this criterion when he states that it applies to "most cases," for if it does not apply to all cases, it cannot serve "as a distinctive feature"

(165). Kruszewski misses, further, the linguistic relevance of the divergents when he describes them in purely physical terms; for though the divergents are not associated, like the correlatives, with morphological functions, they serve as "linguistic cement" and as markers of "the structure of the word or of the sentence" (181; 166).

This review marks Baudouin's departure from the naturalistic conception of the sounds of language, which was still rampant in the phonological theory of the Kazan' period, and anticipates most clearly the tenets of modern phonological theory. Having abandoned, however, the physicalist approach to the speech-sounds, Baudouin came to embrace a psychological viewpoint which still left unresolved the tension between their psychological and physiological aspects, i.e. the relation between the phoneme as a psychological entity and the phoneme as a complex of articulary-acoustic properties (1889 (2) [152]).

Baudouin never tired of emphasizing that the phonemes are "combinations of more basic articulatory-auditory activities of a definite type," that they "are not like separate notes, but like chords composed of several elements" (1910 [271]). The basic units of language are, for him, in a descending order, the syntagms, the morphemes, and the phonemes:

> However, requirements of scientific analysis . . . do not allow us to stop with the phonemes. The phonemes consist of ultimate psychological (articulatory and acoustic) elements which, from the point of vitw of pronunciation . . . , are *kinemes*, and from the point of view of perception are *acousmemes*. I consider these terms indispensable for the greater precision of the abstract concepts of our science. (1910 [267]).

He furthermore emphasizes that what is semasiologized and morphologized are not the phonemes, but their articulatory-auditory elements (1922 [324ff.]), which are "bound and interconnected with each other" (1910 [270]) and which form a system of "oppositions" (1876/77 [83]; 1922 [470]). In his treatment of the phoneme as a psychological entity, he imputes to it, however, properties which do not appear in the actual speech-chain, but are projected on the basis of fuller, nonelliptic forms (1929 (2) [293]), or because it alternates with other phonemes in grammatically related forms as, for example, the feature of voicing in final devoiced consonants, or the presence of zero phonemes in various derived and inflected words. Furthermore, he never explains why this posited capacious mental entity should encompass only the distinctive features of a sound, and not include all the other, non-distinctive elements that are present in the speech-chain.

Baudouin's conception of the phoneme as a "complex of articulatory-acoustic properties" thus only superficially resembles the modern theory of the phoneme as "a bundle of distinctive features" which was introduced into linguistics by R. Jakobson. While for Jakobson the distinctive features are the *invariant* properties of a speech-sound which are present in all its manifestations "on the motor, acoustical or auditory level,"[38] for Baudouin they remain representations of acoustic-articulatory attributes that are divorced from the actual speech-sounds and are unified into a "sound-image" only in the mind. Baudouin does, it is true, often assert that in considering the psychological aspect one must not forget the social aspect of language ("everything constant belongs to the psychological world . . . but is possible only in society" (1915, 157), but the twentieth-century dichotomy between an internal, psychological and an external, physiological (or physical) reality is not thereby overcome. That is why one also finds in Baudouin's writings a tendency to identify the properties of the phoneme with those of its "primary variant" or "imagined psychological unit" (1895 [000]), or to group the variants in terms of their presumed psychological similarity ("although the Russian *i* and *y* are pronounced differently, they are psychologically closer to each other than they are to other sounds" (1903, 36–37)). This uncertainty and vacillation also explains why the phoneme was identified with the "primary," contextual variant also in the work of some of Baudouin's students (e.g., Ščerba). One must not forget, on the other hand, that a whole generation of linguists after Baudouin kept groping for an adequate definition of the phoneme, defining it either in physical terms (as a "class" or "family of phonetically similar sounds"), or in psychological terms (as an "ideal sound"), or as neither one nor the other, i.e., as a "fiction."

As far as Baudouin's psychological theory of the phoneme is concerned, we may discern in it a weaker and a stronger variant. In his earlier writings Baudouin merely states that "an analysis from a psychological viewpoint (as opposed to "a purely phonetic analysis") deals with the relationship between the psychological content of language and the psychological equivalents of sounds, i.e. with the "sound-images" (1884 [313]), or that the phoneme is "a psychological equivalent of the sound complex" (1899, 351; 1903, 39). The psychological significance of the phoneme lies here primarily in its connection with the meaningful, "central, psychological" level of language. Baudouin himself had on various occasions expressed reservations with regard to the psychological dogma that dominated late nineteenth-century linguistics. "Linguistics," he wrote, "must be regarded as an independent science, not to be confused with either physiology or psychology" (1871 [60]); "the question of what is psychological in the strict sense must be left to philosophers and psychologists" (1884 [313]) because linguistics has its own psychology (which he proposed to call "glotto-psychology" (1909 (2), 267)), and, although "linguistics may be considered a socio-psychological science," psychology and sociology are only its "ancillary sciences" (1889 (2) [139]).

In its "stronger" variant, Baudouin defines the phoneme (or phonemes) as "a sound of the same intention," but of "different anthropomorphic realization" (1895 [171]; 1910 [266], as "phonetic notions which exist objectively in men's souls" (1910 [272]) and as a "sound-image which is mobilized in the mind not being strong enough to reach the world of the sense or to become perceptible" (1929 (2), [294]), as or "the periphery of the speech apparatus" (1929 (2), [288]). In refusing to view sound as a sum of physical data governed by natural laws, Baudouin thus came full circle to embrace a view of the phoneme as an incorporeal and inaccessible mental image, a noumenon which is prior to and richer than the world of phenomena. In this too, then, he found himself in accord with Humboldt and his idealistic conception of the speech-sound: "Man muss die Sprachbildung überhaupt als eine Erzeugung ansehen, in welcher die innere Idee, um sich ze manifestieren, eine Schwierigkeit zu überwinden hat. Diese Schwierigkeit ist der Laut und die Überwindung gelingt nicht immer in gleichen Grade."[39]

In departing from the earlier morphophonemic interpretation of phonemes which he had shared with Kruszewski, Baudouin was free to examine the speech-sounds in their mutifarious aspects and functions. In the lectures for the year 1876/77 he had already broached the question of the "dynamics" and "mobility" of sounds, i.e., their role in "phonomorphology" as opposed to the "statics" of sounds, which deals with "the parallelism of sounds," and "the distinctive properties that give rise to certain oppositions" ([83]). He repeatedly underscores the distinctive capacity of sound, which goes beyond its morphological function: "Psychophonetic alternations are one of the morphological means on a par with other inflectional and derivational devices and belong, in fact, to morphology, not to phonology, whereas it is the task of phonology to define those phonetic features that are associated with morphological nuances and differences" (1899, 360) and "morphologization affects only certain articulatory-auditory distinctions . . . while semasiologization affects all articulatory-auditory distinctions" (1927 [282]; 1912, 174). Baudouin cites the use of rhyme, alliteration, and other poetic devices as evidence of the "double affinity of sounds" (1884), i.e., of their "phonological-morphological" and "phonological-semasiological" functions. The latter function is illustrated by such "minimal" pairs as Russian *tom/dom, bal/pal, sdal/stal, d'en/t'en* (1912 (2), 174; 1927, 395). The morphophonemic processes of a language use the distinctive features selectively, as, for example, in Russian, where they involve primarily the features of palatalization and of stressed and unstressed vowels (1917, 254). Under "statics of sounds" Baudouin considers also the different utilization of sounds in various grammatical classes and forms, or the association of certain phonetic elements with certain morphological forms (1915, 205ff.) and the role of "prohibitive analogy," which prevents phonetic change in some grammatical forms (1903, 41). Sounds are, further, distinguished in terms of their active or passive role in the system, which accounts for their different psychological intensity and strength (1884 [313]). The sounds that occur in grammatical morphemes carry a "psychological stress"; they are the "strong phonemes" which serve to differentiate morphological categories and are resistant to change (1884 [313]; 1899, 358; 1903, 40; 1910 [266]; 1929 (2) [292]).

The phonemes of a language, according to Baudouin, form "groupings" of "paired" and "nonpaired sounds" which are at the basis of "the equilibrium of language" (1877/78 [266]). Certain oppositions are basic and stable, whereas others vary and fluctuate, and are bound to disappear (1889, 188; 1910 [371]). The difference in "the phonetic make-up of languages," according to Baudouin, can serve as a useful criterion for a typological "characterization" of languages (1876/77 [92]; 1902 [321]). Phonetic relations can also be studied statistically (1876/77 [84]; 1876/77 [92]). Thus one may compare "percentages of various sounds in a given language," the "ratio of single phonemes to clusters, of "kinakemes" to phonemes, of phonemes to syllables, or of syllables to phonetic words (1876/77 [84]; 1915, 171).

The sounds of language may further be utilized in a "syntactic function," to mark boundaries between words and word-groups ("syntagms"), or as "phonetic cement" (1876/77 [109]; 1881 (1), 149; 1889 (1), 181; 1908, 171), i.e., as features which signalize units of the higher, semantic level of language and which integrate them into wholes. These, as we would say now, configurational and re-dundant functions of the speech-sounds Baudouin studied from the point of view of word and sentence morphology ("morphology of the second degree"). For example, stress, which in Russian is "mor-phologized and semasiologized," is also utilized to indicate the unity of a phonetic word, whereas in Polish it performs only the latter function; a similar function is in the Turkish languages, performed by vowel harmony (1876/77 [109]; 1908, 171). Voicing, which is distinctive in Polish, can at the same time mark a word boundary in some of its dialects (e.g., *głoz narodu* vs. *wiosna;* 1908, 171). Baudouin's concern with the stability and instability or fluc-tuation of sounds inevitably led him to the study of the "facultative sounds" of language (1929 (2) [291ff.]), though he obscured this problem by reference to latent psychological forces that strive to, but cannot, be realized in the speech-act. As was his wont, he ex-amined the question of stylistic variation from a variety of view-points: from a paradigmatic and syntagmatic point of view (e.g., the varying stability of phonemes and the tendency to "weaken" some of them at the end of a word); with reference to morphology (e.g., the omission of phonemes in certain grammatical forms); with relation to writing and other conservative forces which con-tribute to the preservation or restoration of some phonemes. The existence of faculative sounds was to him further proof of the dynamic character of language and of the intrusion of the factors of time and space into synchrony.

Baudouin's inquiries into phonology and morphophonemics are closely related to his work on writing and on "visual language" in general. Though he devoted most of his efforts to clarifying the role of sound in language, he was, like de Saussure, aware of the importance of signs that employ other physical means and that sup-plement or even replace the verbal sign (as in the case of deaf mutes). He was not affected by the mystique of the speech-sound that was the legacy of the Romantics, and he predicted "the vindication of the rights of visual language, which is now held in contempt by linguists who still confuse letters with sounds" (1909, 264). He envisaged two lines of approach to the study of visual language: one that would explore gestures that accompany the spoken word or are used in its stead; the other that would study systems of writing and various types of scientific notation. To the last two Baudouin devoted a number of penetrating studies that deal both with the orthographic systems of various Slavic languages (especially Russian) and with general theoretical questions. In considering the role of writing in the perception and use of spoken language, he urged attention to the three types of members of a speech community: language-learners who are in the process of acquiring spoken and written language; illiterates who are only in command of spoken language; and the educated who have a mastery of both spoken and written language (1909, 265). "Even the simplest elements of writing," Baudouin declared, "are the result of a deeper analysis of the complex linguistic representations" (1910 [271]). Writing systems that refer to the phonemic level of language are "phonemographic," whereas those that refer to the semantic level are "morphemographic" or "syntagmographic." Systems that utilize only one principle of representation are "monistic," whereas most systems incorporate more than one principle and are "dual" or "pluralistic," 1917, 280; 1929 (1) [286]). Baudouin's concern is directed primarily to phonemography, i.e. to the type "in which the division of the sentence into syntagms or syntactic elements is not taken into consideration" (1929 (1) [285]). He points out that the letters, or "graphemes" of conventional alphabets are not the equivalents of phonemes, for the latter consist of more elementary components, while the former are global, "synthetic" units. But in addition to "synthetic" graphemes, some languages make use of "analytical," "diacritic" graphemes which correspend to the distinctive features; e.g. the Polish diacritic marks in *ą, ę, ś* etc. (1915, 211ff.). The graphemes, like the phonemes, may also indicate morphological relations, as in the European alphabets which employ capital letters, or as in Arabic or Hebrew, where special letters are used to mark word boundaries. Of equal interest to Baudouin are those writing systems that omit certain features, as for example the Semitic system, which ignores vowels, or those of various European languages that do not mark the prosodic features. Baudouin constantly calls attention to the "confusion of concepts" which results from the identification of phonemes with letters. On the other hand, he emphasizes the conservative role of writing and the existence of double—written and spoken—norms, and he reminds us that "without the representation of graphemes there would not have been formed in our minds the representations of phonemes as discrete articulatory-acoustic units" (1915, 211). In this way he makes the point that as a derived, secondary system which selects and gives prominence to certain features of the verbal code, writing itself exerts an influence on that code.

5. We shall now consider Baudouin de Courtenay's contribution to morphology, typology, and diachronic linguistics, which were no less pioneering than those he made in phonology and morphophonemics. In the nineteenth century, morphology was the only branch of linguistics that had a direct bearing on typology, as it provided the criteria for the classification of genetically unrelated languages. Historical linguistics, on the other hand, was a strictly genealogical, reconstructive science, and it was Baudouin who gave it a broader, typological outlook.

Baudouin's ideas on grammar and morphology are intimately related to his synchronic approach to language and must be seen, like his phonology, as an attempt to outflank the difficulties which emerged within traditional comparative grammar. The morphological analysis of the Indo-European word, which was so brilliantly initiated by Bopp, gave rise to doubts by the sixties and seventies of the last century about the possibility of an objective reconstruction of the Indo-European inflection and the decomposition of the word into its ultimate components. Linguists like Fick and Sayce had come to question the "empty clatter of stems and suffixes,"[40] which to B. Delbrück had become no more than "useful operational terms" without objective reality. In his disillusionment Delbrück called for a return to the grammatical practice of the Greeks, for whom the word, rather than its parts, was the ultimate unit of language, while adding that "the Greeks were naive, whereas we are resigned."[41] Far from rejecting the attainments of historical grammar in breaking up the word into its morphological components, Baudouin sought rather to put the analysis of the word on a realistic, synchronic basis. He had little patience with Delbrück's pessimism and criticized him for ignoring "the objective-psychological factors" which make morphological analysis possible (1909, 259). Baudouin's main effort during his Kazan' period was, in fact, directed toward a deeper and general linguistic interpretation of the morphological structure of the word.

In his review of Kruszewski's work (in 1889), Baudouin points out that the proper title of Kruszewski's *Outline of the Science of Language* (1883) "should have been *The Word and its Components*, for "the problems we discussed in Kazan' concerned mostly the structure of the word and not the totality of language" (1889 (1), 176). He reiterates the idea in his remarks on Bogorodickij's work: "Analysis of complex wholes into their components has been the central interest of the Kazan' school . . .; analysis, decomposition into features is in all sciences the beginning of precise investigation" (1903, 54). But in further elaboration of his ideas Baudouin progresses inevitably toward a more comprehensive view of morphology as a branch of linguistics that encompasses not only the external, formal side of language, but also its internal, conceptual aspect. Having thus begun as an adherent of Steinthal and under the shadow of Schleicher, who emphasized the material morphological differences between languages, Baudouin at the end of his career moves closely to the Humboldtian conception of "inner form" as the organizing force of the external elements of language, and thereby concludes the great cycle of nineteenth-century linguistics, which moved from the general and universal to the individual and particular, and then back to the universal and general properties of language. While Baudouin's first paper (in 1869) dealt with the morphological analysis of the Slavic word, one of his last papers (1930) boldly resumes the question of the influence of language on the organization of our perceptions and knowledge. But in this paper, as elsewhere (1909, 187ff.), Baudouin rejected Humboldt's idealistic interpretation of the relation of thought and language, treating language rather in the rationalist and modern spirit, as a system of signs, and linguistics as a pivotal science among other semiotic sciences. "Linguistics," he wrote, "is one of the sciences of mental, human phenomena which are expressed by means of signs and symbols drawn from the physical world" (1909, 247–48), and in the future, he predicted, "a linguistic mode of knowledge" will take its place alongside the "intuitive-artistic" and the "analytic-scientific" modes of cognition (1909 (2), 270; 1904 [253]).

In his early work on morphology Baudouin sought first of all to identify the basic units of the sentence and the word. Words and fixed expressions are "the syntactic atoms" (or "syntagms"), whereas "roots in the broad sense" are the "morphological atoms" (1877/78 [114]; 1912, 19) of language. To the last he later assigned the term "morpheme," which would cover any component of a word (Meillet found it to be a "joli mot" and borrowed it in his translation of Brugmann's comparative grammar). Baudouin questioned the Indo-Europeanist theory according to which only the endings are subject to change, whereas the stems are of a fixed, immutable nature. In a study submitted for publication to Schleicher in 1869 (which was turned down for its unorthodox views and was published only thirty years later), Baudouin tried to demonstrate the historical transformations that the Indo-European nominal stems have undergone in Slavic as a result of phonetic and morphological processes. In this study, which advances the theory of "reinterpretation" (*pererazloženie*) or "morphological absorption" (later developed in greater detail by Kruszewski), Baudouin is able to show that far from being opposite and antagonistic forces, phonetic and analogical developments do interact to produce a new type of (consonantal) stem and new types of endings. Through this study Baudouin posits, in addition, the question of the exchange of functions between the lexical and grammatical elements, a question that was broached only later by Meillet.[42] He also puts into a new context the problem of analogy that had been raised by the Neogrammarians to the rank of a psychological "law" on a par with the phonetic laws (though they used it only as a last resort), and which they treated as a kind of "quantitative" proportion between disparate forms selected at random. For Baudouin analogical levelling is primarily a "qualitative," grammatical process (1903, 47) which is possible thanks to the existence of "fixed yet mobile systems" (1908, 164), i.e., morphological patterns that allow the speaker to interpret and to regroup the elements of a word. "Reinterpretation," analogy, and folk-etymology are for him the three types of processes that prove "the reality of the morphemes" and show that "linguistic creativity takes place not only in the field of syntax, i.e. in the combination of ready-made words into phrases and sentences, but also in the combination of morphemes into words" (1917, 281). The live and constant process of "semantic interpretation" and "reinterpretation" is continually confirmed by the use of puns, the creation of new "roots," and the "mistakes" in the language of children (1876/77 [98]; 1903, 44ff.; 1917, 284ff.). Baudouin examines and classifies the morphemes of a language according to various criteria: their central vs. peripheral position in the word; their degree of independence; and their lexical, syntactic, or morphological functions (1909 (1), 183ff.; 1912, 85ff.). Morphology "in the broad sense" is defined by Baudouin as including both the study of word structure (i.e. morphology proper) and the study of sentence structure (syntax). Morphology together with semasiology and lexicology pertain to the "central aspects of language," to its "psychological content" (1884 [313]; 1889 (1), 200). Of these three fields only morphology is truly a part of linguistics, since it exists "exclusively in language and nowhere outside language" (1909, 182), whereas semasiology (which includes the study of grammatical categories and the parts of speech) deals with "extra-linguistic representations." This distinction, which is drawn in most of Baudouin's early writings, must be seen as his tribute to the nineteenth-century tradition (by no means dead even now), which identified the study of structure with that of its external form, relegating the study of meaning to psychology or to other sciences. In his later works Baudouin abandons this antinomy, emphasizing the "linguistic reality" of grammatical concepts (1922; 1930), and defines morphology more generally as the combination "of objective phonology" and "objective semasiology." "These two," he writes, "constitute the basis of linguistics as a separate science" (1915, 166). The question of the "correspondence between these two qualitatively different (*różnogatunkowe*) representations" (1915, 219) and of its expression in different languages is one of Baudouin's central preoccupations, one that, as we have seen, guides his entire approach to phonology and morphophonemics. The formal and meaningful elements of language are, according to Baudouin, in constant interplay, yielding either "complete harmony" or "disorder and chaos" which languages perpetually strive to correct. The optimal type of "correspondence" is achieved in the Uralo-Altaic languages, which are for Baudouin (as they were for Sapir) "sober and orderly," whereas the Indo-European languages that were so glorified by the Romantics as the realization of the synthesis of "matter" and "form" present a picture of "disorderly linguistic thinking" (1909 (1), 185; 1922, 82). Despite his bias in favor of the agglutinative languages, Baudouin succeeds in unravelling the systematic, though far more complex, "harmony" in such a typically synthetic language as Polish, where he shows that the difference between various parts of speech and grammatical categories is matched by a corresponding difference in the structure of their stems, by their different types of endings and morphophonemic processes (1915; 1922). In his study on the *Influence of Language on World-View and Mood* (1929), Baudouin posits the question of the relation of language to thought, and examines the nature of various grammatical categories. Language, he points out, must not be identified with the world of outside reality, for it is a system of abstract ideas, a "mythology" which, like Midas converting all he touched into gold, converts all our experience into linguistic form. The grammatical categories of a language are obligatory and affect every lexical item, like "the obligatory designations of religion which are written in passports even of professed atheists" (234). Baudouin illustrates the obligatoriness of grammatical meaning with various types of gender that give rise to "etymological myths" and put their stamp on religious beliefs, on poetry, on folklore, and on the arts. The grammatical categories are further discussed in terms of their mutual, binary relations, within which the particular categories are opposed to each other as specific and less specific, i.e., as marked and unmarked terms (1922, 122ff.). Within the category of person, for example, only the first and second persons designate persons proper, while the third person is opposed to these as a "non-person," which explains why the third person also figures in impersonal constructions. Within the system of tenses the present is opposed to the past and the future as a "tempus aeternum" that may designate either, while "in extra-linguistic thought" the present does not even exist, for it is "an infinitely small point that moves continuously from the past to the future." In his relentless quest for generalizations, Baudouin subsumes under a common heading grammatical categories that at first glance seem to be of a totally different order. Thus he sees in the formation of a new class of numerals, in the high frequency of zeroes, in the use of "arithmetical" or "geometrical" aspects (such as the semelfactive, iterative or punctual and durative), and in the use of argumentatives and diminutives, the reflection of increased "quantitative" or "mathematical" thinking in Polish (1922, 142ff.). These, and many other such novel ideas, are scattered in all of Baudouin's mature writings.

Equally timely is Baudouin's work in the field of linguistic typology. Beginning with his earliest lectures and programs, he raises the question of a "scientific characterization of various groups of languages and dialects" (1877/78 [118]). "Under close scrutiny," he argues, "all the genealogical schemes which have absorbed so much energy appear to be inadequate" (1884 [311]). At the same time, he came to recognize the one-sided and "anti-quated" character of the prevailing morphological classification of languages which was based on a single, external principle and according to which the inflected, "synthetic" languages (with their "internal flexion") represented the "apex of development" (1876/77 [108]). It is important to remember that typological comparisons, which enjoyed some vogue at the beginning of the nineteenth century, had fallen into disrepute at the time of Baudouin's activity, when linguistics was declared (e.g. by Paul) to be a strictly "historical science" and when Brugmann denied, on theoretical grounds, the value of such comparisons.[43] Even Meillet, who expressed a vivid interest in typology, believed that it could not be done without a prior historical description of a maximal number of languages,[44] a requirement that would have postponed the enterprise indefinitely. Baudouin, on the other hand, saw in the structural comparison of languages simply an extension of the internal analysis of a single language, because he was convinced that the two approaches were complementary aspects of the same inquiry into the general properties of language. "A morphological or structural classification of languages," he wrote, "is based upon the similarity of their actual states independent of their historical relations . . . and depends on universal conditions, and properties common to all people regardless of their origin" (1889 (2) [137]). But such a classification, he stipulated, presupposes the existence of descriptive grammar which states the facts of language in their mutual relation at a given period of history (1909, 189). In his early lectures and programs he believed only in the fruitfulness of a morphological classification which would "define first the psychological character of language, and then its external form as a reflection of internal activity" (1877/78 [119]; 1871 [65]; 1884 [313]). But later he came to acknowledge that "the current state of our science hardly permits such a characterization of the Indo-European languages or of the Slavic languages either. Such a characterization is, at any rate, far more difficult than a characterization of phonetic features and of their historical development"

(1884 [313]). The success of such a classification, he warned, would depend entirely on the selection of features of "general signif-icance," and not of "disparate facts" (1884 [312]). In his program of lectures for the year 1877/78 (published in 1881), he him-self offered the first phonological typology of the Slavic lan-guages which is based on two such features of "general significance" for the Slavic world, stress and quantity. The presence of one or both of these features enables Baudouin to single out five different Slavic areas: (1) Serbo-Croatian, which combines stress and quan-tity; (2) Slovenian, which admits the long/short opposition only under stress; (3) East Slavic and Bulgarian, which lack the opposi-tion of quantity; (4) Czech and Slovak, which lack free stress; and (5) the other West Slavic languages, which lack a free stress (where the stress is of an "anthropophonic" nature). With some minor corrections, this classification is still valid today and is, in effect, the neatest classification that can be made for the modern Slavic languages. "In comparing systems," Baudouin wrote, "we should not compare individual sounds, but the various elements of sounds, their phonic components" (1902 [312]). Thus he raised the question of the different utilization of the feature of nasality or stress in the various Slavic languages, the relation of stress to the quality of the vowels (1884 [315]), and the different character of the palatal *č* in Polish and in Russian. In traditional "comparative grammars," he complained, "such comparisons have [hitherto had] almost no place" (1902 [321]). From a typological point of view he also examined the Slavic categories of gender (1929, 223ff.) and dis-tancing (1912 (1)), and he offered a typological comparison of the Indo-European with the Turanian and Uralo-Altaic languages that makes reference at the same time to their phonological, mor-phological, and syntactic features (1876/77; 1903). Among the salient facts of the Turkic languages, he mentions the configura-tional function of stress and the morphologized character of vowel-harmony, the progressive character of its alternations, the auton-omy of syllables as morphological units, the nominal character of these languages, their lack of gender and of syntactic congruence. At the same time he emphasizes the "contradictions in their word and sentence structure," i.e., the initial position of the dominant morpheme or the root within the word, and the final position of the dominant syntagm, the subject, within the sentence (1930 [306]).

In addition to comparing languages in terms of their phonological and morphological properties, Baudouin also recognized the need for classifications based on phenomena of linguistic diffusion showing the role of geographic contact and cultural influence in the formation of "mixed" languages (1902, 1909; 1930).

Baudouin's approach to diachronic linguistics, like his work on typology, rests on the premise that any comparison of systems in time presupposes the description of their discrete, synchronic states. "This approach," he declares, "attempts to establish two actually given periods in the development of a language and to determine the direction of change of various categories of sounds and of the sound system as a whole" (1884 [313]). Phonological change is, in Baudouin's conception, not merely a replacement of sounds and of their inventories, but a "rearrangement of . . . the articulatory-auditory combination of the phonemes" (1910 [270]). In his early formulations, Baudouin identifies synchrony with statics, and diachrony with dynamics (1877/78 [116]); but the laws of the former, in his opinion, are connected with the laws of the latter (1870, [71]), since "the beginnings of dynamic sound changes [take place] in the synchronic state of a language" (1876/77 [92]). The possibility of change or of the dynamics of sounds is, in other words, conditioned by the "stability" or "variability" implicit in the sounds of language, i.e., by the internal stratification of the phonemic oppositions. "Through all the fluctuations and deviations the linguistic facts and their causal relations exhibit remarkable uniformity and regularity . . . which characterize both the stability of the combinations of the articulatory and auditory elements and their fluctuations and changes" (1910 [270]). The various sounds of a language, writes Baudouin, have a different "potential" for change, and "they carry in their very nature the germ of their relative stability and variability" (1889 (1), 187). The proper description of historical development must, like typological comparison, consider the two interconnected aspects of invariance and variation, and can be accomplished only by "generalizing the entire line of historical development" (1903, 35) through the study of linguistic "tendencies" that pervade the history of a particular language (1876/77 [118]).

Baudouin's historical treatment of Polish phonology (1922, 323ff.) is an illustration of such a description that focuses both on the permanence of a given phonological system and on its "drift," or its movement along a more or less determined path. The direction of change, Baudouin reminds us, is not "an exact formula of phonetic law, but rather a statistical constant" (1910 [270]). Looking at the history of the Polish phonological system as a "whole" beginning with Indo-European until its modern dialectal differentiation, Baudouin underscores first of all the "conservatism" of some phonemes (or, rather, of some "distinctive features and their combinations") that have remained intact throughout the history of the language. Second, he distinguishes in this history two main phases of development, one of which extends from Indo-European to Common Slavic, and the other from Common Slavic to modern Polish. Each of these stages is characterized by a different trend which lends meaning and unity to each of its particular changes. In the first stage there is a tendency to strengthen the vowel system at the expense of the consonants, whereas in the second stage the trend is reversed. The first tendency is manifested in the loss of Indo-European aspirates and palatals, in the elimination of final consonants and clusters, in the formation of nasal vowels, in the influence of vowels upon consonants, etc., whereas the second tendency leads to the loss of diphthongs and syllabic sonants, to the closing of the syllable, to the introduction of palatalized and palatal consonants, and to the influence of consonants on the distribution of the vowels. This interpretation of the phonological development of Polish is no doubt oversimplified and is open to criticism on several points. First, the Polish dialects do not conform to this dyadic scheme, for some of them belong rather to the vocalic type, having preserved (or transcoded) certain vocalic distinctions of Old Polish and having relinquished some of the consonant differences of Common Polish (e.g., the loss of palatalized consonants and of the palatals $č, ž, š, ž$); second, it is questionable whether the paradigmatic and syntagmatic (distributional) changes of Polish (or of any other lagnuage) can be reduced to a single formula, as either of them may occur independently of the other. But the importance of Baudouin's study lies in its insistence on the "limits of the variability of sounds," i.e., on the constraints that are imposed on the range of change which account for the recurrent character of certain kinds of change within the history of a given language. This approach must not be confused with teleological explanation, which Baudouin specifically rejects: "Between the starting and ending point of historical change . . . there is no relationship that could be interpreted as a law of evolution. On the contrary, the path of evolution taken by a series of generations presents an infinite number of discrete points, such that each successive stage depends directly on the conditions of the . . . articulatory-auditory representations" of the preceding stage (1910 [272]). What Baudouin tries to emphasize is rather that "comparison is not a goal in itself," and that the quest for general laws must guide the linguist both in vertical (i.e., historical) and horizontal (i.e., typological) comparisons of languages.

6. This introduction is not the place to discuss Baudouin's significance in Slavic linguistics, which was the main field of his professional activities. I shall indicate here only the main areas of his interest and his major achievements. As is apparent from the foregoing, it is almost impossible to separate Baudouin's contributions to Slavistics from his work in general linguistics, for the study of empirical facts was for him always a springboard for broad theoretical generalizations. In all of his general linguistic studies he draws on his vast knowledge of the Slavic languages and dialects, with which he had first-hand familiarity both as a student of Slavic texts and as a dialectologist. He was an extremely talented organizer of field work (as, for example, in Slovenia, where he secured the cooperation of scholars, teachers, farmers, and newspapers), and was an indefatigable collector of linguistic and ethnographic data (which include Serbo-Croatian texts from Southern Italy, Lithuanian folksongs, and a vast store of Slovenian material, most of which remains to be published). His main fields of interest, besides comparative Slavic, were Polish, Slovenian, and Russian. In each of these areas he left a large body of work dealing with the history, structure and/or dialectology of these languages. In Slavic historical linguistics his name is associated with the so-called third palatalization of velars, with the "euphonic" *n* in the oblique cases of personal pronouns, and with "Linden's law" (the treatment of initial *wr* in Slavic). His major comparative works deal with the relationship of Polish, Russian, and Church Slavonic, and with Slavic phonology and morphology.

Boudouin's book on *Old Polish Before the Fourteenth Century* is still unsurpassed. On the basis of toponymic and anthroponymic material culled from Latin medieval texts, Baudouin succeeded in reconstructing the picture of Old Polish phonology and in defining its principal phonological development (the change of the palatalized consonants *t'*, *d'*, *s'*, *z'*, *r'* into the palatals *ć*, *ʒ́*, *ś*, *ź* and *ř*). His *Psychological Description of the Polish Language* and his *Outline of the History of the Polish Language* not only give a compact and profound analysis of the synchronic and diachronic aspects of Polish, but are among his most mature works on general linguistics. The formerly much-disputed question of the position of Kashubian among the Slavic languages was solved once and for all by Baudouin's penetrating analysis, which proved it to be a member of the Lekhitic group of the Slavic languages most closely related to Polish (in Baudouin's catching phrase, it is "plus polonais que le polonais même").

Baudouin was the first Slavic scholar who put the study of the Slovenian dialects on a scientific foundation. He was also the first to identify the fundamental character of the phonological development of Slovenian, which consisted in transforming the opposition between the long, accented and short, unaccented vowels into a maximally differentiated qualitative opposition. Slovenian linguistics is only now beginning to recognize the significance of Baudouin's insights, after years of haggling over his obviously misguided theory about the Turanian origin of the Rezija dialects. Baudouin also emphasized (contrary to some authoritative opinion of his day) the basic historical unity of Slovenian and Serbo-Croatian as opposed to Macedo-Bulgarian.

Baudouin's contributions in Russian are scattered in all of his general linguistic works, as he believed that only live languages provide a solid basis for the verification of linguistic hypotheses. Among his specifically Russian works are his analysis of Russian orthography with relation to the sounds of Russian, his lexicographical additions and introduction to Dal's dictionary, and his study on thief-slang (in the introduction to Trachtenberg's monograph). His lectures on Russian clarified for the first time (after the efforts of Böhtlingk, Grot, and Tulov) the basic principles of Russian phonology, and prepared the ground for an outstanding school of Russian phonologists.

Such, then, was the scope of this remarkable scholar and teacher.

The present translation is the first rendering into English of Baudouin de Courtenay's works, which were written originally in Russian, Polish, German, and French. I have profited mostly from the Russian edition of these writings, which was published in Moscow in 1963 under the editorship of V. P. Grigor'ev and A. A. Leont'ev. I have consulted the original publications for ambiguous or difficult passages and have translated items VII, XII, XVII, and XXI directly from the German and Polish.

This selection of articles and books is intended to give a diversified, though fairly compact, picture of Baudouin's representative works. The *Statement of Linguistic Principles* (VIII) has a purely historical value and is included here because it is well known and has been frequently cited. The first eighteen studies are entirely within the field of general linguistics, and the last four deal with Slavic topics. The material is otherwise presented in a chronological order.

In addition to the omissions in the Soviet edition (marked in this book by . . .), I have omitted a number of passages and phrases, most of them in the nature of introductory or concluding remarks, plus some metaphors, and the mathematical tables which would now appear obscure and have no bearing on the arguments (these omissions are marked by ⟨. . .⟩). In a number of cases I have added (in brackets ⟨ ⟩) explanatory notes and minor corrections.

Baudouin's writings present a serious challenge to the translator. Succinct, epigrammatic, and almost classical formulations are embedded in a stream of redundant statements, piled-up metaphors, and poorly organized sentences which are bound (especially in their German form) to test the patience of any reader. This translator can only concur with Meillet's verdict on Baudouin's style: "Sa manière de s'exprimer était gauche, peu idiomatique; on dirait que jamais il ne se sert d'une langue maternelle."[45] Total fidelity to the original text would have been as much a disservice to the modern reader as to Baudouin's basically lucid ideas. I have therefore chosen to be faithful first of all to Baudouin's thought, without departing too drastically from his wording. On the other hand, I have tried to adhere to Baudouin's linguistic terminology, although he himself was not always consistent. For the benefit of the English reader I have included a glossary of Polish and Russian words which he did not translate (in his German and French texts).

It is my pleasant duty to thank Professor Thomas A. Sebeok of Indiana University for his encouragement for me to undertake this onerous though rewarding task of bringing Baudouin to the English reader, and Mr. Bernard Perry of Indiana University Press for his support and patience with this endeavor. I also wish to thank my students, David Henderson and Terry Merz, for helping with the translation of certain chapters.

EDWARD STANKIEWICZ

June 1971   Yale University

NOTES

1. A. Meillet (1), *Introduction a l'étude comparative des langues indo-européennes* (8th ed.), Paris, 1937, p. 475.

2. R. Jakobson, "De Saussure's Unpublished Reflections on Phonemes" (quoted from manuscript by courtesy of the author; forthcoming in *Cahiers Ferdinand de Saussure*, 1971).

3. R. Godel, *Les sources manuscrites du Cours de linguistique générale de F. de Saussure* (henceforth quoted as *SM*), Paris, 1957, p. 29ff.

4. F. de Saussure, *Cours de linguistique générale* (4th ed.), Paris, 1949, pp. 153, 154.

5. *SM*, p. 51.

6. op. cit. (1), p. 478.

7. A. A. Leont'ev, "Boduèn de Kurtenè i francuzskaja lingvistika," *Izvestija AN, Serija literatury i jazyka*, 1966, 25, 4, pp. 329–32.

8. See F. M. Berezin, *Očerki po istorii jazykoznanija v Rossii* (Konec XIX-načalo XX vekov), Moscow, 1968, p. 259.

9. *Cours*, p. 172.

10. *SM*, p. 65.

11. A. Meillet (2), (Necrology), *Revue des études slaves*, 10, 1930, p. 175.

12. V. Bogorodickji, "Kazanskij period professorskoj dejatel'nosti I. A. Boduèna-de-Kurtenè," *Prace filologiczne*, 15, 2, 1931, p. 467.

13. op. cit. (2), p. 174.

14. H. Ułaszyn, "Jan Baudouin de Courtenay. Charakterystyka ogólna uczonego i człowieka (1845–1929)," *Biblioteczka Koła Slawistów imienia Baudouina de Courtenay*, 1, Poznań, 1934, pp. 1–43.

15. R. Jakobson, Kazańska szkoła polskiej lingwistyki i jej miejsce w światowym rozwoju fonologii, *Bulletin de la Société polonaise de linguistique*, 19, 1960, p. 20.

16. W. von Humboldt (1), "Über das vergleichende Sprachstudium in Beziehung auf die verschiedenen Epochen der Sprachentwicklung," *Werke*, 3, *Schriften zur Sprachphilosophie* (ed. A. Flitner, K. Giel), Darmstadt, 1969, p. 2.

17. idem (2), "Über die Verschiedenheit des menschlichen Sprachbaues und ihren Einfluss auf die geistige Entwicklung des Menschengeschlechts," *Werke*, p. 473 (VII, 95).

18. Note that according to F. Schlegel "comparative grammar" was intended to reveal the "internal structure" of the related languages ["die innere

Struktur der Sprachen oder die vergleichende Grammatik"], *"Über die Sprache und Weisheit der Indier," F. v. Schlegels sämmtliche Werke,* 7, Vienna, 1846, p. 291.

19. H. Osthoff, K. Brugmann, *Morphologische Untersuchungen auf dem Gebiete der indogermanischen Sprachen,* Leipzig, 1878, p. XIII; see also K. Wechssler, "Gibt es Lautgesetze?," *Forschungen zur romanischen Philologie,* 1900, p. 422ff.

20. H. Osthoff, *Schriftsprache und Volksmundarten,* Berlin, 1883, p. 17.

21. For further comments on this subject, see E. Cassirer, *The Philosophy of Symbolic Forms,* 1, *Language* (7th printing, New Haven, Conn., 1968, p. 170ff.

22. H. Paul, *Prinzipien der Sprachgeschichte* (4th ed.), Tübingen, 1920, p. 24.

23. op. cit., p. 37.

24. op. cit., p. IX.

25. Quoted from Cassirer, p. 173.

26. *SM,* p. 38.

27. op. cit., p. 15.

28. For an account of the controversy concerning the reality of dialects, see L. Gauchat, "Gibt es Mundartgrenzen?," *Archiv für das Studium der neueren Sprachen und Literaturen,* 111, 1903, pp. 365–403.

29. Meillet (3), *Linguistique historique linguistique générale,* Paris, 1 (1929), 1948, p. 107.

30. Fr. Techmer, *Phonetik,* Leipzig, 1880, p. 59.

31. op. cit., p. 20.

32. A. Camilli, *Il sistema ascoliano di grafia fonetica,* Città di Castello, 1913, p. 22.

33. E. Sievers, *Grundzüge der Lautphysiologie,* Leipzig, 1876, p. 37.

34. *ibidem,* p. 42.

35. *Cours,* p. 221.

36. The following quotations are from the Polish translation of Kruszewski's works *Wybór pism* (translated by J. Kuryłowocz, K. Pomorska), Wrocław-Warsaw-Cracow, 1967.

37. *Cours,* p. 218.

38. R. Jakobson, M. Halle, *Fundamentals of Language,* The Hague, 1956, p. 8.

39. op. cit. (2), p. 459 (VII, 82).

40. A. H. Sayce, *Introduction to the Science of Language* (3rd ed.), London, 1890, p. XVI. There also the reference to Fick.

41. B. Delbrück, *Einleitung in das Sprachstudium,* 1880, p. 75. Cf. the references to Delbrück in Baudouin, 1909, p. 258ff. and in Kruszewski, p. 50.

42. op. cit. (3), p. 130ff.

43. K. Brugmann, *Zum heutigen Stand der Sprachwissenschaft,* Strassburg, 1885, p. 11ff.

44. "La linguistique générale qu'on obtient en faisant abstraction de l'histoire est encore une science peu faite, difficile à faire, et qui pour se faire suppose du reste qu'on ait déjà décrit aussi complètement que possible l'histoire du plus grand nombre de langues possible" (3), p. 101.

45. A. Meillet (2), p. 174.

47

WORKS BY BAUDOUIN DE COURTENAY
CITED IN THE INTRODUCTION

For the full titles of Baudouin de Courtenay's works see the Table of Contents and the Bibliography.

Page numbers referring to the English translation are given in square brackets; otherwise they refer to the Soviet edition, with the exception of the following, which come from the original publications: 1881 (2), 1888, 1909 (2), 1912 (2), 1915, 1922 (Ch. II).

1871	General Remarks. . .
1875	*Opyt fonetyki*. . .
1875/76	Program of Readings. . .
1876/77	Program of Lectures. . .
1877/78	Program of Lectures. . .
1881 (1)	*Nekotorye otdely*. . .
1881 (2)	Neskol'ko slov o sravnitel'noj grammatike indoevropejskix jazykov, *ŽMNP*, 213.
1884	The Slavic Linguistic World. . .
1888	Zametka k nekrologu N. V. Kruševskogo, *RFV*, 20, 297–302.
1889 (1)	Mikołaj Kruszewski
1889 (2)	On the Tasks of Linguistics
1895	*An Attempt at a Theory*. . .
1897	Statement. . .
1899	Fonologia. Fonema.
1901	On the Mixed Character. . .
1902	Comparative Grammar. . .
1903	Lingvističeskie zametki. . .
1904	Linguistics of the Nineteenth Century
1908	O związku wyobrażeń. . .
1909 (1)	Zametki na poljax soč. V. V. Radlova
1909 (2)	*Zarys historii językoznawstwa*. . .
1910	Phonetic Laws
1912 (1)	*Ob otnošenii russkogo pis'ma*. . .
1912 (2)	*Sbornik zadač*. . .
1915	*Charakterystyka psychologiczna*. . .
1917	*Vvedenie v jazykovedenie*
1922	*Zarys historii języka polskiego*
1927	The Difference between Phonetics. . .
1929 (1)	The Influence of Language on World-View. . .
1929 (2)	Facultative Sounds. . .
1930	Problems of Linguistic Affinity. . .

I

Some General Remarks on Linguistics and Language

Inaugural lecture for the Chair of Comparative
Grammar of the Indo-European Languages, given
December 17/29, 1870, at St. Petersburg University

GENTLEMEN: Inaugurating these lectures on the so-called comparative grammar of the Indo-European languages, I consider it
appropriate first to characterize, in general terms, the object of
our studies and to define its relationship to other studies. The
science to which the subject of my present talk belongs is linguistics; it follows that whatever is related to linguistics is also applicable to the comparative grammar of the Indo-European languages,
although the latter has some features of its own which do not pertain to linguistics in general. This fact is inherent in the nature of
the subject as well as in the methods which have been elaborated
for it historically.

In the general characterization of our science, I shall try first of
all to define its limits showing (1) what should not be expected of
it, and (2) its essence. I shall then try to define its subject, i.e., the
nature of language. My lecture will thus be divided into two parts:
(1) linguistics in general and the so-called comparative grammar
of the Indo-European languages in particular, and (2) language in
general, and especially the Indo-European languages. Both these
parts are closely related to each other, overlap, and condition each
other, making a precise division between them almost impossible.

As a starting point in defining the science of linguistics, I shall
take up the commonly held belief that grammar is the science
which teaches us how to speak and write correctly in a certain
language. This continues to be the view of many grammarians,
who, in fact, define the subject of their science this way. Obviously,

49

no one may impose on another a particular interpretation of a term, especially of a technical term. Thus we cannot demand that the general public or a certain school of grammarians discard their current definition of grammar. But we have a perfect right to tell them that such a definition and the attitude toward language which corresponds to it exclude grammar from the realm of science and class it with the arts, whose aim is the application of theory to practice. But can the student of language afford to limit his task in this way, and is this indeed the way in which the discipline of linguistics, as it has developed historically, presents itself?

The distinction between art in the broad sense (which includes more than the fine arts) and science in general corresponds to the dictinction between practice and theory, between invention and discovery. Art operates with technical rules and procedures, whereas science deals with generalization from facts, with their implications, and scientific laws.[1] Art has two aspects: (1) a continuous practice based on tradition, and (2) improvement in the means of realizing practical tasks. Analogously, the historical development of science presents: (1) the transmission of knowledge from one generation to another, and (2) the broadening and improvement of knowledge by diligent and talented scientists. Each step forward in art is made through invention; each step forward in science is made through discovery.

In the realm of language (as distinct from the science of language) one may also speak of art (or rather of arts) as applied to language in general and to individual languages. Among others these arts include:

A. Those which apply the results of science to everyday needs:

1) The first of these is the mastery of a language or languages, beginning at an early age and lasting throughout life. This process is partly a problem of didactics and partly a matter of independent work, the success of which depends on the ability and practical aptitude of the student. It may involve the mastery of (a) a native language, and (b) of foreign languages. Sources here depends to a large extent on the application of discoveries of linguistic science, which in the case of one's native language provides an insight into (a) the acquisition of the language by the young child, and (b) its free and skillful use by the older child.[2] In the case of foreign languages it provides an informed and conscious approach that

facilitates understanding, correct use, and fluency. The application of art in this area consists in the improvement of practice, exercises, and teaching methods.[3] Midway between the study of a native language and the study of foreign languages is the study of the literary language, that language which unifies a whole people and facilitates the mutual understanding of its members, and which usually represents (with some modifications) the colloquial speech of the so-called educated class (in contradistinction to folk dialects). In countries where the literary language differs considerably from the local dialects (for example, in Germany), its study is for many people not much easier than that of a foreign language.[4]

2) The art of teaching language to deaf-mutes is characterized by methods all its own. Audible language is not accessible to deaf-mutes who possess only the language of pantomime. And although they may produce sounds which resemble language sounds, these sounds exist only for the hearer; the movements of the articulatory muscles are to the deaf-mutes of the same order as a grimace or gesture of the fingers. The training of deaf-mutes to pronounce words audibly takes into account the anatomical and physiological aspects of grammar.

Only a clear knowledge of the sounds of language (as opposed to their graphic representations) and of the origin and structure of words can provide

3) a good method of teaching children (and adults) to read and write a given language, and

4) an orthography and spelling which reflect the achievements of our science.

B. Everyday needs, the tendency toward convenience, simplicity, and facilitation of social intercourse, have brought forth in each nation possessing a literature of its own a single, more or less standardized, and educated language which serves to unify the members of the nation and which serves as a link between successive generations. Because of this very function, such a language unavoidably tends to be conservative and to resist the course of natural development. The role of human consciousness in this matter is of paramount importance.

The conscious and unconscious striving toward regularity, order, and correctness may, in turn, give rise to a linguistic purism which borders on pedantry[5] and which leads to constant interference with the natural course of language, to the proscription of phenomena that appear to be irregular, and to prescriptions of how things should be. The grammarians concoct "inexorable" rules, together with exceptions to the rules,[6] that are supposed to enable a foreigner to speak a given language "more correctly" (i.e., in accordance with the grammar) than the native. But grammarians, approaching language from such a viewpoint, do not understand its development: they do not know that seeming grammatical exceptions can be explained by the history of the language and are either remnants of past "rules" or harbingers of future ones.[7] It is pleasant to legislate, if only in the field of language, and every (or almost every) practically oriented grammarian tries to arrogate to himself the right to pass verdicts in this area. It is very difficult to resist this temptation, and the disposition to organize and to improve one's native tongue is shared even by enlightened and objective minds.[8]

If to the above-mentioned factors we add the effect of ever greater politeness and flattery, accuracy and logic, we obtain a more or less complete picture of the interference of man's consciousness upon language, which at a certain point of development introduces true *artificiality* into language. Although the extent of this interference is limited, it leaves a definite mark on the structure and make-up of language.

C. In addition to the linguistic skills which form a bridge between science and life, between theory and practice, there is that skill which enables science to operate, namely its technical aspect. It includes, among others, the practice, continuity and dissemination of science, and allows for its growth, new discoveries, and methods; it speeds up the research of scholars and facilitates its mastery by beginners.

The main conditions of the pursuit of science are, in my opinion, the availability of adequate data and proper scientific method.

Adequate data can be gathered only through the study of pertinent phenomena, through the identification of the scientific facts which circumscribe the object of inquiry. In the case of language this means the practical study of languages, the categories of which we wish to comprehend scientifically and treat theoretically.[9] Only by acquiring a practical knowledge of the languages one is dealing with can one avoid the kind of errors committed, for example, by

Th. Benfey in his *Griechisches Wurzellexicon,* where the author interprets the Old Church Slavonic *prazdĭnujǫ (ferior)* as "they beat me" instead of "I celebrate," or *ukradǫ (furor)* as *toben* "to rave, make noise" instead of *stehlen* "to steal," etc.[10] For our purposes it is sufficient to understand the languages; to speak them fluently and to write them is desirable,[11] but not necessary.[12]

The gathering of data goes hand in hand with the elaboration of a scientific technique, or *method,* for (1) the analysis of facts and the inferences drawn from them, and (2) the presentation and transmission of scientific results. The latter includes all kinds of teaching aids and exercises, and such auxiliary means as translations from one language into another or from one form into another (e.g., morphological and phonetic translations), etc.

One may now ask whether the subject of our course, linguistics, falls within one of the above-mentioned practical pursuits. Will we attempt to provide instructions for the successful study of languages by people with the gift of speech or by deaf mutes? Or will our course be a guide for the study of reading and writing, including orthographical prescriptions and rules? Or shall we be concerned with the purification and improvement of language and its application to everyday needs? Or will our lectures, finally, be an exposition of technique, methodology, and propaedeutics?

I must answer all these questions in the negative. The subject of our courses will not be the acquisition of a skill, nor its practice, nor a technique, but primarily the pursuit of *science,* theory, scientific knowledge, with science being interpreted as the exercise of the human mind on the sum total (or complex) of more or less homogeneous facts and concepts.

But the theoretical study of language can also be heterogeneous, depending on the interpretation of the tasks and methods of our science. If we ignore the purely practical aspect, whose aim is the mastery of foreign languages with a maximum of fluency and a minimum of reflection (which is in direct contradiction to the requirements of science, since it calls for a passive attitude toward foreign languages plus an ability to imitate, whereas science aims at a conscious mastery of facts by means of independent reflection— cf. the remarks above concerning linguistic skills[13]), linguistics or the historically developed, conscious, scientific investigation of languages and human speech in general can be discussed in terms of its three distinct approaches:[14]

1) A *descriptive* approach, an extreme empirical one, which sees its task in gathering facts and generalizing from them in a purely external manner, without attempting to explain their causes or to establish their affinity and genetic relationship. The adherents of this approach see all the wisdom of science in the preparation of descriptive grammars and vocabularies, in editing linguistic records, in preparing material without any conclusions, which for some reason or other are always considered overly bold or premature. This attitude stems in part from too strict a critical or skeptical turn of mind which flatly denies the possibility of any real science for fear of reaching the wrong conclusions or of stating hypotheses that might eventually be disproved; in part, however, this attitude must be ascribed to a kind of mental laziness and a desire to avoid the question of the usefulness and goal of gathering data, a desire which thus reduces science to a purely empirical endeavor, to some sort of meaningless game. These scholars defer the explanation of data *ad acta, ad meliora tempora,* losing sight of the important fact that the accumulation of details and their primitive, slavish, purely external explanation may eventually be useful not to themselves, nor to science directly, but to other investigators who will profit from these data if they are trustworthy and conscientiously prepared. It is obvious that if science is to avoid this situation of not seeing the forest for the trees, its practitioners must by all means abandon this approach.[15] Nevertheless, as the first, preliminary step in science, pure description is indispensable. Accurate and faithful observation is, indeed, the first requirement of science, and it is given to few to do it to a high degree of perfection; many can look, but only few can see. Good descriptive grammars, text editions, and dictionaries will always remain a vital need of our science; without them theoretical conclusions of genius will lack a factual foundation.

2) The contrary of this modest and restrained approach is the speculative, philosophizing, aprioristic and childish approach, whose adherents recognize the need to explain phenomena but do not know how to go about it. They think up certain aprioristic (both general and particular) principles and force the facts without much ado, into the strait jacket of these principles. Herein lies the source of the most heterogeneous, biased grammatical theories concerning both the development of language and such language-related fields as history, the study of antiquities, mythol-

ogy, ethnography, etc. These theories are the source of innumerable arbitrary and unfounded explanations which merely attest to the lack of common sense in their authors. Who has not heard the queer etymologies for which one would like to put Messrs. Etymologists in a lunatic asylum? As the alchemists tried to reduce all existence to primitive matter and a mysterious universal force, so some of the representatives of the aprioristic approach try to derive all the wealth of human speech from one or several consonantal groups.[16] Nowadays alchemy is obsolete but linguistic alchemists are still with us; as a matter of fact there is little hope in the near future of driving fantasy and arbitrariness out of the field of linguistics.

The aprioristic trend in linguistics has in recent times given rise to the so-called *philosophic* school, which uses speculation and a limited knowledge of facts to construct grammatical systems that force linguistic phenomena into a logical strait jacket. Of course such systems may represent more or less sophisticated schemes of scholarly minds, products of the art of logic, impressive in their harmony and order; but because they violate and distort the facts for the sake of a narrow theory, they are no more than castles in the air and cannot satisfy the requirements of positive thinking.

If the descriptive, blunt, empirical approach merely holds back the development of science, the aprioristic, arbitrary, and childish approach leads it astray. Because of this, it is decidedly harmful.

3) The truly scientific, *historical,* genetic approach views language as the sum total of actual phenomena, of actual facts, and the discipline analyzing them as an inductive science. The task of an inductive science is (1) to explain phenomena by comparing them with each other, and (2) to establish forces and laws or the fundamental categories and concepts that connect the phenomena and present them as a chain of cause and effect. The first of these tasks is to present to the human mind a systematic knowledge of a certain sum of homogeneous facts or phenomena, whereas the second introduces into the inductive sciences an ever more prominent deductive element. In the same way, linguistics as an inductive science (1) generalizes the phenomena of language and (2) looks for the forces operating in language and for the laws that govern its development, its life. Of course, all facts have equal rights and can be viewed only as more or less significant; by no means can some be deliberately ignored, and it is simply ridiculous to sneer

at facts. All that exists is reasonable, natural, and lawful; this is the watchword of any science.

Many see in "comparison" a special, distinctive mark of the modern science of language, and therefore quite readily and almost exclusively use such terms as "comparative grammar," "the comparative study of languages" (*vergleichende Sprachforschung*), "comparative linguistics" (*vergleichende Sprachwissenschaft*), "comparative philology" (*philologie comparée*), etc. It seems to me that this view is motivated by a certain narrowness and clannishness; if we consider the intentions of the "comparative" grammarians and other "comparative" investigators of language, we can say that every science could be adorned with the epithet "comparative." And thus we could speak of comparative mathematics, comparative astronomy, comparative physics, comparative psychology, comparative logic, comparative geography, comparative history, comparative political economy, etc. Indeed, comparison is one of the indispensable operations of all sciences, as it is the basis of thinking in general. The mathematician compares magnitudes, obtaining in this way data for his synthetic and deductive reasoning; the historian arrives at his conclusions by comparing different phases of a certain kind of human events. Comparison in linguistics plays the same role as it does in the other inductive sciences: it enables us to generalize from facts and opens the road to the deductive method. From another viewpoint, however, "comparative grammar" has a historical meaning: it owes its origin to a new school, a new trend that has made significant discoveries. For this school comparison has meant the comparison of related languages and, more generally, of similarities and dissimilarities of languages;[17] but it does not mean comparison of linguistic facts in general, for the latter is a necessary prerequisite of all scientific analyses of language. A similar historical meaning attaches to the names "comparative anatomy," "comparative mythology," and so on. However, we must not forget that this is only a single moment in the history of a science, when comparison applied in a novel, hitherto unknown way, has yielded vast and completely new results. But if we are to name a science, not after its transient phases or particular scientific procedures but after its subject matter, then we should forgo such names as comparative grammar or comparative linguistics or explanatory grammar[18] (*erklärende Grammatik*) or explanatory linguistics (*erklärende Sprachwissenschaft*) or comparative philology.[19] The most appropriate name for the science of language (which is not unlike the natural sciences) would then be simply *the study of languages* and of human speech in general, the *science of languages (jazykovedenie, jazykoznanie)*, or *linguistics (lingvistika, glottika)*. The name should not commit us to anything but only indicate the subject of the field in which the scientific questions arise. At any rate, a science may be called by any name, and in particular it may be called "comparative," so long as it is clear that comparison is not the end but only a means,[20] and that it is not the monopoly of linguistics but the common property of all sciences without exception.

I have noted that linguistics investigates the life of language in all its manifestations, correlates the phenomena of language, generalizes from the facts, sets up laws of the development and existence of language, and looks for its operating forces.

Law here means a formulation, a generalization that states that under certain conditions, after *a* or *b*, there appears *x* and *y*, or that *a* and *b* in one domain of phenomena (for example, in one language or in one category of words or forms of a given language) corresponds to *x* and *y* in another domain.[21] For example, one of the general laws of the development of language holds that a more difficult sound or group of sounds is replaced in the course of time by one more easily pronounced; another holds that abstract notions develop from more concrete ones, etc. There are seeming exceptions to these laws; nevertheless, under closer scrutiny the exceptions appear to be governed by certain causes, by forces that have prevented the causes or forces accounting for the general law from embracing the seeming exceptions. Once convinced of this, we must realize that our original generalization was inaccurate and incomplete and that the *genus proximum* of our law must be corrected by a limiting *differentia specifica*. Only then does it become clear that the seeming exception is, strictly speaking, only a corroboration of the general law.[22]

It is appropriate to call the common causes, the common factors, which effect the development of language and determine its structure and composition, *forces*. Such forces are, for example:

1) *habit,* that is, unconscious memory;

2) a *tendency toward convenience,* which expresses itself (a) in the transition from more difficult sounds and groups of sounds to easier ones (in order to conserve muscular and neural activity),

(b) in the simplification of forms (through the analogical influence of stronger forms on weaker), and (c) in the transition from the concrete to the abstract in order to facilitate abstract thinking;

3) unconscious *forgetting* and failure to understand (forgetting what was not known even consciously and failure to understand what could not even be understood consciously); but not fruitless, negative forgetting and lack of understanding (as is the case in conscious mental operations), but productive, positive forgetting and lack of understanding, which produce something new by encouraging unconscious new generalization;

4) unconscious generalization, *apperception,* i.e., the force by which a nation groups all the phenomena of mental life into certain general categories. This force is analogous to the force of gravity in planetary systems: just as the force of gravity produces certain systems of heavenly bodies, so the force of unconscious generalization accounts for certain systems and families of linguistic categories; and just as a heavenly body when it leaves the field of attraction of a given planet, moves in space alone until it is drawn into a new system, so certain words or forms whose connection with related forms is lost to the feeling of a nation (or, like loan-words that have at first no connection with the native words of a given language) stand by themselves until they are attracted into some family of words or category of forms through the speakers' ability to create new words through analogy, etc.;

5) unconscious *abstraction,* the unconscious tendency toward separation and differentiation. If apperception is the centripetal force in language, this force (based on unconscious abstraction) can be compared with the second, or centrifugal force,[23] while both forces together make up the force of gravity in general.

The action of the above linguistic forces is deployed in two areas and presents, as it were, two aspects:

1) the purely physical aspect of language, its system of sounds and groups of sounds which is connected with the organic make-up of a given speech community and which is subject to the continuous influence of inertia (*vis inertiae*);

2) the *feeling for the language* of a given speech community. The speakers' feeling for a language is not a fiction, not a subjective invention; it is a real, positive category (function) that can be defined in terms of its properties and effects, and which can be objectively confirmed and proven by facts.

The struggle of the above-mentioned forces determines the development of language. Of course, this struggle and the action of linguistic forces in general must not be personified; science does not deal with myths, but with representations and concepts. Laws and forces are not living beings; they are not even facts; they are products of man's intellectual activity, whose purpose is to *generalize,* to correlate facts, and to find their common denominator, their common formula. Nor are they demonic ideas, as suggested by philosophers of a certain school; they are generic concepts (*Artbegriffe*), which are all the more powerful the wider the range of the phenomena which they encompass and explain. On the other hand, these laws and forces, as, in general, all concepts and conceptual categories, are not global in their kind, but sums of innumerable specific representations and concepts.

I shall refrain from a more detailed analysis of forces and laws, since (1) time does not permit, and (2) strictly speaking, it is the subject of logic, that science which deals with the foundation of knowledge and abstract thought in general. I shall only pose the question: can the general categories of linguistics[24] be treated as laws and forces in the same sense as the laws and forces of physics and other natural sciences? Indeed they can, since the forces and laws of the natural sciences are nothing but unifying formulas of thought, more or less successful generalizations. Their superiority lies only in the simplicity of the phenomena and facts which they examine and in the uninterrupted development of the sciences themselves, which have allowed them to apply mathematical computations and thereby to acquire a high degree of clarity and accuracy, while the highly complex processes of language and the brief history of the science of linguistics have kept its generalizations in a more or less precarious and unstable state. This, however, should not perturb us, considering that the general categories arrived at by the most recent schools in the biological sciences (zoology and botany) are hardly more accurate and clear; they too are only more or less successful generalizations and not forces and laws, if they are to be measured by the same exacting standards that we have become accustomed to apply in the fields of astronomy, physics, chemistry, etc.

It should be apparent from the foregoing remarks that two elements are inseparably linked in language: a *physical* and a *psychological* one (of course, these terms must not be interpreted as metaphysical but as generic concepts). The forces and laws and the life of a language in general are based on processes which are of concern to physiology (to anatomy and acoustics) and to psychology. But the same physiological and psychological categories make up a rigidly defined subject which is investigated by the historically developed science of linguistics. Most of the questions raised by the linguist are never broached by the physiologist or psychologist; consequently, linguistics must be regarded as an independent science, not to be confused with either physiology or psychology. Similarly, physiology examines the same processes, laws, and forces of whole organisms whose abstract analysis is of concern to physics and chemistry; nevertheless, one cannot dismiss physiology in favor of the latter sciences.[25]

Having thus defined, though only in an approximate and inexact manner, the subject of our discipline and the scientific approach that reflects best its present-day state, I shall try to draw an outline of its internal organization, that is, to present to you, gentlemen, the basic branches of linguistics as they have developed historically.[26]

One must first distinguish *pure linguistics,* linguistics *per se,* whose subject is language itself as the sum total of more or less homogeneous facts that belong totally to the so-called manifestations of human life, and *applied linguistics,* whose subject is the application of the results of pure linguistics to questions pertaining to other sciences.

Pure linguistics presents two large areas of research:

A. the exhaustive study of empirically given, fully formed languages.

B. the study of the origin of human speech, the original formation of languages, and the investigation of the general psychophysiological conditions of their uninterrupted existence.[27]

A. *Empirical linguistics* is divided into two parts: (1) in the first, language is examined as a composite of parts, that is, as the sum of heterogeneous categories which are organically (internally) interrelated; (2) in the second, languages as wholes are investigated according to their affinity and formal similarity. The first part is *grammar,* the analysis of the structure and composition of language; the second is systematics, or *classification.* The first can be compared to anatomy and physiology, the second to plant and animal morphology in a botanical-zoological sense.[28] It should be understood that, as everywhere in nature and in science, there are no sharp borderlines between them and that research in one field is based on and delimited by the results obtained in another field. In order to analyze the structure and composition of a certain language, it is very useful, perhaps necessary, to know to what formal type the language belongs; and in order to explain its phenomena by corresponding phenomena of related languages, one must define its place within a certain linguistic branch or family. Similarly, only an examination of the structure and composition of languages provides a solid foundation for their classification.

I. To give a step-by-step analysis of a language, one may subdivide *grammar* into three basic parts: (1) phonology (phonetics), or the study of sounds, (2) word-formation, in the broadest sense of the word, and (3) syntax.

1. The first condition for a sucessful *study of sounds* must be a strict and clear distinction between sounds and their graphic representations. Since no orthography is completely consistent or accurate in rendering sounds and sound combinations, and since inadequate methods of teaching and practice have contributed, or, to be more fair, have not removed the misconceptions stemming from a primitive *concrete* conception of reality, the observance of the above-stated condition requires that one approach the analysis of sounds in parallel ⟨with writing⟩; each sound or group of sounds must be compared with the corresponding graphic sign or letter or group of letters. The subject of phonetics includes:

a) the analysis of sounds from a purely *physiological* point of view, the natural conditions of their formation, their development, their classification, their division (even here we cannot approach language apart from man, but must regard sounds as acoustic products of the human organism);[29]

b) the role of sounds in the mechanism of language, their value for the feeling of a speech community, is determined not so much by their physical properties as by their physiological nature and their origin and history, which involves the analysis of sounds from the viewpoint of morphology and word formation;

c) the analysis of sounds from a *historical* viewpoint: the genetic development of sounds, their history, and their etymological and morphological affinities and correspondences.

The first, physiological (a), and the second, morphological (b) parts of phonetics analyze the laws and conditions of the existence of sounds at a given stage or moment of the language (the statics of sounds). The third, or historical part studies the laws and conditions of the development of sounds in time (the dynamics of sounds).

2. *Word formation,* or morphology, traces the gradual development of language: it reconstructs the three periods of this development (monosyllabism, agglutination or free juxtaposition, and inflection). The parts of morphology are:

a) *etymology,* or the study of roots;

b) *stem formation,* or the study of derivational suffixes and of stems or bases;

c) *inflection,* or the study of desinences and complete words that are found in highly developed, inflected languages.

As generally in nature and science, here too it is difficult to draw clear-cut boundaries and to decide whether a given question falls into one or another category. The transition from a lower to a higher stage of development (or from an earlier to a later stage) is, after all, accomplished, not by leaps and bounds, but slowly, gradually, and imperceptibly.

3. *Syntax,* or word combination, investigates words as parts of sentences and defines them by their function in connected discourse in the sentence (a function which determines their division into parts of speech); it studies the meaning of words and forms in their interrelation. It, furthermore, analyzes whole sentences as parts of larger units, and the combination and relationship of these units.

Just as anatomy is not applicable to the study of all organisms (for example, osteology applies only in the study of vertebrates), not all of the above-mentioned parts of grammar apply to all languages. Thus, for example, the study of monosyllabic languages (whose main representative is Chinese) involves only phonetics and syntax; of word formation there remain only the problems of etymology, that is, the analysis of particular kinds of roots.

The grammatical study of a language requires adherence to the *chronological* principle, that is, the principle of genetic objectivity with regard to the development of language in time. This principle is founded on the three following propositions:

1) No language is born suddenly; it is the result of a gradual and unique development through different periods spanning many

centuries. The periods of development do not replace one another as one sentry replaces another, but each period creates something new which, in the imperceptible transition from one stage to another,[30] prepares the basis for the subsequent development. The cumulative effects of changes occurring over a period of time can be observed only at discrete stages; in the natural sciences they are called strata. Similarly, one may speak of *strata* with regard to language, and the separation of strata is one of the principal tasks of linguistics.[31]

2) The mechanism of a language (its structure and composition) at any given time is the result of all its preceding history and development, and each synchronic state determines in turn its further development.

3) It is inappropriate to apply to the structure of a language at a given period the categories of a preceding or following period. It is the task of the investigator to describe a language structure precisely as it is at each period and only then to demonstrate how the structure and composition of that period could give rise to the structure and composition of the following period. The requirement of genetic objectivity also applies to the investigation of different languages; it is unscientific to ascribe arbitrarily the categories of one language to another language; science must not impose alien categories on its object of study, but must seek in it only what really exists, what defines its structure and composition.[32]

Grammatical problems can be tackled in two ways: they can be discussed in terms of the general categories of ⟨our⟩ science, in terms of the homogeneity of the particular facts, or they can be treated in terms of their genetic development.[33] The first approach identifies similar phenomena in various areas of human speech, or in all languages accessible to the investigator, or within a strictly defined group of languages (or even in one language), with the ultimate goal of formulating general categories, the laws and forces which explain linguistic phenomena. The second approach describes the natural course of a language, abstracting and systematizing only as much as is indispensable for any science; otherwise it traces the internal development of its subject matter (either from the oldest to the most recent period or only of one particular period). This *internal history* of a language (or languages) must be clearly distinguished from its external history,[34] which approaches language ethnologically, from the point of view of the fate of its speakers, and which is consequently a part of applied linguistics, inasmuch as it applies its systematics to ethnography and ethnology (it is in this sense that we speak of applied linguistics as bearing on other sciences). Ordinary grammars select and describe only a certain period in the history of a language. But in order to be truly scientific, one ought to compare the state of the language at this period with the entire development of the language.

The degree of scientific perfection reached by contemporary linguistics is such that, with the amount and precision of available empirical data, and with the knowledge of the history and current tendencies of a language, and drawing upon comparable findings in other languages, we can generally predict the future internal development of that language or construct its past in the absence of written records.[35]

For lack of time I shall not give examples, the more so because in this course many examples will be brought to your attention. Of course, with regard to the future, these scientific (but not prophetic) linguistic predictions are by no means as exact as the predictions of, let us say, astronomy. They are only capable of pointing out in general terms a future phenomenon, but are incapable of determining the exact moment of occurrence of such a phenomenon. But even this is quite encouraging and proves the validity of current research methods, and brings linguistics closer to the goal of all inductive sciences, that is, the broadest possible use of the deductive method.

II. *Systematics,* classification of languages, must not be undertaken with a view to superficially facilitating their study by ordering them on the basis of randomly selected or preconceived characteristics. A truly scientific and modern classification of languages must take into account their natural development and be founded on their genuinely distinctive properties.

In the field of cognate languages,[36] that is, of languages that have developed from a common language and have merely modified the same original material (as a result of the diverse conditions that affected the speakers of these languages), classification itself is only a different aspect of the history of a language. We need only regard these languages as entities, or better, as complexes of meaningful sounds and sound groups presenting a unified whole in the mind of a given people and, on the other hand, to single out the properties of individual languages which set them apart from others or which they share with a larger group in order to realize that the history of language yields *eo ipso* a *genetic* classification of languages. At the same time one must keep in mind that the principle of the genetic differentiation of related languages must be sought not, as is usually done, in phonetic, lexical, and formal differences, but in the general tendencies that determine the unique development of the entire mechanism of a language, since only these tendencies constitute characteristic and invariant properties which enable us to identify individual languages in a family of more or less closely related languages.

Along with genetic classification, there is *morphological* classification, which distinguishes languages in terms of their structural properties, i.e., of those properties which make up the second part of grammar: morphology, or word formation.[37] The morphological difference between various groups of languages is the result of an original and fundamentally different world view of the speakers of these languages, which must have preceded the actual formation of these languages and contributed, in fact, to their formation.[38] Therefore, morphologically different languages cannot be genetically related.[39] Conversely, genetically different languages may belong to the same morphological type, exhibiting an identical, or at least similar structure.[40]

Cutting across the genetic and morphological classification there is the division of inflected languages into *primary* and *secondary,* synthetic and analytic. In the primary languages the composition of words is still keenly felt and flexion is still expressed by means of endings, etc. In the secondary languages, words are made up of mere sequences of sounds, and inflectional relationships are expressed by means of independent words. The basic character of the two types is, nevertheless, the same: they only employ different means to render similar tendencies and functions. Here too, one can hardly draw sharp boundaries, in view of the great variety of transitional states. Moreover, even the most evolved flexional languages exhibit rudiments of the secondary type, while the languages that have moved furthest in the direction of the secondary type retain traces of their original primary structure.

Of the seven known, scientifically described, and genetically ordered groups of languages,[41] two have attracted the greatest attention, for they are most highly advanced in their morphological, flexional structure and their speakers have formed the most civilized and influential nations in world history. These are the *Semitic* and the *Indo-European* groups (branches) of languages.[42] The latter has been subjected to a particularly close scientific scrutiny, and the method of studying it has been applied to the study of other groups as well.

The method of our science can best be understood when it is applied to a strictly defined family or branch of languages. We shall study the Indo-European languages exclusively, investigating their structure and composition during their historical development and their mutual relationships. The *Indo-European* (Aryo-European) branch is divided into eight separate families: (1) Indic, (2) Iranian, (3) Greek, (4) Romance, (5) Celtic, (6) Germanic, (7) Lithuanian, and (8) Slavic. These families separated at different times from a common original language, but some of them remained together longer than others and present more resemblances. On the last matter scholarly opinion is divided, and one must confess that the methods used for resolving it are far from satisfactory (cf. the discussion above on the principle of the genetic classification of languages). We may regard as settled the close kinship of Indic and Iranian, of Slavic and Lithuanian, and probably, of Greek and Romance.[43]

The oldest written records of the Indo-European branch are represented by the Vedas, the sacred literature of the Indians. Their language, Sanskrit, later became, in a somewhat modified form, a common literary vehicle. Thus Sanskrit is not a popular language, but rather a sacred literary language of the same order as Old Church Slavonic (for the ancient Slavs) and contemporary High German (for the Germans). Sanskrit is very important for the study of the Indo-European branch in general both because of the detailed and sucessful analysis which it received at the hands of native grammarians and because of its transparent structure. However, Sanskrit is only one of the members of the Indo-European branch of languages (it is not the proto-language, being but one of the derived languages with the oldest records), and it does not exhaust the wealth of questions raised in the study of this branch; strictly speaking, similar questions arise in a detailed historical study of any other language or family (for example of Slavic, Germanic, or Greek). But a thorough knowledge of the grammatical structure of Sanskrit will do no harm, as long as one avoids the widespread fetishization of Sanskrit and as long as one does not force its categories on the study of other languages.

B. Grammar and systematics complete the scientific investigation of historically existing languages. The second part of pure linguistics deals with questions that lie outside the domain of historically attested facts, such as the beginnings of human speech, its original formation, the general psychological-physiological prerequisites of its existence, the influence of a people's world view on the development of their language and, conversely, the influence of language on the world view of its speakers, on the psychological development of a people, etc. Many investigators of language relate these questions to anthropology and psychology, but it seems to me that since they refer to language, they should also be studied from a linguistic viewpoint, the more so as their solution depends on data provided by the empirical part of our science, by historical linguistics.

Applied linguistics includes:

1) the application of grammatical data to quesions of mythology (etymological myths),[44] antiquities, and the history of culture (by comparing cuturally and historically important words, which are especially pertinent to the reconstruction of a prehistoric period, the study of which constitutes the field of so-called linguistic paleontology). Grammatical investigations are also relevant to the study of mutual relations between various peoples;

2) the application of systematics to ethnography and ethnology and to the history of peoples in general (the classification of languages in relation to the classification of peoples); and, finally,

3) the application of the results of the second part of linguistics (the beginning of language, etc.) to questions of anthropology, zoology, etc. (the contribution of the linguist to these fields is, however, secondary).

In the preceding exposition, I have tried to define linguistics, to point out its basic questions, and to present its internal organization and historical development. But so far I have not posed the question of what is language, though a clear, even a negative, definition would be quite instructive.[45]

Before answering this question, I consider it necessary to refute most emphatically the prejudice held by some scholars that language is an organism. This view was formed on the basis of analogy, though it must be apparent that analogy does not constitute a proof. The recourse to analogy is, in effect, a way of avoiding genuine, serious analysis. It gives rise to empty talk, to scholarly phrase-mongering, which misleads superficial minds and serious people alike. Without entering into a more detailed analysis and critique of the thesis that language is an organism, and without bothering to define the nature of an organism, I shall only remark that an organism, like an inorganic substance, is something tangible that fills a certain space and which, furthermore, eats, drinks, breeds, etc.,[46] whereas man's speech (and the existence of language depends on that, of course) is connected with the movements of his speech organs and the resulting vibrations in the air that produce the sense impressions which are associated with corresponding representations in the mind of the hearer and the speaker.[47] To treat language as an organism is to personify it, to detach it completely from the speakers, from man, and to lend credence to the story of a certain Frenchman who was supposed to have said during the winter campaign of 1812 that his words did not reach his listener's ear but froze in the air halfway. If language is an organism, it must indeed be a very delicate one, and the parts of this organism, words, could hardly be expected to brave the severe Russian cold.

I shall forgo analyzing all the errors and fallacies that ensue directly or indirectly from the misconception that language is an organism.[48] But before I submit the final definition of language, I shall draw your attention, first, to the distinction between human speech in general (as a sum of all present and past languages) and between separate languages, dialects (or the languages of each individual).[49] Second, I would like to point out the distinction between language as a complex of constituent parts and categories that exist only *in potentia,* as a sum of all possible individual variations,[50] and language as a continually recurrent process based on the social character of man and his need to give concrete expression to his thoughts and to communicate them to other human beings (language—speech—the human word).

In the light of all that I have said, as well as what has not been fully said, and even of what has been left unsaid, I propose the following definition of language: Language is the audible result of the normal activity of muscles and nerves.[51] Or: language is a complex of separate and meaningful sounds and groups of sounds which are unified into a whole by the feeling of a certain people (as a collection of perceiving and unconsciously generalizing individuals) who form, in turn, one category, one intellectual species, owing to the language which they all share ⟨. . .⟩.

NOTES

1. In the historical development of any art (not the fine arts only), one must distinguish between unconscious art, that is, ordinary practice preceding theory (although even here unconscious invention is possible), and conscious art guided by theory and knowledge. In the same way, in science one can distinguish between the accumulation of fragmentary knowledge by the savage or uneducated man and the critical analysis of facts and the conscious generalizing of the educated and capable man.

2. See "On the Study of the Native Language in General, and in Particular during Childhood. From the Discussions of I. I. Sreznevskij" (*Izvestija imp. Akademii nauk po otdeleniju russkogo jazyka i slovesnosti*, vol. IX, 1860, pp. 1–51, 273–332; special reprint; fasc. 2, SPb, 1861). Here we also include all textbook-grammars and other books whose aim is to facilitate the study of their native language and the mastery of foreign languages by children.

3. Here we include the art of translating well from foreign languages into one's own language and vice versa.

4. The study of rhetoric pertains to linguistics only externally, i.e., as so-called orthoepy; internally, i.e., in terms of the choice and arrangement of thoughts, rhetoric pertains to dialectics or logic.

5. Cf. Jakob Grimm, "Über das Pedantische in der deutschen Sprache," *Kleinere Schriften*, I (Berlin, 1864), pp. 372–73.

6. Such rules and exceptions can only evoke an aversion for grammar in an independent, positive, and objective mind. Goethe said of grammatical rules and exceptions: "Die Grammatik missfiel mir, weil ich sie nur als ein willkürliches Gesetz ansah; die Regeln schienen mir lächerlich, weil sie durch so viele Ausnahmen aufgehoben wurden, die ich alle wieder besonders lernen sollte" (*Aus meinem Leben. Dichtung und Wahrheit*, I).

7. "Alle grammatischen Ausnahmen schienen mir Nachzügler alter Regeln, die noch hier und da zucken, oder Vorboten neuer Regeln, die über kurz oder lang einbrechen werden" (J. Grimm, Über das Pedantische in der deutschen Sprache," p. 329).

8. Thus, for example, even Schleicher, who considered himself strictly an observer of the natural development of language and made no allowance for the interference of free will upon the natural development of human speech, was concerned with the purity of his native language; he frequently spoke out against various "nonorganic," as he called them, phenomena in the German language that had been introduced by ignorant schoolmasters and called upon

his fellow countrymen to avoid such transgressions. In particular, the second part of his *Deutsche Sprache* is full of passages remarkable for their sermonizing vein and patriotic zeal. Here the practical approach was carried to an extreme. This book had the incidental purpose of awakening the "Nationalgefühl" of the Germans; in my opinion this is almost the same as trying to stimulate an appetite by an article on cooking.

9. "As an 'empirical' linguist," says Schleicher, "I am firmly convinced that only a working knowledge of languages can be the basis for linguistic studies and that one must first strive, as far as possbile, to become acquainted with the languages selected as the subject of research. Only on the basis of solid, positive knowledge can one do anything worthwhile in our science. *Didicisse juvat.* Thus, one who wants to devote himself to Indo-Germanic linguistics must first thoroughly study all the older Indo-Germanic languages, read texts, etc. Anyone who neglects some languages as less important will surely regret this later." (Schleicher, in *Die Wurzel AK im Indogermanischen von Dr. Johannes Schmidt. Mit einem Vorworte von August Schleicher* [Weimar, 1865], p. iv).

10. Cf. Aug. Schleicher, *Die Formenlehre der kirchenslawischen Sprache* . . . (Bonn, 1852), p. xi.

11. It is desirable to develop as fine a feeling for the languages studied as the general education of former times (the 16th and 17th centuries in Western Europe) enabled one to acquire for the so-called classical languages (Latin and Greek, but mainly Latin).

12. Knowledge and understanding of languages differ from command more or less as knowledge of physiological processes differs from their performance (of course, the disparity between the respective subjects makes for the inaccuracy of the comparison).

13. And for one who studies the theoretical side of linguistics, it is quite useful to acquire the widest possible knowledge of various languages, as I mentioned above.

14. Cf. *System der Sprachwissenschaft von K. W. L. Heyse,* . . . (Berlin, 1856), §§ 5–9, pp. 6–21; *Geschichte der Sprachwissenschaft und orientalischen Philologie in Deutschland . . . von Theodor Benfey* (München, 1869), pp. 1–12 ff.

15. The natural consequence of this approach is a narrow particularism which denies the propriety of comparing similar phenomena in different languages and restricts itself to the confines of a single language.

16. Thus, for example, all the words of all languages are regarded as arising from consonant groups signifying "rooster" in *Dr. Max Müller's Bau-Wau-Theorie und der Ursprung der menschlichen Sprache . . . von Dr. Christoph Gottlieb Voigtmann,* . . . (Leipzig, 1865); cf. Johannes Schmidt, in *Zeitschrift für vergleichende Sprachforschung*, XV, pp. 235–37. Voss concludes that all the words are from the original groups *phyō, feo,* and *geo;* cf. J. Grimm, "Über Etymologie und Sprachvergleichung," *Kleinere Schriften*, I, p. 307.

17. Recently there has been a tendency to compare human language with that of animals; this kind of comparison may be expected to yield completely new results.

18. As is known, the explanation of phenomena is the basic goal of all

70

science; explanation, therefore, cannot be considered the monopoly of one or a few of them.

19. To identify philology with linguistics means, on the one hand, to narrow the scope of their respective subjects (since philology deals with all phenomena of the mental life of a people, not only with language), and on the other hand, to define them too broadly (since philology has so far confined itself to a certain people or group of peoples, while general linguistics investigates the languages of all peoples). Philology, however, as it has developed historically, is not a homogeneous science but a conglomerate of parts of different sciences (linguistics, mythology, history of literature, cultural history, etc.) which find their common denominator in the fact that the carriers of these heterogeneous phenomena, which make up the subject and scientific problems of philology, are the same. Hence we can speak of classical (Graeco-Latin) philology, Sanskrit, Germanic, Slavic, Romance philology, and many others.

20. Some scholars, in fact, see all the wisdom of linguistics in comparison for comparison's sake (*ars gratia artis*), and they forget that there are many other interesting aspects of scholarly pursuit.

21. This is the basis for distinguishing laws of development in time from laws that define the synchronic state of a subject in space (or at any given moment of its existence), that is, for distinguishing that which undergoes change from what is essential and fundamental. The laws of one type pass into the laws of the other type; they are mutually related.

22. The necessary conditions for a scientific law are: (a) with regard to the subject: identification, clarity, and accuracy; (b) with regard to the object: generality.

23. Besides these and similar forces that affect the whole life of language, we must assume the existence at a certain stage of the development of mankind of another force (albeit a comparatively weak one): the influence of man's *consciousness* on language. This influence unifies the forms of language and in its own way improves it, since it is a consequence of the striving toward the ideal, as discussed above (in the analysis of linguistic skills). Although the influence of consciousness on language is manifested fully only in some individuals, its results are, nevertheless, transmitted to the whole speech community, slowing down the development of language, counteracting the influence of unconscious forces, which generally tend to accelerate development, all this for the sake of making language an agent of unification and the mutual understanding of all the present, past, and future members of a speech community. This ⟨force⟩ produces a certain stagnation, whereas languages which are not subject to the influence of human consciousness develop rapidly and without inhibitions. The role of consciousness also expresses itself in the (conscious and unconscious) influence of books (and literature in general) on the language of a literate people (e.g., the influence of Church Slavonic books on the pronunciation of the clergy in the Orthodox Slavic countries), the influence of literary on the popular language (e.g., the influence of Church Slavonic not only on the inventory of words but on the structure of spoken Russian) or the acceptance of certain bookish and newspaper expressions as

stereotyped phrases and clichés in everyday language; cf. *Zeitschrift für Völker-psychologie und Sprachwissenschaft* . . . , ed. by Lazarus and Steinthal, V, pp. 106–9.

Sometimes, despite all the efforts of investigators, it is impossible to discover what forces or causes bring about particular phenomena. In such a case, the question of cause must remain unanswered until more favorable circumstances allow the explanation of the phenomenon in terms of cause and effect. For a methodical mind, it is impossible to accept the existence of phenomena without cause and at the same time to pursue science seriously. Nevertheless, many scholars, in analyzing the various manifestations of the so-called inner life of man, prefer mystical explanations to natural ones and introduce into science completely unscientific categories such as purposefulness, chance, interference of demonic forces, etc., not only in cases where definite causes have not yet been discovered but even in cases where the phenomenon in question is explainable by forces and laws already known to science. To seek an objective purpose in phenomena in order to explain them is inadmissible. To say, for example, that "every historically formed nation lives *in order to* manifest and fully develop the capacities and traits bestowed upon it by Nature (!), *in order to* create a special culture, to contribute its share to human civilization" amounts to imposing upon science heartfelt and even noble intentions, letting loose one's fantasy, forgetting that the development of science (the preachings and the daydreams of idealists notwithstanding) is predicated on the question "why?" (and not "for what purpose?") and on the answer "because" (and not "in order to"). Scholars of this nonscientific stamp explain the general character of the manifestations of a given people, which is determined by its disposition and external conditions (or what we usually call "culture" and "civilization") as something bestowed upon them from above. These preachers of supernatural forces readily speak of the "spirit of a people," the "spirit of language," the "spirit of an age" (for example, in explaining particular phenomena by the spirit of the age), and the like, forgetting Goethe's cogent remarks:

> Was ihr den Geist der Zeiten heisst,
> Das ist im Grund der Herren eigner Geist.

A positive-thinking man first asks: *aut* . . . *aut,* i.e., whether purposefulness, destiny, free will, chance,* dogma, etc., and similar beautiful ideas can serve as instruments of explanation or not. If we begin to explain the most trivial phenomenon by purposefulness, destiny, free will, and the like, we must henceforth always admit similar explanations. To treat reality as a heap of incoherent and disconnected phenomena is to dismiss all causality, all science. I repeat: a methodical mind cannot at one and the same time admit the existence of phenomena without cause and not reject science. Science does not allow for compromises: it demands cool, unprejudiced, and abstract thinking.

24. We must distinguish between the categories of linguistics and the cate-

---

*The expressions "chance," "chance similarity," etc., as used by scientists signify either that the cause of the phenomenon is not known or that there is a similarity between various phenomena which have no genetic or natural connection.

gories of language: the former are pure abstractions; the latter, however, are the living part of language: sound, syllable, root, base (theme), ending, word, sentence, different categories of words, and the like. The categories of language are also categories of linguistics, but they are based on the speakers' feeling for the language and on the objective and unconscious conditions of the human organism, while the categories of linguistics in the strict sense are predominantly abstractions.

25. Cf. Theodor Benfey, *Geschichte der Sprachwissenschaft,* pp. 8–9. On the whole, however, all sciences constitute but one science, whose subject is reality. Individual sciences are the result of the attempt to divide the labor; yet this division is based on objective data, that is, on the greater or lesser similarity and affinity of phenomena, facts, and scientific questions.

26. In addition to linguistics proper as the study of language, linguistics includes two kinds of scientific pursuits which have been left aside here: (1) *the history of linguistics* (the investigation of the development of linguistic concepts and their realization in literature and pedagogy) which forms a part of the general history of the sciences, but which must be practiced by students of language, since they alone have a special interest in it and are sufficiently equipped to deal properly with the history of their science; and (2) linguistic propaedeutics, *methodology,* the theory of scientific techniques, whose task it is to work out the best methods of studying and furthering a science in all respects (to work out rules for study, research, and presentation).

27. Here it is apropos to mention a question of linguistic methodology which may contribute to the more accurate definition of some problems that arise in the various branches of pure linguistics. Such is the question of gathering material and the preliminary operations performed on it.

The material utilized in the first, positive section of pure linguistics falls into three categories:

1) The directly given material, or the multifarious variety of *living languages* accessible to the investigator. This also includes the national language in all its variety, the spoken language of all classes of society, be they rich or poor, the language of the peasantry as well as of the educated class ⟨. . .⟩. This material should include the language of all layers without exception: the speech of street urchins, tradesmen, hunters, workmen, fishermen, etc.; the language of different age groups (children, adults, old people) and of people under special conditions (for example, the language of pregnant women), the language of personalities, individual language, the language of families, etc. Of further interest are place names, proper names, and traces of foreign influence (something akin to linguistic fossils).

2) *Records of language* (in chronological order), literature not in the sense of esthetic or cultural products, but as a record of language. The contemporary literature of modern languages is only a document; it is not the language itself. For the reading of ancient monuments, paleography is a necessary linguistic tool. But documents are never a sufficient record of a given language, and data derived from their investigation must be supplemented by the study of the structure and composition of the contemporary language, if one exists, and by deductive reasoning and comparison with other languages, if it is extinct.

73

Usually the documents of a less civilized people transmit information about their language more faithfully than do those of peoples which have created artificial literary languages and writing systems. In the same way, present-day material that is of interest to linguistics includes, for example, letters of uneducated and semiliterate people. Linguistic records include not only entire works, but also single words and phrases occurring in a foreign language (cf. my *O drevnepol'skom jazyke do XIV stoletija*, sections 1–3). While the study of a living language can be justly compared with zoology and botany, it would be inaccurate to compare the analysis of documents with paleontology, inasmuch as language is not an organism and words are not parts of an organism; consequently, words cannot leave visible traces, real imprints (fossils) of their former existence, as do organisms or parts of organisms of animals and plants. Written records present only arbitrary, visual signs (graphs) of the audible sounds of language and allow conclusions about language only by analogy. The linguist cannot even see the structure of living languages (although he may hear their sounds), and he can judge the language of written records only by comparison and other scientific means. At the same time, the naturalist can sometimes re-create the structure of extinct organisms on the basis of fossils.

The preliminary operations based on the material of living languages and documents consist of the presentation of all the richness of languages in a published form, through the preparation of descriptive grammars and dictionaries.

3) Indirect material for inferences and conclusions about language is provided by: (a) children's language (which throws light on the formation of sounds, their alternation, the feeling for the root, the tendency to differentiate, etc.; (b) natural flaws in the pronunciation of individuals; (c) the pronunciation of deaf mutes; (d) the pronunciation of foreigners and their general treatment of a foreign language (this throws light on the difference between languages and on the nature of the languages compared).

The second part of pure linguistics, which deals with the beginning of the human word, with the primordial formation of sounds, etc., provides us no direct, only indirect, material, from which we can draw analogical inferences and conclusions:

1) The linguistic development of an individual illuminates the primordial formation of language, since we are taught by the natural sciences that the individual recapitulates, on a smaller scale, the changes of the species. Of primary interest here is the observation of the infant, of the young child, beginning to babble (revealing from the earliest age the rudiments of his future language). Observations thus made can be projected *mutatis mutandis* into the epoch of primordial speech. Nevertheless, analogical statements in this area should be made with great caution, since our baby differs from the primordial man who is about to begin or has just begun to speak: (1) zoologically: (a) in a collective sense, in that it represents another degree of development of the human species, a different brain structure and nervous system; (b) in an individual sense, in that it represents another degree, another stage of individual development; (2) the baby finds himself among people speaking a ready-made language, which has been formed over many generations, each of which added something to the language of its predecessors; the baby faces

from the start ready-made cultural relationships, while primordial man lived in a close relation with nature and submitted to its influence passively.

2) The comparison of various degrees of cultural and intellectual development of various peoples leads us to the conclusion that the contemporary state of humanity simultaneously presents different stages of its development ranging from half-wild savages to the highly advanced Caucasian tribe (race) (cf. the simultaneous existence in a society of children, adolescents, adults, elders, etc.). To gain an approximate picture of the primordial state of language, it is most instructive to investigate the languages of savages. When direct observation is impossible, one may draw this information from works of other scholars and from dependable descriptions by travelers.

3) The study of the general trends and direction in the development of languages enables one to retrace this development backward and to arrive at more or less tenable conclusions concerning the formation of primitive languages, even though these appear to us in advanced stage of development. It is clear that some modern languages retain, if only in a rudimentary state, much that constituted the essence of primitive languages.

The indirect observations concerning the original formation of languages should be corroborated by anatomical and physiological studies of man's nervous system, which should, perhaps, serve as a point of departure.

28. This comparison must not be taken literally for, as we shall see below, language is not an organism, whereas anatomy and physiology, just as the morphology of organisms, deal with actual organisms. The correctness of the comparison is based on the identity and similarity of the mental processes that occur in both areas.

29. The investigation of the sounds of language from a physical point of view must take into account the findings of physiology and acoustics. Some investigators of language show no interest in acoustics and physiology, depending in this matter on their own resources. I think that the scientific study of a subject can profit from various kinds of investigation and must not ignore the results of related sciences. Otherwise one is always performing the work of a Sisyphus ⟨. . .⟩.

30. The imperceptible transition from one state to another, the imperceptible effect of the slowly but thoroughly operating forces in language (as of other phenomena in life) can be expressed by the algebraic formula $O \times \infty = m$, which means that when an infinitely small change occurring at a given moment is repeated an infinite numbers of times, the final result is a noticeable, definite change. In the passage of time, extension of space, the action of a drop of water on a stone, etc., there is always an elusive, critical point when something vanishes without even leaving a tangible trace.

31. The first attempt to bring together and to synthesize this kind of investigation and to establish the separate layers in the formation of Indo-European is Georg Curtius' treatise, "Zur Chronologie der indo-germanischen Sprachforschung," *Abhandlungen der philologisch-historischen Classe der Königl. Sächsischen Gesellschaft der Wissenschaft*, 111, Leipzig, 1867. Curtius distinguishes seven main periods in the formation *(Organisation)* of the Indo-European languages: (1) the period of roots *(Wurzelperiode)*; (2) the

period of root determinants (*Determinativperiode*); (3) the period of primary verbs (*primäre Verbalperiode*); (4) the period of stem (base) formation (*Periode der Themenbildung*); (5) the period of complex verbal forms (*Periode der zusammengesetzten Verbalformen*); (6) the period of the formation of cases (*Periode der Casusbildung*); and (7) the period of adverbs (*Adverbialperiode*). One of the main conclusions of his work is that language employed the same means at different times in completely different ways (*dass die Sprache dieselben Mittel zu verschiedenen Zeiten in ganz verschiedener Weise verwendete* [p. 193]). The different changes of identical sounds under identical conditions can likewise be explained only by assuming a different chronology of these changes.

32. The error of many scholars is that in a genetic classification they carelessly compare languages of different stages of development, such as Sanskrit and Slavic, Sanskrit and English (the first is a very ancient, and the second a highly advanced Indo-European language).

33. As for the two main approaches of the inductive sciences (see above), it should be observed that the second approach chiefly generalizes and explains phenomena in terms of their genetic and synchronic relationship, whereas the first approach seeks to establish general laws and forces.

34. The external history of a language is closely connected with the fate of its speakers, the fate of its people. Its study comprises the geographic and ethnographic diffusion of a given language and the influence upon it of foreign languages (and vice versa). It deals, further, with the literary or spoken use of a given language, with the social status of its speakers, with its expansion in space (e.g., the spread of French, German, English, and the so-called universal languages) or in time (e.g., Latin, Greek, Church Slavonic), with its use by and function for other peoples, and other such questions. The internal history of a language, on the other hand, deals with its natural development apart from the fate of its speakers but of course not apart from the physical and psychological make-up of its speakers. The internal history can ignore the fate of the language, focusing only on the changes which occur within the language. Internal history investigates how a people speaks at a certain time or over the course of many centuries, and why it speaks in this way, while external history asks how many people speak the given language and where. The first approach concentrates more or less on the question of quality, the second on the question of quantity ⟨. . .⟩. The external and internal histories of a language (which are the object of a science, not the sciences) are related. The effect of the former on th latter seems to be stronger than the converse. The influence of foreign languages, literary treatment, native command, geographic conditions of the country determine the more or less rapid development of a given language and its specific character. The internal history of a language, the degree of its flexibility (though by itself an insignificant factor) determine the faster or slower development of its literature and are decisive factors in determining the question of the change of language, that is, when a given language is to be viewed, because of its deep changes, as a new language and its dialects as new and autonomous entities. The subject matter of the external history of a language is largely the same as that of history and history of lit-

erature. The historian often touches on the external history of the language when he discusses the expansion of a people, its education, and the flowering of its literature.

35. One of the important tasks of scholarship is to re-create the so-called original and basic languages (*Ursprachen* and *Grundsprachen*), i.e., the languages represented in modified form by actually existing languages. But one must keep in mind that the reconstruction of the original and basic languages represents not real phenomena but deductively obtained scientific facts.

36. The external test of the genetic relationship of languages is the possibility of phonetic translation from one language into another, that is, the possibility of rendering each word (except borrowings) of one language in the form of another language in accordance with specific sound laws and sound correspondences.

37. From this point of view, languages are most generally divided into monosyllabic, agglutinative, and flexional.

38. For an example, let us take the two extremes, the monosyllabic and the inflected languages. Inasmuch as language determines the national frame of mind, people speaking monosyllabic languages have never had (as a people or nation) and never will have a need to express conceptual relationships by means of material forms, sounds, and sound groups; we may even assume that speakers of such languages lack the conception of formal relationships altogether, which is not the case with speakers of flexional languages. The effort of abstraction which has led to the distinction of noun, verb, and other parts of speech is in the monosyllabic languages rendered through a strictly defined word order (e.g., the predicate follows the subject, the attribute precedes the subject, etc.). In the flexional languages, this task is achieved by means of purely formal elements.

39. This, of course, does not prevent a people from substituting a language of one structure with a language of another structure, and from breaking away from a given ethnic group or national language; it is sufficient to point to the Negroes in America who have adopted French or English; but when such a change takes place, there is probably a change also in the frame of mind of the people. On the other hand, the morphological structure of one language may combine with the material of another language (of course, only through borrowing); an example of this is the combination of Chinese structure with Russian material discussed in an article of S. I. Čerepanov, "Kjaxtinskoe kitajskoe narečie russkogo jazyka," in *Izvestija imp. Akademii nauk po otdeleniju russkogo jazyka i slovesnosti*, II, pp. 370–77.

40. However, this may be due to our inadequate and narrow morphological classification. Given a more precise and less narrow classification of the structure of various languages, the distinctions may turn out to be more numerous than has generally been assumed until now.

41. These groups are: (1) Indo-European, (2) Semitic, (3) Hamitic, (4) Finno-Tartar or Uralo-Altaic, (5) Dravidian, (6) Polynesian or Oceanic (Malayan), (7) South African.

42. The original basic difference between the Indo-European and Semitic languages is matched by an original basic difference in the religious beliefs of

their speakers or nations. The seeds of their religious differences must have been planted at a time when man was beginning to be man, beginning to speak: the form in which the deity enters into contact with man is personified for the Indo-Europeans and is endowed with prophetic powers for the Semites.

43. The close kinship between the Balto-Slavs and the Germans, posited by Grimm and Schleicher and now accepted by most scholars, was, surprisingly enough, expressed as early as the 13th century by a Polish chronicler, Boguchwał: "sic et Theutonici cum Slavic regna contigua haventes simul conversation e incedunt, nec aliqua gens in mundo est, sibi tam communis et familiaris, veluti Slavi et Theutonici" (cf. my *O drevnepol'skom jazyke do XIV stoletija*, dictionary entry *slavjanin*). The close kinship of the Slavs and the Lithuanians was recognized by the Poles of the 17th century. Here is what the well-known Polish writer Pasek writes on this subject: "Taka właśnie rożnica mowy Jutlandczyków od niemieckiej, jak Łotwy albo Żmudzi od Polaków" [There is the same difference in speech between the Jutlanders and the Germans, as between the Latvians or Lithuanians and the Poles.] *(Pamiętniki Paska* [Petersburg, 1860], p. 19).

44. Cf. the attempts to explain the biblical tale of the Tower of Babel. "In dem letzten Worte sehen wir sogar, wie die Sage von dem Bischof Hatto durch die Volksetymologie veranlasst wird, ähnlich wie man im Pentateuch mehrere dergleichen etymologischen Sagen, die Mythe vom babylonischen Thurmbau (die bekanntlich nur auf der falschen Anknüpfung des Namens Babel an hebr. *balal* beruht) an der Spitze, längst erkannt hat" (Förstemann, "Über deutsche Volksetymologie" in *Zeitschrift für Vergleichende Sprachforschung.* . . . , ed. by Aufrecht and Kuhn, I, 6).

45. Here one must remember the dictum *omnis definitio periculosa* and forgo a real definition that would implicitly include all properties of language in one condensed formula, since these properties can be known only through a study of details; it is sufficient to give a nominal definition that indicates only the subject of study without defining *a priori* all its properties and peculiarities.

46. We can observe an organism with our eyes, but language only with our hearing; what appears to our eyes in books is not language, but its graphic representation (e.g., an alphabet). An organism appears to us globally; it has continuous existence from the time of its birth until death. Language as a whole exists only *in potentia*. Words are not bodies and not elements of a body: they appear as complexes of significant sounds and sound groups only when man speaks, and they exist as representations of significant sound groups only in the brain, only when man thinks in them.

47. The word presents primarily two sides to observation: the sound form and the function which, as body and spirit in nature, never appear separately; even in actuality it is impossible to separate them without destroying the other side (cf. Dr. Johannes Schmidt, *Die Wurzel AK im Indogermanischen* . . . , [Wiemar, 1865], p. 2). Form and content, sound and thought, are so inseparably linked that neither can be changed without producing a corresponding change in the other (ibid., p. 1). In this view of the nature of language there is obviously something missing that might link sound and meaning; namely, the conception of sound as an interpretation of the external side of the word.

This shortcoming is the result of treating language apart from man. For where is the sound-form of thinking and writing, the processes which require the so-called function of words? These processes are, in fact, carried out by combining concepts of the object (meaning) with representations of sound (in writing, with representations of visual signs), and not with the audible production of sounds. A case in point is the deaf mute whose "speech" produces sound-waves and corresponding sound impressions that are perceived only by the hearer; the deaf mute associates the so-called function, not with sounds and sound-representations, but with certain movements of the organs and their representations; the effect of these movements on the air and on the ear of the hearer is to him incomprehensible. Some people are also known to have learned English (whose sounds are represented by a very difficult orthography) by sight without the help of a teacher. For such people the so-called function of English words is associated not with the sound form of the words, but with their graphic signs (compare the substitution of visual musical notes by tactile ones in teaching the deaf to play music). And could it be claimed that meaning (function) is, on the other hand, inseparable from sound for people endowed with a good ear who listen to a foreign language which they do not know? In all these cases, there is supposed to be some mystical association of the sound form with the so-called function without the participation of the individuals (the speakers who do not hear, the people who only read, or who hear but do not understand). The views referred to above are based on a narrow, falsely interpreted monism which applied consistently would vitiate the notions of birth, life, and death of the organism, and of the organism itself. For a dead organism retains its external form more or less (appearance and bodily structure), but loses its essential functions which give way to functions characteristic of a different organism.

48. Perhaps I shall soon have the possibility of treating more closely and critically the misleading view that language is an organism and similar views, such as that linguistics is a natural science (like botany and zoology), that it is completely different from philology, that language and history are opposed to and incompatible with each other, etc. I shall also try to point out some other errors and false notions about language and linguistics, which are in part unconsciously shared by the public and in part consciously fostered by scholars.

49. The language of an individual can be examined in terms of quality (way of pronunciation, choice of words, forms and phrases peculiar to a given individual, etc.) and in terms of quantity (the store of words and expressions used by the given individual). As for the latter, cf. Max Müller, *Vorlesungen über die Wissenschaft der Sprache . . . Für das deutsche Publikum bearbeitet von Dr. Carl Böttger* (2d ed.; Leipzig, 1866), pp. 227–28. One must also pay attention to the distinction between ceremonial and daily language, family and social language, and generally to linguistic diversity under various circumstances of life, to the distinction between the common language and the language of specialists, to varieties of language according to mood: the language of feeling, imagination, cerebration, etc.

50. From this point of view, language (or dialect, even individual speech) does not form a whole, but is a generic concept, a category into which one

may fit a complex of actual phenomena. Cf. also the concept of science as an ideal, as the complex of all scientific data and inferences, as opposed to science as a repeated scientific process.

51. Language is one of the functions of the human organism in the broadest sense of the word.

I I

A Program of Readings for a General Course

in Linguistics With Application to

the Indo-European Languages in General

and to the Slavic Languages in Particular (1875–1876)

DIVISION OF LINGUISTICS into pure and applied. Pure linguistics includes: (1) the comprehensive analysis of objectively given, existing languages, and (2) the study of the beginnings of human speech or language, the original formation of languages, and the general psychological-physiological conditions of their uninterrupted existence. The first, positive part of linguistics includes: (1) *grammar* and (2) *systematics*. Also of interest to linguists is the *history* and *methodology* of their science.

The *Indo-European languages* in general and their classification. Scholarly views concerning the gradual separation of these languages. The newest theory of J. Schmidt rejecting the possibility of any systematization in this area. The major families of the Indo-European languages.

A more detailed classification of the Baltic and Slavic families of the Indo-European languages. Common features of the Baltic and Slavic families. Their major phonetic differences.

GRAMMAR

Division of pure positive linguistics. *Analysis of language* as the basis of subdividing grammar. The simplest, elementary analysis of a concrete language, proceeding from complete expressions of thought (connected, live, concrete speech) to sentences, from sentences to words, from words to their significant, meaningful parts (words as complexes of significant, meaningful parts), on the one hand, and to purely physiological, acoustic parts of speech, to sounds on the other hand (words as complexes of discrete sounds). Analysis of words from different points of view. Division of grammar into (1) phonetics, (2) morphology, and (3) syntax.

I. Phonetics

Preliminary remarks: (1) The necessity of distinguishing sounds from corresponding letters. (2) The history of the development of writing and the origin (formation) of phonetic writing. (3) The difference between alphabet, graphics, and spelling (orthography). (4) Rendering of sounds of one's native tongue by symbols of the generally used native alphabet and graphics. Detailed survey of (a) the letters of an adopted alphabet which are used to represent the individual sounds of a given language, and of (b) the sounds of a given language that are represented by individual letters of an adopted alphabet.

Letters of incompletely literate persons and so-called illiterate works in general. Their significance in defining the phonetic character of a language. Survey of individual confusions and so-called mistakes, and slips of the pen. (5) Scientific alphabets, graphics, and spelling. Requirements of precision and adequacy.

The Science of Sounds—Phonetics

What is a sound of language? Its definition from the standpoint of (a) acoustics, (b) anatomy and physiology, (c) psychology.

In considering the sounds of language, two factors must be distinguished: (1) the physiological, in the strictest sense of the term, and (2) the physiological-psychological. The sounds of language may be examined from three points of view: (1) the acoustic-physiological, (2) the psychological (word-forming, morphological), and (3) the historical, or etymological. The physiological and the morphological parts of phonetics examine the laws and conditions for the existence of sounds at a given moment of the history of a language (statistics of sounds), whereas the historical part deals with the laws and conditions of the development of sounds in time (dynamics of sounds). Sound analogy.

A. The Statics of Sounds

Part I. The Acoustic-Physiological Aspect.

Purely physiological categories of sounds. In examining them it is necessary to make use of the results of acoustics, physiology, and anatomy.

1. The physiological statics of sounds in the strict sense of the word.

a. Anatomical-physiological and acoustic conditions of the formation and *physical* existence of sounds. Purely physiological categories of sounds. Analysis of sounds in general, apart from their role in the mechanism of language.

More detailed division (classification) of sounds. Division according to quality. According to quality, sounds are primarily divided into *vowels* and *consonants;* their physiological and acoustic differences. Distinctive features of true vowels and true consonants.

Division of consonants. Simple consonantal elements. (1) Anatomical division, according to the speech organs that participate in the production of individual consonants. (2) Physiological division according to the manner of pronunciation. Table of consonants.

Table of vowels. Qualitative distinction: pure vowels and nasal vowels; full vowels and reduced vowels. Quantity of vowels: space and time, stress and length.

Complex (compound) consonants. Identification of simultaneously produced consonants, that is, of consonantal elements pronounced at one and the same time. Aspirates. Nasal resonance. Soft (*mouillierte*) consonants. Affricates. Tables of complex consonants.

Complex vowels. Double vowels, or diphthongs. Definition of diphthongs. Their different categories: (a) phonetic distinctions; (b) genetic distinctions.

Transition from vowels to consonants and vice versa. Simultaneous combinations of vowels and consonants (the unification of a vowel and consonant into one complex sound). Nasal vowels.

The relative clarity and perceptibility of individual sounds.

Table of all the sounds of the Indo-European languages.

⟨a.⟩ Parallelism of sounds based on their distinctive physiological properties. These distinctive properties give rise in languages to certain oppositions (parellels) of sounds. The investigation of these oppositions constitutes the object of the second part of phonetics, inasmuch as in primary languages they are intimately connected with the meaning of words and their parts.

b. Sounds in the syllables. The (physiological) syllable as distinct from the simple combination (complex) of sounds. Various categories of syllables.

c. Sounds in the word. Combinations of sounds in general. The distinction of place in the syllable and in the word with relation to the character of sound. Stability of sounds.

d. Sounds in the overall language of man or of a nation. Relativity of the categories of sounds. Influence of external conditions on the sounds of a language. The relation of language to a nation with respect to sound. The uniqueness of seemingly identical sounds in different languages. The uniqueness of variations of sounds.

The *characterization* of languages in terms of their phonetic make-up. The difference between the Asiatic and European group of the Indo-European languages. Similar differences in the European area, for example, the difference between the Germanic and Balto-Slavic languages. Differences in the Slavic area. Subgroups: Russian (Great Russian and Ukrainian), southern (Bulgarian, Slovenian, Serbo-Croatian), and northwestern (Polish, Czech, etc.).

Statistics of sounds. Ratios of the number of various sounds in a given language. Evaluation of the statistics of sounds.

2. *Dynamic factors.*

Static beginning of changes (substitutions) in sounds conditioned by their physical (physiological) properties. Different categories of sound change based on the difference between the various categories of sounds. The role of habit in using certain sounds and combinations (e.g., combinations of consonants) which are apparently more difficult than other sounds which are avoided. Phenomena of assimilation, etc., encountered among all peoples and at all times.

Physiological explanation of sound change. Theoretical and graphic, psychological explanations of assimilation, permutation, and the general tendency toward economy. Comparisons with everyday events. What appears to be unique and to occur only once produces, through countless repetitions, deep changes in the whole language, i.e., in all individuals speaking the language. What appears to be sporadic can, under certain conditions, become a constant linguistic hábit.

The conflict between habit and the tendency toward economy. Other factors affecting sounds. Compensatory lengthening. Different categories of compensatory lengthening.

Sound laws: (a) laws of the combination of sounds at the synchronic state of a language; (b) sound laws in the evolution of language (they are dealt with in the third part of phonetics).

Part II. The Psychological (Word-Formational,
Morphological) Aspect.

Examination of sounds from the morphological, psychological standpoint. Their significance in the mechanism of language and for the "feeling" of a given speech community.

The mechanism of sounds, their relations and so-called dynamic interaction based on the connection between sound and meaning. Here we examine the influence of certain sounds on meaning and, conversely, the influence of meaning on the quality of sounds. This is the result primarily of the parallelism of sounds, that is, their physiological oppositions. For example, the distinction between soft and hard sounds, based mainly on the mutual relationship of vowels and consonants, the distinction between long and short, stressed and unstressed, voiced and voiceless sounds, etc. Detailed examination of the parallelism of sounds in various languages. The assumed psychological utilization of parallelism of sounds in the primary Indo-European language.

Original quantitative and pre- or postpositive gradation (*gunation*), etc. Stress as the probable cause of original gradation. Distinction of original diphthongs and those due to secondary processes; contractions.

Secondary, qualitative gradation. Replacement of gradation by distinctions of stress.

Gradation of vowels and consonants, based on the previous development of the language and on parallelism of sounds. The (unconscious) use of secondary phenomena and differentiation for internal purposes, for differences of meaning. The psychological role of sound parallelism in parallel roots and in the formation of stems and forms.

The discrepancy between the physical nature of sounds and

their value in the mechanism of language and in the perception of language. The psychological role of sounds in a given language as the result of physiological conditions and of historical sound-changes.

The loss of the psychological, internal role of sounds, i.e., of their mobility (variation) in secondary, analytic languages. The evidence of Romance, Germanic, and Bulgarian. A common tendency in all Indo-European languages.

The difference between sound laws in native and borrowed words. The decline of the morphological significance of sounds in secondary words which are treated as mere conglomerates of sounds. Borrowed words; words not transparent in their composition, whose composition has been forgotten. Secondary languages.

B. The Dynamics of Sounds

Part III. The Historical, Etymological Aspect

Development of languages with respect to sounds. The etymological, historical aspect of sounds. Change and stability of sounds.

1. *General analysis of sound-changes. Common causes and laws.*

Sound-changes conditioned by both static factors discussed above: by the purely physical and the psychological-physiological factors which continually interact with each other in the development of language. In presenting the development of a certain language, it is thus best to discuss the entire development itself, without setting up abstract divisions.

Three common causes (dynamic factors) of sound change: (1) the tendency toward convenience, or conservation of muscular and neurological activity (a purely physiological factor); (2) the loss of connection, or of the awareness of a radical connection between words; (3) the prevalence of the psychological aspect of sounds over the physical one.

The main force behind all purely phonetic sound-changes is the *tendency toward convenience,* which accounts for the shortening, disappearance, and replacement of more difficult sounds by easier ones; in this respect it is important to note the difference between primary and secondary languages.

Phonetic (physiological) or *psychological* explanation of seeming exceptions (deviations) from this tendency. The preservative effect (influence) of some sounds upon adjacent (preceding or following) sounds with the possibility of the disappearance of the influencing sounds. The appearance of new sounds as a result of purely physiological or internal, morphological causes. 1. (a) Insertion (*epenthesis*), its explanation; (b) Compensatory lengthening, its explanation; (c) The German sound shift (*Lautverschiebung*); (d) Influence of stress, etc. 2. (a) Lengthening of radical and word-formational vowels for derivational purposes; (b) Gradation, *polnoglasie*, etc.; (c) The role of analogy, folk etymology, and, in general, of unconscious generalization on the basis of newly formed associations and suppression of older ones.

Relative ease and difficulty of sounds in a given speech community.

Categories of sound change: e.g., (1) simple disappearance of a sound for the sake of easier pronunciation; (2) complete assimilation accompanied most often by disappearance, or by compensatory lengthening. Sound changes: (1) independent of other sounds; (2) influenced by other sounds (a) within the same syllable or (b) in contiguous position, across syllables. Examples of the latter are: (1) the German *Umlaut;* (2) the effect of stressed syllables on the weakening (reduction) and shortening of adjacent syllables; (3) Avestan and Greek *epenthesis;* (4) Slavic compensatory lengthening.

Quality of sound changes with relation to the position in the word: (1) beginning of the word; (2) middle of the word; (3) end of the word.

The law of word-final pronunciation (*Auslautgesetz*) conditioned by habit and the general structure and history of a given language. The development of this law in Greek, Gothic, Lithuanian, and Common Slavic. The disappearance of all unstressed syllables following the stressed one in French, and the resulting generalization of stress on the final syllable.

The category of words and of sound combinations which are subject to unusually great, or sporadic, shortenings.

The tendency toward expressiveness and differentiation of two or more originally identical words or of formal parts of words by varying the quality of sounds. The loss of awareness of the origin of a word. The force of inertia.

The limits on the changeability of sounds.

2. *Common sound changes in the Indo-European languages in general and in the Balto-Slavic languages in particular.*

Historical shortenings and changes of sounds that appeared at a period of transition: (1) from ancient Indic to modern Indic; (2) from ancient Greek to modern Greek; (3) from ancient Romance to modern Romance; (4) from Anglo-Saxon to modern English; (5) from Old High German to Middle High German and from Middle High German to New High German; (6) from Common Slavic to the modern Slavic languages, etc.

3. *Etymological kinship and identity of sounds in one language or in related languages* due to the historical change of originally single sounds.

History of sounds. The basic sounds of basic forms.

Phonetically distinct sounds (and words) can be identical etymologically when they develop from originally identical sounds; conversely, originally distinct sounds can in the course of time become identical phonetically. Examples of complete phonetic identification or of partial similarity of etymologically different words from one or more languages. Homonymy. Ambiguity. The results of identification (including disappearance) of originally different sounds, especially in more advanced languages.

Sound laws and sound tendencies not strong enough to become an established habit.

The law of sound shift (*Lautverschiebung*) in German.

4. *Characterization of the general phonetic tendencies and directions of development of the Indo-European languages.*

In studying the history of the Indo-European languages, one may detect certain tendencies of divergence which vary according to the properties and state of development of the respective languages and which could provide the basis for a genetic classification of these languages. Among these tendencies which are determined by physiological and psycho-physiological (morphological) factors, are, among others, the following:

1) The constant *tendency toward economy* combined with the force of *habit*. The tendency toward simplification and shortening of sounds (including their loss or substitution by zero).

a. The influence of the environment of other sounds. Various types of assimilation and dissimilation. Disappearance and appearance of sounds. Changes in the combination of consonants. Consonantal and vocalic diphthongs.

b. Replacement of sounds by easier sounds without the influence of other sounds. The tendency toward shortening, weakening, and disappearance of sounds. Shortening of sounds (of vowels and consonants) to an acoustic minimum, then to a minimum in the sense of preserving the time needed for their production, but without the actual pronunciation of the sound up to its loss, either without a trace or with [compensatory lengthening]. The law of shortening (or narrowing) in the historic development of vowels. The potential for survival of easier, more conveniently pronounced sounds, and the susceptibility to change of more difficult sounds; stability of sounds.

Seeming exceptions to the above mentioned general tendency. The appearance of new sounds: of consonants in clusters that are difficult to pronounce (insertion); of consonants between vowels (elimination of "hiatus"), etc. The replacement of the *spiritus lenis* by full consonants varying according to the following vowel. Relevant in this respect is also:

2) The *tendency toward compensation* for shortening.

a. Compensation for the shortening (or lengthening) of a given sound completed in the sound itself. Features (moments) of sounds. The reasons for the qualitative (acoustically) change of short and half-short vowels. Lengthening, or the increase in the duration of the air-stream, is neutralized in the case of narrowing of vowels (going from *a* to *i* or *u*).

Likewise, shortening, or the decrease in the duration of the air-stream, is neutralized by opening. Lengthening counteracted by narrowing, and shortening counteracted by opening. The effect produced by increasing the duration of a vowel at the expense of its opening remains, consequently, roughly the same. The strength and intensity of the air, and the duration of its flow as the chief factors of this increase. The law of shortening or narrowing of vowels in a historical perspective.

b. Compensation for the narrowing or disappearance of a certain sound; compensation in preceding or even following sounds (or syllables). Compensation as the result of the conflict between habit and the tendency toward economy. Four types of compensatory extension: (1) compensatory extension for single sounds (cf. above); (2) compensatory extension for the loss of consonants; (3) compensatory extension for the loss of vowels or syllables; (4) so-called contraction. Three types of compensatory phenomena can be distinguished: (1) lengthening of vowels, (2) opening of vowels, (3) stressing of vowels. In general, compensatory extension (or, rather, *compensatory strengthening*) consists in pronouncing a given syllable with greater energy in compensating for the weakening or loss of a certain muscular activity.

3) *The double direction of change.*

The total or partial disappearance of a certain category of sounds brings about a new state or a return to the older state.

4) *The tendency toward balance.*

In the realm of vowels, a tendency toward shortening or narrowing; in the realm of consonants (in which narrowing is more difficult) a tendency toward opening and longer duration.

5) *Gradual loss of the distinctiveness of sounds.*

The definiteness of sounds in primary languages reflects the greater sensitivity of primitive people. The gradual loss of the definiteness of sounds goes hand in hand with the loss of the significance of words. The ever increasing non-distinctiveness and fusion of consonants. Increasing non-distinctiveness and fusion of vowels; fusion of unstressed vowels. Loss of diversity. The loss of musical (esthetic) feeling for language among some peoples.

6) *Qualitative nuances of quantitative distinctions.* Replacement of quantitative types of gradation by qualitative types of gradation. Qualitative shading of quantitative differences: (a) of hard and soft consonants; (b) of short and long vowels, etc.

7) *Loss of the significance of sounds.* The gradual decrease of vocalic and consonantal types of gradation, increasing immobility of vowels and consonants. The distinction in this respect between primary and secondary languages. The gradual development of a fixed stress.

8) *Weakening of the esthetic character of language* in its external and poetic and creative forms. Weakening of the esthetic character of language through the loss of the distinction of stressed and unstressed syllables and long and short ones. Simplification of the plastic aspect of language. Confusion of stress with quantity, etc.

The physical and geographic conditions of a country have an influence on the organic make-up of a people, which in turn determines the character of their language. Conversely, the language influences the make-up of the speech organs and the physiognomy of both the individual person and the entire people. Probably as a result of physical conditions and the specific development of language itself, some languages tend to make predominant use of the front speech organs, and other languages of the back speech organs, etc. The corresponding difference between the Asiatic and the European branches of Indo-European.

Tendencies toward the future state of a language condition its present state.

The importance of phonetics.

I I I

A Detailed Program of Lectures for the

Academic Year 1876–1877

A. PHONETICS

I. Statics of Sounds (Continuation)

1. *The Purely Physiological Aspect of the Statics of Sounds (Continuation)*.

The influence of foreign languages on the phonetics of a given language.

The influence of external conditions on the sounds of a language, on a people's pronunciation. The influence of a people's occupations, its way of life.

The uniqueness of seemingly identical sounds in different languages.

Characterization of languages according to their phonetic make-up. The range of sounds peculiar to each language.

The statistics of sounds. Ratios of individual sounds in the living usage of a given language.

The beginnings of dynamic sound changes in the synchronic state of a language. . . .

The beginnings of sound changes (alterations) conditioned by their physical (physiological) properties.

The stability of sounds.

The relative ease or difficulty of sounds.

Different categories of sound changes: assimilation, dissimilation, metathesis and others. Comparison with similar phenomena in writing (slips of the pen) and in everyday events.

Static features of sounds.

General concepts (categories) of phonetics.

The distinction between sound correspondences, sound laws, and sound processes. Distinction of sound processes, laws, and forces.

Sound laws and correlations of sounds: 1) static ones, appearing at one moment in the existence of a language; 2) dynamic ones, appearing in the development of a language.

2. *The Psychological (Psycho-Physiological) Aspect of the Statics of Sounds.*

Examination of individual sounds in connection with the meaning of words.

Psychological-static mobility of sounds.

Gradation of vowels (*Lautsteigerung*). The original quantitative and prepositional gradation of Indo-European vowels. The secondary, qualitative type of gradation. Gradation of consonants.

The discrepancy between the physical nature of sounds and their significance in the mechanism of language and in the people's linguistic feeling.

Rudimentary gradations that have ceased to be mobile.

Different layers of productive gradations.

The disappearance of psychological mobility of sounds in the secondary, analytic Indo-European languages.

The influence of analogy on sound changes (this, strictly speaking, is a part of the dynamics of sounds). Different types of analogy.

The phonetic factor which plays the role of cement with respect to words, i.e., which connects (unifies) syllables into words or several words into one word. Indo-European stress. The Turanian (Finno-Turkic) harmony of vowels, etc.

II. *The Dynamics of Sounds, i.e., the
Historical, Etymological Aspect of Phonetics*

... 1. Dynamic changes of sounds. Changes of sounds with time. The two major dynamic factors of the changes (alterations) of sounds:

1) The purely physical (physiological) factor, whose operation is determined by sound laws.

2) The psychological factor, consisting of the analogy of sounds.

The properties of sounds, complexes (combinations) of sounds, and words. The property of sound as the product of the tension of muscles and nerves in an infinitely small unit of time and the duration of a sound. The property of a vowel, obtained by multiplying its median breadth by its duration (continuity). The definiteness of a vowel is reduced in proportion to the reduction of its properties.

Stability of sounds:

1) Static stability, i.e., resistance to changes at a given moment in the existence of a language;

2) Dynamic stability, resistance to historical changes. A limit is placed on the changeability of sounds.

2. General cause of dynamic sound changes (substitutions). Changes of sounds:

a) independent of the influence of other sounds, merely as the result of the tendency toward convenience.

b) due to the influence of other sounds, owing to contact with other sounds.

c) as a consequence of the place occupied by a certain sound in a word or phrase. The effect of different positions in the word on the quality of sound changes: the begining, middle, or end of the word. The law of word-final combinations of sounds (*Auslautgesetz*).

The preservative action (influence) of some sounds on others with which they are combined. This influence is reflected, of course, also in the disappearance of the originally influencing sounds.

Sporadic shortenings of sounds in some categories of words.

3. General sound changes in the Indo-European languages in general, and in the Balto-Slavic languages in particular.

The parallel development of sounds. Proportions of sounds in their change in three directions: (1) the historical, the transition from an old to a new state; (2) the geographic, dialectological; (3) the static, at one and the same in the same dialect.

Physiologically identical sounds of different languages have a distinctive value depending on ⟨their place within⟩ the entire sound system, and their relation to other sounds. Another range of sounds. Comparison with the tones of music.

4. Etymological kinship and identity of sounds within one language or in related languages, which is based on their history, i.e., on their development from one and the same original sound. Phonetic translation.

The splitting of one sound into two or more. The fusion of several sounds into one.

5. Characterization of general tendencies in the development of

the sounds of Indo-European languages and of the general directions of this development.

1) The main direction of dynamic, purely physiological changes of sounds. The tendency toward convenience, i.e., toward the reduction of the properties of sounds. The law of shortening or narrowing of vowels in historical perspective.

Seeming exceptions to this direction in the development of sounds. Appearance of a new sound, *polnoglasie*, compensatory lengthening, etc. The explanation of such phenomena, either in purely physiological terms or in terms of the influence of popular word formation, analogy, and other types of unconscious generalization (apperception).

2) The tendency toward compensation for the shortening of sounds.

Compensatory lengthening and, more generally, compensatory strengthening of a sound, i.e., increasing its substance as a result of the conflict between the tendency toward convenience and habit.

Different forms (kinds) of compensatory strengthening of sounds. Compensatory strengthening of the vowel. Contraction. Compensatory strengthening of the consonant.

The increase in stability of sounds, both vocalic and consonantal.

6. Gradual loss of the definiteness of sounds.

The qualitative shading of quantitative distinctions.

The loss of the significance of sounds, as well as of their internal vitality and mobility.

Weakening of the esthetic character of a language regarding its sounds.

Linguistic formulas and abbreviational symbols in phonetics.

B. MORPHOLOGY

. . . Morphological distinctions in languages of different structure. The basis for a morphological classification of languages.

The intimate connection of morphology and syntax.

Subdivision of morphology. Morphological statics and morphological dynamics. Forms and their functions, i.e., their inner meaning.

I. *Roots*

As the main, governing parts of words, i.e., roots from a static-morphological point of view. . . .

Concepts of the root of a word. Determination of the root by its external appearance and meaning.

The three-way principle of the subdivision of roots: (a) phonetic (open, closed, etc.); (b) genetic (primary, secondary, etc.); (c) by meaning, by the role of the roots in a given language (verbal roots, nominal roots, material ⟨lexical⟩ roots, and pronominal, demonstrative, formal roots, etc.).

Reduplication (*geminatio*) of the root.

Root determinants (determinants of roots); (*Wurzeldeterminative*). The distinction between root determinants and suffixes.

Reflexes (representatives, substitutes) of the primordial roots of the Indo-European proto-language in individual Indo-European languages.

Phonetic differentiation of roots, that is, the differentiation of roots as a result of sound laws.

Parallel roots.

The overlapping of formerly distinct roots.

Relative stability of roots.

Change in the form of roots. Change in the form of roots under the influence of analogy. Ascribing a different meaning to a root under the influence of analogy.

Transfer of the center of gravity of a word from one root to another, that is, transfer of the role of the main root to the subordinate root which previously had a secondary role (of prefix, affix, or other) in the word. Cf. my review of the work *"Issledovanija drevneslavjanskogo perevoda XIII Slov Gregorija Bogoslova . . . A. Budiloviča"* (in *ŽMNP,* November 1872, pp. 170–84).

Traces of independent roots in contemporary languages, either only in meaning or in meaning and external form. Sanskrit roots in the meaning of independent words.

The uninterrupted formation of new words.

Verbal particles. Cf. I. I. Sreznevskij, "Glagol'nye časticy" (*Materialy dlja sravnitel'nogo i ob"jasnitel'nogo slovarja i grammatiki,* II, pp. 334–36).

The different form and meaning of verbal particles.

Impersonal verbs. Cf. F. Miklosich, *Die Verba impersonalia im Slavischen von Dr. . . . ,* Wien, 1865. Steinthal, [Review of] Carl Philipp Moritz, *Über die unpersönlichen Zeitwörter* (in *Zeitschr. für Völkerpsychologie und Sprachwissenschaft,* I, 1860, pp. 73–89).

Vocative case and imperative mood.

The gradual elimination of roots. The gradual weakening of the vitality of roots.

Languages with and without roots. The complete elimination of roots as categories of language in analytic languages.

Words with and without roots. Words belonging to a family and isolated words.

Words that have no roots, even in synthetic languages:

1) native words with a forgotten root;

2) alien, foreign, borrowed words from other languages. . . .

Semi-assimilation and full assimilation. The distinction between *foreign* words (*Fremdwörter*) and assimilated words (*Lehnwörter*).

What criteria should be applied to borrowed words?

A) with respect to the source, to the language from which it is borrowed:

1) place: from which dialect was it assimilated?

2) time: when was it assimilated?

B) with respect to the borrowing language:

1) place: by which dialect was it assimilated? by which social class of the people? was the assimilation colloquial or bookish? etc.

2) time: when was it assimilated? The strength of the assimilation process earlier and now. The temporal distance of the assimilation as a factor in the loss of the foreign character of the borrowed word. Cf., among others, my *O drevnepol'skom jazyke do XIV stoletija*, §§113, 114, 44.2.

C) was a certain word borrowed from another language directly or through the intermediacy of other languages, i.e., is it a natural, unborrowed word in the language from which it was borrowed, or was it borrowed from some third language?

The profound distinction between several (two or more) words borrowed from one and the same source, i.e., representing variants of one and the same foreign word.

The fate of borrowed words, their wanderings. Return of a borrowed word, in reshaped form, to the language from which it was originally borrowed.

Assimilated common nouns borrowed from the names of peoples or from the names of persons and surnames or from place names of a particular type.

International words which are, so to speak, the product of a compromise between two peoples.

Thorough assimilation, as a result of which the foreign word ceases to be foreign. Analogously, the root is forgotten in native words.

Different ways of assimilating foreign words:

1) purely phonetic;

2) the borrowed word acquires suffixes and endings by analogy to native words. The converse is the combination of foreign suffixes and endings with native words;

3) assimilation through folk etymology or popular word formation (*Volksetymologie*).

. . . Folk etymology as a force that revives words which have become ossified in their composition and have lost their connection with the former root.

Folk etymology as proof of the vitality of roots as a linguistic category.

The effect of folk etymology on truly foreign (borrowed) words and on native words with a forgotten root.

Comparison of folk etymology with gravitation in planetary systems.

Different categories of folk etymology:

A. *External* categories, producing change in the external form of a word, contrary to sound laws: (1) adaptation to a root of similar meaning; (2) mere adaptation to a comprehensible form.

B. *Internal* categories, consisting in a new interpretation of a given word, without a change in form (its external shape): (1) interpretation by meaning, adaptation to a form with a similar meaning; (2) subsumption under some category and the assignment of a meaning.

Incorrect (false) interpretations of the composition of words in writing.

The role of folk etymology in the confusion of graphic signs.

Etymological myths.

Puns based on folk etymology.

Learned word-formation resulting from ignorance of the laws of a language. Conclusions drawn from it by mythologists, historians, ethnologists, etc. . . .

II. *Affixes, Suffixes, Prefixes and Infixes.*
Stems (Themes). Stem-formation (Derivation).

... *Suffixes,* as distinct from root determinants.

The origin of suffixes.

Primary and secondary suffixes.

Classification of suffixes acording to (a) external form (simple, compound, etc.), (b) meaning, function.

Distinction of primary and secondary, synthetic and analytic languages with respect to suffixes.

Whole words which become suffixes.

The descriptive principle of the analytic stage of development.

Replacement of suffixes by separate words. The complete loss of suffixes as a productive category of language.

Prefixes. Are there prefixes in Indo-European languages? Prefixes in Finno-Turkic (Uralo-Altaic, Turanian) languages.

Prefixes whose meanings have been forgotten.

Origin of the augment in Sanskrit and Greek.

Can prepositions be considered prefixes?

Infixes, e.g., in the Semitic languages.

Seeming infixes in Indo-European languages.

Stems (themes) of different grade.

The independent existence of stems in Indo-European languages.

Stems in primary languages and their loss in secondary languages.

III. *Compounding (compositio)*

... Three degrees of compounding:
1. Compounding of roots
   a) externally
   1) of different roots (the possible source of root determinants and of suffixes);
   2) of the same root, reduplication (*geminatio*);
   b) internally
   1) through the intensification of the meaning (root determinants, *geminatio*);
   2) through the expression of a certain relationship or the addition of a nuance of meaning (suffixes, *reduplicatio*).

Compounding of suffixes.

Tautology in folk poetry and in language generally.

2. Compounding in the narrow sense of the word (σύνθεσις, *compositio, Zusammensetzung*).

Categories of compounds:

compounds of two nominal or verbal stems;

compounds of nouns with nouns;

compounds of verbs with nouns;

compounds whose composition has been forgotten, as a result of either the loss of the autonomy of one of its parts or of shortening; and

compounds of nominal or verbal stems with particles.

3. Compounding of existing forms, juxtaposition (παράθεσις, *Zusammenrückung*).

Juxtaposition of dependent and coordinate forms.

Epitheta ornatia.

Expressions unified into one fixed form. . . .

IV. *Formation (and Origin) of Declined and Conjugated Parts of Speech.* . . .

V. *Inflection (Flexio)*

. . . The distinction between inflection and word formation. Declension, conjugation.

The distinction between the noun (substantive, adjective) and the verb.

Formation of inflected forms. Different theories. The theory of agglutination and the theory of "adaptation."

How is inflection accomplished?

Mobility of endings, mobility of inflection.

1. *Declension (Declinatio).*

The meaning of the cases.

The origin of case endings.

Number. The dual (*dualis*). External expression of number distinctions in the declension.

Gender from a formal point of view.

The development of genders in different languages. Languages that do not now and never have designated genders.

Gender in the Indo-European languages. Fusion of genders. The gradual elimination of this category in the Indo-European languages.

What is meant by gender form (motion) and the case endings in adjectives? Congruence (agreement) of the adjective with the substantive.

What is meant by gender and number in verbs?

The Turanian languages.

The meaning of gender in declension.

The development of forms of declension.

Diversity in declension.

The declension of substantives and pronouns. The declension of pronouns and adjectives. Secondary development of the compound declension of adjectives in the Slavic and Baltic languages.

Change in the forms of declension. Their shortening and simplification.

Stems (themes) of declension.

Primordial stems of the Indo-European proto-language. Primary stems, equal to roots, and secondary stems formed from roots by means of suffixes.

Stems endings in vowels and stems ending in consonants. (Vocalic and consonantal stems).

Different layers in the development and formation of the forms of declension.

Different views on the character and meaning of the stems (themes) of declension. The genetic point of view. What are stems from this point of view?

Change of stems. The transition of ancient stems of the proto-Indo-European language to new stems, for example, in the Slavic languages.

The gradual shortening of the stems of declension as a result of phonetic laws and the interaction of phonetic and morphological factors.

In Slavic there are no vocalic stems of declension. Proofs of this statement.

The loss of endings and, in general, the shortening of the end of a word favors the development of exclusively consonantal stems. The loss of endings, but not of the need to express case relationships by means of inflection. Only two solutions are open to language in such situations. The assignment of new functions to rudimentary suffixes.

Fusion of the end of the stem with the ending.

The rudimentary existence of vocalic stems (themes) in Slavic languages is real from an external point of view as well as from the point of view of their meaning. Traces of original final vowels of stems (themes) in present-day case endings and in compounds. Traces of the distinction between vocalic and consonantal stems in the diverse declensions.

Parts of former stems in the role of endings.

Revival of declension with the help of new, exclusively consonantal stems.

The formation of consonantal stems in place of vocalic ones even at the oldest historically attested stage of the Indo-European languages.

Differentiation of stems. Fusion of stems.

The influence of analogy on the stems (themes) of declension.

Disappearance of the less frequently used categories of stems.

Diversity of the declension in the Indo-European languages.

Strictly, one should not speak of the diversity of the declension of nouns or stems in all ⟨grammatical⟩ cases, but only of the diversity of the declension in some ⟨grammatical⟩ cases.

2. *Conjugation (Conjugatio)*

. . . Stems (themes) of conjugation.

Personal endings. Their origin and development.

Number in the verb in general and in the personal endings in particular.

The significance of voice in general and in the personal endings in particular.

The gradual loss of diversity in personal endings.

The replacement of personal endings by pronouns.

Tense. Different categories of tense. Objective and subjective tenses. The intersection of categories.

Stems of the tenses.

Reduplication, gemination, as a feature of completed action.

Stems of past tenses.

The augment. Its origin.

The future tense and its bases.

Moods. Means of expressing their distinction.

Aspects. Number and duration of action. Means of designating aspects: (1) special suffixes, (2) prepositions ⟨prefixes⟩, (3) gradation of the root vowel.

Deverbal substantives: participles, gerunds, infinitives, supines.

The meaning of the infinitive.

The conjugations. Their subdivision. Different systems of dividing the conjugations of verbs.

Primary and secondary conjugation.

Distinction between verbal stems and present-tense stems. Stems of aspects, moods, tenses.

Vocalic and consonantal stems (themes) of conjugation.

Morphological and phonetic shortenings of the stems of conjugation (cf. the stems of declension).

Compound verbal forms.

The analytic state of verbal forms.

The loss of feeling of stems and endings. Ossification of verbal forms in secondary languages.

The prevalence of the descriptive ⟨periphrastic⟩ principle.

VI. *Analogy*

. . . Analogy as a force of language operating against tradition and sound laws. Analogy as a special case of the force of unconscious generalization (apperception). The difference between analogy and folk etymology.

Factors of analogy: (1) phonetic, (2) syntactic, (3) purely morphological.

The interaction of analogical factors in the historical development of language.

Different manifestations of analogy in the forms of declension and conjugation (in the forms of nouns and verbs).

Analogy of stems and analogy of endings.

Directions in the working of analogy:

1) external, when one form is replaced by another without change of meaning;

2) internal, when the form remains unchanged but acquires a new meaning, is interpreted differently. Its effect upon linguistic feeling.

The effect of the second category on the change of the system of declensions and conjugations, i.e., on the *morphological* shortenening of bases.

On the other hand, the entire declined or conjugated form may become a stem.

Various tendencies and special causes (reasons) for the operation of analogy (evoking the influence of analogy):

1) the preponderance of the feeling of identity of forms over their external diversity and sound laws;

2) the loss of the original function (meaning) of certain forms;

3) the tendency toward distinctiveness of forms;

4) the tendency toward simplification of forms, etc.

The effect (influence) of analogy:

1) at the beginning of a word;

2) within a word;

3) in final clusters, at the end of a word, in desinences, etc.

The effect of the last type of analogy manifests itself in: (1) stems, (2) desinences, and (3) whole, complete forms.

General conclusions about analogy.

VII. *The Elimination of Inflection*

... The distinctiveness of desinences is suppressed (obscured). Substitutes for desinences. Prepositions. Pronouns: (1) demonstrative pronouns in the function of articles, (2) personal pronouns in the function of personal endings.

Analytic (separate from the word) substitutes for desinences appear at first in support of desinences, then take their place.

On the origin of the article, cf. Jakob Grimm, "Über das Pedantische in der deutschen Sprache," *Kleinere Schriften,* I (Berlin, 1864), p. 338.

Which part of grammar should deal with the article, prepositions and the personal pronouns which modify verbs: syntax or the study of inflection?

Ossification of certain forms.

The complete loss of some inflectional categories.

VIII. *Particles*

... Ossified inflected forms in the function of particles and auxiliary words.

Adverbs are by origin case forms of nominal (substantive, adjectival) and pronominal stems, verbal forms or entire expressions.

Prepositions develop from adverbs.

The splitting of one preposition into two or more. The merger of several prepositions into one as a result of sound processes and analogy.

Subordinate particles. Subordinate expressions. Desultory word-expressions and desultory expressions.

Integral, fixed forms and even expressions serve as the basis for further formations. Cf. my "Wortformen und selbst Sätze, welche in der polnischen Sprache zu Stämmen herabgesunken sind," *Beiträge zur vergleichenden Sprachforschung*, VI (1870), pp. 204–10; I. I. Sreznevskij, "Ob izučenii rodnogo jazyka," *Izvestija Akademii nauk*, IX, p. 288.

Statistics in morphology. Cf., among others, F. F. Sławiński, *Obliczenie wyrazów zawartych w trzech słownikach: (1) Lindego, (2) w Wilkeńskim, (3) Rykaczewskiego, przez . . . ego* (Warsaw, 1873).

IX. *Etymology. Kinship of Words*

As a part of morphological dynamics.

The genetic kinship of words, roots, affixes, desinences, stems (themes), etc. . . .

X. *The Meaning of Words. Semasiology*

. . . Changes of meanings. Main tendencies and currents.

Loss of the original meaning of a root.

Splitting of roots with respect to meaning.

Merger of the meaning of different roots under the influence of sound laws and analogy.

Fusion of borrowed and native words.

Directions in the development and change of the meaning of roots: (1) from indefiniteness ⟨vagueness⟩ to definiteness, (2) from the concrete to the abstract.

The substitution of words ⟨of space⟩ by words of time.

Roots of Indo-European languages for which no basic concrete meaning has been found. Cf. George Curtius, *Grundzüge der griechischen Etymologie*, pp. 101, 178, 312, 231.

Internal form (*innere Form*) in language.

The influence of foreign words on a people's world-view with relation to the native language. Foreign meanings present in native words.

C. SYNTAX

. . . Division of syntax:

1) the meaning of parts of speech and forms of words;

2) linking (connection) of words (of separate sentences and the linking of sentences).

Two parts of syntax (as in phonetics and morphology):

A. Statics: (1) the form of expressions and sentences and of parts of sentences; (2) the meaning of expressions and sentences and of parts of sentences.

B. Dynamics: (3) the origin of expressions and sentences and of parts of sentences.

Etymological explanation of syntactic phenomena and, conversely, syntactic explanation of the appearance, development, and loss of various forms.

Interpretation of the various parts of speech as constituents of the sentence.

The meaning of forms as means for linking words into a whole. Languages with and without form.

Analysis of analytic forms. Particles and auxiliary verbs.

Replacement of words of place by words of time.

Replacement of one case by another.

The connection of words, the sentence.

Agreement of words as distinct from their subordination or dependence. Congruence as distinct from attraction.

Congruence and attraction as they appear (manifest their action): (1) in the linking of words, (2) in the linking of sentences.

Congruence, fusion of two concepts into one.

The distinction between the attribute and predicate.

The influence of syntax on inflection. The formation in Slavic (and Lithuanian) of two adjectival declensions. The article.

Attraction (gravitation) in comparison with assimilation of sounds. Different categories of attraction: regressive and progressive, etc. Attraction in the linking of words and sentences. Shortenings and omissions due to attraction. Sporadic, isolated attraction and permanent attraction which lends form to individual expressions and determines the development of a language.

So-called *tmesis* (τμῆσις) of the Scholastics. The gradual transition of adverbs into prepositions. Free juxtaposition of words due to frequent repetition and habit becomes constant and obligatory. Repetition of the same preposition, owing to congruence, before the substantive, the adjective, and the verb.

The synethetic and analytic structure of language from a syntactic point of view.

The linking of sentences.

The transition of independent sentences into dependent ones, and of the so-called natural construction into the artificial construction.

The transition of demonstrative pronouns and conjunctions into relative pronouns and conjunctions. Division into demonstrative, relative, and interrogative particles.

The independent use of different forms and particles, outside any grammatical connection with the sentence or sentences.

The distinction between grammar and logic.

The influence of foreign languages on the syntactic structure (construction) of a given language.

D. A GENERAL VIEW OF GRAMMAR

Parallel development and identical laws of language from the standpoint of phonetics, morphology, and syntax. The generalization of particular data from phonetics, morphology, and syntax. The history of language. . . .

Parallelism between the state and development of a language in phonetics, morphology, and syntax. The similarity between static and dynamic laws in the three domains of grammar.

A brief (concise) survey of the laws and forces operating in a language. Can general categories of linguistics be viewed as forces and laws?

The purely physical and physiological aspects of language, and a people's feeling for its language.

Forces operating in language: (1) habit, i.e., unconscious memory, (2) the tendency toward convenience, (3) unconscious forgetting and misunderstanding, (4) unconscious generalization or apperception, (5) unconscious abstraction, the tendency toward separation, differentiation.

Laws and forces: (1) static, i.e., operating in the synchronic state of a language; (2) dynamic, determining the development of a language. Statics and dynamics in grammar.

Inheritance (*Vererbung*) and adaptation (adjustment, *Anpassung*) in language.

The succession of processes in the development of a language.

Rudiments in language.

Comparison of the development of language with biological and social development.

Changeability of language.

The development of langauge due to individual stimuli, slowly, with no sudden jumps. The formula: $O \times \infty$.

The effect (influence) of inertia (*vis inertiae*) on language.

Explanation of changes in language.

The greater or lesser degree of changeability of a language with relation to geographic, historical, and ethnographic-anthropological conditions. The influence of climate and soil. The influence of the nature of a people and of its education.

The influence of consciousness on language. The influence of books.

The relationships between literary and popular languages.

The history of a language. Methods of re-creating and illustrating the history (development) of a language: (1) individual development of particular persons, investigation of children's language, etc.; (2) literary monuments in chronological order; (3) examination of the structure and composition of living languages in all their diversity and the separation of the various layers of their formation.

Stratification in language.

The chronological principal in the examination of the structure and composition of language and languages. The chronology of phonetic, morphological, and syntactic processes.

Two aspects of the history of language: the *external* and the *internal*.

Having studied the course of the development of a certain language in comparison with others, one should be able to predict its further internal development.

E. CLASSIFICATION OF LANGUAGES

. . . The definition of *morphological classification*. Its principles. Refutation of the theory which sees in individual groups only different degrees of perfection of a single principle (element) of morphological structure that leads gradually from monosyllabicity and agglutination to inflection.

Can a morphological classification (characterization, description) of languages be based on their phonetic properties? The sameness of phonetic processes and laws in languages of completely different morphological structure. Compare the sameness of chemical and physical processes in organisms of morphologically different structure. To what extent and from what standpoint are the data of phonetics suitable for a morphological classification?

Which morphological and syntactic aspects (pertaining to the structure of words and sentences) should be considered in a morphological classification of languages?

Is a morphological classification of languages possible at the present time? Is a morphological *classification* altogether possible, and should it not be replaced by a *characterization* of individual groups (branches) of languages? Linguistic geography and ethnography.

What language types have been determined scientifically?

Is it possible to reduce these types to a common denominator, i.e., to derive all of them from a common type? Can we assume the common origin of the inflected Indo-European, the inflected Semitic, and the agglutinative Turanian languages?

The relationship between the morphological and genetic classification. Is genetic kinship between languages of different morphological types possible? Is there a necessary coincidence between genetically related languages and languages of identical morphological type?

Morphological translation from a language of one type (structure) into a language of another type. Its distinction from phonetic translation and translation of meanings.

Characterization of languages of the Indo-European branch in comparison with those of the Finno-Turkic (Turanian, Uralo-Altaic) branch. What is the major morphological difference between the two branches?

The phonetic cement which in both branches conjoins several syllables into a whole, i.e., into one word as a syntactic unit comprising morphological (formal) parts. Stress and vowel harmony. Stress unifies the syllables into one word only phonetically, as syllables, while vowel harmony unifies the syllables not phonetically, but morphologically (roots in the role of suffixes).

On the one hand, preservation of the autonomy of syllables as morphological units, and on the other, subordination of all syllables to one syllable. Variability vs. invariability of the root. Gradation of vowels vs. their psychological immobility; in the latter case, flexional relations are expressed through suffixes instead of vowel gradation, etc. On the one hand, integration of all syllables (including those of the suffixes) into one word, and on the other, distinctiveness and autonomy of the suffixes which enter, so to speak, only temporarily into a union with the main root.

On the one hand, the endings and affixes form a tight unity with the stem (or root); on the other hand, almost all affixes and endings function as autonomous units.

On the one hand, regressive sound change (when following sounds influence preceding ones) and, on the other hand, progressive sound change (e.g., vowel harmony, the assimilation of following consonants to preceding ones, the disappearance of following consonants and not of preceding ones).

[Compare the parallel distinctions in social life and in history in general: (1) (parallel to regressiveness in language) the striving toward ideals of the future influences social and political movements and brings about political upheavals (the life of the mind, ideals, ideas, etc., outstrip reality and are so strong as to evoke at times attempts at their immediate implementation); (2) (parallel to progressiveness in language) social and political conservatism wherein the course (of the present and future) is almost exclusively controlled by the past.]

The Turanian languages lack genders (*genera*) etc., and personification in general is far less often manifested than in the Indo-European languages.

A verbal character prevails in the Indo-European languages, and a nominal (adjectival and substantival) character in the Turanian languages. To compensate for the weak development of independent verbs, the Turanian languages employ a large number of auxiliary verbs.

In the Indo-European languages there is grammatical congruence of subordinate words with the main word; in the Turanian languages, only the main word is logically speaking "declined" and "conjugated"; congruence does not exist at all.

The Turanian languages preclude internal analogy of forms consisting in a new interpretation of the same form, such as the reinterpretation of the former nom. sg. feminine (collective) *gospodá* as a nom. pl. masculine.

The completely different word order in the sentence of the two types of languages.

From a historical, developmental point of view, all Indo-European languages are predisposed, because of their very structure, to change from a synthetic state to an analytic state, while the conservative Turanian languages are safeguarded against this kind of change: because of agglutination, they are, to begin with, "analytic" and have the means of replacing suffixes that have lost their distinctiveness with new, productive, and meaningful suffixes. In the Indo-European languages that are subject to strong sound changes and shortenings, it is possible to preserve the synthetic structure for some time by means of analogy, etc.; but in the end, all such means are exhausted, and the transition to an analytic state follows inevitably.

The *genetic classification* of languages, based on their common provenience from one original language. Original basic forms and derived ones. The importance of geographical and chronological criteria.

Phonetic translation (the rendering of the sounds of individual words of a given language by the sounds of another language by observing strictly defined sound laws and established sound correspondences) as a firm and irrefutable test of the genetic kinship of languages. Is such phonetic translation possible in the case of all genetically related languages? Distinction of stages, different degrees of development (for example, the synthetic and analytic languages of the Indo-European branch). Phonetic translation: (1) between synthetic languages; (2) between synthetic languages and their descendant analytic languages; (3) between analytic languages going back to a single synthetic language (for example, between French, Italian, Roumanian, etc.); (4) between analytic languages that developed from different, but genetically related synthetic languages (for example, between English, French, and Modern Greek). In the last case, phonetic translation is usually impossible; and consequently, it is impossible to establish the genetic kinship between such languages (for example, between Hindu, Modern Persian, Albanian, a Neapolitan or French dialect, Celtic, English, Bulgarian). If these secondary languages were the only representatives of Indo-European, no one would have thought of their genetic relationship. The great importance of the most ancient synthetic languages in defining genetic kinship.

Discrepancies in the lexical material because of the loss of words and roots in some languages, or because of borrowings.

The distinction between *synthetic* and *analytic languages* based on morphological and genetic "classifications." Cf. H. Chavée, "La science positive des langues indo-européennes, son présent, son avenir," *Revue de lingistique. . .*, I, pp. 9, 22–23.

Much more rapid changes and phonetic "decay" in analytic languages than in synthetic languages. The transparency of synthetic languages, whose words are felt not only singly, but also in their morphological make-up. The words of analytic languages are subject to the action of sound laws alone, and are not protected from change by a live awareness of their morphological structure. The lack of mutual intelligibility among peoples speaking closely related analytic languages, as opposed to intelligibility among speakers of synthetic languages which may be genetically more remote. For example, Avestan and Sanskrit vs. the dialects of Milan and Naples.

Identical sound-changes in analytic languages and in synthetic languages from which the former are derived.

The question of mixed languages.

The question of the influence of foreign languages on the syntax of a given language.

The Kjaxta dialect of the Russian language. Cf. S. I. Čerepanov, "Kjaxtinskoe kitajskoe narečie russkogo jazyka. Zapiska . . . ," *IORJaS*, II, pp. 370–77.

The probable influence of the Finnic and Turanian languages in general on Lithuanian and Celtic.

Phonetic influences: (1) between genetically related languages; (2) between languages of differing morphological type (here the influence is much more pervasive, penetrating the entire phonetic structure of a given language).

The probable influence of foreign languages on the phonetic propeties of various Slavic dialects. The loss of vowel length and of mobile stress.

Germanized dialects of the Slovenized Germans of southern Austria.

The Rezian dialects ⟨of Slovenia⟩.

The Romansch dialects of northern Italy, Switzerland, Tyrol, and Gorizia.

The great importance of similar questions for ethnology as ethnic and national history.

The Genetic Classification
of the Indo-European Languages

Different views of the basic question: how are we to interpret the genetic relationship of the Indo-European languages?

The theory of gradual disintegration of a basic, primary language into derivative, secondary languages, which is represented by the genealogical tree *(Stammbaumtheorie)*. The main variants of this theory. The Indo-Italo-Celtic group and the Germano-Balto-Slavic group; the Asiatic and the European groups.

The modern geographic theory which rejects the concept of gradual disintegration of large linguistic entities into smaller ones and which posits instead a series of "wave-like" transitions from one linguistic entity into another *(Wellentheorie)*.

Critique of both theories. Cf., among others, my *Opyt fonetiki rez'janskix govorov . . .* , §300, statements 1–3, pp. 124–25.

IV

A Detailed Program of Lectures
for the Academic Year 1877–1878

... GRAMMAR

Chapter 1. Analysis of Language as the Basis for Subdividing Grammar. (Cf. *A Program of Readings for a General Course in Linguistics,* p. 81).*

Step-by-step analysis of language. Definition of concepts: *speech, sentence, word, expression.* Morphological, etymological parts of the word: *root, prefix, desinence,* etc. Phonetic elements of connected speech: *syllable, sound,* etc. *Words* and *expressions* as *syntactic* atoms, units of the sentence and of connected speech. *Roots* in the broadest sense of the word as *morphological* atoms, units. *Sounds* as *phonetic* atoms, units of words.

The *division of words* from various points of view, phonetic and morphological.

The subdivision of grammar into *phonetics, morphology,* and *syntax. Etymology, semasiology,* and *lexicology.*

A. *Phonetics*

Chapter 2. The Science of Sounds—Phonetics. (Cf. *PR,* pp. 82–95, *Program of 1876–1877,* pp. 92–95).

Necessary preconditions for the precise investigation of sounds:

1) Distinction of letters and sounds.

2) Reduction of subjectivity to a minimum. What is the role of subjectivity in the investigation of sounds?

Breakdown of phonetics:

---

* Henceforth abbreviated as *PR.* Page numbers refer to the English text of the *Programs.*

I. *Physiology of sounds,* as applied to grammar (physiology of sounds from a linguistic, glottological viewpoint).

II. Phonetics in the narrow sense of the word: statics and dynamics of sounds . . .

. . . Definition of the discrete [*členorazdel'nyj*] sound.

Common properties of the sounds of language:

a) "objective" properties: (1) acoustic, (2) physiological;

b) "subjective" properties: (3) psychological.

What is sound as the smallest indivisible phonetic unit of language? The definition of the simple, single, discrete . . . sound from an acoustic, physiological, and psychological standpoint.

Comparison of the phonetic unit of language with the atom as the unit of matter and with the integer as the unit in mathematics. Acoustic, phonetic, indivisible (atoms). The relative magnitude of indivisible atoms. Cf. the indivisible units in anatomy, histology, chemistry, etc.

What three main aspects must be distinguished in each sound? . . .

. . . The *physiological explanation* of sound changes. Nerve reflexes. Comparison of the assimilation of sounds, etc., with analogous phenomena in other areas of reflex motions of the nervous system. Theoretical and graphic interpretations [cf. *PR*, p. 82, *Program of 1876–1877,* p. 92]. Similar phenomena in writing; e.g., assimilation in spelling. *Lapsus linguae* and *lapsus calami.* Everyday occurrences of the same kind. What is here simultaneous and unique, etc. [cf. *PR.* p. 82].

Rapid and slovenly pronunciation enables us to observe the developing phonetic tendencies of language. . . .

Chapter 8. Phonetics as Distinct from the Physiology of Sounds.

Phonetics as the study of the morphological and etymological aspect of sounds, as the application of the physiology of sounds to an examination of the sound structure (mechanism) of a given language. Phonetics = the applied physiology of sounds.

The distinction between the physiology of sounds and phonetics. The *physiology of sounds* concerns all *sounds* of human speech (sound units and their combinations) from an objective physical and physiological (natural and historical) point of view. *Phonetics,* or, more precisely, the grammatical part of phonetics, investigates (analyzes) the *equivalents of sounds* (sound units and their combinations) in terms of their specific properties, i.e., insofar as they *play a role,* for example, ⟨as⟩ soft and hard, simple and complex, consonantal and vocalic, etc., even though from a strictly physio-logical viewpoint, the phonetic equivalents of soft sounds may be hard, and vice versa, etc. The discrepancy between the physical nature of sounds and their role in the mechanism of language, as reflected in the feeling of native speakers.

Chapter 9. The Distinction Between Statics and Dynamics of Sounds. . . . Sound Laws (Lautgesetze):

a) the laws of combination of sounds at a given stage of a language; laws of the equilibrium of language.

b) laws of the development of language; laws of the historical change of language.

The study of the laws of the equilibrium of language is the sub-ject of statics; the study of the laws of development in time and of historical change of language is the subject of dynamics.

Branching ⟨grouping⟩ of sounds. On the one hand, paired sounds, and on the other, non-paired or isolated sounds. Examples. Cor-respondences and groupings of sounds: (a) purely static (static-physiological), (b) dynamic and static (static-etymological).

a) Correspondences and groupings of sounds due to static-physiological changes. Examples.

b) Correspondences and groupings of sounds due to dynamic changes. Examples.

The Ø (zero) sound as a minimal phonetic entity. As a result of the gradual decrease of a sound and then of its complete disap-pearance, there develop dynamic and static relationships (corre-spondences, groupings) of sounds in which one of the members has a certain magnitude and the other is infinitely small, or zero:

$$S : Ø \text{ (where S represents any sound).}$$

Examples of the distinction between:

a) (static) relationships of sounds in a stable state, laws of simul-taneity, and

b) (dynamic) laws of development in time.

Only the latter is based on the comparison of related languages and of different periods in the history of a single language.

Fusion of sounds in their origin.

The stability of sounds is twofold, static and dynamic.

Chapter 10. The Psychological Aspect of Phonetics.

. . . The psychological aspect in the life and development of the sounds of language. The psychological explanation of phonetic phenomena.

In examining the sounds of language one must distinguish two factors: (a) the physiological (physical) in the strict sense of the word, and (b) the physiological and psychological. . . .

The interaction of physical (physiological) and psychological factors of language statically and dynamically.

The psychological part of phonetics:

a) static factors: gradation, phonetic cement, etc.;

b) dynamic factors: sound analogy as a factor counteracting sound laws, etc. Sound analogy as a force in the statics and dynamics of sounds. . . . ⟨. . .⟩

THE CLASSIFICATION OF LANGUAGES

Chapter 1. Genetic Classification in General.

The recognition of linguistic kinship is based not on chance similarity of entire, undivided words, but on the full etymological correspondence of both the main and secondary (subordinate) elements of words according to strictly defined sound laws. For this reason we must first divide words into their morphological parts and then establish their relationship with the same parts in other languages.

The identity or similarity of roots reduced to the simplest form. The identity or similarity of formal (word-forming) elements of the word. The identity or similarity of the functions of these elements. *Grammatical* identity or similarity.

Phonetic translation, or transposition of the sound-form of certain words of one language into the sound-form of another language according to strictly defined sound laws and sound correspondences. The possibility of phonetic translation is a reliable, unmistakable test of the generic kinship of languages, although the impossibility of phonetic translation is no proof of its absence. Cf. *Program of 1876–1877,* p. 108.

The kinship of languages is based on their provenience from one common language. Genetically related languages are, in other words, different variants of one and the same proto-language, of an original primary language.

Observance of *geographic* and *chronological* conditions. One cannot directly compare English words with Russian ones, Modern Greek words with Polish ones, etc., without reducing them first to older and, consequently, closer degrees of development. Cf. *atavism* in biology. The similarity between nephews and uncles is not explained by the descent of the former from the latter, but by their descent from the same grandparents or great-grandparents.

It is even more difficult to deduce the phenomena of one language from the phenomena of another cognate language (e.g., phenomena of Latin from Greek, English from Polish, Russian from Old ⟨Church⟩ Slavic).

Yet it is possible, and even necessary, to compare the relationship between languages related in an ascending and descending line. Thus, for example, it is instructive to compare the relationship between Prakrit and Sanskrit with the relationship between the Romance languages and Latin. . . .

The reasons for the disintegration of one language into several. Cf. Benfey, *Nachr. Gött.* 21, 1871, pp. 553–58.

The views of Max Müller and E. Renan. The appearance of dialects preceded the formation of one homogeneous, unified language ("Dialekte sind überall vor der Sprache dagewesen").

Is it possible at the present state of our science, to have a *generic classification* of any particular branch of genetically related languages? For the time being, one cannot speak (in most cases) of a genetic classification in the strict sense of the word, but only of a scientific characterization of the various groups of languages and dialects. . . .

The requirements for a scientific classification of related languages.

The bases for a classification—

Not sporadic phenomena, but common tendencies determine the unique structure and composition of a given language. It is necessary to seek out those tendencies whose beginnings were present in the once unified, common, base language, and then to determine which tendencies (which aspects) came to predominate in the various groups and languages derived from the base language.

Common tendencies are established by generalizing individual facts and phenomena of the derived languages and by deductions concerning the base language. . . .

. . . From a scientific standpoint, two languages may be considered completely different entities if:

1) the morphological parts (morphemes) of their words, or their simple and indivisible words (which cannot be deduced from preceding forms) have nothing in common in either their phonetic material or their syllabic structure;

2) the laws of the original combinations of the simple words differ absolutely in the two languages being compared. The impossibility of phonetic translation, however, is not sufficient proof of the ultimately different origin of the two languages. . . .

Chapter 2. Principles of Morphological (Structural) Classification in General. (Cf. *Program of 1876–1877,* p. 108.)

Refutation of the theory which sees in separate groups only different degrees of perfection of a single principle (type) of morphological structure, and which considers inflection the apex of perfection, which is arrived at first, through monosyllabicity, and then through agglutination.

Can a morphological (structural) classification (characterization, description) of languages be based on their phonetic properties? The identity of partial phonetic processes and laws in languages of a totally different morphological and syntactic structure. Totally different morphological types of languages, languages with a completely different structure, may be phonetically identical, may share the same phonetic laws, changes, and correspondences both dialectally (geographically) and chronologically (temporally). Compare the sameness of chemical and physical processes in organisms of completely different morphological structure in biology. Animals and plants of different form, origin, and overall structure may share the same laws of blood circulation and feeding, may have the same tissues and perform the same functions.

Which morphological (pertaining to the structure of words) and syntactic (pertaining to the structure of sentences) features need be considered in a morphological (structural) classification of languages? Cf. Steinthal, *Charakteristik* . . .

"Internal form" (*innere Form*) as a basis of classification. The internal feeling of language (*innerer Sprachsinn*) determines the internal form, i.e., the actual system of grammatical categories of a given language.

Internal form simultaneous with phonetic form. However, one should define first the psychological character of language and then its external form as a reflection of internal ⟨psychological⟩ activity.

The definition of language: the form of language in general is defined by combining the two aspects of the internal relation to the psychological material (*Auffassungsweise*) and the means of word formation. Consequently:

I. 1) The primary basis for a classification of languages should be the relationship of matter and form and its morphological manifestation.

2) The relation of subject and predicate. "Etymological" form:

a) Nomen, Nominativus,

b) Verbum finitum.

True nominatives and true finite verbs are alien to formless languages, to those that do not distinguish matter and form.

II. Three morphological devices of word formation:

1) Immutability of words and simple juxtaposition;

2) Agglutination (adding on) of affixes;

3) "Appending" [*priobrazovanie*] (*Anbildung, adaptatio?*). . . .

V

On Pathology and Embryology of Language

1. Physiology is the study of normal organic processes; pathology is the study of deviations and abnormalities. In the field of linguistics, the description and explanation of ordinary, normal linguistic behavior belongs to the realm of physiology, and the description and explanation of linguistic abnormalities to that of pathology.

Just as pathological phenomena may consist of the same elements as normal physiological phenomena, but in a different arangement and different quantitative ratios, so abnormal linguistic behavior is not something utterly different from normal linguistic behavior, but a kind of pathological overgrowth (hypertrophy) of some linguistic elements at the expense of others, or the loss (atrophy) of some elements. In other words, the study of abnormal phenomena deals with certain elements which have developed one-sidedly but are also found in normal behavior, or attempts to explain the loss of some elements.

2. The study of abnormal biological (organic or linguistic) behavior also sheds light on normal changes which take place in the course of generations. A weak and infrequent deviation repeated over several generations may acquire sufficient strength to become, in the end, a characteristic of the entire species. Individual deviations may yield the same result, but in a shorter period of time.

Individual linguistic deviations differ from historical deviations affecting a series of generations. In the latter case we have to do with the sum total of a long chain of minute changes and substitutions of one kind of activity of the speech organs for another (speech organs are here intended in the broadest sense of the word, i.e., including not only the speech organs proper, but also the brain), whereas individual deviations appear in the form of definite, so to speak, macroscopic substitutions. The quantitative and qualitative differences between the substituted and substituting functions in individual deviations is usually far greater than those which affect the entire speech community and lead eventually to historical changes.

3. In the historical development of language, we are dealing with a mass of interacting individuals who inherit linguistic features or adopt them from their contemporaries, whereas in the case of individual linguistic deviations we have to do with one passive individual who is exposed to the influence of his environment, but is incapable of adopting all its linguistic features because of a defective speech apparatus. He is thus forced to replace the difficult features by simpler ones, or to omit them altogether.

It is precisely this defectiveness, the individual character of the deformation, that constitutes the main difference between individual pathological deviations and the historical changes affecting an entire speech community with its organically and linguistically normal individuals.

4. A similar distinction must be made between the language of pathological individuals and that of children learning to speak. The language of children is a subject for a special field of study, which we may call *linguistic embryology*. The phenomena of acoustic and mental substitutions occurring in child language are similar to those of individuals suffering from speech defects. But the deviations in speech of children are transient and due to the underdeveloped state of their speech organs, whereas the linguistic deviations of defective individuals are fixed and chronic and cannot be removed, unless we remove the organic defects themselves, a process which is rarely possible.

5. It is otherwise difficult to draw a fixed line between the language of children and that of linguistically defective persons. Some children develop linguistically very rapidly and quickly acquire the average linguistic norm of the given speech community. Usually, children speak in their own way for a certain period of time, acquiring only gradually a clear pronunciation and correct speech. For the duration of that intermediary period, children, too, must be considered linguistically pathological. In addition, we must distinguish various types of linguistic deviations. Some begin with birth, and some develop later in life as a result of physical

or nervous disorders. Deviations of the first type are either absolutely incurable or may be overcome in part or completely. Deviations of the second type differ from the incompletely formed language of children only quantitatively, i.e., by their degree of duration. The case of Wladek M., presented below, illustrates the type of linguistic deviations which slowly recede but which cannot be completely eliminated.

6. We distinguish two aspects of language: the *psychological* and the *physiological, cerebration* and *phonation,* or: (1) *language* in the proper sense of the word, and (2) *pronunciation.* The essence of language lies, naturally, in cerebration, i.e., in the brain processes, which are inherited through zoological development and tractable to the influence of the environment. Phonation, however is indispensable as the final sign of cerebration, as the connecting link between the cerebration of different individuals endowed with the faculty of language.

In accordance with the above distinction, we may further divide linguistic deviations into *cerebral* and *phonational.* In either case there is either a complete inability to function, or the ability to substitute one function for another. The inability to function may apply only to some elements of the language, or to the language as a whole. In the latter case we deal with complete *alalia,* or *muteness.*

7. Pathological linguistic phenomena are called *aphasia.* Aphasia may be complete or partial. In the first case the individual does not speak at all; in the second, he is incapable of controlling some elements of the linguistic performance.

8. Since I consider the study of such phenomena very interesting and useful, I have devoted particular attention to the language of partial aphasics and to the language of children, whenever the opportunity presented itself. In this way I have collected a great deal of material on the *pathology* and *embryology* of language.

I should add that the material in my possession pertains almost exclusively to the phonational aspect of language, i.e., to the pronunciation of the studied individuals. I have had little opportunity to investigate the cerebral aspect of language systematically.

Gradually I intend to develop and publish the materials I have collected. I will begin with the description of the linguistic deviations of a partial aphasic, Wladek M.

GENERAL REMARKS

... 104. Leaving all generalizations for a special work that will contain the results of a thorough investigation of the different forms of pathology and embryology of language, I shall limit myself to the following remarks:

105. 1. As W.M.'s incorrect pronunciation gradually improved, some of his deficiencies were eliminated, but others were not. It is possible to eliminate, at least partially, deficiencies due to laziness and apathy or to the dynamics of the organism. Thus, for example, instead of the original substitution of the consonant group xn by n, xn was pronounced. But deficiencies due to the structure of the body, to anatomical defects, cannot be eliminated. Thus, W.M. will obviously never regain r, $ł$, or k, g. He will never learn to distinguish in his speech the three series of consonants (1) s, z, c, $ʒ$, (2) $š$, $ž$, $č$, $ǯ$, (3) $ś$, $ź$, $ć$, $ʒ́$, although he distinguishes them clearly by ear. The overall defect of W.M.'s pronunciation, which is muffled and nasal, will also forever remain in his speech.

106. 2. W.M.'s pronunciation is characterized by a prevalent use of dental consonants, i.e., of t, d and their combinations, instead of k, g, and other sounds. Something similar (i.e., the increasing prevalence of dental consonants, or the condensation of speech functions toward the end of the tongue) occurred in the historical development of various language groups, especially Indo-European.

107. 3. At first W.M. replaced both mid vowels o and e by the vowel a; then he replaced only e by a, and finally he acquired both mid vowels. This indicates the physiological difficulty of pronouncing the mid vowels. It is also known that the original Indo-European o and e became a in the history of some languages of that family. For example, Sanskrit has a instead of the original e and o; German and Lithuanian have a instead of the original o, etc.

108. 4. The replacement of consonant clusters in W.M.'s speech at a very early date resembles the replacement of clusters in the Finnic languages (Finnish, Estonian, Hungarian and others); e.g., $st > t, zd > d$.

109. 5. As in all languages (and, more generally, in anything that develops) one can distinguish strata in W.M.'s speech that originated at different periods of time. Cf. my remarks about the words *pamiśnoć, majiti,* etc. (§ 80, 91 ⟨not included here⟩).

V I

On The Tasks Of Linguistics

MY TASK is far more difficult than that of other lecturers. I refer not only to the lack of time for preparing this lecture as I would have liked to and as the subject deserves. What is worse, educated society regards our science with minimal interest. This low estimate expresses itself, by the way, in the view, communicated to me second-hand, that "linguists can only lecture about where to dot the i's."

There may actually be linguists with stores of knowledge this rich, as there may be scientists and physicians who can only explain the art of shearing sheep or milking cows. Yet as natural science is not confined just to these skills, linguistics is not limited to dotting i's and crossing t's. Although I consider myself only an ordinary practitioner of linguistics, I am able to do far more than prescribe calligraphic and orthographic rules.

Mainly to counter this sort of opinion of what linguists do, I will first speak briefly about the goals and tasks of linguistics in general, and then proceed to a more detailed presentation of the nature of our science, and explanation of the causes of linguistic change.

The role played by grammar, a part of linguistics, in the schools helps to propagate and give credence to such lay opinions as the one cited above. School grammar is usually content to give detailed practical rules, in the conviction that its task is to teach how to speak and read a given language correctly. This by itself is, obviously, more than "dotting i's," but it is still a very modest, practical goal.

First of all, I must caution against the very confusion of linguistics and philology.

Philology, as it has developed historically and as it is usually presented by its practitioners, is a conglomerate of knowledge, of detailed information about a variety of matters, and not a science in the strict sense of the word; on the other hand, linguistics is a monolithic and well-defined discipline. The aim of philology is to reproduce and re-create the life of a particular nation in all its manifestations. Philology's leading position is held by classical philology, which aims at the multifaceted investigation of the Greeks and the Romans, the two most celebrated peoples of European antiquity. The benefits of this philology, which was born at the time of the Renaissance and Humanism, have been immeasurable in the education of generations of European peoples. The ancient Romans, and especially the Greeks, stood head and shoulders above the fanatic and backward men of the Middle Ages. Acquaintance with classical antiquity, with its literature and philosophy, must have shaken the monastic minds, freed them from the bonds of scholasticism, and implanted the broader views characteristic of those ⟨ancient⟩ times.

Classical philology has had a long and uninterrupted existence. It is still being developed, and it is zealously watched over. But its civilizing role has ended. The travesty of classical philology which is perpetrated in our high schools can only harm young minds. As a science, philology must be regenerated and its horizons widened; otherwise, it will be but a remnant of antiquity, unsuited to the modern requirements of science.

Recently, new branches of philology have arisen in Europe. These are in part distorted replicas of classical philology: Indic philology, Semitic philology, Chinese philology, Germanic, Romance, Slavic philology, etc. Some of these branches (Indic, Semitic, Chinese), while only recently making their appearance in Europe, flourished long ago in the homelands of the people they study; Chinese and Indic philology, for example, are far older than classical philology, the brain child of Europe.

In a more precise sense, one may treat, for example, Polish philology as the many-sided study of Polish society and the Polish nation together with its literature.

Regardless of the people or nation investigated, philology collates information from various fields of science pertaining to a given society. It is a kind of encyclopedia which includes the history of philosophy; the history of literary and intellectual accomplishments; the history of society and socio-political struggles (i.e., general history and sociology); the history of legal organizations and legislation; the history of customs and morals, or ethnology; the history of beliefs, or mythology; the history of language, or grammar in the broad sense of the word—in other words linguistics.

In origin, linguistics is everywhere in the debt of those philologists who first studied language for special purposes, that is, as a means of investigating other aspects of the intellectual life of a nation, but then discovered the pleasure of studying language for its own sake and created the science of grammar. So it was in India, among the Arabs, and finally, in Europe. As a result, linguistics long bore, and even now to some extent bears, the stamp of its origin in philology. Hence the peculiar character of philological linguistics, which still employs improper, perverted methods of investigation. Today it would be inconceivable for a natural scientist to begin his investigations on forms which had long ago disappeared or which were preserved only in fragments and only then to proceed to the study of the world around him. But this is the method that is still dominant in linguistics. From old to new, from inaccessible to accessible, from the monuments of a language to the language itself, from letters to sounds—this is the order in which most linguists pursue their object of study. Thus history of language degenerates into a history of literary monuments, or even into a chronological survey of works about language, into mere erudition, into a bibliography of opinions, into a knowledge of books. Hence the scorn for the surrounding world, for the *linguae vulgares,* and hence the "aristocratic" contempt for facts. In his discussions of language, the philologist asks: what is its parentage? Does it boast ancient written records? Does it have a history of several dozens of generations who used it for literary purposes? Only a language which can thus attest its nobility is deemed worthy of investigation by these learned men. Hence the overestimation of Sanskrit's importance vis-à-vis the study of less ancient languages; the overestimation of Latin and ancient Greek, of Gothic and Old Church Slavonic vis-à-vis the later representatives of the same linguistic family. In fact, however, the study of modern languages, accessible to us in all their facets, is far and away more important. My statement may strike some people as eccentric, but the natural scientist will understand me immediately. The study of paleontology presupposes the study of zoology, botany, etc., and not the reverse.

As the name itself indicates, linguistics is the scientific investigation of language, or human speech, in all its diversity.

Like other phenomena, linguistic phenomena give a first impression of chaos, disorder, confusion. But the human mind has an innate ability to shed light upon seeming chaos and to find harmony, order, system, and causal relationships in it. Linguistics is the goal-directed activity of the human mind to find order in the phenomena of language.

Even the most ordinary and least scientifically trained mind performs tentative, unconscious, and partly conscious operations. Every human mind systematizes, generalizes, seeks causes. As far as language is concerned, everybody learns first to distinguish himself from others and his own speech from the speech of others; everybody can distinguish his native language from other languages, given the opportunity to hear them; everybody can distinguish a sentence, containing a thought, from something that is not a sentence; everybody can isolate words and their particular meanings from what is not a word. The distinction between meaning (the internal content, as it were) and the combination of sounds which serves to render meaning is strange to no one. Perhaps not everyone is fully aware of it, perhaps not everyone is able to express or formulate it, but the distinction is undoubtedly grasped, if only subconsciously, by every normal person. The science of linguistics introduces absolutely nothing new in this respect; it only perfects and refines our thinking ⟨about these processes⟩, frees it from the accidents of chance, and substitutes a chain of conscious and clearly defined concepts for a mass of vague and diffused ideas.

Linguistics is concerned with the investigation of language, i.e., human speech in all its diversity. But bearing in mind the fact of the existence of perhaps several thousand tribal and national languages and recognizing that a lifetime—given even the greatest of abilities—is hardly enough to acquire knowledge of even a small fraction of them, we submit that the ideal of linguistics as complete knowledge of languages is unattainable. No book could present the entire system of linguistics. No human brain could comprehend the whole mass of pertinent facts. Each investigator masters only a small fragment of the whole, through which he gains a view of the whole and creates for himself a more or less adequate picture of the nature of language in general.

Here a comparison with the crystal as an ideal mathematical form and with those fragments of crystals that are encountered in reality, naturally suggests itself. As the mineralogist re-creates a picture of the whole crystal from a piece, so we can reconstruct the homogeneous whole ⟨of language⟩ on the basis of knowledge of some of its parts.

Let us now take a look at the variety of problems facing linguistics. These problems may be divided or classified in various ways, depending upon where one begins.

I

Thus, for example, starting with the distinction between the individual and tribe or nation, we draw the distinction between the individual and tribal or national language, and between individual linguistic development and the history of a tribal or national language.

Individual language may develop normally from the speech of an infant to the fully fledged speech of a child, and from child speech to that of an old man; or its development may be abnormal and defective.

Whatever is individual is at the same time general, universal. Since the simplest elements of individual development are shared by all people, embryology and pathology of language are a part of general linguistics, as distinct from the study of particular languages or language families.

Alongside the study of individual language, one must place the study of tribal and national languages, i.e., languages that are distinguished from each other by the names of tribes or nations that use them, such as Polish, Czech, Serbian, Russian, Ukrainian; German, Danish; French, Italian; Lithuanian, Latvian; Estonian, Hungarian.

But can we speak about the development of such languages?

Real development is uninterrupted as, for example, the development of the cells of an organism, of the parts of a plant or animal, or of seeds into plants, etc. In all such instances there is a constant, invariant base and gradual uninterrupted change of properties and their arrangement.

There are different types of development. The simplest form of development is represented by the purposeful growth of individual organisms. In animals and human beings, this refers both to the physical and mental development from the embryonic state throughout the life cycle.

The periodic development of individuals is a more complex kind of development. The reproductive process of living beings must be mentioned first. The ovum is transformed and becomes an animal, a living being; this being develops individually but, at the same time, part of it is transformed into an ovum, which in turn is able to generate a new living being, and so on indefinitely. Similarly, a seed becomes a plant, part of the plant becomes a seed, and the seed becomes a plant again, etc.

Continuous periodic development may be complicated by the metamorphoses to which an individual may be subjected during his lifetime. Thus, for example, a butterfly's ovum gives not a butterfly, but a caterpillar; from the caterpillar, a chrysalis; and only the chrysalis, a butterfly, which again lays eggs that undergo the same metamorphoses. This kind of development is fairly common in the animal and vegetable kingdoms.

All this pertains to the development of entire organisms. Similarly, there is continuous development of various properties, such as the nervous system, the muscles, etc.

In the case of language, development concerns only individual linguistic peculiarities, and not the peculiarities of a collective language. To begin with, the development of individual languages, up to the point when the child acquires full linguistic mastery, must be separated from the study of collective languages. Can there be uninterrupted development in linguistic communication between different individuals? Each individual acquires his language anew, inheriting perhaps only a different degree of general linguistic ability. He receives the stimulus to speak by means of the senses, especially voice, from individuals about him, and in turn affects their speech. There is not and cannot be a direct way, a direct link between the linguistic images of one individual and those of another. There is only the indirect link through the mediacy of sound symbols and, in general, of mental connections, that is, the so-called associations and arrangement of concepts. Linguistically, the individual can develop only in society; however, language, as a social phenomenon, cannot develop; it can only have a history.

History is the succession of homogeneous, but different, phenomena conjoined by indirect, rather than direct, causality. Such a succession of phenomena is found, for example, in geology; we shall probably learn about this concept of history in geology from the forthcoming lectures on the past and future of the earth.[1]

A similar kind of succession is found in language. Language as a social phenomenon, the language of a group or nation, cannot have development; it can only have a history.

Thus, one of the first tasks of linguistics is to face the difference between the individual and society.

II

We face the second task of linguistics when we turn to the problem of the origin of language, i.e., to the formation of language within the human species, as opposed to language as a fully developed, finished product.

For the individual, the beginning of speech is the beginning of his linguistic development, whereas for the human race the beginning of language is the beginning of its history.

In his gradual development from lower, prehuman species, man became man only when he developed language, or speech, as we know it.

Do animals therefore completely lack the faculty of speech? Careful investigations have shown that many animals have the rudiments of speech. Thus, for example, cats in feeding and guarding their young use some ten different voice modulations to express danger, threat, endearment, encouragement, enticement, etc. The rudiments of speech have also been found in apes and monkeys, the species nearest to man, e.g., the orangutan and the howler monkey (*Brüllaffe*). The great diversity in the language of birds, especially the domesticated varieties, is known to everyone who has had the opportunity to observe them. In any case, it is undeniable that some animal species use modulations of voice as a means of communication. However, none of this is the equivalent of human language, which employs arbitrary symbols in great number and in most complex combination. The language of animals is characterized by necessity, directness, and invariability, i.e., by traits directly the opposite of those which constitute the essence of human language. At least this is true of the language of domesticated birds and animals observed by me. I know nothing of the language of the orangutan which I have not had the occasion to study or to read about in scientific works.

On the other hand, there obviously exist human tribes whose language is in a rudimentary state and cannot possibly be viewed as human in the full sense of the word; consequently, such tribes are halfway between animal and man.

In view of the fact that the structure of the languages of various groups differs in principle and cannot be reduced to a common denominator, i.e., to an originally common state, and since some languages are in the process of being created, while others have gone through many stages of development lasting perhaps thousands of years, we must conclude that the myth of the common descent of all men (from one couple) is contrary to science.

Similarly, one must discard the hypothesis of the origin of the whole human race in one place from some kind of animals of a lower species. Man as a social being endowed with language originated in different places and at different times from different lower species of anthropoids.

In this connection the question arises why human communication employs only the voice, an organ that affects only our hearing, and not other sensory organs.

The organs of smell and taste are out of the question. To be sure, "nature often speaks to us by means of taste and smell" as in warnings of danger. But how far would we get if mutual understanding were to depend on the nerve endings of the mucous membranes of our nose and the surface of our tongue? The sense of touch requires direct contact at a minimal distance. It is, indeed, possible to express one's feelings and intentions by pinching, kicking, elbowing, stroking, kissing, but all these are too confined to serve as a means of linguistic communication.

Thus only sight and hearing remain as senses which can function at a distance and carry the greatest variety of impressions. Only the eye and ear can compete with each other to fulfill the communicative needs of language. That visual language may exist side by side with acoustic language is, in fact, attested by the existence of highly developed and diverse sign-languages, e.g., among the Indians of North America or the deaf-mutes as well as by the various systems of writing which employ visual symbols to convey meaning directly (as in Chinese writing) or indirectly, through the intermediacy of sound.

We may hypothesize that, in its primitive stage, human speech employed sight and hearing constantly and simultaneously, the voice being assisted by vivid mimicry, as is still the case among some tribes and with some individuals. Why, then, did the voice prevail, while gestures were discarded? Why did linguistic communication confine itself to acoustic means, forgoing the use of visual means?

The answer seems simple enough. The voice can be heard in the dark, through obstacles that would curtail sight, or when one's back is turned to the speaker; the voice can be heard from a distance at which only an exceptionally sharp eye would be able to make out gestures, even in the best light. Light waves travel in a straight line, whereas sound waves move in all directions. Air as a vibrating medium surrounds man everywhere and at all times; light is not always and everywhere present. That is why we speak with our voices and not with grimaces and finger movements; that is why mimicry, which formerly accompanied speech, gradually was reduced to playing a very modest role.

In concluding this section on the foundations of language, I shall venture to add that people were able to begin to speak only when they ceased to walk on all fours, when they stood up on two legs with their heads raised and their necks straight, so that their larynxes and windpipes were placed vertically and not horizontally to each other. The extent to which the standing position facilitates the production of speech is best demonstrated by birds, which may learn to imitate human speech, a feat completely unattainable for more highly developed quadrupeds. A child begins to utilize his speech organs as adults do only when he is able to walk, or at least to hold himself erect. If we attempt to speak standing on all fours, we can see how much more difficult it is than when we stand erect on our two feet.

III

I shall now proceed to the tasks of linguistics in the investigation of fully developed tribal or national languages.

The concept of language as a complex and integral whole is merely an ideal. The ideal and actuality are not the same. Thus it is possible, for example, that the concept of a Polish language comprises something that may not exist, and may never have existed or been established. Here we may again recall the analogy of the crystal. As crystals found in nature are but parts of ideal crystals, the native language that any Pole carries in his mind is but a fraction of the whole.

What aspects of the total language, the full and ideal model, does grammar consider? (For I am now thinking specifically about grammar.)

The central core of the ideal model consists of the average and fortuitous cross section of the languages of individuals of a given speech community.

Each individual language comprises an internal, central aspect and an external, peripheral aspect, i.e., a mental or cerebral aspect and a sensory aspect lying outside the cerebral region. Every language consists, in other words, of language proper and speech. But do both aspects exist on equal terms in each individual? Can they not be reduced to one common term?

Only the linguistic images of an individual have extension and development. The sounds uttered at any given moment and the activity of the speech organs are transient, just as is any combination of tones produced in singing or instrumental playing. Only the competence of the organs, only habits are subject to gradual development, but never the external acoustic aspect of individual language. Speech sounds and the corresponding movements of the speech apparatus may exist and be repeated only insofar as they leave an impression on the nervous centers, on the brain or mind, in the form of permanent representations.

Everything concerning human language as such is located in the brain. Without a brain, without a mind, there might be a talking machine, but not a man who thinks and is part of society. Thinking and membership in society are thus the basic conditions for language in the proper sense of the word.

This being the case, what aspects of this ideal model of collective language are of interest to grammar?

First, we must identify the movements of the speech apparatus that have been acquired through practice, through habit, but which are conditioned by the nervous system and the brain; these movements are at the same time intimately connected with voice, with the acoustics of speech.

Second, there is an internal (central) or psychological aspect, also closely connected with articulatory and auditory representations.

In the first case we deal with phonation, or speaking; in the second, with cerebration, or speech in general.

The external aspect of language, or phonation, is the subject of phonetics, or the science of sounds, at present the most advanced and most thoroughly elaborated part of grammar. Phonetics investigates the various kinds of pronunciation, the nature of sounds and the activity of the speech organs, the interconnection of sounds and their formation and production at each moment of their historical development. It examines the organs, or instruments, of speech which participate in the pronunciation of the different categories of sounds of a given language, the production of speech in different parts of the speech apparatus, the relationship between musical and purely linguistic aspects of language, the role of tones or sounds in distinguishing meanings of words, and their historical origin.

Here belong such questions as: the difference between the vowel sounds *e* and *a* in *gnieść–gniatać;* the difference between the vowel sounds *o* (or *ó*) and *a* in *dogodzić–dogadzać, chodzić–chadzać, prosić–upraszać, ⟨skrócić–⟩ skracać;* the difference between the vowel sound *i* and the combination of sounds *oj* in *pić–poić, gnić–gnoić;* the difference between the consonant sounds *s* (or *ś*) and *ch* in *włosy–włochy, nos–noch, kluski–kluchy, kalosze–kalochy*, etc. How were they pronounced by earlier generations, and how are future generations likely to pronounce them?

What were the operations and movements of the speech organs of our ancestors and what sounds were uttered in certain positions of particular words at a given stage of a language? From what sounds did the consonants and vowels *s, ž, č* and *e, o* develop historically in words such as *sadzić, sen* (alongside *sto, słoma*), or *żelazo, cztery, może, piecze, sierota, wiode, sen*, etc.

Phonetics should provide an answer to these and similar questions.

The other parts of grammar investigate the central aspects of speech, the cerebration of a given language.

First, we must distinguish between the simplest psycho-linguistic elements which appear in the guise of sound (the morphemes) and their combinations. For example:

> po-*łoż*-y-l-i-śmy na pod-*łodz*-e,
> *leż*-y na *łóż*-k-u. . . .

This part of grammar poses such questions as: what is the form of the main, central elements of words (the roots)? What internal relationships of words do they ⟨the morphemes⟩ mark, and do such markers exist in general? What is their place with relation to the main element? What is the origin of these meaningful segments or elements of words?

The part of grammar that deals with these and similar questions is called morphology, or the study of words and their constituent parts. It is divided into:

1) the study of the formation of words, or word-formation;

2) the study of changes of words, or inflection, which, in the case of our type of language, has two main parts: declension and conjugation.

After morphology in the narrow sense of the word comes syntax, or the study of the sentence as a simple unit and as a unit consisting of words. It studies the combination of words into sentences, and the principles of such combinations.

Morphology in the narrow sense, plus syntax, constitute morphology in the broadest sense of the word.

Finally, the psychological content itself, the linguistic concepts which exist independently but manifest themselves through linguistic forms, are the subject of a separate part of grammar, semasiology, or the science of meaning. This part of grammar investigates the images of the outer and inner worlds in the human mind apart from linguistic form. The questions it poses are: what types of concepts are expressed (or designated) in the given language? What are their relations? What is their origin? How do meanings change? And so on. As an illustration, I might mention the recurrent process of increasing meaningfulness [*osmyslenie značenija*], the process of transition from the concrete to the abstract. For example, *skutek, raz, obowiązek, pojmować, lękać się, wstyd, wstydzić się,* Germ. *Scham; dowcip, wątpić, badać, łączyć, bluźnić, dusza, duch, Bóg, Zeús; bies; niebo, wiara, kryzwda, część. . . .*

IV

Grammar treats the phonetic and cerebral elements of collective (tribal) languages. But for the sake of a general characterization and classification of the linguistic world, we can treat these languages as indivisible wholes, as separate entities.

The classification of languages presupposes a precise definition of their differences and, in the first place, of their similarities. These similarities may be due to:

1) the genetic kinship of languages of certain peoples and tribes, or

2) the general similarity of the nature and change of languages, independently of their historical or genetic relations.

Similarity between genetically related languages is due to the fact that these languages present but modifications of the same linguistic material. Thus, for example, the Slavic languages are related to and resemble each other as modifications or variants of a common Slavic linguistic state. The same principle accounts for the more remote similarity and affinity between Slavic and such other Indo-European (Indo-Germanic) languages, as Sanskrit (together with the whole Indic group of languages), Iranian (Bactro-Persian), Armenian, Greek, Latin (together with the Romance languages), Celtic, Germanic, and the Baltic languages—Lithuanian and Latvian, the languages nearest the Slavic group.

The parallel investigation and comparison of genetically related languages is the subject of so-called comparative grammar.

The other kind of classification, the morphological or structural classification of languages, is based upon the similarity of their actual states, independently of their historical relations, and on the linguistic changes which appear to depend on universal conditions, on properties common to all people regardless of their origin.

Morphological classifications up to now have been very inexact, mainly because a great many languages have not yet been investigated at all. One of the most popular classifications, though probably not the most successful, divides all languages of the world into three main groups, or classes: (1) isolating monosyllabic languages, whose chief representative is Chinese; (2) agglutinative, affixing languages, among which Turco-Altaic, Hungarian, etc., have been the most studied; and (3) inflected languages, which include the Semitic languages and the above-mentioned Indo-European languages.

Through lack of time, I shall not dwell on the basis of this classification, but I shall only remark that its accuracy is very questionable.

Even if it were most accurate, however, we should have to remember that the state of a language or languages under consideration is not eternal, fixed, and unchangeable, but transitional. The best proof of how deeply the structure of a language may change is the transformation from "synthetic" inflected languages, in which the internal form of a word is varied, into analytic languages with external affixes, which has taken place repeatedly in the history of the Indo-European tongues.

It is enough, for example, to compare the structure of Latin with that of the Romance literary languages (French, Spanish, and Italian), and especially their most recent varieties (i.e., the various French and Italian dialects), to realize the extent of their difference.

Among the Germanic languages, literary English has moved the furthest in this direction; among the Slavic languages, Bulgarian is a representative of the new type of language differing from the old state of Slavic in approximately the same way as, for example, French differs from Latin.

In classifying languages, we must reserve a special place for mixed languages, which include, in a certain sense, both the language of migrants, *korzennopolski* ⟨root-Polish⟩, and the *polska szpracha* of the students of Dorpat. To this category also belong such crystallized and well-defined languages as Yiddish-German, the Chinese-Russian dialect of Kjaxta and Majmačina, the Chinese-English dialect of the southern coast of China, and others. We tend to look down on these languages, contemptuously labeling them "jargons," but we ought not to forget that such jargons often grow into very respectable and powerful languages. It is sufficient to mention the example of English. In general, we have the right to doubt the purity of a great many languages; it does not take a linguist to know that almost every language includes many foreign elements.

Classification of languages must, furthermore, take into consideration the existence of special languages for social groups and trades (legal or illegal) and, especially, of secret dialects and argots (e.g., of criminals, thieves, vagrants).

Finally, we need to stress the difference between naturally developing languages and artificially cultivated, literary languages, a difference analogous to that between wild and domestic animals or between wild and cultured plants. This kind of distinction may evolve in any language family. Thus, for example, the Romance family produced Latin first, and then six other of the best known literary languages (French, Italian, Spanish, Portuguese, Provençal, and Roumanian); I shall say nothing of the different provincial and territorially circumscribed literary languages. In the Germanic family there is German, Dutch, Danish, Swedish, English, etc.; in the Slavic family, Church Slavonic, Russian, Polish, Czech, Serbian, Croatian, Slovenian, Bulgarian, Ukrainian, Slovak, Lusatian, and there are others.

Another, completely separate, category is represented by *Volapük,* the "invented" artificial language par excellence.

V

The forgoing remarks pertain to the history of language, i.e., the investigation and description of existing languages and the causal changes occurring within them.

Recently a new science, or branch of science, has come of age; it concerns itself with the factors that support the life of language and bring about its changes.

As I have already noted, the basis of language lies exclusively in the central nervous system. Sounds and their combinations, or the sensory, external, peripheral aspect of language, mean nothing by themselves. Proof of this is the fact that an unknown foreign language, the sounds of which we can distinguish quite precisely, is not a language for us. This is further corroborated by the fact that some people have the ability to utter over a long period of time various sounds and combinations of sounds which neither they nor anyone else can comprehend.[2] But would anyone call such "senseless gibberish" language? And since the basis of language is purely psychological, linguistics must be considered a branch of the psychological sciences. But, insofar as language exists only in society, and the psychological development of man is possible only through intercourse with other people, we shall rather say that linguistics is a psychological-sociological science. Those who consider language an "organism" and linguistics a natural science are obviously in error.

In view of the fact that both psychological and social factors operate in language, we must regard both psychology and sociology (the science that deals with the interaction of people in society) as ancillary sciences of linguistics.

Proper comprehension of the external aspect of language (phonation) requires the help of anatomy, physiology, and acoustics.

Physiology, in combination with microscopic anatomy or the histology of the brain, might help us understand the psychological essence of language if it could replace psychology, if it were in a position to explore and systematize ⟨the structure of⟩ the brain tissues, if it could reveal the physical and chemical changes of these tissues in the process of speaking and thinking. However, as far as I know, nothing has been done in this field to date, except the general localization by natural scientists of language (strictly speaking, of its motor functions only) in the human brain: it is located in the third left temporal lobe of the brain of people who are primarily right handed. Be that as it may, this discovery is still too insignificant to justify replacing psychology with anatomy and physiology.

Until now we have considered linguistics as a thing in itself, in isolation from life, without asking whether it has or can have any practical applications. At the same time, many people measure the value of science, and to some extent justifiably so, by its applicability to practical ends: "kein Geschäft, kein Vergnügen." Most people respect only things which seem to be practical and useful.

All sciences can be applied in either or both of two ways: a science can serve the needs of other sciences, and it can serve practical life. Thus, for example, logic applies to all sciences without exception, although its practical usefulness is very limited. Mathematics is used in every science which deals with any quantities whatsoever, but its application to practical life is far more modest. Physics and chemistry have their purely scientific applications primarily in physiology, but they also are of paramount importance in practical life. Astronomy's application to practical life is highly restricted. Why then bother to investigate the starry worlds and to determine their relations? And why study geology and the past and future of the earth? For, aside from satisfying our idle curiosity, we get nothing out of it. We cannot use its information directly, and we cannot convert it into money.

As far as the "application of linguistics" is concerned, its purely scientific usefulness is very considerable, but its applicability to practical life is extremely modest.

Linguistics could probably be applied to the study of the history of ideas, to psychology, to mythology, etc. It could also be applied to the history of culture and legal concepts. Thus, for example, the present meaning of the Polish word *dziedziniec* from *dziad* ("ancestor, grandfather") harks back to the period of private land ownership in contrast to *pole* "field," which represented the property of an entire community. The word *gościniec* from *gość* (compare the Latin *hostis* with *hospes*) designates the road by which the *goście*, i.e., "outsiders," usually merchants, arrived, while the word *gospoda* (*Herberge*) designates a place or settlement of the *goście*. The etymological connection between *chłop* "peasant" and *chłopiec* "boy" and between *rob* "slave" (OCS *rab*), *robota* and Czech *robě*, *robátko*, Russian *rebënok, robënok* "child" etc., as well as the use of *otrok* (*infans*) with the double meaning "slave" and "child" show that the legal position of children and slaves at one time was more or less identical: neither children nor slaves had a voice; both were considered "infants" in the family. The foreign origin of the words *szlachta, szlachcic, herb, hrabia, książę, król,* and *cesarz* supports other, historical evidence that these institutions and concepts were imported to Poland from the outside.

The importance of this aspect of applied linguistics is that it enables us to reconstruct the culture of a people who have left us neither written records nor material objects. With the help of linguistics we can learn how a given people lived, how it dressed, what kind of dwellings it had, what kind of domestic animals it kept, whether it was agricultural or nomadic, what kind of grains and plants it knew, what kind of family relations it had, how it was organized legally, etc.

No less important is the application of linguistics to ethnogenesis, i.e., to the science of the origin of peoples, although here the ground is less firm.

The application of linguistics to practical life has hitherto been very modest. Of particular relevance is its application to pedagogy, or rather didactics. Its main task is the design of the most suitable methods for the teaching and study of one's "native" and foreign languages. (The study of one's own literary language is of central importance.)

The application of linguistics to rhetoric is less pertinent, for it is limited, in fact, to instructions on the correct pronunciation of words, on the correct use of forms, and of word order. Oratory in general is based on logic and psychology.

Linguistics could be applied with great success to teaching deaf mutes how to read and write.

Rational instruction of normal people in reading and writing (including spelling) ought to be based on linguistic knowledge; anybody who knows how to read and write will probably admit the importance of such an application of linguistics.

Linguistics could also be applied to practical politics. Its findings could be most helpful in objectively and theoretically defining states and national entities. Such political groups as Switzerland and Austria present particularly interesting problems.

The transmission of a national tradition, the possibility of preserving the heritage of one's ancestors, can be best accomplished through the study of the national literary language, and the preservation of the purity and integrity of one's literary language requires a knowledge of grammar, one of the most important parts of linguistics. I should also mention the importance of Latin for all of Europe (particularly during the Middle Ages), and of the Italian literary language for the politics and ethnography of modern Italy.

Contained within the right limits and without degenerating into a mania, grammatical purism (or concern for linguistic norms) should be guided by the recommendations of theoretical linguistics.

In the field of invention, I should mention the universal language, *Volapük,* whose value and practicality is often exaggerated; however, it seems to me that in a modified form it might actually serve as a universal vehicle of commerce and industry. Indeed, the inventor of this artificial language must have acquired a thorough acquaintance with the grammars of many languages before he set out to realize his ambition of inventing an artificial international language.

From what I have said, it should be apparent that the contempt in which linguistics is held as a science of little practicality and applicability is to some extent justified. I do not intend to influence the minds and feelings of the majority of people holding this view. I shall only take the liberty of calling attention to the difference between man and animals.

Leaving aside the question of language, I shall dwell on a more important and more obvious difference. As man emerged from the animal state, the scope of his activities was enlarged through the help of instruments of the external world. At first he fought with his teeth and his claws; but then he turned to the club, the stone, the spike, the arrow, the rifle, and the cannon. At first he was protected from atmospheric changes by furs and hides, but his further progress was marked by the use of clothes and of the hearth. Primitive "man" devoured raw food, but man has invented pots and roasting spits, plates, spoons, knives, and forks. Primitive "man" propelled himself from place to place using his own legs, but man invented the use of the wagon and of domestic animals, of steam and of complicated machines. Primitive "man" could only sing, i.e., play on the flute situated in his throat, whereas man started out with the pipe and tin box and finished with splendid modern music. . . . Primitive "man" communicated by means of his own organism, with his hands, vocal cords, throat, tongue, teeth, nose, etc., but man proceeded to invent writing, artificial light, and electricity. Thus the primordial primitive being was transformed into civilized and socially organized man. These differences are of enormous importance, the more so that they developed unconsciously and spontaneously. But what was the driving force, the guiding idea? At bottom there was the striving toward comfort and convenience, a striving that is also shared by animals. For even animals show a tendency to use the external world for protection against its harmful effects. Suffice it to mention ant hills, beehives, bird nests, beaver lodges, and sticks and stones in the hands of orangutans, chimpanzees, and gorillas.

But no animal, be it the gorilla or chimpanzee, shows the slightest striving for intellectual gratification, satisfaction based on knowledge. The thirst for knowledge and its gratification is proper only to man, and especially to highly organized, conscious man.

Let there be, then, a large part of educated people who refuse to rise above the intellectual level of animals; let them look to science for profit and comfort only. But there will always be some eccentrics dedicated to the pursuit of knowledge and to the widening of their own intellectual horizons. Among the latter there will always be a handful who recognize language as a subject worthy of study and linguistics as a science equal to other sciences.

NOTES

---

1. These lectures were given by S. Tugutt on the 3rd and 10th of April, 1888.
2. I myself possess this ability to a high degree.

V I I

An Attempt at a Theory of

Phonetic Alternations:

A Chapter from Psychophonetics

CONTENTS

⟨. · .⟩

FOREWORD

I have published a larger work, "Próba teorji alternacyj fonetycznych" ⟨An Attempt at a Theory of Phonetic Alternations⟩ in
Rozprawy Wydziału filologicznego ⟨Transactions of the Philological Section⟩ Cracow Academy of Sciences (now Polish Academy of
Sciences in Cracow), vol. XX, 1894, pp. 219–364 (also published separately). According to usual procedure, I was also
supposed to supply a short summary in German or French for
the *Anzeiger* (or *Bulletin*) of the Academy. However, since I felt it

necessary to make available to non-Polish-speaking scholars the particulars of the exposition and the course of my argument, and especially the formulas which I have advanced, I had greatly to exceed the maximum length of such a résumé and instead of a short summary, give a German version of the same material. Nevertheless, my entire manuscript was accepted without reservations for preparation by the editors of the *Anzeiger,* set up completely in galley proofs, and painstakingly corrected by me with the kind assistance of Mr. St. Rosznecki, Cand. Mag.; then nearly half the type was set under the heading of the *Anzeiger* and my German spelling was changed to conform to the style of the *Anzeiger.* Suddenly, however, toward the end of October, I was told it was impossible to accept such a long work for the *Anzeiger* (of which a single volume could under no conditions exceed four folios and still cost only 40 Kreuzers). And, in fact, the *Anzeiger* is not the most suitable place for a work which has cost so much effort. Therefore I decided to publish it as a separate book, even though this entailed the tiresome, not very profitable, and time-consuming task of changing the résumé style into a direct scholarly exposition and the expression "the author" into "I." It also entailed the division into individual chapters and so forth. And I had to do this with the material already in type.

The history of the origin of this modest contribution likewise explains why I have taken my examples primarily from Polish and have cited them generally without translation. If I had composed the German version independently of the Polish original and had not been forced to merely transform an *Anzeiger* résumé into a separate study, I would have aimed at a greater selection of examples from various languages. Nevertheless, I believe that the Polish examples are quite comprehensive and that anyone will be able to test the general propositions of my work on any other language he might like.

The subtitle, "A Chapter from Psychophonetics," sounds somewhat pretentious; however, by this I merely wanted to indicate that I consider myself an adherent of the linguistic school which emphasizes the psychological factor in all linguistic phenomena.

I would advise the beginner as well as the reader who is not accustomed to such explanations not to read this book through from beginning to end without interruption, but rather to study it in the following order: after the "Explanation and Definition of Some

Technical Terms" and the "Explanation of Symbols and Abbreviations" (p. 132), read through Chapter I (p. 153) attentively, then pass over Chapter II and go directly to Chapter III (p. 170) and after that go through the four following chapters, IV–VII (p. 175 ff.) in sequence; after Chapter VII one can return to the Introduction, followed by Chapters II (p. 161) and VIII (p. 197).

INTRODUCTION

At present I am giving only the first part of my work. The second part should encompass: (1) an analysis of the conditions under which alternations arise; (2) a classification of alternations, at the time of their emergence and (3) during their further existence, when they are maintained through the force of tradition and linguistic intercourse; (4) an account of the different means of utilizing alternants for psycholinguistic purposes; (5) a specification of the limits within which the alternants may move in various directions; (6) an analysis of the different layers of alternation; and (7) an analysis of the correspondences of alternations, i.e., of alternations which correspond in different languages. Moreover, I intend to give special consideration to: (1) the alternations of Sanskrit, (2) the alternations of the Indo-European (Indo-Germanic) languages, which are of common Indo-European origin, and (3) the alternations common to all Slavic languages.

The etymological relationship of speech sounds has been observed for a long time, roughly since the time when man began to be seriously concerned with grammatical and especially with phonetic questions.

The greatest heights here were attained by the Indic grammarians, who developed a very refined theory of the "laws of sandhi," on the one hand and the "laws of guṇa" and "vṛddhi" on the other hand. But the Indic grammarians lacked a feeling for history and were unable to grasp the significance of gradual development, historical sequence, or chronology in general. As a result, their findings lay, so to speak, on a single temporal plane; everything happened simultaneously, as though there were neither a past nor present nor future. Thence also the purely mechanical character of their gramamtical rules; they give excellent prescriptions for the formation of all kinds of grammatical forms, but we would look in vain for a scientific explanation of the ways and means by which these forms originated.

The concepts of *guṇa* and *vṛddhi* have been taken over by European grammarians under the names "Ablaut," "phonetic gradation" and the like, and the theory of phonetic changes has now reached a high level of sophistication. Although European linguists have been dependent on the views of the Indic grammarians, they have surpassed the latter in two ways: first, they have introduced the concept of chronology into their investigations and have made use of it with greater or lesser success; second, they have formed their conclusions on a much broader "comparative" base, using material of a greater variety of languages, including not only related but also unrelated languages.

According to the most recent studies of phonology, the relationship between two different but etymologically related sounds is completely the reverse of what was supposed by earlier linguists; what had passed earlier for the basic form turned out to be a derivative (secondary) form, and vice versa. A characteristic example of this change of viewpoint is the replacement of the theory of "vowel gradation" by the theory which posits the weakening of a stronger phonetic structure and the loss of a part of that structure (F. de Saussure, Brugmann, Osthoff, Hübschmann, and many others).

But even the most recent linguistic works deal with the alternations themselves only indirectly, focusing attention on the determination of phonetic changes and the establishment of the historical priority or origin of the speech sound in question. Furthermore, these works fail to give a satisfactory account of the very concept of alternation or coexistence. One of the works which most closely approaches the concept of alternation developed in my preceding study, and which affirms first of all the existence of alternations, is August Leskien's *Der Ablaut der Wurzelsilben im Litauischen* (Leipzig, 1884).

The expression "alternation" in the sense in which I use it does appear, however, here and there in contemporary linguistic works. Thus, for example, de Saussure says (*Mémoire sur le système primitif des voyelles dans les langues indoeuropéennes*, Leipzig, 1879, p. 12): "The Italic languages have too greatly leveled the inflection of the verb for us to expect to find in them the alternation of weak and strong forms."

I arrived at the concept of alternation developed in my preceding study more than eighteen years ago, when I was giving lectures on certain aspects of comparative grammar and general linguistics at Kazan' University and at the Kazan' Theological Seminary.

The customary approach to phonetic differences in the works available to me at that time was to determine the change of one speech sound into another, and particularly to establish "sound laws" and so forth. This approach could not satisfy me for, first, it gave an inadequate account of the chronology or order of the historical layers and, second, it gave an inexact formulation of the actual facts. One such overriding fact is the *coexistence* of phonetically different but etymologically related speech sounds; only after establishing this fact can one proceed to the investigation of its causes.

My views on the subject at that time were expressed, or rather noted in passing, in my Detailed Program of Lectures for the Academic Year 1876–77, pp. 92–95, 107; in my Detailed Program of Lectures for the Academic Year 1877–78 p. 114ff.; in *Iz Lekcij po latinskoj fonetike*, Voronež, 1893, and even much earlier in "Wechsel des *s* (*š*, *ś*) mit *ch* in der polnischen Sprache" (*Beiträge zur vergleichenden Sprachforchung von Kuhn*, VI, pp. 221–22) (where in 1868 this alternation *s* || *ch* was called a "constant gradation *used to differentiate meaning*"). My ideas on this matter have gradually become more refined and precise. In my Russian lectures I used the word *čeredovanie* 〈"alternation"〉 to indicate the co-occurrence in one and the same language of phonetically different but etymologically related sounds.

One of my Kazan' students, M. Kruszewski, in his dissertation *Nabljudenija nad nekotorymi fonetičeskimi javlenijami, svjazannymi s akcentuaciej* 〈Observations of Some Phonetic Phenomena Connected with Accentuation〉, Kazan', 1879, collected the material available in the *Rig-Veda* to study the alternations caused by the influence of the accent. He acquired a clear and independent view of similar phonetic phenomena and presented it in the introduction to his master's thesis *K voprosu o guṇe. Issledovanie v oblasti staroslavjanskogo vokalizma* 〈On the Question of Guṇa. A Study in the Area of Old Church Slavonic Vocalism〉, Separate offprint from *Russkij Filologičeskij Vestnik,* Warsaw, 1881 and also in the German version of this introduction *Über die Lautabwechslung,* Kazan', 1881.[1]

Kruszewski developed the "theory" of alternations more "philosophically," more comprehensively, and more precisely than I myself have done, thanks mainly to his strict application of the analytic method. It cannot be denied, however, that Kruszewski merely gave another, finer form to what he had learned from someone else. (This was admitted by Kruszewski himself; cf. *Über die Lautabwechslung,* p. 1.) One might take exception to certain shortcomings in Kruszewski's presentation of the theory of alternations. Despite his rigor and analytic method, Kruszewski left many things unnoticed; he did not define the boundaries between the individual classes of alternations precisely enough, and he set up alleged characteristic features of individual classes that could by no means be considered characteristic; on the other hand, he ignored other features which should have been mentioned as the most characteristic for a given class. Moreover, Kruszewski made occasional mistakes in logic. All of this, however, should not surprise us in view of the novelty and difficulty of the subject, and especially if we consider that Kruszewski based his general conclusions on facts drawn from the limited area of phonetic changes caused in Russian by palatalization or "softening" of consonants.

Kruszewski's terminology is not satisfactory and cannot be retained today. After all, both works of Kruszewski, his master's thesis and his brochure *Über die Lautabwechslung,* belong to a time when the Kazan' linguists became infatuated with nomenclature, developing a mania for inventing new and unusual techical terms; Kruszewski was wise enough to use some restraint in this respect in his works. This disease reached monstrous proportions in my own *Nekotorye otdely "sravnitel'noj grammatiki" slavjanskix jazykov,* the reading of which could only be hampered by such technical terms as *coherents, homogenes, heterogenes, monogenes, polygenes, amorphism* and *secondary heterogeneity of morphemes, amorphous correlatives, divergence and anthropophonic coherence, mobile correlation and morphological coincidence, coincident correlatives, coexistent correlatives,* etc.

However, despite this frightful number of newly coined techical terms, there is a sound kernel of useful observations in this work. Among one of its most original ideas (which was, however, nothing new for me personally, since I had been developing it for several years in my lectures) was the requirement to distinguish *native alternations* from *foreign (borrowed) alternations*. Of a certain methodological value are also: first, the distinction of the concepts *sound* and *phoneme*[2]; second, the unification of the concepts of root, affix, prefix, ending, and the like under the common term, morpheme; third, the distinction between a purely anthropophonic, physiological, and acoustic analysis of human speech and an analysis based on a morphological and semasiological viewpoint; fourth, the distinction between basic (primary) and derived (secondary) members of an alternation.

Another work of mine appeared almost simultaneously with this selection, "Otryvki iz lekcij po fonetike i morfologii russkogo jazyka, čitannyx v 1880–1881 akad. godu . . ." This work was mainly devoted to an analysis of the divergents in Russian.

The renowned Orientalist Dr. V. Radloff (at present a member of the Imperial Academy of Sciences in St. Petersburg) in his article devoted to the application of Kruszewski's principles to the Turkic languages "Die Lautalternation und ihre Bedeutung für Die Sprachentwicklung, belegt durch Beispiele aus Den Türksprachen," *Abhandlungen des fünften internationalen Orientalisten Congresses gehalten zu Berlin im September 1881,* Berlin, 1882, has replaced the term "phonetic interchange" by "phonetic alternation." The alternations of the first type he calls, as I do, *phonetic divergence, divergents;* alternations of the second type which in my present terminology are called "traditional alternations" he calls *phonetic compensations, compensatory sounds* (a not particularly apt expression), and finally he has restricted the term *correlation, correlative* to alternations of the third type, as I do, too. In R. Brandt's recently published book *Lekcii po istoričeskoj grammatike russkogo jazyka, čitannye Romanom Brandtom, Vypusk I, Fonetika* ⟨Lectures on Russian Historical Grammar by Roman Brandt, vol. 1, Phonetics⟩, Moscow, 1892, we also find a chapter entitled "Čeredovanie zvukov" ⟨Phonetic Alternation⟩. But Brandt evidently understands under this term something different from what I have always understood; for he is concerned not with the phenomenon of simultaneity, or coexistence, but with the explanation of phonetic changes which he divides into "changes" (*perexody*) and "substitution" (*podstanovki*) depending on whether they occur now or whether they occurred in the past. Professor Brandt is absolutely right when he reproaches me for the mass of newly coined technical terms in my *Nekotorye otdely sravnitel'noj fonetiki*. But the same reproach also applies to him, for he has probably invented more than a hundred completely new technical terms, which make the reading of his works infinitely more difficult, and which, in comparison with my own terms, have the sole advantage of having been coined from native Russian rather than from Latin. This is, however, a very dubious advantage, for a Latin technical term can be easily understood by scholars in Europe and America, irrespective of nationality, while an exclusively national term, coined under the influence of puristic tendencies, only increases the difficulty of mutual understanding. Our times, infected as they are by international animosities, cannot well afford them.

My attempt at presenting a theory of alternants will perhaps receive no recognition. It cannot, however, be denied that the concept of "alternation" and "alternants" is relevant to an enormous mass of linguistic facts, for there is probably no sound in any language which is completely isolated and does not alternate with another sound, just as there is no word to which the study of phonetic alternations cannot be applied.

Explanation and Definition of Certain Terms

The *phoneme* = a unitary concept belonging to the sphere of phonetics which exists in the mind thanks to a psychological fusion of the impressions resulting from the pronunciation of one and the same sound; it is the psychological equivalent of a speech sound. The unitary concept of the phoneme is connected (associated) with a certain sum of individual anthropophonic representations which are, on the one hand, articulatory, that is, performed or capable of being performed by physiological actions, and on the other hand, acoustic, that is the effects of these physiological actions, which are heard or capable of being heard.

Phonetics, as a whole, concerns all phonetic phenomena, both anthropophonic (whether these be of a physiological or auditory nature) and psychophonetic in which the former, sensory phenomena are reflected. Phonetics consists thus of two parts, of an *anthropophonic* and *psychophonetic one.*

The *morpheme* = that part of a word which is endowed with psychological autonomy and is for the very same reason not further divisible. It consequently subsumes such concepts as the *root* (*radix*), all possible *affixes*, (*suffixes*, *prefixes*), *endings* which are exponents of syntactic relationships, and the like.

Explanation of Symbols and Abbreviations

= . . . identity in the mathematical sense.

| . . . alongside, one occurring alongside the other.

|| . . . symbol of alternation or co-occurrence, of a unilingual correspondence, of etymological relationship in one language.

≠ . . . symbol of correspondence, of a multilingual correspondence, or of etymological relationship in different languages.

⇒ . . . symbol of transition, change; whatever stands on the left side of the symbol had changed into whatever stands on the right side.

⇐ . . . the reverse symbol, symbol of the origin of whatever stands on the left side of the symbol from whatever stands on the right.

≷ . . . symbol of the lack of any connection from either point of view.

. . . symbol of parallelism.

* . . . assumed, reconstructed form.

«+» . . . denied, impossible, or invented form.

CHAPTER I

DEFINITION OF ALTERNATION AND ALTERNANTS.
ESTABLISHING THE NOTION OF ALTERNATION
ETYMOLOGICALLY AND PHONETICALLY.
THE ORIGINAL CAUSE OF EVERY ALTERNATION.

In every language and in the speech of every individual we observe a partial phonetic difference between etymologically identical morphemes. In other words, in every language there are etymologically related morphemes which differ phonetically in some of their parts. For example, in the etymologically related morphemes *mog–* and *moż–* of the Polish words *mog–ę* | *moż–esz*, the first two phonemes *m* and *o* are identical, but the final phonemes *g* and *ž* are different. Such phonetically different phonemes, which are parts of etymologically related morphemes and which occupy the same position in the phonetic structure of the morphemes (in the cited example, the third position), we shall call *alternants,* and their relationship to each other, an *alternation.*

Similarly, there are two obvious alternations in the root morphemes of the Polish words *mróz* | *mroz–u* ⟨gen. sg.⟩: *u(ó)* ‖ *o* and *–s(–z)* ‖ *–z–*. A distinct alternation also occurs at the juncture between the root morpheme and the formal morphemes in the Polish words *płac–i–c* | *płac–ę*: *ći* ‖ *c*. In the base morphemes of the German words *lad–en* | *Las–t, Ver–lus–t* | *ver–lor–en, Fros–t* | *frier–en, geb–en* | *gab* . . . , we find the following clear alternations: 1) *d* ‖ *s, ā* ‖ *ă*; 2) *s* ‖ *r, ŭ* ‖ *ō*; 3) *s* ‖ *r, ŏ* ‖ *ī* (ie); 4) *g* ‖ *g₁, e* ‖ *a, –b* ‖ *–p* (b).

Strictly speaking, in all such cases we could consider the alternating units to be not phonemes, but morphemes, since only the latter form semantically indivisible linguistic units. Thus, from the point of view of the psychological reality of language, there is an alternation between entire morphemes and their combinations; e.g., Polish *mog–* ‖ *moż–, mrus* ‖ *mroz–, płać–i* | *płac–*; German *lād–* ‖ *lăs–, lŭs–* ‖ *lōr–, frŏs–* ‖ *frīr–, g₁eb–* ‖ *gap.* The phonetic difference between related morphemes we shall call a *phonetic alternation.* (This alternation is connected with a semantic alternation between the morphemes and entire words.) The phonetic alternation of entire morphemes, however, can be reduced to alternations of their phonemes, or the phonetic components of the morphemes.

In terms, then, of phonemes, we shall call *phonetic alternants* or *alternating phonemes* such sounds or phonemes which differ from each other phonetically, but are related historically or etymologically. *Phonetic alternants,* or *alternating phonemes* are, in other words, sounds or phonemes which, though pronounced differently, can be traced back to a common historical source, i.e., originated from the same phoneme.

Establishing the Notion of Phonetic Alternation and Phonetic Alternants by Etymology.

The semantically basic morphemes of the Slavic words, Pol. *prosi–ę* | Cz. *pras–e* | Rus. *pəras'–ónək* (*porosënok*) | Ukr. *poros'–á* (*porosja*) | SCr. *prās–àc* | Slov. (Krajna) *pras–c* are etymologically related, since they can be traced back to a common historical source, *pors–*. But this common historical source *pors–* can, in turn, be compared with etymologically related morphemes of other Indo-European languages: Slavic *pors–* | Lith. *parš–as* | Lat. *porc–us* | Germ. *fahr–*. Likewise, Slavic *vez–* {Pol. *wiezi–e* | Cz. *vez–e* | Rus. *v'ez'–ót (vez–ët)* | Ukr. *vez–é (vez–e)* | SCr. *vèz–e* ...} ≠ Lith. *vež–* ≠ Germ. *vig–* ≠ Lat. *veh–* ≠ Gk. *ϝεχ–* ≠ Skt. *vah–* and others.

Any such comparison of words and morphemes of different languages rests on the assumption that the morphemes in question are etymologically related. The etymological relationship is established on the basis of semasiological similarity, on the one hand, and partial phonetic similarity of the morphemes, on the other hand.

The phonetic similarity must be neither accidental nor arbitrary, but must recur in a series of morphemes comprising at least partially the same phonemes. Thus, for example, we posit the etymological relationship of the basic morphemes of the above-quoted Slavic words *prosi–ę* | *pras–e* | *poros'–a* ... first, on the grounds of their semasiological similarity (they all mean "pig," "boar," "swine"), and second, on the grounds of the occurrence of identical phonetic correspondences in a whole series of words (*p*; *s* with different reflexes; *ro* ≠ *ra* ≠ *oro*...). The etymological relationship of morphemes belonging to various Indo-European languages (e.g., *pors–* ≠ *parš–* ≠ *pork–* ≠ *farh–* ...; *vez–* ≠ *vež–* ≠ *vig–* ≠ *veh–* ≠ *ϝεχ–* ≠ *vah–*) is likewise founded on the semantic similarity of the morphemes and the occurrence of regular phonetic correspondences in a series of words (*p* ≠ *p* ≠ *p* ≠ *f* ..., *or* ≠ *ar* ≠ *or* ≠ *ar* ... *s* ≠ *š* ≠ *k* ≠ *h* ...; *v* ≠ *v* ≠ *v* ≠ *v* (*ϝ*) ..., *e* ≠ *e* ≠ *i* ≠ *e* ≠ *e* (*ε*) ≠ *a* ..., *z* ≠ *ž* ≠ *g* ≠ *h* ≠ *χ* ≠ *h* ...).

It is on the basis of similar comparisons that we say: Polish *ro* corresponds to Czech and South Slavic *ra* and to Russian *oro*; these diverse Slavic sequences can be derived from a proto-Slavic sequence *or*; all these Slavic sequences, as well as the assumed proto-Slavic sequence *or*, have correspondences in other Indo-European languages, i.e., *ar* in Baltic (Lithuanian and Latvian) and Germanic, *or* in Latin; Slavic *s* corresponds to Lithuanian *š*, German *h*, Latin *k*, etc.

It would be a mistake however, to regard the historical-phonetic inference as being unimpeachable. What is etymologically related in the different languages are not independent phonemes, but the morphemes in which they occur, i.e., those simplest, indivisible semasiological parts of a word which have an autonomous psychological existence. Consequently, when we speak of the affinity of Slavic *z* with Lith. *ž,* Germ. *g,* Lat. *h,* Gk. χ, Skt. *h,* we do not mean the aboslute relationship of these phonemes, regardless of the morphemes in which they occur, but the relative relationship of these phonemes in particular morphemes (*vez–, liz–ać, zim–a*). The phoneme *z* is related to certain phonemes of other Indo-European languages in words such as *ząb, zn–ać, ziarno.* . . . Similarly, Slavic *s* corresponds to Lith. *š* $+$ Germ. *h* $+$ Lat. and Gk. *k* $+$ Skt. *ç* in the word **pors–ę (prosi–ę),* etc., but not in such words as **sedmĭ, sebe, sÿn–, bos–,* etc.

Thus, all etymological comparisons of words belonging to different languages are based on the recognition of an etymological relationship between the morphemes comprised in these words. But the etymological relationship of the morphemes can be treated as an etymological relationship of the particular phonemes and their combinations.

Etymological relationship based on the comparison of various languages, we shall call *correspondence,* or *interlingual correspondence.* But in addition to this type of relationship, there is also the etymological relationship of morphemes belonging to one and the same language. Since we recognize the etymological relationship of different, though similar morphemes, belonging to various languages, e.g. {*pros– | pras– | poros– | *pors–*} | *parš– | pork– | farh–,* we should with even more reason admit the etymological relationship of morphemes belonging to the same language; e.g., *mog– | mož–, rod– | rut, mroz– | mrus, plot– | pleś–,* etc. The second, or intralingual type of etymological relationship, we shall call *alternation,* and the alternation concerning specifically the phonetic elements of the morphemes, *phonetic alternation.*

In the case of alternation, or intralingual etymological relationship, we are dealing with speakers belonging to the same speech community, while in the case of correspondence of interlingual etymological relationship, the speakers, or more specifically the carriers of elements forming a relationship of correspondence, belong to multiple and ethnically diverse speech communities.

As in the case of correspondence, we can treat the alternation of morphemes, in their identity and difference, as an alternation of their constituent phonemes (*mog–* $\parallel$ *moż–* can be broken down into the phonemes *m* $\parallel$ *m, o* $\parallel$ *o, g* $\parallel$ *ż*; and *mroz–* $\parallel$ *mrus–* into *mr* $\parallel$ *mr, o* $\parallel$ *u, z* $\parallel$ *s*. . .). The existence of corresponding and alternating morphemes is due to the fact that the respective morphemes were in either case historically the same.

What has been said with respect to correspondence—namely, that it concerns morphemes, and not individual phonemes, and that the latter form a relation of correspondence only insofar as they are a part of certain groups or types of morphemes (i.e., not every Slavic *o* corresponds to the Latin *o*, but only the *o* of some morphemes)— holds likewise with respect to alternation. Thus, for example, not every Polish *ż* alternates with *g*, but only the *ż* which occurs in morphemes that alternate with morphemes containing *g*. But while the correspondence of phonemes implies a correspondence of morphemes, there are also purely phonetic alternations (variations, ramifications) of phonemes that are not bound to one or another morpheme. These variations I have called *general phonetic divergents*. Thus, for example, the Polish i_2 (y) $\parallel$ i_1 (i) in the phonetic sequences *py, by, my, ty, dy* . . . , *cy, dzy, sy, ry* . . . , *czy, dży, szy, ży* . . . , *p'i, b'i, m'i* . . . , *ći, dżi, śi, żi* . . . , *k'i, g'i, ch'i* . . . , *ji*, do not depend on the semantic value of these sequences. The same holds true of Polish e_2 $\parallel$ e_1 (*pe, be* . . . $\mid$ *p'e, b'e* . . .), *s* $\parallel$ *ś* (*st, sp* . . . $\mid$ *ść, śp'* . . .), *ę* $\parallel$ *en* $\parallel$ *em* $\parallel$ *eṅ* $\parallel$ *eń* (*ęs, ęz, ęš, ęž, ęch* $\mid$ *ęt, ęd, ęc, ędz* $\mid$ *ęp, ęb* $\mid$ *ęk, ęg* $\mid$ *ęć, ędż* . . .).).

Establishing the Notion of Alternation Phonetically

In almost all works and studies dedicated to phonetic questions we find pronouncements concerning the "transition" of some sounds into others, the "transformation" (or "change") of some sounds into others, and so forth. Thus, for example, Polish grammars speak of the change of *k* into *cz* in the words *piecz–e, rącz–ka* . . . ⟨dim.⟩, from *piek–ę, ręk–a,* and of *ę* into *ą* in the words *mąż, dąb* . . . from *męż–a, dębu* . . . ⟨gen.⟩. . . .

Such a formulation of the relationships in question is misleading. Whoever uses it is confusing an arbitrary, subjective ⟨linguistic⟩ experiment with the objectively given historical processes.

In an arbitrary experiment, we can pass from one sound to another by substituting, according to need, the various movements of the speech organs. Thus one can easily pass from *b* to *m* if one merely keeps open the nasal cavity by lowering the soft palate without changing the position of the other speech organs. In the same way, one can pass from a "hard" ⟨nonpalatalized⟩ p to a "soft" ⟨palatalized⟩ p', from o to u, from e to o, etc. In this manner, by changing only one property at a time, one can move from p to a through almost the entire scale of the speech sounds: $p - p' - b' - b - m - n - d - z - \check{z} - \check{s} - s - x$ (ch) $- k - g - g' - \gamma'$ (h') $- [-\jmath] - i - e - o - u - y - a$.

But what do we actually do in such an experiment? We gradually alter the groups of phonetic representations and perform the corresponding physiological processes. But we need not confine ourselves to such a gradual change; after pronouncing p we can directly imagine the representation of a and implement it phonetically. And then we are indeed entitled to say: "p has changed into a."

But what does actually happen? One group of phonetic representations is substituted by another, and their successive implementation gives us a certain right to say: "p passes into a," "x passes into y." In reality, though, the various associations of representations follow each other, like slides in a kaleidoscope, only in the head of the experimenter. The successive production of sounds corresponding to these associations is only coincidental and certainly not obligatory. Thus even at this stage there is no change from one pronunciation to another, but only replacement of one mental image by another.

In the objective historical development of a language such sound changes are purely fictitious, to say nothing of the types of "transition" such as k into cz, g into $\dot{z}$ or ϱ into ϱ. *There are neither pronetic changes nor phonetic laws, and there can never be such,* if only for the simple reason that human language in general, and the sounds of a language in particular, are not endowed with continuous duration. A word, or a sentence, once uttered, disappears at the moment of its utterance. There is no physical connection between utterances. What links the separate speech acts—be they sounds, phonetic words, or utterances (that are heard and perceived by the ear)—are representations, or *images of the memory,* which during the utterance itself serve as a stimulus to set the speech organs into appropriate motion.

⟨The production of sounds⟩ allows for two possibilities: the physiological conditions determining the activity of the speech organs may allow the full realization of the processes intended by the

brain center, or they may inhibit them. In the first case, the phonetic intention coincides with its realization (for example, *za, ra,
ar, ła* . . . Pol. *mech, jabłek* ⟨gen. pl.⟩ . . . ; *rodu, mrozu, męża* ⟨gen.
sg.⟩; *woda* ⟨nom. sg.⟩ . . .); while the second case produces a discrepancy (e.g., Pol. *zła*—monosyllabic and with a voiced *z, rtęć*—
with an ordinary voiced *r, atr, łka, mchu, piekł, jabłko* . . . , *rud
(ród)*—with *–d, mruz (mróz)* with *–z, mąż* with *ž, wud-ka (wódka)*
with *–d–*). In the second case, our phonetic habits and the universal conditions determining the production of phonetic sequences,
compel us to modify the pronunciation of the intended sequences;
e.g., *sta* (with *s* instead of *z*), *ŗtęć, atŗ* (with voiceless and weakened
r), *ļka, m̦chu, piekļ, japļko* . . . , *ruţ* (with a weakened *t*), *mrus,
mąș̌, wut-ka.* . . .

But even in forms such as *cnót* or *matka*, the phonetic environment prevents us from pronouncing the *t* as clearly and independently as in *cnota* and *matek*, . . . and compels us to substitute for
it a *t* which is weakened and dependent on the following sound.

An intended *"pieke"* instead of *piecze* or *"rąkek, rąkka"* instead of *rączek, rączka* could, on the other hand, be pronounced
without the slightest difficulty and without necessitating a "change"
of *k* into *cz*.

The discrepancy between the phonetic intention and its realization is solved by substituting an intended impossible activity by a
possible one.

The substitution can be of two kinds: (1) if the intention, which
is founded on related words and forms, cannot be realized, the intended phoneme is replaced by one which is closest to it phonetically (examples above); or (2) the actual pronunciation is imitative
of foreign sounds in the speech of others which we intend to reproduce. The latter type of substitution is known to occur (a) in the
speech of children and, more generally, within the limits of the
native language; and (b) in the rendering of foreign words whose
pronunciation is modified in accordance with our own phonetic
habits (for example, when French *sur* is pronounced in Polish *śur*
[*siur*]).

Phonetic change or "transition" results in all these cases from
the discrepancy between the intention and its realization.

Only the first type of substitution applies to the alternations
and alternants.

The substitution of an intended pronunciation by a possible one constitutes the only type of phonetic change or "transformation" that may occur in the synchronic state of a given language. What is ordinarily called phonetic "change" or "transformation" of one sound into another is, from an objective point of view, only co-existence, or alternation.

Such *coexistence*, or *alternation, is neither phonetic change in the present nor succession in the historical sequence. It is simply the phonetic difference between etymologically related morphemes.* However, its cause is still considered something of a puzzle.

If it is claimed that the *č(cz)* in such contemporary words as *pieczę, rączka,* etc., is derived from *k,* then one could with equal right insist that on the contrary, the *k* of *piekę, ręka* is derived from *č.* Notice the complicated alternation:

$$c \;\|\; \begin{array}{l} k\;(g) \\ ć \end{array}$$

| *ciec, siec, móc, strzec* | *ciek–ę, siek–ę, mog–ę, strzeg–ę,* |
| | *by–ć, da–ć . . . ;* |

It would be a sign of poor thinking, and a historical error, to claim that the *c* in *ciec, móc* . . . is based on *kć* (or *gć*).

In short, *phonetic change, as it is ordinarily understood, is a fiction, a delusion.* There can be only:

1) *substitution of intended activities by possible ones, ⟨stemming from⟩ the lack of coincidence or discrepancy between the phonetic realizations and intentions,* and

2) synchronic phonetic differences, i.e., *alternations of a historical origin of morphemes and of their phonetic components, the phonemes.*

The two types of phenomena are closely interconnected. Active, dynamic substitutions give rise to embryonic, incipient phonetic alternations; while the alternations which from a contemporary point of view seem to have no cause, can be traced back to substitutions which took place in the past.

Causes of Alternations

If the history of a given language is viewed as something continuous and uninterrupted, it appears that the cause or stimulus (impulse) of a given alternation is a purely phonetic or anthropophonic one. But in the case of mixed languages, the situation must be defined more precisely: the primary stimulus of an alternation is probably always of an anthropophonic nature, but it may have its roots (1) in the native language, as is most frequently the case, or (2) in a foreign language from which the given speech community has borrowed the entire alternation or one of its elements.

The original cause of the alternation may still be active in the present, synchronic state of the language or it may have been active in the past. In the latter case it can be discovered by way of hypotheses and historical inferences.

C H A P T E R   I I

CLASSIFICATION OF ALTERNATIONS AND ALTERNANTS.

I. Classification of Alternations according to their Causes

The complexity of causes accounting for the emergence and preservation of alternations must ultimately be ascribed to communal life and the physical (anatomico-physiological) and psychological make-up of the members of a speech community.

1. *Classification of alternations according to the possibility of determining the anthropophonic causes operating in the synchronic state of a language.*

All alternations are either due to living anthropophonic tendencies and to fixed and constantly repeated anthropophonic habits, or they are not due to them. Hence we may divide them into two large classes:

1) *neophonetic alternations,* and

2) non-neophonetic, *paleophonetic* alternations.

Alternants of the first class we shall call *divergents,* and their relationship *divergence*; alternants of the second class we shall call *nondivergents,* and their relationship, *nondivergence.*

2. *Classification of alternations according to the possibility of establishing their psychological causes.*

All alternations are either associated with representations of certain psychological differences (nuances) of a semasiological (significative) or morphological (structural) nature, or they are not associated with them. On this distinction we base the division into:

1) *psychophonetic alternants,* or *correlatives,* and

2) *non-psychophonetic alternants,* or *non-correlatives.*

The relation of correlatives forms a *correlation,* while the relation of noncorrelatives forms a *noncorrelation.*

3. *Classification of alternations according to traditional and, more generally, social causes.*

All alternations are either the result of repetition and imitation (including transmission from one generation to another) or they are independent of this factor.

All genuine paleophonetic alternations are preserved through tradition and are, consequently, due to social conditions.

Divergences, or neophonetic alternations, arise and are maintained independently of tradition, although there are some divergences whose anthropophonic connection with their causal factors is supported by tradition and linguistic intercourse.

Finally, the correlations or psychophonetic alternations are due, above all, to tradition and linguistic intercourse; but when they become associated with psychological distinctions, the influence of the social factor upon the speaker ceases.

4. *Classification of alternations according to internal (autoglottic) or external factors.*

All alternations arise *either* in the uninterrupted historical evolution of a given language, *or* they are borrowed from other, closely related languages. In other words, the present or past causes of some alternants *either* lie within the given speech community *or* result from linguistic contact of this community with other communities or literatures.

Divergences are always of internal origin, for their difference is the result of the varying pronunciation of the members belonging to the same speech community. On the other hand, traditional or even psychophonetic alternations (correlations) may have their origin in foreign sources (Polish *h* ‖ *z* in *błahy* ∣ *błazen* of Czech origin; or the Russian *er* ‖ *ra* in *smerdet'* ∣ *smrad* of Church Slavonic origin).

From a synchronic point of view all alternations are internal and peculiar to the given language. They are foreign only from the viewpoint of their provenience.

Alternations stemming from a foreign source are: (a) either totally foreign or (b) partially foreign (e.g., Polish *g* ‖ *h* in *gardzić* ∣ *hardy, ganić* ∣ *hańba*; Russian *olo* ∣ *la* in *golová* ∣ *glavá*).

In terms of their origin, the alternations of the first type could be called *foreign monolingual,* and those of the second type, *foreign-native bilingual.*

5. *Classification of alternations according to the difference between individual and social causes.*

Divergences and correlations are essentially due to individual or, at best, collective-individual causes, whereas traditional paleophonetic alternations are due exclusively to social causes.

The individual or collective-individual causes of divergences are anthropophonic.

The individual or collective-individual causes of correlations are psychological.

Inasmuch as we attribute the traditional alternations of one language to social causes, we have even more reason to attribute foreign alternations to such causes; the social factor here embraces not one, but two speech communities.

6. *Classification of alternations according to the simplicity or complexity of their causes.*

a) All alternations have either one or two causes.

One cause is involved in

divergences which are not supported by tradition, and in

traditional alternations which are neither divergences nor correlations.

Two causes may be involved in

divergences which depend not only on anthropophonic conditions but also on linguistic intercourse, i.e., divergences which are transitional between divergences in the strict sense and traditional alternations; and in

traditional alternations which are at the same time correlations, or psychophonetic alternations.

The combination of divergent, or neophonetic, with correlational, or psychophonetic causes, is impossible.

Change of causality comes about in the historical succession:

when divergences become traditional alternations;

when alternations of foreign origin become traditional alternations;

when traditional alternations become correlations, or psychophonetic alternations;

when correlations become traditional alternations.

b) The causality of certain alternations is either simple or complex.

One cause accounts for

pure *divergences,* or purely neophonetic alternations, which are not affected by tradition and linguistic intercourse in general, and purely *traditional alternations.*

Two causes account for *correlations* which depend, on the one hand, on tradition and, on the other, on individually formed psychophonetic relationships.

II. Classification of Alternations according to the Conflict of Different Tendencies

1. *The conflict of tradition with individual needs and tendencies.*
Such a conflict pertains to traditional alternations which are not at the same time correlations. Because of their very nature, correlations exclude the conflict between individual tendencies and tradition.

Such a conflict arises when divergences are about to emerge; the final establishment of a divergence marks the unconsciously won victory of individual peripheral tendencies over tradition and linguistic intercourse in general.

However, there are divergences in which the individual tendencies not only do not contradict, but are supported by tradition (e.g., *s* || *ś* in Polish *kostka* | *kość*). Such a state is transitional between divergence in the strict sense and a traditional alternation which, in time, produces the above-mentioned conflict.

In the case of traditional alternations, tradition supports the complexity of phenomena and taxes the memory, while the individual tendencies strive to reduce this complexity and to relieve the memory.

Conversely, in the case of emerging divergents, tradition lends simplicity and unity, while the individual tendencies introduce previously nonexistent distinctions.

Finally, in the case of correlatives, there is agreement and harmony between tradition and individual tendencies.

2. *A conflict between individual anthropophonic or peripheral-phonetic tendencies with individual central-psychological tendencies* must necessarily appear in divergents which differ because the phonetic intention of one of them could not be realized. In the case of other alternations there can be no such conflict.

III. Classification of Alternations according to their Genesis, or Distance from their Causes

Strictly speaking, we consider here not only clear and distinct alternations, but also incipient (embryonic) and residual alternations. Accordingly, we shall distinguish (a) embryonic, (b) live, and (c) petrified alternations.

1. *Classification of alternations according to their distance from the source of anthropophonic causality.*

Here we shall distinguish the following stages:

a) embryonic alternations, due to individual tendencies;

b) alternations that develop both individually and socially;

c) developed alternations;

d) established alternations;

e) transitional alternations that are gradually receding and are felt to be obsolescent;

f) petrified, residual alternations.

Stages (c) and (d) are preserved mainly through tradition and social intercourse in general; stages (e) and (f) persist as a result of the conflict between individual and social tendencies, in which the former gain the upper hand.

Stages (a) and (b) represent divergences, or neophonetic alternations; (c), (d) and (e) represent traditional or psychophonetic alternations; a variety of stage (d) forms correlations, or psychophonetic alternations; stage (f) represents an alternation only in retrospect, for by itself ⟨from a synchronic point of view⟩ it lacks the kind of phonetic difference which is required to view it as an alternation proper.

2. *Classification of alternations according to their distance from the source of psychological causality.*

Here we shall distinguish the following stages:

a) incipient alternations; paleophonetic alternations which are beginning to be utilized for psychological distinctions; alternations whose psychophonetic associations are rudimentary. Each member of a speech community must accomplish for himself this process of associating concepts;

b) established, i.e., clear and distinct alternations;

c) disappearing alternations;

d) obsolete alternations.

The last three stages, (b), (c), and (d), are due to both individual tendencies and social factors.

3. *Classification of alternations according to the distance from a source originating in a related language.*

Here we shall distinguish the following stages:

a) borrowing of foreign alternations by single individuals of a given speech community;

b) individual as well as collective adaptation of foreign alternations and their estrangement from the original source;

c) ultimate establishment of the foreign alternations (in the borrowing language) and their preservation through tradition and social intercourse in general.

Established alternations of this category as subsequently subject to the same changes or loss as the other types of alternations (III.1 and III.2).

With regard to the last type of alternations (III.1–3), one must mention the role of *turning points* in the history of a language which affect alternations no less than other phenomena of language. Such a change takes place most conspicuously when the phonetic representations and peripheral activities (i.e., activities involving the speech organs) and their corresponding acoustic results form new combinations which differ ⟨. . .⟩ from previous ones. ⟨. . .⟩

IV. Classification of Phonetic Alternants and Alternations according to their Etymological Relationship

The phonemes which constitute alternating pairs must always be etymologically related, that is, they must originate from a single proto-phoneme; but this relationship can be of a dual nature:

a) either the phonemes alternate in etymologically related, and hence alternating, morphemes (e.g., $g \parallel \check{z}$ in Pol. *mog–* | *moż–*, etc.);

b) or the phonemes alternate as components of whole groups of morphemes having a similar phonetic structure (e.g., Pol. $i(y) \parallel e$ in the verbs *wy–cin–a, wy–żyn–a, na–gin–a* | *roz–bier–a, wy–cier–a, po–żer–a* . . . ; $e \parallel o$ in *piek–ę, ciek–ę, strzeg–ę, grzeb–ę* | *bior–ę, wiod–ę, nios–ę, płot–ę* . . . ; Lat. $i \parallel e$ in *col–lig–o, con–tin–et, ab–ig–it, af–fic–it* . . . | *con–fer–o, at–ter–it, im–per–at* . . . ; Goth. $i \parallel e(r)$ . . .).

As to the degree of etymological relationship between the alternating phonemes, the two types of alternations differ only quan-

titatively, not qualitatively. The morphological relationship between the morphemes, i.e., their relationship as members of certain
morphological categories, is simply a result of generalization. This
generalization is based not only on the comparison of a whole
series of morphologically related morphemes, but also on their
etymological relationship. Thus the comparison of the Polish forms

1.

	ciek–	*ciecz–*
	strzeg–	*strzeż–*
	grzeb–	*grzeb'–*

2.

	bior–	*bierz–*
	wiod–	*wiedź–*
	nios–	*nieś–*
	płot–	*płeć–*

3.

ciek–	*ciecz–*	*tok–*	*tocz–*
strzeg–	*strzeż–*	*strog–*	*stroż–*
grzeb–	*grzeb'–*	*grob–*	*grob'–*

4.

bior–	*bierz–*	*bor–*	*borz–*
wiod–	*wiedź–*	*wod–*	*wodź–*
nios–	*nieś*	*nos–*	*noś–*
płot–	*płeć–*	*płot–*	*płoć–*

leads us to establish an alternation which can be regarded as an
abstraction of all of these cases, namely to the alternation *o* ǁ *e* in

piek–	*bior–*
ciek–	*wiod–*
strzeg–	*nioś–*
grzeb–	*płot–*.

The comparison of morphemes according to their morphological, formal relationship, and the discovery of phonemic alternations
of such types as *e* ǁ *o* in *piek–* ... *bior–* ... , has proved to be extremely fruitful in the recent historical studies of Indo-European
phonology which were so auspiciously launched by Brugmann and
de Saussure.

The distinction between two types of alternation according to the
degree of relationship between the alternating phonemes is closely
related to the question of the different directions of the morphological assimilation of morphemes, i.e., to the directions of leveling trig-

gered by psychological factors. Two directions are most important:

a) assimilation according to etymological relationship, and

b) assimilation according to morphological or structural relationship.

V. Classification of Phonetic Alternations according to the Simplicity or Complexity of their Relationship

1. *The distinction between equivalent and nonequivalent phonemes.*

If one phoneme corresponds etymologically to another phoneme, or if two phonemes correspond to two other phonemes, their relationship is simple. But if one phoneme corresponds to two or more phonemes, then the alternation is one of nonequivalent phonemes. This type of alternation also includes the alternation of a specific phoneme with a zero-phoneme, i.e., the absence of a phoneme.

There are, furthermore, cases in which a particular phoneme alternates not with another phoneme, or with two or more phonemes, but with a part of another phoneme, or with a phoneme plus a part of a neighboring phoneme.⟨. . .⟩

2. *Classification of alternations according to the number of their constitutive members.*

Ordinarily there are only two alternants in an alternation, as in the relationship of a unified causality. However, there are also some (though quite rare) cases when an alternation arising from a single cause, a single anthropophonic tendency, includes three or even four phonemes in the various degrees in which it is manifested. An example is the Russian divergence of vowels depending on the accent ($ó \parallel \breve{a} \parallel \breve{y}(ə)$ in *gód–, gód–a | gắd–á | gy̆dắvój pól–gy̆d–a*. . .).

3. *Classification of alternations according to the simplicity or complexity of the morphemes containing the alternating phonemes.*

A series of contiguous morphemes is opposed to a single morpheme. In such a case we either deal with simple morphemes, or we must compare the phonemes of two contiguous morphemes.

Examples of the first type have been cited above; as an example of the second type we can adduce the Polish alternation $ći \parallel c,$ $dźi \parallel dz$ in *płac–i | płac–ę, rodz–i | rodz–ę.*

4. *Classification of alternations according to the distinction between morphemes belonging to a single word and the etymological relationship of morphemes belonging to different words.*

All the above-mentioned alternations occur in morphemes belonging to a single word. But if we were to look for a phoneme or a combination of phonemes which alternates, for example, with the final *c* of Polish *ciec,* we would find that it consists of two morphemes which can never be combined: 1) *ciek–,* and 2) *–ć* in the infinitive:

$$ciec \;\left|\right|\; \begin{matrix} ciek- \\[4pt] \qquad -\acute{c} \end{matrix}$$

The pertinent alternation is:

$$c \;\left|\right|\; \begin{matrix} k- \\[8pt] -\acute{c}. \end{matrix}$$

Thus, we shall distinguish two types of alternations and alternants:

a) simple ones, which involve sets of phonemes belonging to a single word (e.g., Polish $\{d\acute{z}i \parallel dz\} \Leftarrow \{di \parallel d\underset{\cdot}{i}\}$), and

b) complex ones, in which at least on one side, the phonemes belong to two different words ⟨sic!⟩:

$$\left(c \;\left|\right|\; \begin{matrix} k- \\ -\acute{c} \end{matrix} \quad \text{in } ciec \;\left|\right|\; \begin{matrix} ciek- \\ -\acute{c} \end{matrix} \quad \text{etc.} \right).$$

5. *Comparison of simple alternations and simple alternating pairs with alternations of alternations, or of alternating relations.*

Simple alternations require no further elucidation here. As an example of an alternation of alternations, we can adduce the Polish:

$$\{t \parallel \acute{c}\} \parallel \{k \parallel \check{c}\}$$

$$\{plot-\varrho \mid pleci-e\} \parallel \{piek-\varrho \mid piecz-e\}$$

$$\{e \parallel e\} \parallel \{o \parallel e\}$$

$$\{piek-\varrho \mid piecz-e\} \;\left|\right|\; \left\{ \begin{matrix} nios-\varrho \mid niesi-e \\ plot-\varrho \mid pleci-e \end{matrix} \right\}$$

$$\left\{ c \;\left|\right|\; \begin{matrix} k \\ \acute{c} \end{matrix} \right\} \left\{ \acute{c} \parallel \acute{c} \right\}$$

$$\left\{ ciec \;\left|\right|\; \begin{matrix} ciek- \\ -\acute{c} \end{matrix} \right\} \left\{ by-\acute{c} \;\left|\right|\; \begin{matrix} by- \\ -\acute{c} \end{matrix} \right\}.$$

Alternations of alternations, or of alternating relations, are based on a purely formal or structural relationship of morphemes.

One could actually set up many more criteria for the classification of alternations. But I shall limit myself for the time being to those discussed in this chapter and shall proceed to a more detailed analysis of some alternating types.

CHAPTER III

ALTERNATIONS CLASSIFIED ACCORDING TO
    ANTHROPOPHONIC CAUSALITY.
THE ANALYSIS OF DIFFERENT TYPES AND
    THEIR CHARACTERISTIC FEATURES.
DIVERGENCES.

As is apparent from the forgoing remarks, every language has gone through the process of splitting originally homogeneous phonemes for purely anthropophonic reasons, regardless of their occurrence in one or another kind of morphemes or morphemic categories. For example, the original phoneme k in Polish has split into k, k', $\check{c}$ (cz) and c. A special, psychologically conditioned case of phonetic splitting is the split of phonemes in etymologically related morphemes; for example, of k into k, $\check{c}$ and c in the morphemes *wilk–*, *wilč–*, *wilc–* (*wilk, wilczysko, wilcy*).

In both cases we find a split of what constitutes, or at one time constituted, a psychological unity. But a phoneme considered apart from meaning-carrying morphemes forms a unity only as a phonetic representation, as an image imbedded in memory, while the phoneme as a component of a morpheme owes its psychological unity to the etymological connection of morphemes.

We must keep in mind another important fact: the conclusion that phonemes which are now distinct, without any apparent reason for their distinction, must have formed at one time a single phoneme is suggested only by etymology, i.e., by etymological comparisons within one language (alternations), or between two or more languages (correspondences). Where we cannot prove the existence of alternations or correspondences, we have no right to assume that one phoneme is derived from another.

One could speak of the splitting of a particular phoneme into several phonemes independently of the etymological connection of the morphemes containing them only if the causal factors are still at work, if they are still fully alive, if one can pin them down, so to speak, *in flagranti*.

Neophonetic factors operate independently of etymological relations. Phonemes or sounds of the same intention but different realization can thus be compared without regard to their etymological connections.

Compare, for example, the split of the Polish "nasal vowels" according to the environment into $ę, ą \mid ęn$ (*en*), $ąn$ (*on*) $\mid ęm$ (*em*), $ąm$ (*om*) $\mid ęn$ (*eń*), $ąń$ (*oń*) $\mid ęń$ (*eń*), $ąń$ (*oń*) $\mid e, o$ or the Sanskrit anuṣyāra.

The Russian vowels *a, e,* and *o,* particularly *a* and *e,* exhibit different variants according to the following consonant (*mat, mel, zakon . . . | mat', mel', kon'. . .*).

In literary German *s* varies its pronunciation according to its environment.

This kind of contemporary, live split of a psychologically homogeneous phoneme into two or more phonemes we shall call *divergence*. Divergence is of a *purely anthropophonic phonetic nature*; it is a divergence of the phoneme itself, regardless of its membership in related morphemes.

But when the differentiation is determined by the etymologically (psycho-historically) related morphemes, the result is a *phonetic-etymological divergence or a neophonetic alternation,* i.e., a rudimentary alternation of morphemes and their constituent phonemes. Examples:

Pol. $s \parallel ś$ [*kostka* | *kość, cząstka* | *część, piosnka* | *pieśń*];
Pol. $ń \parallel \dot{n}$ (voiceless *ń*), $ł \parallel \dot{l}$ (vl. *ł*), $r \parallel \dot{r}$ (vl. *r*) [*pieśni* | *pieśń jabłek, jabłko, wiatru* | *wiatr . . .*];
Pol. $i_2(y) \parallel i_1(i)$ [*głowy, cnoty . . .* | *postaci, soli . . .*];
Pol. $-t- \parallel -\dot{t}$ (weakened *t*) [*cnota* | *cnót*]; . . .
Pol. $ęn$ (*en*) $\parallel ęń$ (*eń*) [*będę* | *będzie . . .*];
Rus. $o \parallel o_1, a \parallel a_1, e \parallel e_1$ [*vóza* | *vozít', bába* | *bábe, ètot* | *èti . . .*];
Rus. $i_2(y) \parallel i_1(i)$ [*balý darý . . .* | *korolí, carí . . .*];
Rus. $ó \parallel ă \parallel \ў$ [*gód, góda* | *godá* | *godovój pólgoda . . .*];

Germ. –*b*– || –*p* [*Grabe, Stabe* . . . | *Grab, Stab* . . .];
Germ. x_a(*ch*) || x_i(*ch*) [*brach* | *bricht, Loch* | *Löcher*. . .].

In both the purely anthropophonic and alternating divergences there occurs either:

a) substitution, necessary adaptation to the conditions of pronunciation, or

b) in addition to adaptation, unconscious recollection of individual anthropophonic modifications of the psychologically homogeneous phoneme.

In the first case (a) there is a discrepancy between the intention and its anthropophonic realization: we *desire* to pronounce a given phoneme with all its properties, but we are *able* to pronounce only the modification of this phoneme, substituting possible characteristics for intended ones.

The proof of this lies, first, in the orthography, and second, in the frequent discussions concerning the actual quality of a sound perceived in a particular case. The perception of educated people is often influenced by orthography.

For example, the expression "⟨German⟩ *z* is pronounced like *s*" is in some sense justified: the *z* represents the imagined psychological unit, but the *s* represents its implementation on the linguistic periphery.

An example of the second case (b) is the Polish *ś* in *kość, gość, pieśń, pieśni* . . . , *s in śpi* (also pronounced *spi*), in which adaptation and substitution are supported by the unconscious recollection of individual characteristics.

The unconscious recollections of individual characteristics occurring in etymologically related morphemes represent a transitional stage between divergents and traditional alternants.

The anthropophonic splitting of psychologically homogeneous phonemes, which accompanies purely anthropophonic or alternational divergents, is caused by:

a) the development of different properties in one member of an alternating pair or, rather, through the substitution of some properties in place of others [–*ț*– || –*d*– in *rad* | *rada,* –*s* || –*z*– in *mróz* | *mrozu, r̦* || *r* in *wiatr̦* | *wiatru, m* || *m* in *mchu* | *mech* . . .], or

b) the weakening of the autonomy of one member of the alternating pair.

Here we must distinguish between conditions which favor the manifestation of the properties of a given phoneme and those which prevent it. Thus, for example, the position of *t* in *ta, sta* is favorable for the manifestation of the properties ⟨of *t*⟩, while in a*t* it is unfavorable. The same holds true of *r* in *ra, rydz, ar* as opposed to *rda, rdza* . . . , of *l* in *ligać* as opposed to *lgnąć,* and of *m, m̀* in *my, migać* as opposed to *mgła, mgnie.* . . .

The cause of any particular divergence is either universal or ethnic, i.e., spatially and temporally conditioned. In other words, the combinatorial-anthropophonic changes, which provide an impulse for the splitting of a phoneme, come about either

1) as a result of continuous, one might say, eternally acting forces, or

2) as a result of transient, temporary forces which act only in a particular period of a given language.

In the latter cases these forces operate

a) synchronically, or

b) they belong to the past of a given language.

Within both the purely anthropophonic and alternational divergences we must distinguish:

1) phonetic *habits* (e.g., beginning any syllable with a consonant, which accounts for, among other things, the use of the so-called prothetic consonant to avoid *hiatus*), and

2) *accommodation,* for the sake of easier pronunciation.

This latter is, in turn, either

a) *mandatory* and *without exceptions* in "normal," correct pronunciation (e.g., the divergence of *t* in *ta | tr | tl | ts | tn | at | ant* . . . ; the alternation of *d* in *dno | den* . . .), or,

b) reduced to a weak anthropophonic tendency, a tendency curtailed by "prohibitive analogy," i.e., by the striving toward phonetic leveling of psychologically different morphemes.

Features of Divergence

1) The first and basic feature of any divergence can be formulated as follows: the *alternating phonetic properties are not individual and independent properties of the anthropophonic variants (modifications) of a given phoneme in a given phonetic position of a morpheme, but are conditioned combinatorially,* i.e., they depend on the combination with other phonemes or, more generally, on the conditions of the anthropophonic environment.⟨. . .⟩

Two other features are closely allied with the first feature of

divergence or with the alternations that are caused anthropophonically:

2) *Direct definability ("Bestimmbarkeit") and the presence of
anthropophonic causes for the alternations,* and

3) Generality and anthropophonic necessity of the alternation.
Which means that such an alternation

a) occurs without exception in all words and phonetic combinations containing the given phonemes in the given language, and

b) is causally connected with anthropophonic alternations in
such a way that

x' may combine with y', and

x" may combine with y", but

x' ... y" or

x" ... y' are impossible.

4) *Divergence is independent of psychological (morphological
or semasiological) factors. It occurs on the periphery of language, in
the articulation of phonemic complexes which need not be speci-
fied syntactically or morphologically.*

5) *Since the properties of the phonemes* x', x" *are not individual,
psychological properties that are stored in the brain center, but
conditioned variants which depend on the phonetic environment*
(y', y") *rather than on psychological factors, the anthropophonic
variations of the dependent phoneme may go unnoticed.* These
variations are established automatically by the peripheral phonetic
conditions. The possibility of perceiving and marking these variations is, however, by no means excluded and may, in turn, establish a link between divergence and the traditional alternations.

Within the area of divergence or neophonetic alternations, we
may, further, distinguish different degrees and varieties, such as:

a) *embryonic alternations,* which we can discover by means of
minute, as it were, microscopic observation, or which we can
simply postulate;

b) *alternations* with clearly *definable consequences,* i.e., alternations which cannot be perceived in a state of weakened consciousness, but which can be discovered in a state of sharpened or
intensified consciousness [e.g., Pol. *m* || *m* in *mech* | *mchu, r* || *r* in
Piotra | *Piotr, t* || *t* in *kota* | *kot,* Rus. *a* || *a* in *brata* | *brate*]. Here
a psychologically homogeneous phoneme appears together with its
anthropophonic bifurcation;

c) *alternations* which can be *perceived* not only consciously but also *unconsciously,* and which come about, on the one hand, from a split (bifurcation) of the psychological unity and are, on the other hand, supported by tradition [for example, Pol. *–b–* || *–p* in *łba* | *łeb, p'(pᵢ)* || *p* in *kupiec* | *kupca* . . . ; Rus. *t* || *d* in *svatat'* | *svad'ba* . . .].

In deciding whether a given alternation belongs to type (b) or to type (c), we can examine the pertinent facts of language and of writing (the test of writing applies, of course, only to literary languages and literate individuals). Thus Polish *–b–* || *–p* in *łba* | *łeb* belongs to type (c), since there is also a form *łepek* ⟨dim.⟩; so does Russian *d* || *t* in *búdok* | *búdka* in view of *bútočnik,* and *t* || *d* in *svátat'* | *svád'ba* in view of *svádebnyj* ⟨adj.⟩ The Polish spelling *tchu* ⟨gen. sg.⟩ *tchnąć* shows that *d* || *t* in *dech, oddech* | *tchu, tchnąć* belongs likewise to type (c). In the speech of Polish children who pronounce *vrušek (wruszek)* instead of *vružek (wróżek* ⟨gen. pl.⟩), the *ž* || *š* alternation *wróż–yć* | *wróż–ka* also belongs to type (c) or, to be exact, is not yet established as a proper alternation.

The three types cited obviously admit in each language a series of transitional stages and oscillations in one direction or another.

CHAPTER IV

CORRELATIONS, OR PSYCHOPHONETIC ALTERNATIONS.

A correlation is an alternation of phonemes in which the phonetic difference is connected (associated) with some psychological difference between forms and words, that is, with some morphological or semasiological difference.

Strictly speaking, the alternation concerns not isolated phonemes (sounds), but entire morphemes, or even words.

At this stage of the development of alternational relations, morphology utilizes homogeneous phonemes (i.e., phonemes stemming from an originally single phoneme) as mobile correlatives in the same way as it utilizes mobile *word-forming morphemes* (affixes), i.e., prefixes, suffixes, desinences, etc. The mobile correlatives form a necessary link, an integrating part of some mobile homogeneous morphemes. And like the suffixes or prefixes, the correlatives may serve to distinguish morphological categories.

Thus, in Polish, as in other Slavic languages, one class of denominal verbs is still productively formed by means of adding the suffix *i* to the primary stem; the final consonant of the stem corresponds to the palatalized consonant which had developed historically by way of spontaneous degeneration at the time of the first Slavic palatalization (which applies at least to the velars *k, g, ch*): [*brud–* | *brudź–i–ć, łup* | *łup–i–ć, tok–* | *toč–y–ć, trwog* | *trwož–y–ć* . . .].

The locative case of Polish substantives is marked not only by the desinence *–e*, but also by the change of the final thematic consonant into a sound which developed by way of spontaneous degeneration from a palatalized consonant at the time of the second Slavic palatalization (which applies at least to the velars): [*narodź–e, wol–e, boř–e, strać–e, ręc–e, wódc–e, nodz–e, strudz–e* . . .].

To cite other examples:

In the Polish conjugation, 1st p. sg. *nios–e* (*nios–ę*), *plot–e, gn–e, bior–e, piek–e, mog–e* . . . 3rd p. sg. *nieś–e, pleć–e, gń–e, bieř–e, pieč–e, mož–e* . . . ;

also in the Polish conjugation 3rd p. sg. (2 sg., 1–2 pl.) {*lub'i mów'i, woli, rańi, twořy, točy, trwožy, sušy,*} *noši, woźi, świeći, chodźi* | 1st sg. (3rd pl.) *lub'e, mów'–e, wol–e, rań–e, twoř–e, toč–e, trwož–e, suš–e,*} *noš–e, wož–e, świec–e, chodz–e* . . . ;

noši–, woźi–, świeći–, chodźi– | *noš–enie, noš–ony, wož–enie, wož–ony, świec–enie, świec–ony, chodz–enie, chodz–ony* . . . ⟨verbal nouns and past passive participles⟩;

simple verbs vs. duratives and iteratives: *pali–ć, czyńi–ć, trudźi–ć* | *pal–a–ć, –czyń–a–ć, –trudz–a–ć* . . . , but *stroi–ć, točy–ć, trwožy–ć, chodźi–ć, množy–ć* | *–straj–a–ć, tač–a–ć, trwaž–a–ć, chadz–a–ć, –mnaž–a–ć* and *gnieś–ć, pleś–ć, mieś–ć, leć–e–ć, siedź–e–ć* | *gniat–a–ć, plat–a–ć, miat–a–ć, lat–a–ć, siad–a–ć* . . . ;

the same relationship holds in Russian verbs: *bros–á–t'* | *brás–yva–t', koló–t'* | *kál–yva–t', strói–t'* | *–stró–iva–t', (strá–iva–t'), próči–t', –proč–iva–t', ljubi–t'* | *–ljúbl–iva–t', dolbít'* | *dálbl–iva–t', xodi–t'* | *xáž–iva–t', nosi–t'* | *nášiva–t', zapodózri–t'* | *zapodózr–iva–t' (zapodázr–iva–t').* . . .

The nom. pl. masc. of Polish nouns ⟨also adjectives and past tense of verbs⟩ in combination with the desinence *–i* (*–y*) has a final consonant which underwent palatalization (in the case of the velars, palatalization of the second period) by way of spontaneous degeneration [*chłop–i, kać–i . . . , silń–i, mil–i . . . , wilc–y, ptac–y . . . , wielc–y, drudz–y . . . , szl–i, chodzil–i, dal–i . . .*].

In Modern High German the plural of certain masculine and neuter substantives is formed not only by adding the desinence –*e* or –*er,* but also by changing the nonpalatal stem vowel into a palatal (by so-called Umlaut): *Wolf, Dorf, Grab, Loch, Wurm* | *Wölfe, Dörfer, Gräber, Löcher, Würmer. . . .*

In ancient Indic ⟨Sanskrit⟩ some derived names are formed simultaneously through the addition of the suffix –*ya*– and the correlative change of the simple vowel of the stem morpheme into the second degree of the "vowel gradation" (*vṛddhi*–): *kāunteya–, sāubhagya, vāirya, pārthava*– . . . from *kunti–, subhaga, vīra, pṛthivī–. . . .*

As is well known, some suffixes or subordinate morphemes (suffixes, prefixes) can give a word a nuance of coarseness, abstraction, etc. A word can acquire similar nuances through a correlative relation of morphemes, as, for example, in the correlation *x* (*ch*) || *s* in Polish *włoch–y, kluch–y* | *włos–y, klus–ki* . . . ; Russian *ra, la* || *oro, olo;* and *šč, žd* || *č, ž* as in *graždanin* | *goroždánin, glavá* | *golová, prevraščát'* | *voróčat'* . . . ; French *k* || *š* as in *cause* | *chose* . . . (in this last case one could hardly speak of an actual, live correlation that is still perceived by the speakers).

The so-called vowel gradation found in proto-Indo-European and in the older stages of various Indo-European languages is closely connected with a correlative alternation of phonemes in which one member of the alternating pair has a zero-phoneme, i.e., lacks any phoneme:

$$x \parallel \emptyset$$

This "vowel gradation" may continue to be alive and productive, or its productivity may be waning.

In this context we can also mention the so-called infixes, which are widely used in the Semitic languages.

The possibility of forming new alternating pairs may serve as a proof of the productivity of correlative alternations, particularly when such alternations could not have arisen by way of simple phonetic change. This is the case of the *c* || *č* (*cz*) correlation which is used in the formation of Polish diminutives from simple substantives. Having developed phonetically in words where both *č* *(cz)* and *c* were the result of various palatalizations of *k* in different periods of the language, the correlation is now also found in words in which the *c* goes back to a *ti̯*, and not to a *k*. The correlation *c* || *č* *(cz)* was caused by a phonetic development in the words *donica, miednica, krynica, lice, słonce, kupiec* | *doniczka, miedniczka, kryniczka, liczko, słoneczko, kupczyk* . . . , just as the correlations *k* || *č, g* || *ž, x* *(ch)* || *š* *(sz)* in *ręka* | *rączka, noga* | *nóžka, mucha* | *muszka.* . . . But the correlation *c* || *č* in correlative pairs of the type *świeca* | *świeczka* . . . was brought about by morphological assimilation ("analogy").

The older nom. pl. of the possessive pronouns *nasz–y, wasz–y,* has in modern Polish been replaced by *naś–i, waś–i,* because the consonant *ś* is felt to be a characteristic feature of this case for stems ending in the consonants *s, š* *(sz)* or *x* *(ch)*: *naš* | *naś–i.* . . .

The older diminutive forms of the Polish *grosz, arkusz* were *groszyk, arkuszyk* (as they are still in some parts of the Polish linguistic territory, e.g., in Lithuania, the Ukraine, etc.); at present these forms have a palatal *ś* as in *arkuśik, grośik.* (A similar "palatalization" is used in children's speech to express endearment and affection.)

The vowel alternations of Sanskrit which are subsumed under the general term *guṇa–,* were originally mostly correlative, i.e., morphologically mobile; in the period from which Indic literature dates, this mobility began to change into the psychological immobility of a purely traditional alternation. The so-called *vrddhi*–on the other hand, became a living, mobile, and productive correlation.

Correlations are always in a state of transition between one type of simple traditional alternations and another. A correlation arises only as a result of the utilization of alternational distinctions for psychological purposes, and this utilization may be repeated generation after generation until it ceases; and when it ceases, the psychophonetic alternation or correlation is converted into a simple traditional alternation. We shall illustrate this general statement with some examples.

The Polish alternation $\emptyset$ || *i* (*n* || *in*) in *pn–ę, pń–e* | *pin–a;* *–čn–ę, čń–e* | *–čyn–a; tn–ę, tń–e* | *–ćin–a* . . . was at first a mobile correlation, as shown by its extension to the pair *gn–ę gń–e* | *g'in–a* . . . ; but at present it is shifting into a state of total psychological immobility, as are the other alternations closely related to it (*čt–ę, čć–e | čyt–a, słać | syl–a–c, tk–a–ć | tyk–a–ć, br–a–ć | b'er–a–ć.*

The category of rudimentary psychophonetic alternations also includes the Polish $o \parallel u(ó)$, as in *chod–u, bor–u, stoł–u, grod–u | chód, bór, stół, gród* . . . ; *'ę, 'ą $\parallel$ ę, ą*, as in *ćęž–ki ćąž–a | tęg–i ws–tąž–ka; u $\parallel$ Ø* as in *such–y | sch–ną–ć* . . . ; German *i (e) $\parallel$ a* in *bind–e | band, ess–e | aβ* . . . ,

$$
\begin{matrix}
in \parallel & & & bind\text{–}e & \\
& un & in & & ge\text{–}bund\text{–}en. \ldots \\
an \parallel & & & band &
\end{matrix}
$$

We can assume that even the Polish alternation $o \parallel e$ in *bior–e, nios–e, wioz–e | bierz–e, niesi–e, wiezi–e* . . . was once felt to express a relation of different forms or in other words was a true, albeit short-lived, correlation. Now, of course, it shows no trace of correlativity, for otherwise there could not be any tendency to level the stems and to change such forms as *bior–e, nios–e, wioz–e* . . . into *bier–e, nies–e, wiez–e.*

There are also cases in the history of a language when a particular correlation seems to disappear, but in actuality only changes its outward appearance to be subsumed under a broader, more general correlation.

An interesting example of such a change is found in Russian, where the alternation $k \parallel č, g \parallel ž$ in the present tense of verbs of the literary language, e.g., p_iek–ú, t_iek–ú, b_ier_ieg–ú, st_ier_ieg–ú . . . $p_ieč$–ót, $t_iieč$–ót, $b_ier_iež$–ót, $st_ier_iež$–ót . . . is replaced in dialectal spech by the alternation $k \parallel k_i, g \parallel g_i$, e.g., p_iek–ú, b_ier_ieg–ú . . . | p_iek_i–ót $b_ier_ieg_i$–ót . . . on the model of the alternations:

$b \parallel b_i, t \parallel t_i, d \parallel d_i, s \parallel s_i, z \parallel z_i, r \parallel r_i, n \parallel n_i$ . . . (in the forms gr_ieb–ú, pl_iet–ú, v_ied–ú, n_ies–ú, v_iez–ú, b_ier–ú, gn–ú . . . gr_ieb_i–ót, pl_iet_i–ót, v_ied_i–ót, n_ies_i–ót, v_iez_i–ót, b_ier_i–ót, gn_i–ót. . .). All these alternations can be reduced to the single correlation:

$$P\emptyset \parallel PY$$

{where **P** indicates palatalization, "softening," **Ø** – absence (in this case, of palatalization), and **Y** – presence (in this case, of palatalization)}.

If one considers this process of substitution of the alternation $k \parallel č, g \parallel ž$ by the alternation $k \parallel k_i, g \parallel g_i$ superficially, one might conclude that a correlation, or psychophonetic alternation has been lost. Such a conclusion would, however, be misleading. One could speak of the loss of a correlation only if, instead of the pairs $k \parallel k_i$, $g \parallel g_i$, we found the pairs $k \parallel k$, $g \parallel g$, i.e., if all forms of the present tense were leveled. But such a leveling should also have affected the other consonants, so that we would find not only the forms $p_ie\!k{-}\acute{o}t$, $t_iek{-}\acute{o}t$, $b_ier_ieg{-}\acute{o}t$, $st_ier_ieg{-}\acute{o}t$, . . . but also $gr_ieb{-}\acute{o}t$, $pl_iet{-}\acute{o}t$, $v_ied{-}\acute{o}t$, $n_ies{-}\acute{o}t$, $v_iez{-}\acute{o}t$, $b_ier{-}\acute{o}t$, $gn{-}\acute{o}t$, ... Actually the situation is quite different, and the development of the forms $p_iek_i{-}\acute{o}t$, $t_iek_i{-}\acute{o}t$, $b_ier_ieg_i{-}\acute{o}t$, $st_ier_ieg{-}\acute{o}t$ . . . testifies to the great vitality of the correlation $P\emptyset \parallel PY$ in the present tense of this type of verbs.

Characteristic Features of Correlations and Correlatives

1. From the viewpoint of anthropophonic causality—*the alternating features concern the various points of articulation or the phonemes, individually, autonomously, and independently.*

2. *At any given stage of a language, the cause of the phonetic alternation lies only in tradition (transmission), in social intercourse, in usage.* We have learned to speak in a certain way from our environment and our ancestors; such an explanation is completely sufficient.

3. *The anthropophonic causes of an alternation, its anthropophonic causal connections, lie in the history of the language and can be established only through historical-linguistic studies.* At one time an anthropophonic cause was at work, but later it ceased to operate, and now it is absent.

(These three characteristic features are common to correlatives with simple traditional alternations.)

4. *As a result of the ever-recurring process of associating representations, each alternation of this sort was endowed with psychological differences of a formal morphological or semasiological, meaning-carrying nature.* ⟨. . .⟩

Thus we see that the correlatives, or psychophonetic alternants, carry corresponding psychological differences. Anthropophonic distinctions and nuances are here always accompanied by psychological, morphological, or semasiological nuances and distinctions.

5. From what has been said above, it follows that *it is the nature of the psychological, morphological, or semasiological correlatives to be general and without exceptions.*

A particular correlation encompasses all words of a given category without exception, e.g., within the conjugation all verbs of a *particular type,* within the declension all nouns of a *particular type,* a *particular type* of derivatives, etc.

6. *The degree of phonetic similarity of the alternating phonemes is in such cases completely immaterial.* It is only necessary that there be a psychophonetic association of the representations of particular anthropophonic activities with the corresponding psychological distinctions. ⟨. . .⟩

7. *The seeming phonetic changes which occur in the area of correlations are as a rule not gradations, not a movement in a particular anthropophonic direction, but leaps which from an anthropophonic point of view are totally incomprehensible and which are often in contradiction with the general course of historical-phonetic changes.*

A striking example of this type is the previously mentioned replacement of Russian $p_i e\check{c}$–*ót, $b_i er_i e\check{z}$–ót* . . . by $p_i ek_i$–*ót, $b_i e$–$r_i eg_i$–ót* . . . or the use of the Russian imperative $p_i ek_i$–*í, $b_i er_i eg_i$–í,* pomog$_i$–*í* . . . instead of the earlier $p_i ec$–*í, $b_i er_i ez$–í, pomoz–í* . . . , or the Polish *piecz, pomóż* . . . in place of the earlier **piec– (piec–y), *pomódz– (pomodz–y).* . . .

8. Neither the divergents nor the traditional alternations tolerate a change of the alternational correlation or innovations of a particular type. However, one of the characteristic features of the correlatives is the creation of *innovations according to a certain model, the possibility of transferring a ready made correlative relation to new words, the possibility of the incessant reestablishment of the relation.*

The transference of a correlative relation can occur

a) within a group of words of a certain type (semantic or lexical transferability), or

b) within a specific morphological category.

9. [*The feature which arises from the generalization of a whole series of correlatives.*] In the case of divergents, some causal relations are universal. *In the case of correlatives, only the ability to form correlative relations is universal; the specific types of correlatives are conditioned temporally and spatially.*

10. [*The genetic feature, the feature which characterizes the formation of correlatives in individuals.*] Each member of a speech community arrives at the divergents by himself directly, by means

of immediate, physiological accommodation, whereas the correlatives are acquired step-by-step, gradually, in proportion to the strength and intensity of psychophonetic associations already formed in one's mind.

In this context it is necessary to indicate that the correlations developed from traditional alternations within one and the same language differ often in their semantic function from those correlations in which at least one member has been borrowed from another related language.

In correlations of the second kind the borrowed member of the alternation generally has a more abstract, loftier, more literary or more solemn meaning than the member formed within the native language whose meaning is usually more concrete and colloquial. Thus, for example, Polish *h* || *g* in *hańba* | *ganić, hardy* | *gardzić* . . . (if, indeed, these pairs can be treated as examples of a developed correlation);

Russian *ra* || *oro, ła* || *oło, re* || *ere, le* || *oło, ra–* || *ro–, šč* || *č, žd* || *ž, o* || *Ø* in *grad, graždanin* | *górod, gorožánin; glavá, glávnyj* | *golová golovnój; prédok* | *peredók; plen, plenít'* | *polón, polonít'; rázum* | *rózysk; rávnyj* | *róvnyj; rab, rábskij* | *róbkij, robét,' osveščát', prosveščénie* | *svečá, prosvéčivat'; čúždyj* | *čužój; roždát'* | *rožát'* . . . ;

French *k* || *š* in *cause* | *chose, caniculaire* | *chien, camp* | *champ* . . . (if again, these represent at all a developed correlation).

As a very rare example of conscious and arbitrary interference with the spoken language in forming a correlative, or psychophonetic alternation, I shall report the following case which I myself observed. In a Slovenian school in the province of Goricia, in the Karst region, the teacher required the children to replace the word- and syllable-final consonantal *u* (*ṷ*) characteristic of that dialect (as of almost all Slovenian dialects) with *l* in conformity with the spelling, not only in reading but even in speaking; hence, *dàl, bìl, prósil* . . . instead of *dàṷ, bìṷ, prósiṷ*. . . . But since this dialect has an *ł* (resembling the Polish, Russian, or Lithuanian *ł*) in word-initial and word-medial position, the *–ł–* || *–ṷ* correlation peculiar to the native dialect was in the speech of the school children replaced by the correlation *–ł–* || *–l–*, i.e., the pairs *dáła* | *dàṷ, bìła* | *bìṷ, prosíła* | *prósiṷ, déłała* | *déłaṷ* were replaced by *dała* | *dàl, bìła* | *bìl, prosíła* | *prosíl, déłała* | *déłal*. . . .

A correlation introduced so artificially could obviously not endure and was in time replaced by the normal correlation *–ł–* || *–ṷ*.

However if one did not know the local dialect, he might have concluded on the basis of the speech of these children that the dialect had, in fact, the correlation $-t-\ ||\ -l$. It is almost certain that if the teachers had continued to demand that the children pronounce $-l$ in place of $u̯$ for a number of generations, the alternation $-t\ ||\ -l$ would have eventually become an established fact of that language.

Finally, we might mention the various layers of alternations, which go back to different periods in the history of a language and which replaced each other as psychologically mobile, psychophonetic alternations, or correlations. Several such layers can be distinguished in Polish: (a) alternations of proto-Indo-European origin, (b) alternations of Common Slavic origin, and (c) properly Polish alternations of more recent origin which have, in part, retained their full psychological vitality.

For with time, correlations may lose their psychophonetic value and become purely traditional alternations that could be compared with extinct volcanoes.

"Analytic" languages, whose morphology shows a tendency toward decentralization, lack morphological correlations.

CHAPTER V

TRADITIONAL ALTERNATIONS.

The phonetic and psychological causes of alternations are, like those of other linguistic phenomena, both individual and social. They are social in that they are not individually phonetic or individually psychological, but *collectively* phonetic and *collectively* psychological. Their "social" character is, nevertheless, secondary, since they are not the result of imitation and repetition, but of psychological organization, and serve the psychological needs of each individual belonging to a given speech community.

Although both the divergents and correlatives must be examined from the viewpoint of traditional and social causality, the characteristic feature of divergents is their anthropophonic causality, and of correlatives, their psychological causality, whereas in the case of purely traditional alternants we can speak only of traditional and social causality.

As has been mentioned above, the original cause for the emergence of all alternants is always purely anthropophonic.

Hence it follows that purely traditional alternants are never original but are the historical continuation of neophonetic alternants or divergents, whose anthropophonetic cause has ceased to function as a living factor and belongs now only to the past.

Consequently, all traditional alternations are simultaneously paleophonetic.

Let us illustrate this otherwise simple statement with a few examples:

Polish *ród* | *rod–u,* in which *–t(d)* || *–d–* is a neophonetic alternation, or divergence, but *u(ó)* || *o* is a traditional, paleophonetic alternation.

mróz | *mroz–u*: divergence *–s(z)* || *–z–*; traditional alternation *u(ó)* || *o*;

mąż | *męż–a*: divergence *–š(ž)* || *–ž–*; traditional alternation *ą* || *ę*;

płot–ę | *pleś–ć*: *o* || *e* and *t* || *ś* are both traditional alternations;

płaci– | *płac–ę, rodzi–* | *rodz–ę*: only one traditional alternation, *ći* || *c, dźi* || *dz*;

Literary German *geb–en* | *gab*: two divergents, *g*ᵢ || *g* and *–b–* || *–p (b)*; one traditional alternation, *e* || *a*;

lad–en | *Las–t*: two traditional alternations, *ā* || *ă, d* || *s (d* as occlusive, *s* as spirant), and one divergence *d* || *s* (if one considers these phonemes from another point of view, viz. *d* as voiced, and *s* as voiceless);

Fros–t | *frier–en, Ver–lus–t* | *ver–lier–en, ver–lor–en*: the traditional alternation *s* || *r.*

Fros–t | *frier–en*: the traditional alternation *ŏ* || *ī (ie)*;

Ver–lus–t | *ver–lor–en*: the traditional alternation *u* || *o*;

verlier–en | *Ver–lus–t, ver–lor–en*: the traditional alternation *ī (ie)* $\left\|\begin{array}{c} u \\ o \end{array}\right.$;

Sanskrit *nāmn–* | *nāma*: the traditional alternation *n* || *a*.

From the point of view of their origin and historical evolution, the traditional alternations fall into two main groups:

1) those that developed directly from divergents, or neophonetic alternations that have lost their live anthropophonic cause;

2) those that have gone through several stages; at first the di-

vergence became a traditional ⟨*sic!* the author obviously means neophonetic⟩ alternation which was, in turn, utilized as a correlation that subsequently lost the ability to express psychological distinctions and became a plain traditional alternation.

1) Examples of traditional, paleophonetic alternations, which are derived directly from divergents of neophonetic alternations:

a) alternations which had developed as a result of palatalizing or dispalatalizing accommodation, i.e., "softening" or "hardening"—

Polish *š* ‖ *x* (*ch*) [*szed–ł chodz–i* . . .]
ć ‖ *t* [*ciek–, ciec* | *tok; cież–ki, ciąż–a* | *tęg–i, ws–tąż–ka* . . .],
b ‖ *b'* [*br–ać* | *bior–e, bierz–e* . . .],
o ‖ *e* [*bior–ę* | *bierz–e, nios–e niesi–e* . . .],
a ‖ *e* [*świat* | *świec–i* . . .];

b) the alternation found, among others, in Latin, in some German-speaking areas, and Čuvaš:

$$s \parallel r;$$

c) the alternation of a phoneme with zero, i.e., with the absence of a phoneme; e.g., Polish *e* ‖ *Ø* [*pies* | *ps–a, sen* | *sn–u* . . .],

$$\varnothing \left\| \begin{matrix} e \\ o \end{matrix} \right. [br–ać \mid bierz–e, bior–ę. . .].$$

2) Examples of traditional alternations which have gone through three stages of evolution (from divergents to traditional alternants, from traditional alternants to correlations, and from correlations back again to traditional alternants).

The Indo-European alternation *e* ‖ *o* which for some time marked the difference between primary verbs and certain types of nouns and which is preserved until now, for example, in Polish as

$$_{i}e, \begin{matrix} {}^{i}e \\ {}_{i}o \end{matrix} \left\| \right. o: [grzebi–e, grzeb–ę \mid grob–; ciez–e, ciek–ę \mid tok–; wlecz–e,$$

$$wlok–ę \mid włok–; pleci–e, plot–ę \mid płot–. . .].$$

The Polish and other Slavic alternations *Ø* ‖ *i*, *Ø* ‖ *y* [*pn–ę* | *pin–a, czt–ę* | *czyt–a*. . . , *tk–a* |*tyk–a, tch–nę* | *dych–a*. . .].

The Polish alternation *o* ‖ *u* (*ó*) [*chod–* | *chód*. . .].

The alternation in the conjugation of the literary German "strong" verbs: e.g., *i, e* ‖ *a* [*bind–e* | *band, geb–e* | *gab*. . .],

$$\begin{matrix} i, e \\ a \end{matrix} \left\| u, o \left(\begin{matrix} in \\ an \end{matrix} \right. \right\| un, \begin{matrix} er \\ ar \end{matrix} \left\| or \right)$$

[*bind–e, band* | *ge–bund–en; werf–e, warf* | *ge–worf–en*. . .].

In view of the fact, emphasized above, that the correlations characteristic of a given speech community are acquired through the individual effort of its speakers who often fail to develop the feeling (awareness) of a correlation, it would appear that all the correlative or psychophonetic alternations mentioned in Chapter IV lack, for such speakers, a correlative character and fall into the category of purely traditional alternations. ⟨. . .⟩

Features of Traditional Alternations

1. *The alternating properties are associated with certain points of articulation, i.e., with specific phonemes, individuallly and autonomously.* ⟨. . .⟩

2. *It is then apparent that at any given stage of a language, tradition (transmission), social intercourse, or usage are the sole causes of an alternation.* We have learned to speak in a certain manner from our environment and our predecessors; this type of explanation is completely sufficient. The preservation of a particular alternation cannot be ascribed to any indivdual factor.

3. *The anthropophonic causes, the anthropophonic causal relations of an alternation lie in the past history of a language and can be discovered through historical-linguistic studies.* An anthropophonic cause was operative for a certain time, after which it ceased to act.

The above three features apply to simple traditional alternants and the correlatives.

4. *Psychological associations, which support the preservation of traditional alternations, are in constant conflict with the tendency to eliminate phonetic distinctions that are justified neither by individual anthropophonic tendencies nor by individual psychological needs.* Such a conflict leads either to the introduction of a correlative meaning in traditional alternations ⟨. . .⟩ or to the elimination of differences, to leveling ⟨. . .⟩.

186

CHAPTER VI

FOREIGN ALTERNATIONS, i.e.,
ALTERNATIONS WHICH ARE DUE TO THE
INFLUENCE OF ANOTHER LANGUAGE.

The correspondences or formal equivalents of different languages are not used by the same speakers and lack a common psychological substratum, except for the special case of bilingualism, when one and the same person speaks two (or more) languages. But even outside such cases, a correspondence can become not only a historical but a live, psychophonetic phenomenon. This happens when a language has borrowed words from historically related neighboring languages as, for example, when Polish has borrowings from Russian dialects (and vice versa), Lithuanian from Slavic (and vice versa), or Latin from Italic. These borrowings may be due not only to geographical proximity, but also to literary or cultural proximity. Such are, for example, the borrowings from Latin into French and other Romance languages or from Old Church Slavonic into Russian and other Slavic languages.

In this way there arises a live phonetic correspondence, which is perceived as such by the speakers. But in addition to producing an awareness of correspondences, borrowings may also account for introducing:

a) paleophonetic alternations from a closely related language;

b) a live relationship between native and borrowed forms of etymologically cognate morphemes; such a relationship might be called an *alternation of correspondences* (or correspondence-simultaneity).

It is clear that such borrowings and exchanges are ordinarily found only between closely related languages, such as Polish and Czech, Polish and Ukrainian, Serbian and Bulgarian, Russian and Church Slavonic, French and Latin, Latin and Italic dialects, etc. For if there is no close linguistic relationship, we can hardly expect to find a sufficient number of morphemes having a constant etymological or psychophonetic relationship, which is required to produce in the borrowing speech community an awareness of a

187

thorough-going correspondence between the respective languages. And the existence of such an awareness is an absolute prerequisite for recognizing this type of alternation.

An example of a totally "foreign" alternation, i.e., of an alternation in which both members are of foreign origin is the Polish alternation *h* || *z* [in *błah–y* | *błaz–en*. . .], which was borrowed from Czech.

As examples of "mixed" alternations, i.e., of alternations in which one member is of native and the other of foreign origin, we may cite the Polish *g* || *h* [*gan–ić* | *hań–ba, gardz–ić* | *hard–y, błog–i* | *błah–y*], Polish *ło* || *ła* [*błog–i* | *błah–y, błaz–en*. . .], Latin *b* || *f* [*rub–er, ruf–us*. . .], French *š* || *k* [*chose* | *cause, champs* | *camp*. . .] and other such doublets which are partially felt by the speakers themselves to be etymologically related and which can partially be established only through scientific, theoretical study.

Different types of alternations which are due to borrowing can be studied to great advantage in literary Russian, since this language was for a long time subject to strong Church Slavonic influence, to which it owes a significant number of alternations.

In accordance with what was said above, we must distinguish first of all two basic types of alternations occurring in Russian:

1) alternations which are entirely of Church Slavonic origin, and

2) mixed alternations, which are half Church Slavonic and half Russian.

The alternations of the second type are far more numerous than those of the first type. The phonetic quality of a mixed alternation in which one of the members is of Church Slavonic and the other of Russian origin may sometimes give rise to uncertainty as to whether one member of the alternation or both members are of Church Slavonic origin.

Russian alternations which are entirely borrowed from Church Slavonic are:

a) *ti* || *šč, di* || *žd* in *o–sveti–t'* | *o–sveši̇̌č–át', rodi–t'* | *rožd–át'*. . . .

The corresponding native alternations are *ti* || *č, di* || *ž* in *sveti–t'* | *sveč–ú, rodi–t'* | *rož–át'*. . . .

In both types of alternations, the first members are identical, but the second ones are different. The properly Russian *šč, žd* come from another source and participate in another type of alternation: *sk* || *šč* [*isk–át* | *išč–et, pisk–* | *pišč–ít*. . .], *sti* || *šč* [*pustí–t'* |

pušč–ú, svist–ít | svišč–ú. . .]; *žĭd ⇉ žd, žd* || *žĭd* [*žd–át' | o–žĭd–át' . . .*
vražd–á ⇐ vraž'd–a. . .].

The alternations borrowed from Old Church Slavonic also in-
clude: ${}^{t}_{\;i}$ || *šč* in *pit–át, | pi–šča* ⟨sic⟩, *klevet–át' | klevéšč–et . . . ,*
tvi || *ščvl'* in *u–mertvi–t' | u–merščvl–ját' . . . , stri* || *ščr'* in *iz–ostri–t' |*
iz–oščr–ját'. . . , ${}^{z}_{\;ž}$ || *žd* in ${}^{iz-}_{\;živ}$ || *iždiv–énie,* ${}^{voz-}_{\;žel–át'}$ || *vożdel–*
énnyj. . . ;[3]

b) *sk* || *st* in *blesk | blist–át', blest–ét. . . ;*

c) *er* || *ra* in *mérz–kij | mraz', smerd–ét' | smrad, vert–ét' |*
vrat–á, vrat–ít', vrašč–át. . . ;

l'e || *ła* in *vlek–ú, vleč', –vlek–át' | vlač–ít' ób–lak–o. . . .*

Examples of mixed alternations in Russian, i.e., in which one of
the members is of native origin and the other a borrowing from
Church Slavonic are:

a) *g* || *γ (h)* in *gospod–in | γospód', gosudár' | γosudár', bogátyj |*
bóγa. . . .

One should not conclude from this example that *γ* (i.e., a voiced
x (ch) or spirant (*g*) was the original Church Slavonic pronunciation. On the contrary, since *g* is used by the Slavs of the Balkan peninsula where the Church Slavonic literary language originated, we
may assume that this pronunciation was also characteristic of Old
Church Slavonic. But Church Slavonic penetrated into Great Russia
through Kiev, or more generally through the Ukraine, and the
Ukranian clergy and scholars have in this case imposed their pronunciation upon Church Slavonic, i.e, they pronounced the original
letter *γ* as *γ (h)*. Sanctioned by the ecclesiastical academy of Kiev,
the one-time center of Orthodoxy, this pronunciation became the
standard obligatory in all Russia, including the Ukraine and Great
Russia. This is why the Russian Orthodox clergy adopted this *γ*
pronunciation in reading, and why it is still maintained in Russian
words of Church Slavonic origin that are still perceived as borrowings.

The *g* || *γ* alternation can, of course, be treated as an alternation
only in the speech of those Great Russians who use *g* in their
native pronunciation. But in Byelorussia and in the many other
areas of the Great Russian linguistic territory where only (*h*) is
pronounced, the alternation is lost without a trace.

b) *ó* || *é* in those cases where an *ó* should have developed in Great Russian and where only spelling and a desire to pronounce the letters in accordance with their names in the alphabet account for the *é* pronunciation in words of Church Slavonic origin, and for the alternation *ó* || *é* (where *ó* is of Russian and *é* of Church Slavonic origin); e.g.,

in root morphemes: *nëb–o* | *nébo, o–dëž–a* | *o–déžd–a, mërt–vyj* | *s–mért–nyj, mërz–nut'* | *mérz–kij, na–përst–ok* | *perst.* . . . ;

in suffixes: *–óž* || *–éž* [*grab–ëž, pad–ëž* | *mjat–éž, pad–éž.* . .]; *óv–a* || *év–a* [proper name *Korol–ëva* | *–korol–éva*]; *–ónn–* || *–énn–* [*počt–ënn–yj, soverš–ënn–yj, osvjašč–ënnyj, vljubl–ënn–yj.* . . | *počt–énn–yj, soverš–énn–yj, preosvjašč–énn–yj, nezabv–énn–yj...*]; *–ó* || *–é –e* [*–t'jó* || *–t'íjé* and *–n'jo, –en'jó* | *–n'ie, –en'ie*: *žit'ë–byt'ë ži–tié, by–tié, vra–n'ë, žra–n'ë lga–n'ë pisá–nie, poslá–nie, zaklá–nie, vved–en'ë* (dialectal) | *vved–énie, javl–énie, voznes–énie, vozdvíž–enie.* . .].

In the last case, *–ó* || *–é, –e* [*–t'jó –t'ijé, –n'jo, –en'jó–n'je, –én'je*], *–ó* appeared in Russian not by way of a phonetic process, but by way of morphological assimilation ("analogy") to other nouns of this type. In all other cases the Russian *–ó–* developed from a short *e* (corresponding to Common Slavic *ě* or *ĭ*) before a "hard" or non-palatalized consonant.

c) *č* || *šč, ž* ||*žd*:

in the roots: *sveč–á* | *o–svešč–át', voróč–at'* | *vrašč–át', rož–át'* | *rožd–át', xož–ú* | *xožd–énie, čuž–ój* | *čúžd–yj.* . . ;

in the suffixes: *–uč–, –ač–* | *–ušč–, –ašč–*: *drem–úč–ij, plov–úč–ij, pax–úč–ij, kip–úč–ij* | *dréml–jušč–ij, plyv–úšč–ij, kip–jášč–ij* . . . , *gor–júč–ij, kol–júč–ij, von–júč–ij* | *kól–jušč–ij, vonjá–jušč–ij* . . . , *gor–ják–ij, vis–ják–ij, sto–ják–ij* | *gor–jášč–ij, vis–jášč–ij, sto–jášč–ij* . . . ;

d) *–oro–* || *–ra–, oło–* || *–ła–, –ere–* || *–re–, –oło–(–ele–)* || *–le–, ro–* || *ra–*: *vorot–* || *vrat–, gorod–* || *grad–, norov–* || *nrav–, storon–* || *stran–, porox–* || *prax–* . . . , *golov–* || *glav–, molod–* || *mlad–, volok–* || *vlak–, solod–* || *slad–* . . . , *berem–* || *brem–, bereg–* || *breg–, vered–* || *vred–, sered–* || *sred–, pered–* || *pred–, pere–* || *pre–, čered–* || *čred–* . . . , *volok–* || *vlek–, molok–* || *mlek–, polon–* || *plen–* . . . , *rab–* || *rob–, rov–* || *rav–, roz–* || *raz–, rost–* || *rast–* . . . ;

e) *Ø* || *o* in *s–bor* | *so–bór, v golové, v glavé* | *vo glavé*.

The mixed alternations could have formed by virtue of a mental process reminiscent of the mathematical formula: "two entities which are equal to a third entity are equal to each other," or "two entities which are similar to a third entity are similar to each other."

Let us compare, for example, the native Russian alternation *ti* ‖ *č* [*vărót'i* ‖ *vỹ–răč–ú* ... (*voroti–* | *voroč–u*)] and the *alternation ti* ‖ *šč* of Church Slavonic origin [*sỹvrăt'i–* | *sỹ–vrăšč–ú* ... (*sovrati–* | *sovrašču*)]. Both of these alternations share a common member, *ti*, which alternates with *č* in Russian and with *šč* in Church Slavonic. In accordance with the above mathematical formula we may say: *two psychophonetic entities* (that is, *two phonemes* or *groups of phonemes*) *alternating with a third entity, alternate with each other.* In the given case we obtain the bilingual alternation *č* ‖ *šč* of which Russian makes, in fact, extensive use.

On the basis of the above analysis of alternations from the viewpoint of the history of inter-ethnic relations we may conclude that the paleophonetic alternations, whether they be purely traditional or correlative (i.e., psychologically mobile) form two types:

1) they develop within a particular language without any foreign influences, they are the result of the linguistic activity of one speech community; or

2) they arise under the impact of a closely related speech community from which a whole category of words has been borrowed containing phonemes that are part of a particular alternation.

The process of borrowing takes place (a) through oral transmission, or (b) under the influence of a foreign literature.

The alternations resulting from the influence of another language can be of two types: (1) either the entire alternation, i.e., both of its members are borrowed, or (2) only one of its parts (members) is borrowed and the other part is of native origin.

In a homogeneous (with respect to its alternations) speech community, all alternations owe their origin to an internal anthropophonic impulse. But when a speech community is mixed (with respect to its alternations), we can distinguish in terms of the original anthropophonic impulse (1) monolingual and (2) bilingual alternations. Monolingual alternations may owe both parts (members) (a) to the native language, or (b) to the foreign language from which they were borrowed. The following possibilities obtain:

1) monolingual native, or internal;

2) monolingual foreign;

3) bilingual, or internal–external.

Only in the case of the first type can it be asked whether the original anthropophonic cause is still active in the given state of the language, or whether it belongs to the past. In the case of the second type, such a question is totally irrelevant.

Paleophonetic alternations, whether internal or external, can either

1) have a purely traditional causality, or

2) be utilized for a psychological, morphological, or semasiological purpose.

Characteristic Features of Foreign Alternations

1, 2, 3. The first three characteristic features are the same as in traditional alternations and correlations. In addition, they have a fourth and fifth feature:

4. *The original anthropophonic causes for the transition of an originally homogeneous phoneme into an incipient (embryonic) alternation and then into a neophonetic alternation (divergence) as well as the anthropophonic causes for the further transformation of a divergence into a traditional alternation do not belong to the given speech community, but belong either to a related speech community* (more precisely, to the speech community from which the particular alternation was borrowed), *or in part to the borrowing speech community, and in part to the speech community from which one of the members of the alternation was borrowed.* Thus the Russian alternations *di* || *žd, ti* || *šč* arose not within the confines of Russian, but among the Slavs who settled the Balkan peninsula; one of the members of the Russian alternations *ž* || *žd, č* || *šč* is rooted, however, in the past of the Russian language itself, while its other member was formed in the past among the Balkan Slavs, since it was they who originally formed the Church Slavonic language.

5. *Fully or partially borrowed alternations cannot be explained by anthropophonic causes. But as far as the neophonetic aspect of the borrowed alternations is concerned, it should be noticed that the phonemes making up the alternations must obey the requirements of the native language of a given period.* The "sound laws" governing the language of a given period apply equally to the native phonemes and alternations and to the naturalized or borrowed phonemes and alternations.

The fourth characteristic feature of traditional alternations pertains only to those borrowed alternations which remain within the sphere of purely traditional alternations, without being utilized for psychological purposes. When such a utilization takes place features 4, 5, 6, 7, 8, 9, and 10, which characterize the correlations or psycho-phonetic alternations, apply also to the borrowed alternations.

CHAPTER VII

INCIPIENT (EMBRYONIC) ALTERNATIONS.

As in nature in general, we must also distinguish in language two kinds of phenomena: macroscopic phonomena which are immediately apparent and accessible to observation without any special effort, and microscopic phenomena which can be detected only as a result of a concentrated effort.

This distinction also holds with respect to observable entities and their differences. In the first case the "entities," whether they are bodies, impressions, or representations, are macroscopic or become accessible to our senses by means of magnifying devices. In the second case however the entities in question and their differences may at first glance appear to be clear and transparent, or they may be infinitely small and, as it were, unreachable, unless we apply magnifying instruments and exercise an effort of maximal attention and concentration.

For this reason we should consider, in addition to the *clear and easily definable alternations, alternations involving minimal differences, embryonic alternations.*

What is in question here is not merely the desire to satisfy an idle curiosity or the fruitless exercise of our powers of discrimination, but the discovery of the germinal beginnings of anthropo-phonic causality. For it is precisely at this stage that we find the original influence of different phonetic conditions which produce those incipient differences that, as they increase with time, lead to a split of an originally homogeneous unit into two or more clearly distinct units.

On the basis of the positive results obtained in the study of phenomena due to diverse anthropophonic conditions, we should examine such conditions even though at first sight they do not seem to account for any palpable effects.

And, if for no other purpose, the embryonic alternations should be studied for the simple reason that they may point up the possibilities of linguistic change and provide a stimulus for further objective microscopic linguistic investigations, where we need no longer depend on our subjective impressions but on physical, acoustically and optically reliable equipment.

Thus we may investigate the factors of anthropophonic change and the emergence of *phonemic divergence* in morphemes containing the respective phonemes independently of their etymological relationship. What we are concerned with is the pronunciation of divergent phonemes in phonetic words or in any phonetic combinations of the given language, regardless of their meaning. Thus the embryonic divergences of the phoneme *k* in the combinations *ka* | *ke* | *ki* | *ko* | *ku* | *ką* | *kę* | *kr (kraj)* | *kł (kłaść)* | *kl (kląć)* | *kš (krzywy)* | *ks (k sobie)* | *km' (kmin)* | *kń (kniaź)* | *kt (kto)* | *kp' (kpić)* . . . do not depend on the meaning of the morphemes and words containing these combinations. Compare the similar independence of meaning of the phoneme *a* in the combinations *ka* | *ta* | *pa*, where the phonemic divergence of the vowel is determined only by the preceding consonantal phonemes. These embryonic differences in seemingly identical phonemes may further depend on their occurrence in word-initial, word-final, or word-medial position [*x–* || *–x* || *–x–*], on the degree of intensity (accent), on their occurrence in autophthongal or symphthongal position {*u* | [*a*] *u, i* | [*a*] *i* . . . , i.e., *u* || *u̯, i* || *i̯* . . .}, etc.

But if we are to consider this type of divergence within the framework of alternations, we should concentrate only on related morphemes. In the pair *dn–o* | *den–ko,* the phoneme *d* is only seemingly identical. While the main point of articulation, the moments of pause and closure produced by the respective speech organs are indentical in both *d*'s, they differ in the transition to the following phonemes so that their pronunciation is, in effect, different both acoustically and physiologically.

In the Polish words *ród* | *rod–u,* *mróz* | *mroz–u,* *mąż* | *męż–a* we have, in addition to the transparent traditional, paleophonetic alternations *u(ó)* || *o, ą* || *ę,* and the equally clear neophonetic alternations or divergences *–t (–d)* || *–d–, –s (–z)* || *–z–, –š (–ż)* || *–ž–,* the following embryonic neophonetic alternations:

a) *r*[ód] || *r*[odu], [m] *r* [óz] || [m] *r* [ozu],

b) *m* [ąż] || *m* [ęża],

c) [ró] *t* ‖ [ro] *d* [u], [mró] *s* ‖ [mró] *z* [u], [mą] *š* ‖ [mę] *ž* [a]. . . .

These alternations, –*t* ‖ –*d*–, –*s* ‖ –*z*–, –*š* ‖–*ž*–, require further comment. We are not here concerned with such transparent divergences which stem from the different activities of vocal chords in the larynx, or the weaker quality of –*t*, –*s*, –*š* with respect to –*d*–, –*z*–, –*ž*–, but rather with those that are due to the influence of the preceding vowels *u*(*ó*), *ą* and *o*, *ę* upon the consonants. ⟨. . .⟩

In Russian *góda* ‖ *gădá* there are two embryonic alternations, *g* ‖ *g*, and *d* ‖ *d*, since the vowels following these consonants carry in each case a different stress.

In short, an enormous number of phonetic facts are caused by such phenomena. One could affirmatively claim that there is not a single group of etymologically related words in any language that does not display a whole series of such embryonic alternations or, to put it differently, that there is not a single phoneme in any language that always occurs in the same anthropophonic environment.

Embryonic alternations are to be interpreted as alternations of imperceptible differences in the respective phonemes. As these differences are infinitely small, we may designate them by Ø:

$$d(x' - x'') = \emptyset$$

where *d* indicates the difference, and x′, x″—any phoneme in different anthropophonic environments, which may in time produce a split of the phoneme into two or more phonemes.

The very fact that the words containing the respective phonemes differ on the one hand anthropophonically, i.e., in their phonetic combinations and structure (e.g., the different place of stress), and on the other hand psychologically, i.e., semasiologically or morphologically, introduces a difference between the seemingly identical phonemes that may eventually become perceptible.

Thus the anthropophonic difference between *a* ‖ *a* in the Polish words *matka* ‖ *macierz* (where the first *a* occurs in a closed syllable before a nonpalatal consonant, and the second *a* in an open syllable before a palatal consonant) may in time lead to a transformation (degeneration) of the *a* in two different directions; for example, to the change of *a* in *macierz* into an *e*-type vowel.

Such a change, we may hypothesize, would in turn entail an alternation *m* ‖ *m*, since the *m* before *a* in *matka* is in a different anthropophonic position than the *m* before *e* in our hypothetical **mecierz*.

A similar anthropophonic difference may affect the vowel *a* in *matka* | *mateczka* (the first in a closed, the second in an open syllable) which may eventually split into two distinct phonemes.

On the other hand, we must keep in mind that because of *psychological reasons* the phonemes belonging to the morpheme *mat–* in *matka* may undergo different changes than the same phonemes of that morpheme in *mateczka,* since the word *mateczka* is a diminutive, affectionate, hypocoristic term, which the word *matka* is not. The morpheme *mat–* and its phonemes *m . . . a . . . t* are, consequently, subject to quite different conditions in the two words.

But the potential changes of phonemes caused by psychological differences are not to be confused with anthropophonic causality and must not be subsumed under the concepts of either embryonic or other kinds of alternation.

It is, nonetheless, a fact that each phoneme (sound) is subject to different kinds of influence depending on whether it is treated as a simple sound or a phonetic constituent of a morphological unit. In a similar fashion, each human is subject to different influences as a psychological individual, as a member of a family, of a society, of a state, etc., just as each body is exposed, in turn, to physical conditions, chemical conditions, and so forth.

Embryonic alternations involve two degrees of differences depending on the *particular combinations of the phoneme:*

1) *Truly embryonic, potential* alternations in which the difference between the phonemes equals zero ($\emptyset$).

For example, the perceptual difference to the ear between *s* || *s* in the Polish *kos* | *kosa* is $\emptyset$, as long as our perception is not sharpened by means of optical and acoustical equipment.

2) *Overt* and discernable alternations. The difference between the phonemes can here be designated as $\alpha \rightarrow \emptyset$, i.e., as a discernable difference with the limit $\emptyset$.

The latter alternation is transitional to *divergents*.

The embryonic alternations include, however, only alternations with minimal phonemic differences which are not immediately perceived but can be discovered through the conscious effort of analysis.

In the chain of historical development these alternations form only an intermediary link between embryonic alternations proper and neophonetic alternations or divergents which can be detected by minimal perception.

That such minimal perception is at work is confirmed by "analogical" formations, such as Polish *z wusa*, instead of *z wozu* "down from the wagon," which appears not only in the language of children, but also in the language of adults, due to the influence of ⟨the nom. sg.⟩ *wus* (*wóz*).

CHAPTER· VIII

THE ⟨GENETIC⟩ RELATIONSHIP
BETWEEN DIFFERENT TYPES OF ALTERNATIONS.
GRADUAL TRANSITION FROM ONE TYPE TO ANOTHER.

Let us take as an example a pair of etymologically related Polish words: *plotę* | *plecie* (now pronounced *plote* | *pleće*). The constituent phonemes of these words form the following alternations:

l [o] || l [e]   embembryonic alternation,
[t] e || [ć] e neophonetic alternation or divergence,
  o || e paleophonetic or traditional alternation,
  t || $ć$ psychophonetic alternation or correlation.

The present state of alternations in these words has developed from earlier stages in which the constituent phonemes belonged to different classes of alternations.

Historical and comparative studies enable us to posit the following succession of alternations dating back to the Indo-European period:

1) **plet–o–* | **plet–e–*.

This period was characterized only by the embryonic alternations t [o] || t [e], e [to] || e [te], in which t and e were differentiated in the same way in all anthropophonic sequences of *eto* | *ete* regardless of etymology.

2) **plet_o–o–* | **plet_i–e–*

with the neophonetic alternation or divergence t_o || t_i and the embryonic alternation $e[t_o]$ || $e[t_i]$.

3) **ple_ot_o–o–* | *ple_it_i–e–*

with two divergences, t_o || t_i and e_o || e_i,

or **ple_ot–* | **ple_it'–*

with the traditional alternation $t \parallel t'$
and the divergence $e_0 \parallel e_1$.

This period was marked by a gradual accumulation of anthropophonic tendencies. It was also a period of individual oscillations, when an individual speaker, following earlier usage, might retain the alternation *plet– || plet'–*, while another speaker would yield to the strong anthropophonic tendencies and introduce a new alternation *plot– || plet'–* into his speech. Moreover, the same individual might use *plet–* and *plot–* interchangeably, that is, *plet– || plet'* or *plot– || plet'*. The language of the children of the speech community had an important role in this process.

4) The established norm
$$*plot– \parallel *plet'–$$
$$(\rightrightarrows plot– \parallel pleć–)$$
with the paleophonetic or traditional alternations $t \parallel t'$ ($\rightrightarrows t \parallel ć$), $o \parallel e$, and the embryonic alternation $l[o] \parallel l[e]$.

5) The state of conflict between a feeling for the unity of the morpheme and the impression made by its outer form. One consequence of this is the tendency to eliminate external differences and unify the phonetic form of a morpheme which is felt to be a psychological unit, or else to utilize the phonetic differences for psychological purposes, so that phonetic divergence comes to be associated with psychological divergence.

In the case we are discussing, the alternation $t \parallel ć$ is associated with certain verb forms, *plot–ę, plot–ą | pleci–e | pleci–esz, pleci–emy, pleci–ecie*; the other alternation $o \parallel e$ is also to some extent associated with the psychological alternation of verb forms, but it is psychologically much weaker, leading to analogical formations such as *plete, pleto* instead of *plote, ploto (plotę, plotą)*.

Let us consider more closely the history of the different alternations in the morphemes *plot– | pleć–*.

Let us take first the alternation

$$t \parallel ć.$$

In the first stage this was an embryonic alternation $t[o] \parallel t[e]$; then it became a divergence $t[o] \parallel t_i[e]$; in the third stage it became a paleophonetic alternation $t \parallel t_i \rightrightarrows t \parallel t'$ (t_i denotes a t with palatalization caused by a following palatal phoneme, while t' is the same phoneme t with concomitant independent palatality). In the fourth stage palatalization increases, so that finally the original phoneme splits in two, $t \parallel t'$, and eventually t' becomes $\acute{c}$. In the fifth stage the traditional alternation $t \parallel t' \rightrightarrows t \parallel \acute{c}$) becomes a correlation, and has remained so until the present.

Now let us take the alternation

$$o \parallel e.$$

In the first stage it was merely embryonic and remained so in the second stage. In the third stage it became a divergence, i.e., $e[t] \parallel e[t_i] \rightrightarrows o[t] \parallel e[t']$. In the fourth stage this divergence became a paleophonetic or traditional alternation. Finally, in either the fourth or the fifth stage, the alternation $o \parallel e$ became psychophonetic, i.e., a correlation; today, however, it seems to have retreated, so to speak, to the status of a traditional alternation which, as a result of the tendency to level the phonetic form of identical or etymologically closely related morphemes, is gradually being eliminated.

As for the embryonic alternation

$$l[o] \parallel l[e]$$

this appeared in the third or fourth stage, but has remained embryonic.

Many other examples could be cited to illustrate this gradual development.

We can make two general conclusions from our study of these alternations:

a) first we can give a survey of the genetic development of alternations in the history of a particular language;

b) then we can examine how this process is implemented in the language of individual speakers of a given speech community, especially in the language of children.

I. Historical Sequence of Various Alternations in the National Language (the Language of a Speech Community).

All alternations owe their origin to a splitting of a unity into variety as a result of special circumstances and general causes.

The original cause or impulse of any alternation will always be found in the various anthropophonic conditions in which an originally unified phoneme is bound to appear.

As a consequence of anthropophonic differences, the emerging embryonic distinctions of a phoneme give rise to distinctions which are minimal both in terms of their own objectively observed magnitude and in terms of the impression of them perceived by members of the speech community; and as is well known, the greater or lesser force of the observable image depends on the force of the perceived impression.

Later in the historical succession, the minimal distinctions cease to be minimal; they increase, become intensified and apparent to the naked eye.

This increase of distinctions is first brought about by the same conditions which provided the first impulse for the development of minimal distinctions; but it lasts only a limited period of time, for the phonemes which have now been endowed with new properties begin to change spontaneously in a certain direction. Thus, originally combinatorial changes are replaced by later spontaneous changes, and a conditioned neophonetic alternation or divergence becomes an anthropophonically independent, paleophonetic, traditional alternation.

However, in addition to this possibility of development, i.e., the possibility of increase and ultimate independence of the embryonic minimal distinctions which are at first due to the role of the environment, there also exists another possibility, the possibility of the disappearance of minimal distinctions, namely at a point when the conditions responsible for these distinctions cease to operate.

Thus, for the elimination of neophonetic alternations, irrespective of whether they are embryonic or already plainly divergent, it is sufficient that there no longer be a causal relationship between the anthropophonic modifications of the given phoneme and the conditions responsible for them. Subsequently, however, a neophonetic alternation can be eliminated in either of two ways:

1) the anthropophonic distinctions between the alternating variants of a given proto-phoneme (*Urphonem*) are totally dependent on the influence of the environment, owing to anthropophonic factors, but by themselves they lack individual traits and are committed to memory neither by way of tradition nor through linguistic intercourse in general;

2) or else, in addition to dependence on the anthropophonic environment, the new features developing in this manner acquire a sort of individual independence and *eo ipso* are transmitted by tradition and linguistic intercourse in general. The phoneme in

question is subject to such a strong anthropophonetic influence that the new features which are thus being formed force themselves upon our perception as independent and autonomous.

1) In the first case anthropophonic variants (variations, modifications) of the phonemes disappear along with the loss of the functional dependence, and the embryonic variants return to a state of absolute identity. When the causes are eliminated their results, too, disappear.

2) In the second case the loss of dependence on anthropophonic conditions does not entail the loss of the features which have been acquired by way of anthropophonic adaptation; on the contrary, having ceased to be functionally dependent, the new features become individualized and autonomous; as such they are capable of further strengthening and growth and are able to impress themselves ever more strongly on the memory of the speakers. In this way the properties of the phonemes which are acquired by way of anthropophonic adaptation become individual, independent properties of a given phonetic segment of a given morpeme in a given word.

This unconscious remembering of individual features, insofar as it affects etymologically related morphemes, provides the point of transition between the category of divergents and that of traditional alternations.

Thus we enter the field of traditional alternations, which are maintained by force of linguistic intercourse between the members of a given speech community. However, although tradition is a force capable of preserving alternational distinctions inherited from earlier generations, it is not sufficient to endow these distinctions with a causal relationship to serve for the expression of specific needs. But it is precisely in terms of these needs that the individual speaker, and eventually the entire speech community becomes aware of the lack (absence) of a *raison d'être* (for the distinctions) and this awareness cannot but lead to a conflict with tradition.

Nevertheless, the distinctions between phonemic alternants which have already lost their *raison d'être* can be retained for two reasons:

1) one, psychological—when individually unmotivated distinctions are committed to memory not as types, but precisely because of their specific, individual character. This is especially true of frequently used, everyday verbs such as *be, eat, know, give* . . . , nouns

like *father, mother . . . , eyes, ears, hands, feet . . .* , pronouns like *I, you . . .* ;

2) another, sociological—when the preservation of individually unmotivated distinctions facilitates communication between members of the same and different generations. Here tradition is an important factor of conservatism in maintaining the cohesion of a given speech community.

However, there may arise an individual need to liquidate distinctions that are motivated neither anthropophonically nor psychologically, i.e., alternations that are neither divergences nor correlations; superfluous traditional distinctions may be eliminated in one of three ways:

1) The feeling for an etymological connection between the morphemes containing the alternating phonemes may bring about a phonetic assimilation (leveling) of their form by generalizing one of their variants. For example, in Polish

po–syl–ać | *po–sel* $\Rightarrow$ *po–sel–ać* | *po–sel*
od–dych–ać | *od–dêch* $\Rightarrow$ *od–dech–ać* (dial.) | *od–dech*

glech–nąć | *gluch–y* $\Rightarrow$ *gluch–nąć* | *gluch–y*
dzwęk | *dzwięcz–eć* $\Rightarrow$ *dzwięk* | *dźwięcz–eć*

and in Russian, on the contrary,

zvuk | *zvjačát'* $\Rightarrow$ *zvuk* | *zvučát'*.
Another example of partial leveling in Polish is:

u–biór	*u–bier–ać*		*u–bór*	*u–bier–ać*
u–bior–u		$\Leftarrow$	*u–bor–u*	
z–biór	*z–bier–ać*		*z–bór*	*z–bier–ać*
z–bior–u			*ż–bor–u*	

Compare further *z–bór, po–bór, na–bór, wy–bór . . . , –bor–u. . . .*

2) The feeling for the etymological connection of the words in which the morphemes containing the alternating phonemes occur is lost, causing lexical differentiation between words that were previously felt to be etymologically related; this differentiation, however, enriches the vocabulary of a given language; e.g.:

Polish *częś–ć*⟩⟨*kąsa–ć, kęs;* 'Russian *čas–t'*⟩⟨*kus–át'*,
       "   *po–czą–tek, –czyn–ać, –czn–ę* ⟩⟨ *koni–ec;*
             Russian *na–čá–lo* ⟩⟨ *kon–éc;*
    "   *po–kój* ⟩⟨ *spo–czy–wać;*

    "   *bod–e*)(*bad–am;*
    "   *wierci–eć*)(*wart–ki*)(*wars–twa*)(*wrzeci–ono*)(*wrot–a*
)(*po–wrót, po–wrot–u;*
    "   *wodz–ić*)(*wad–a;*
    "   *po–czet*)(*cześ–ć*)(*czyt–ać*)(*za–c–ny;*
    "   *ciag–nąć*)(*tęg–i*)(*ws-tąż–ka.*

Even *jes–* (*jes–t. . .*))(*s–(s–ą)* or *chodz–ić*)(*szed–ł, sz–ła* are now
phonetically speaking two separate roots which maintain their connection only through their semasiological association.

The complexity of alternating relations of a given morpheme
facilitates its mixing with morphemes, its attraction to a different
class of morphemes. Pertinent Polish examples are:

od–po–czn–ę | *od–po–czą–ć* | *od–po–czyn–ek* . . . from *od–po–*
czy–nę | *od–po–czy–ną–ć* | *od–po–czyn–ek,* and attracted, at least
morphophonemically, to the class of *za–czn–ę, po–czn–ę* | *–cza–ć* |
–czyn–ać | *za–czyn–, roz–czyn–* . . .

rzn–ąć | *rzn–ę* | *–rzyn–ać,* from *řz–nąć* (*rz–nąć*) | *řz–ne* | *rzez–ać*
(⇐ *rzaz–ać*), drawn into an alternation with *žą–ć* ⇒ *žn–ąć* | *žnę* |
žyn–ać.

3) The third way of eliminating unmotivated alternations is the
utilization of these alternations for psychological purposes, that is,
for the association of phonetic differences (nuances) with morphological or semasiological ones. This is the source of *psychophonetic
alternations,* or *correlations,* which every member of a given speech
community is bound to acquire by his own mental effort through
accumulating and generalizing individual associations.

Regardless of the subjective feeling of the speaker, traditional
alternations may regularly occur in certain types of forms which
are semasiologically distinct; e.g., Polish:

nog–a, ręk–a | *nóž–ka, rącz–ka* . . . ;
pi–ć, gni–ć | *poj–ić, gnoj–ić* . . . ;
tok–, bok– | *tocz–yć, bocz–yć sie* . . . ;
po–mog–ę, chodz–ę, mocz–ę, robi–ę | *po–mag–am, chadz–am,*
    macz–am, rabi–am . . . ;
gniot–ę, miotę | *gniat–am, miat–am* . . . ;
sł–ać, tk–ać | *sył–ać, tyk–ać* . . . ;
u–br–ać, wy–pr–ać | *u–bier–ać, wy–pier–ać* . . . ;
u–mrz–eć, wy–prz–eć, wy–trz–eć | *u–mier–ać, wy–pier–ać, wy–*
    cier–ać. . . .

However, if the speaker becomes aware of a constant relationship, a fixed association between the phonetic form of such words and their meaning, then the traditional alternation *eo ipso* becomes a correlation, and the native speaker acquires a richer repertory of psychophonetic devices for the expression of morphological and semasiological distinctions.

But despite repeated efforts to eliminate irrational, i.e., neither anthropophonically nor psychologically motivated phonetic distinctions, there can always remain a considerable substratum of distinctions which do not affect the semantic relationship between the individual variants, i.e., distinctions constituting the paleophonetic or traditional alternations, such as are found in (Polish):

sen | snu; dzień | dni–a; wiedzi–e | wiod–ę | wiód–ł | wieś–ć |
wy–wod–u | wy–wód | wodz–ę | wodz–i | wódź | wódz . . . ;
ś–mier–ć | mar–twy | –mor–u | –mór | u–mier–a . . . ; br–ać |
–bier–ać | bierz–e | wy–bor–u | wy–bór | wy–borz–e . . . ;
wrzeci–ono | po–wrot–u | po–wrót | wróc–ę | wróc–i | wrac–a |
wierc–i | wart–ki. . . .

This substratum constantly decreases as a result of the above-mentioned changes in three directions; on the other hand, it constantly increases at the expense of former divergences, as well as of former correlations.

The tendency to eliminate distinctions lacking individual motivation (causality) affects alternations of both divergent and correlative origin. In the latter case, i.e., when the previously live psychophonetic connection disappears, only the first two ways of eliminating the alternation manifest themselves: either the morphemes assimiliate (level, make uniform) their phonetic form or the feeling for the etymological relationship of the words and morphemes containing the alternating phonemes is lost. The third way, i.e., the restoration of the psychophonetic character of traditional alternations of correlative origin, is a very rare phenomenon altogether.

Thus, traditional alternations can be classified according to their origin as:

1) *paleophonetic alternations,* which have lost their anthropophonetic causality ⟨motivation⟩;

2) *paleopsychological alternations* which have lost their psychophonetic causality ⟨motivation⟩.

In time both of these alternations either can be eliminated by analogical leveling of the constituent phonemes (either $x' \mid\mid x'' \Rightarrow x' \mid\mid x'$ or $x' \mid\mid x'' \Rightarrow x'' \mid\mid x''$) or can lose their alternational character altogether when what were at first phonetic variants of one basic morpheme split into two morphemes which are no longer felt to be related, so that the alternations become merely residual (rudimentary):

$$(x' \mid\mid x'' \Rightarrow x' \, \rangle\langle \, x'').$$

Since we are dealing with the psychological value of phonetic phenomena, and the feeling for this value ebbs and wanes with the individual characteristics of all the members of a given speech community, we must assume a whole scale of indeterminate transitional states which are reminiscent of the flickering of a flame about to die out.

In this gamut of countless indeterminate transitional states three classes of alternations stand out conspicuously, and have been discussed in Chapters III, IV, and V:

traditional alternations which are motivated purely socially (being due only to tradition and communication); these alternations are either paleophonetic or paleopsychological (but the latter are likewise ultimately of a paleophonetic origin; Cf. Chapter V);

neophonetic alternations, or *divergences,* which have an individual anthropophonic motivation absent in the other two classes (Cf. Chapter III);

psychophonetic alternations, or *correlations,* having an (individual) psychological motivation absent in the other two classes (Cf. Chapter IV).

From the viewpoint of their historical development these classes can be presented in the following sequence:

1) *divergences,* characterized by a live physiological process and individual anthropophonic relationship, preserving the original motivation of all alternations $\langle . . . \rangle$ (examples: $d \mid\mid t$ in *wod–a | wód–ka*, $\acute{s} \mid\mid \dot{z}$ in *pros–ić | proź–ba*, $i_2(y) \mid\mid i_1(i)$ in *słom–y | ziem–i*);

2) *paleophonetic,* or *traditional alternations,* characterized by active social factors, with loss of the originally anthropophonic motivation of the alternations$\langle . . . \rangle$ (Examples: $p \mid\mid p'$, $t \mid\mid \acute{c}$, $ar \mid\mid er$ in *na–parst–ek | pierśći–eń*, $ł \mid\mid l$, $o \mid\mid e$ in *czoł–o | czel–e*);

3) *correlations* characterized by vitality of the psychological factor, individual psychological correlation, secondarily developed

psychological motivation ⟨. . .⟩ (Examples: *o* ‖ *a* in *chodz–ić* | *chadz–ać, trwoż–yć* / *trważ–ać, s* ‖ *ch* in *włos* | *włoch, klus–ki* | *kluch–y*).

From the standpoint of space, i.e., of place of origin, the traditional alternations fall into two classes:

a) *native formations* developed within a given speech community, and

b) *foreign formations* adopted from another speech community by interlingual oral communication or through writing.

From the viewpoint of transition from an earlier to a later state, the traditional alternations in turn form two classes:

a) those that developed directly from *divergences,* and

b) those which are a continuation of *correlations,* and have switched to the category of traditional alternations.

In the former alternations we can, in turn, distinguish three classes:

a) those directly derived from divergences;

b) those which have passed through only two stages of alternational evolution—that of divergences and that of traditional alternations; and

c) those which have passed through four stages of evolution before their disappearance—divergences, traditional alternations, correlations related to tradition, and purely traditional alternations.

In the correlations we can distinguish two principal *levels of psychological intensity*:

a higher level which involves an *active and creative association of the phonetic variants with psychological differences (nuances),* and which makes possible the formation of new alternating pairs on the model of an existing productive type (for example, the alternation *o* ‖ *a* in Polish verb stems: *nos–i–ć* | *nasz–ć*); and

a lower level on which the association between the phonetic variants and psychological differences, though present, is not strong enough to create new analogical formations; this is then the level of *psychophonetic weakness and passivity* (for example, *i* ‖*oj* in *pi–ć, gni–ć* | *poj–ić, gnoj–ić* . . .).

Between these two levels there is a whole range of intermediate stages.

We have shown above that the traditional character of simple traditional alternations always finds itself in conflict with the tendency to eliminate phonetic distinctions which are not motivated physiologically or psychologically, and that when these individual tendencies prevail, the traditional alternations assume a psychophonetic character and become correlations, or else there is phonetic leveling of the alternating pair.

Similar conflicts can also develop in the case of correlations. For example, in the Russian correlations $k \parallel č$ in verbs such as *pekú | pečóš, tolkú | tolčóš* . . . we can detect a conflict which leads ultimately to the substitution of the $k \parallel č$ correlation by a new $k \parallel k'$ correlation (*pekú | pek'óš, tolkú | tolk'óš* . . .).

If we were to regard the alternating phonemes $k \parallel č$ as indivisible entities, we would have to deny the presence of any conflict and expect the correlation $k \parallel č$ which forms a closed unity to remain without change until its psychophonetic character is finally replaced by a purely traditional one. However, if we consider the articulatory components of the phonemes and the verbal type to which they belong, the conclusion imposes itself that the correlation $k \parallel č$ disrupts the harmony of the ⟨verbal⟩ type and that only the alternation $k \parallel k'$ does it justice, since it is in full agreement with such other partial alternations as $b \parallel b'$ (*grebú | greb'ot*), $d \parallel d'$ (*vedú | ved'ót*), $s \parallel ś$ (*nesú | nes'ót*), etc., which can be subsumed under the general formula

$$P\emptyset \parallel PY$$

(where $P\emptyset$ designates the absence of palatalization, and PY the presence of palatalization in the consonant).

This generalization of Russian correlations in the above-mentioned verb type is taking place at present in various Russian dialects. The same phenomenon occurred at a much earlier time, for example, in possessive adjectives which have come to serve primarily as patronymics and family names, such as *súkin syn, Súk–in, Sobák–in, Kóšk–in, Sipjág–in, Múx–in* . . . ; the old correlation $k \parallel č, g \parallel ž, x \parallel š$ (*súk–a | suč–in, sipjág–a | sipjaž–in, múx–a | múš–in* . . .) has been replaced by the new correlation $k | k', g | g', x | x'$ on the model of a large number of partial alternations of the same general type, $b \parallel b', d \parallel d', s \parallel ś$ (*rýb–a | Rýb–in, Marúd–a | Marúd–in, pláks–a | Pláks–in* . . .).

Thus we see how correlations can grow, how partial correlations can be absorbed by more general ones, and how the generalization of correlations may make them more efficacious and supple.

However, as is the case with all linguistic forms, the alternations too must ultimately be weakened and disappear, no matter how transparent and productive [*mächtig*] they may be at first. Having absorbed a series of partial correlations and having reached the highest degree of strength and clarity, the general alternations in time lose their force and psychophonetic character, become plain traditional alternations, and are finally lost in the mass of unproductive extinguished alternations.

II. The Development of Alternations in Individual Language, especially in that of Children

Language can not be inherited; only the faculty of speech and the tendencies toward a certain direction of changes incipient in the structure of the language are inherited. Heredity is a biological factor, while the language of any individual develops through social intercourse. Nevertheless, we must fall back on heredity in order to explain the persistence of repeated historical changes.

The most radical changes take place in the language of children. The most far-reaching are phonetic changes and morphological leveling. Thereafter the children gradually acquire the speech habits of the adult members of the community, but a certain number of changes inherited from children's language may remain in their individual speech, and, more importantly, the tendencies toward such changes, even if they arise again spontaneously in later generations, become a part of their inheritance. Insofar as they accrue in successive generations, these changes eventually become ingrained in the language.

In alternations we are dealing first of all with the inherited accumulation of phonetic tendencies and with their gradual intensification.

Since every individual acquires on his own the language of his speech community, he necessarily also acquires the alternations by himself.

During the gradual acquisition of his native language, every child proceeds through several stages: at first he does not understand anything; then he begins to understand the language of his environment, although he is still unable to speak, i.e., he is still in a state of audition and passive linguistic perception; finally, he begins to speak, adding to audition and perception the factor of phonation. Linguistic cerebration or thinking, once set in motion,

208

now finds a solid foundation in the acquisition of individual language.

To be sure, in the earliest stages of this process, when the child is just beginning to understand the language of his environment, there can be no question of alternations. Alternations develop only later. But in any case we can regard pairs of phonemes which enter into words and morphemes understood by the child, and which form alternational pairs in the language of his environment, as *embryonic*, or *germinal* (incipient) in the speech of the child.

At this stage, when the child has not yet begun to talk but is already aware of the properties of the native language and can understand it within certain limits, that is, when the child has reached the state of advanced audition and perception, but without phonation, there naturally cannot be any question of neophonetic alternations or divergences, since these depend on *individual* pronunciation. Whether there also develop ⟨at this time⟩ correlations or psychophonetic alternations depends on the personality of the given child, or his psychological capacity and agility. In any case, there are no correlations in the very first stages of this development; they emerge only by way of associations from traditional alternations. The simple traditional alternations apparently exist in children's speech in the stage of audition and perception; the ability to distinguish phonetic modifications (variants) of morphemes which are felt to be etymologically related then develops spontaneously. That is why the clear distinctions between divergents or neophonetic alternants also leave a definite imprint on the memory by dint of their own traditional quality. Thus, for example, before the child begins to distinguish in his own pronunciation such a divergence as $d \parallel t$ in Polish *broda | bródka*, he has already observed the anthropophonic difference in the pronunciation of the two phonemes. And this is how the element of tradition becomes added to the neophonetic alternations or divergences⟨. . .⟩.

When the child begins to talk, imitating the speech of his environment, he also imitates the alternations, although the neophonetic alternations or divergences may develop independently, inasmuch as they are determined on the one hand by the shape of the speech organs and on the other hand by inherited tendencies. This allows for wide individual variations: some children develop divergences to a much greater degree than others. However, the tendency to develop new divergences is, on the whole, much more typical of the speech of children than that of adults, whose language represents the linguistic norm. What is only embryonic in the latter can become apparent and palpable in the speech of children. The various conditions implicit in the combinations of a single phoneme quickly yield definite results here when the phoneme splits into two or more phonemes; the anthropophonic causes in the language of children are far more prominent than in that of adults, and their effects are, consequently, more immediate.

In short, as in the realm of phonology and morphology, children anticipate the normal development of language in the area of alternations.

At any rate, children's speech has far more neophonetic alternations or divergences and fewer correlations or psychophonetic alternations than the normal language of a given speech community. However, we cannot ignore one correlation which is highly developed in children's speech: the alternation of palatal with nonpalatal consonants for the expression of endearment (*d'* || *d*, *ś* || *s*, *l'* || *ł* . . .).

As children's language comes to resemble that of adults, the child regresses, so to speak, in the field of alternations; he loses the most innovative variants (modifications) and replaces the stage of transparent divergence with that of an embryonic alternation.

Now that we have examined, although only in rough outline, the development and transformation of various types of alternation in the language of children, we shall briefly and schematically present in tables and formulas *the historical sequence of the various stages of alternation, and the transition from one stage to another in the language of an entire speech community.*

I. Divergences encompass the whole language, but arise spontaneously, through anthropophonic adaptation. Every period in the history of a language is characterized by its own divergences, although there are some which are external and universal.

II. Correlations develop from traditional alternations.

III. Traditional alternations develop either from divergences in the native language or from traditional alternations of foreign origin.

Monolingual (native) divergences	Foreign alternations
↓	
Traditional alternations	
↓	↓
either become correlations	or else remain traditional alternations
↓	↓
these either remain correlations	or else cease to be correlations and again become traditional alternations

II–III. Phonemes, which express traditional alternations, whether merely traditional or traditional-psychophonetic (correlations), must at the same time fulfill the requirements of divergences or anthropophonic alternations of the particular period. ⟨. . .⟩

While the alternations, after completing a certain evolutionary cycle finally disappear, the sources for new alternations never do. Consequently, there is an unending process of reconstruction of alternational relationships resulting in the accumulation of new layers of alternations.

Some kind of anthropophonic change is always taking place at every stage of the language, some kind of adaptation of the phonemes to anthropophonic conditions. The effects of these adaptations are transmitted by tradition from one generation to another, until they are, in turn, replaced by new changes.

NOTES

1. Cf. Brugmann's review (*Literar. Centralblatt*, 1882, No. 12, p. 401), where in any case Brugmann erroneously states that the author defines as "phonetic interchange" what is usually called "phonetic transformation" or "phonetic change."

2. However, at that time I understood phoneme to mean something different than now; i.e., I interpreted it as the sum of the phonetic properties representing an indivisible unit within either a single language or a group of languages.

(The proposal to use the term "phoneme" instead of "sound" came from Kruszewski.)

3. In the case of this alternation, there is a striking parallelism between *šč* and *žd*. Why don't we have *št* like *žd*, or *ždž* like *šč?* It is not too difficult to answer this. In the Old Church Slavonic documents there was an abbreviated symbol ɰ instead of ⁄. This sign, which had the form of a single letter, was pronounced like *šč* in words of Russian origin that were not influenced by Church Slavonic such as *pušč–ú, i–ščet, pišč–it*. . . . It was then quite natural for this pronunciation to spread as well to words with the letter ɰ, borrowed directly from Church Slavonic texts such as *osveščát', prosveščénie, sovraščát', prekraščát', pišča, umerščvljat'* . . . , and not *"osveštát'," "prosvešténie,"* although this second pronunciation, with *št*, was characteristic of Old Church Slavonic itself. The matter stands somewhat differently with *žd*. The Church Slavonic texts use no abbreviated sign for *žd* of the type ɰ in place of ⁄, and therefore it did not occur to any Russian to pronounce the words *roždát', roždestvó, ograždát', ubeždát', iždivénie, voždelénnyj* in any way other than with *žd*.

VIII

Statement of Linguistic Principles

1) There are no "phonetic laws."

2) To treat language as an "organism," and linguistics as a natural science, is a fallacy without any scientific basis.

3) Language is exclusively psychological. The existence and development of language is governed by purely psychological laws. In human speech, or language, there is not a single phenomenon which is not psychological.

4) Since language exists only in human society, the social aspect must always be considered, in addition to the psychological aspect. Linguistics must be founded not only on the psychology of the individual, but also on sociology (which, unfortunately, has not yet been developed well enough to afford any fruitful conclusions).

5) The laws of the life and development of language have not been discovered yet, but they can be arrived at only through careful inductive research. Present-day linguistics is well on the way toward this goal.

6) The cause, the impulse for all linguistic change, is a tendency toward convenience, toward a minimum of effort in three areas of linguistic activity: in pronunciation (phonation), in hearing and perception (audition), and in linguistic thought (cerebration).

7) All existing and extinct languages arose by way of mixture. Even individual speech, which originates and is formed in contact with fully developed individuals, is the product of mixture and interaction.

8) Many characteristics of historically formed languages can be explained if we assume the previous occurrence of mixture of the peoples and languages in question.

9) The history of language is a process of gradual "humaniza-

tion," that is, a growing departure from the linguistic state of animals of a higher order.

10) The historical evolution of the morphology of a language consists in the alternate shifting of emphasis from the end of the word to its beginning, and vice versa. The life of words and sentences can be compared to a *perpetuum mobile* consisting of constantly oscillating weights which at the same time continuously move in a certain direction.

11) There is no immobility in language. The assumption of invariable roots contained in the same, invariable stems of declension and conjugation, etc., in all related languages is a scholarly invention, a fiction, and at the same time, a hindrance to objective research. In language, as in nature in general, everything moves, everything is alive and changing. Rest, standstill, stagnation are seeming phenomena; they are but special cases of movement with minimum change. The statics of language is only a special case of its dynamics or, rather, its kinetics.

12) In language there is an unending process of shifting the place of contact of the ultimate, no longer divisible linguistic units. A given linguistic unit is either expanded at the expense of another, or it cedes a part of its structure to another unit. One unit disappears and another is formed.

13) The dictum *ex nihilo nil fit* finds complete confirmation in linguistics. Linguistic units seemingly originating in nothing (e.g., the phonemes or "sounds," the morphemes) are created from material already at hand which only acquires new form.

14) The object of investigation must be treated as it is, without forcing upon it alien categories.

15) In linguistics, perhaps even more than in history, one must adhere strictly to the requirements of geography and chronology.

16) "The monosyllabism of roots" in the Indo-European languages is an unproven dogma.

17) "Roots" are by no means the monopoly of any one period of development of a language. Every language has roots. New roots can be created endlessly, at any time.

18) For linguistics, as a science dealing with generalizations, the study of living, existing languages is much more important than that of languages which have disappeared and can be reconstructed only on the basis of written records. Only the biologist (zoologist or botanist) who has thoroughly studied living flora and fauna can

undertake the study of paleontological remains. Only the linguist who has thoroughly studied a living language can venture to make assumptions about the characteristics of dead languages. The study of living languages must precede the study of extinct languages.

19) According to the doctrine now accepted by Darwinian biologists, the embryo reflects on a smaller scale the changes and transformations of the entire species. Just the opposite takes place in the linguistic development of the child. The child in no way repeats on a smaller scale the linguistic development of an entire nation; on the contrary, he reaches into the future, anticipating in his speech the future state of the national language, and falls back, so to speak, only later, conforming more and more to the language of his environment.

20) The impetus for essential changes in the national language come principally from the language of children. Chidren introduce certain substantial changes in pronunciation and morphological structure. Later they learn to speak "correctly," on the model of their environment, but the original tendencies leave their traces. The children of these children inherit a disposition toward similar changes, toward the future state of the language, reiterating on their part the same changes. They also subsequently master the linguistic norm of the environment, but the inclination to change is transmitted with ever greater force to the following generations. The accumulation of such traces over a number of generations leads, finally, to definitive changes in the language.

21) Mankind, as an aggregate of individuals endowed with language, has emerged at various times in various places. The beginning of language is not monogenetic, but polygenetic.

22) In investigating language we must strictly distinguish between development and history. History consists in the succession of homogeneous, but different, phenomena. Development consists in the continuity of essential, and not merely phenomenological (concerning only the phenomenon) changes. Development is characteristic of individual language; history, of collective language.

I X

On the Mixed Character of All Languages

... THE USUAL CONCEPTION of a "comparative grammar of the Slavic languages" or a "comparative grammar of the Indo-European languages" is based on the assumption that languages are pure, that the history of languages is an uninterrupted and undisturbed development of an original system in various directions without the interference of foreign languages. Fundamental linguistic studies, such as the *Grundriss der vergleichenden Grammatik* by Brugmann and Delbrück, give such an impression in fact by working with several dozens of "roots" or groups of etymologically related words. Yet it is sufficient to consult any dictionary of such a supposedly pure language as Indo-European or Slavic to convince oneself that it contains a far larger number of assimilated words or words of obscure or unclear origin than words suitable for "comparative grammar" in the current sense of the word. The latter, indeed, constitute a negligible number, if we consider that ordinary "comparative grammars" do not cover entire languages, do not give an insight into the entire structure of the languages in question. Many people, however, seem to be unaware of this, treating the thesis of the absolute purity of language as a linguistic dogma. They admit, it is true, the possibility of foreign elements being borrowed, but at the same time add that the basic character of a given language remains unchanged. Thus, for example, they do not deny that many Romance elements have entered English, but they insist that all these foreign elements have been completely assimilated without in the least affecting the Germanic base of the language. And once such an allegation is made by an authoritative scholar, it is bound to be repeated by a whole crowd of imitators.

It is well known that teachings drawn from foreign grammars

which have been obsolete even within their own areas have hampered the development of original but true-to-fact views on the nature of particular languages.

How a country's "public opinion" may be offended by any attempt to emancipate a given science from prevailing views, from prejudice and preconceived ideas, can be shown by an example from the history of Russian grammar. Thirty-five years ago, N. P. Nekrasov attempted to treat the Russian verb in an independent fashion (in his *O značenii form russkogo glagola,* St. Petersburg, 1865). He was shouted down and bitterly attacked. How dare he, a Russian, look with his own eyes at the facts of the Russian language and see in it what actually exists instead of what is supposed to exist according to the stereotypes of medieval Latin grammars! This peculiar kind of "Westernism" was inspired by the fear that the acceptance of Nekrasov's teaching would force one to think and, as is known, "denken ist schwer und gefährlich!" It is all right to go on repeating the ideas of others, but, for goodness' sake, let us not stir things up!

Do not think, however, gentlemen, that my remark is intended to champion the ideas of the Slavophile imitators of those German philosophers who claimed special originality for the Russian or Slavic mind. On the contrary, I do not recognize any national logic, but only identical laws of thought for all mankind. There is no European, American, French, English, German, Russian, or Polish science—there is only one science, common to all men. For the same reason I believe that Western European scholars have no monopoly on scientific discoveries and generalizations, that a Russian or Pole may also have original ideas, and that there is therefore no need to slavishly follow so-called "European science" and to hold to its tenets blindly and uncritically.

Each of us has a duty to look with his own eyes. And if we examine the question of the mixing or non-mixing of languages with our own eyes, we will have to admit that no language is pure or unmixed.

Mixing, be it of a physical or psychological nature, is the beginning of all life. Mixing takes place in the development of any individual language beginning in early childhood. The child is influenced by his parents and other persons of his immediate milieu. The language of any of these persons is surely, even if negligibly, different from the language of other persons, and the various individual languages shape the language of the child who will almost invariably select those linguistic peculiarities which he can master more readily and with less effort.

For example, if in a Russian or Polish family, at least one person pronounces ŭ instead of ł, or a velar r instead of an apical r, the children of this family will, in the majority of cases, tend to make the same sound substitution, pronouncing ŭa instead of ła, and ra (with a velar r) instead of ra (with an apical r).

Marriage produces mixed family languages, and the contact of tribes and nations leads to interaction and mixing of dialects and, on a wider scale, to mixing of linguistic groups and of tribal and national languages.

Nations and tribes live in close proximity or are interspersed. Along the boundaries of tribal and national languages, multilingualism inevitably arises, and with it, mixed languages.

Nomadic life, military campaigns and war service, abduction of foreign women and slaves, trade, scientific exchange, etc.,—all these factors contribute to the mixing of languages.

We could easily hypothesize that at a certain time the Slavs of Eastern Europe were scattered among the Finns (to a certain extent this is still the case even now); in other parts of Europe the Finns mixed with Germanic and Lithuanian tribes; in Central Europe Slavs lived among Germans; Celts, who were scattered over almost all Europe and in Asia Minor, underwent the influence of peoples of different origin who, in turn, influenced their languages; the Aryans of Eastern India were scattered among peoples of Dravidian origin; in Western Europe, tribes related to the modern Basques were constantly in contact with Celtic, Romance, and other tribes; the language of the nomadic Gypsies, who are still nomads, absorbed all kinds of foreign elements; the Jews, who have lived among other peoples, have felt the impact of the languages of their fellow citizens and have influenced their languages to a greater or lesser extent.

But this interaction and mixing of languages is determined not only geographically and territorially, but also chronologically. An old language used as a language of the church, of ritual or in traditional formulas and expressions, may influence the living language of a given period which in turn undergoes the influence of the latter. It is enough to think of the interaction between modern

Latin and the Romance languages, or between the varieties of Church Slavonic and the modern South and East Slavic languages.

The formation of a mixed language, that is, of a language whose elements prevail over another language, though not without being seriously modified by the language spoken by the linguistically assimilated people, can in some cases be documented by historical records. Thus, for example, Pastor Bielenstein[1] was able to trace the formation of Latvian, a language of the Baltic or Aistian branch of the Indo-European languages, and to show the indelible traces which Finnish has left in its phonetics, morphology, etc.

The Armenian language is, for a variety of reasons, justly treated as one of the Indo-European languages, but there are good reasons (considerations of its basic structure, as well as its peculiarities) why it should be grouped also with the Turco-Tatar or Uralo-Altaic or some such closely related group of languages. For example, external, physical, and spatial relations are in the Armenian declension expressed in the Tatar manner (in the *locative, ablative,* and *instrumental* cases), while social relations continue to be expressed through Indo-European forms (in the *genitive, dative,* and *accusative*). The Armenian suffix of the plural is obviously not of Indo-European origin, but a borrowing, if not from Tatar, at least from some other language. The loss of gender distinctions and the lack of sexualization of reality must be due to "foreign," non-Indo-European influence. The question of the ethnic origin of the Armenians is even more complicated by the fact that the Armenians have historically mingled with the Jews and other Semites who had shared their habitat with Caucausian, and especially Georgian peoples whose languages must have affected to a noticeable degree the character of the Armenian language.

The influence of foreign peoples upon the development of the Romance languages from vulgar Latin dialects can likewise be traced historically.

In recent times, mixed dialects have been formed in border areas where Chinese have come into contact with Europeans. Such are, among others, the *Kjaxta* or *Majmak* dialect of Russian-Chinese and the international dialects of English-Chinese and Portuguese-Chinese.[2] Recent decades have witnessed the creation of artificial mixed languages which are to serve as vehicles of international communication: *Volapük, Esperanto, Bolak.*

The effects of language mixing are twofold: on the one hand, they enrich a given language with elements of another, "foreign" language (with a stock of new words, new syntactic phrases, forms, pronunciation), and, on the other hand, they weaken the distinctions peculiar to the given language. They bring about a more rapid simplification and fusion of forms, the disappearance of irrational distinctions, the assimiliation of some forms to others (through the process of "analogy"), the loss of declension and its replacement by single forms with prepositions, the loss of conjugation and its replacement by single forms with prefixes of a pronominal origin and auxiliary particles, the loss of a morphologically mobile stress, etc.

In the contact and interaction of two languages that mix in a "natural way," the victory goes in each case to that language which is marked by greater simplicity and clarity. Simpler and clearer forms prevail over difficult and irrational ones. Thus, if one language has gender distinctions and the other language lacks them, the language resulting from the mixture will either lack these distinctions completely or exhibit them in a weakened form. If only one of the two interacting languages has an article, or personal possessive suffixes (that is, suffixes denoting the belonging of an object or person to another person: "my," "your," "his," "her," "our," "your," "their"), it is much more likely that the resulting mixed language will inherit this "analytic" or decentralizing feature than not.

The same can be said regarding the predominance of one of two mixing languages in their "struggle for survival": victory belongs to that language which is more easily acquired and which requires less physiological and psychological energy. Thus, for example, in localities where Roumanians live side by side with Germans or Slavs, the predominating language, the language of intertribal communication, is Roumanian; this is understandable, since Roumanian is more easily mastered by Germans and Slavs than the other way around. Similarly, because of the relative simplicity of Tartar as compared with the far more difficult Russian, the language of communication between Russian and Tartar peasants within Russia is usually Tartar. Of course, this takes place only in the "natural" course of things, in the absence of conscious interference on the part of administrative authorities and of other political and social forces which employ preventative or coercive measures.

Looking, then, at the whole Slavic linguistic world, we can find in it a considerable number of cases of language mixing. In some instances this mixing is occurring now and can be observed in *actu*; in other instances, we are faced with the results of mixing that took place a long time ago.

Right now mutual influence can be seen to take place, for example, between literary Russian and the various dialects of Great Russian and Ukrainian or varieties of Polish, with Great Russian gaining the upper hand as a result of existing peculiar conditions. Similar mutual influence takes place between Polish and Ukrainian, Polish and Czech, Polish and Slovak, Polish and Kashubian, Serbian and Bulgarian, etc. Mutual influence is also observed between the various Slavic literary languages and the territorial dialects where the respective literary languages are being used.

Several peripheral Southwest Slavic areas (mainly the "Slavic" areas of Northern and Southern Italy) are subjected to Romance influence, as are Slavic areas bordering on Roumania. Some Southwestern and Northwestern Slavs (e.g., the Lusatians and the Poles of Prussia, including the Kashubians) are subject to strong German influence. The Slavs of the Hungarian kingdom are exposed to the influence of Hungarian. Within Russia, the Slavic linguistic element is in a state of interaction with various "foreign," non-Slavic elements (Lithuanian, Latvian, Estonian, Tartar, Čuvaš,[3] etc.). In America, the speech of Poles, Czechs, Slovenes, and other Slavs is subjected to the influence of English and to gradual Anglicization.

Conversely, we can note the Slavicization of foreigners. Thus, the Russians are gradually assimilating the ethnic minorities; the Czech and Slovenes are partially assimilating the Germans; a partial, though negligible, Polonization and Russification takes place in Lithuania.

The final results of language mixing can be seen in the different parts of the German linguistic territory where Slavs have been absorbed, not however without leaving more or less clear linguistic traces in the German dialects which they have made their own. The same can be said of those parts of the Romance linguistic territory where we find descendants of Romanized Slavs.

Within the boundaries of the Russian state there are quite a few regions whose populations constitute a mixture of a "foreign" and a preponderant Slavic element. In the Northwest such Slavicized areas are the former territories of Lithuania and Estonia. The Polish cities were at one time occupied, in addition to the Jews, by settlers from various parts of Germany; now these cities are mostly Polonized, but the formerly predominant German element is of necessity reflected in the language of their present ethnically mixed populations.

With our own eyes, so to speak, we could observe the final Slovenization of several settlements of German exiles or colonists in *Krajna* and *Gorica*: in Nemški Rovt (*Deutschruth*), in Koritnica, in Stržišče, etc. As early as the first half of the 19th century, the inhabitants of these villages spoke a characteristic South German dialect (which is closely related to the dialects of Tyrol); in the 1870's, only the old people could express themselves in this dialect; their children, who were then middle-aged, could still understand this dialect, but they no longer could speak it; but the youngest generation could not even understand this language of its forefathers. The commonly used dialect at that time was a Slovenian dialect, borrowed from nearby Slovenian neighbors. The local dialect, however, preserved clear traces of the German origin of its speakers in its phonetics, morphology, and syntax. Phonetically it was so thoroughly German that at a distance it gave the impression of a German dialect. Later, of course, under the influence of the school, sermons, and communication with the adjacent "purely Slovenian" villages, this German-Slovenian dialect has more and more relinquished its German imprint, though it is unlikely to lose it completely.

In view of such historically proved cases of the influence of foreign linguistic traits on the basic structure of Slavic languages, we have the right to admit a similar influence of foreign traits in wide areas of the Slavic linguistic world. We can regard Bulgarian, Macedonian, Upper and Lower Lusatian, Great Russian, Ukrainian, Slovenian, Serbo-Croatian and other areas as being linguistically mixed. The tiny group of the *Rezija* dialects shows certain basic features that cannot be explained without admitting external, non-Slavic influence. Czech, Slovak, and Polish exhibit peculiarities which are reminiscent of the Finno-Ugric branch of languages. Among these is the fixation of stress on a certain syllable of the phonetic word (on the penultimate syllable in Polish, and on the initial syllable in Czech and Slovak), and the loss of distinction in most Polish territorial dialects between the "hushing" consonants, *š, ž, č,* and the "hissing" consonants, *s, z, c,* in favor of the latter. The original Slavic stress was morphologically mobile, and characteristic of certain morphemes, i.e., morphologically connected with significant parts of the word, and not bound to a definite syllable of the phonetic word. The mobile stress could not have disappeared spontaneously while the original structure of the Slavic word remained unchanged. The basis of this structure was a centralized and cohesive unity of the various significant parts of the word; such a structure is even now characteristic of all varieties of Czech, Slovak, and Polish. Only the impact of ethnic mixing with tribes incapable of perceiving the morphological mobility of stress could have caused the loss of this stress among the linguistic ancestors of the present-day Slovaks, Czechs, Poles, as well as of the Upper and Lower Lusatians.

The inability to pronounce "hushing" consonants (which characterizes most Polish dialects) is peculiar to the western Finns (Estonians, Suomi, etc.), but there is no doubt that in former times the Finns reached farther west, and it is most probable that some of them lived scattered amidst the Northwestern Slavs. That the Finns once lived together with the Lithuanian (Baltic, Aistian) tribes is attested by the development of the Latvians who formed a nation only in historical times, as is shown by the investigations of Bielenstein, which I mentioned above. And, in fact, the number of "hushing" consonants is much smaller in Latvian than it is in Lithuanian, whereas the "hissing" consonants prevail in the Latvian dialects and are less common in Lithuanian. The patterns of old Lithuanian stress were likewise destroyed in Latvian, evidently under the influence of the Kurs and Livonians, who are closely related to the present-day Estonians, and who were totally absorbed by the Lithuanian-Latvian tribes. The relationships of stress and quantity of vowels and syllables in the Latvian dialects are very similar to those found in the Estonian linguistic area.

In view of all the above-mentioned instances of interaction between Slavic and foreign elements, of all the completed and continuing influences of foreign dialects upon Slavic and of Slavic upon foreign dialects, we believe that the "ideal Slavic linguist" should master not only all the Slavic languages in their multifarious variety, but also all the languages that influenced or might have influenced the Slavic languages, and vice versa. Such a goal is, of course, only an ideal. I myself am quite remote from it; in the first place, I do not have perfect mastery of all Slavic languages, and in the second place, I am completely or almost completely unfamiliar with some foreign dialects that influenced or were influenced by the Slavs. But I can, at least, console myself that there is hardly a scholar who fits this ideal, that is, who knows the Slavic languages in all their variety together with all the above-mentioned foreign languages.

Realizing full well the demands of such an ideal, we shall be content with a more modest goal: we shall limit our investigation to certain phenomena of the Slavic linguistic world and examine them in their mutual relation from a scientific, primarily psychological, point of view; on the basis of this investigation we shall then attempt to arrive at conclusions of a general linguistic nature.

Thus, we shall "compare" languages "in their mutual relation." But the "comparison" and examination of languages "in their mutual relation" opens up two possible approaches.

In one approach, we can compare languages independently of their genetic (or historical) relationship. We can examine the identical features, changes, historical processes, and transformations of languages which are unrelated historically and geographically. From this viewpoint we can compare the development of the Romance languages with that of the modern Indic languages, the development of the Slavic languages with that of the Semitic languages, the development of Russian with that of Coptic, the development of English with that of Chinese, etc. Everywhere we are confronted with the question of the cause of the similarities and differences in the structure and evolution of language. This kind of linguistic comparison provides the basis for the broadest linguistic generalizations in the fields of phonetics, morphology, and semasiology (the science concerning the meaning of words and expressions).

The other approach enables us to compare languages on the basis of their historical kinship and geographic, social, and literary proximity. The comparison of historically related languages constitutes the foundation of "comparative grammar" in the current sense of the word. On it are based the comparative grammars of the Indo-European, Semitic, Uralo-Altaic (or Turco-Tatar), Germanic, Romance, Slavic, and other languages.

Less common is the comparison of languages on the basis of their geographic, social, and literary proximity, that is, the kind of comparison which takes into consideration their mutual influence in the widest sense of the word. Geographic contiguity, compact or diffuse proximity, commercial and other relations, wars, various types of cultural influence, even at a geographical and historical distance—all these provide the basis for comparative studies of two or more languages against a historical background. A most rewarding topic of study along these lines would be a comparative grammar of the Slavic and Baltic (Lithuanian-Latvian) languages as representatives of both the Indo-European and Finno-Ugric languages. Of equal interest would be comparative studies of the Slavic and Uralo-Altaic (Turco-Tartar) languages, of the West Slavic dialects and the neighboring German dialects (including the German literary language), of some Slavic languages and Hungarian, of the South Slavic languages and Roumanian, Albanian, modern Greek, and others.

Having entitled my course "Comparative grammar of the Slavic languages with relation to other Indo-European languages," I intend to present, of course, a comparison based on the posited historical, or genetic, kinship of these languages. We shall, consequently, consider not the borrowed, but the internal material as it has evolved in time in various directions along the line of historical succesion from proto-Indo-European to Common Indo-European, and from proto-Slavic to Common Slavic. Thus, we shall devote our main attention, first, to the comparison of those aspects of the Slavic languages which are considered purely Slavic with those aspects of other Indo-European languages which are considered purely Indo-European, and second, to the formulation of general linguistic conclusions on the basis of these comparisons.

N O T E S

1. *Die Grenzen des lettischen Volksstammes und der lettischen Sprache in der Gegenwart und im 13. Jahrhundert. Ein Beitrag zur ethnologischen*

Geographie und Geschichte Russlands von Dr. A. Bielenstein. (Mit einem Atlas von 7 Blättern.), St. Petersburg, 1892.

2. Through the study of mixed languages, Professor Hugo Schuchardt of Gratz has rendered a great service to science.

3. I call attention to the very interesting investigation by V. A. Bogorodickij, *Dialektologičeskie zametki, II. Nepravil'nosti russkoj reči u Čuvaš*, Kazan', 1900.

X

A Note on the Changing Character of Declensional Stems, especially on their Reduction in Favor of Endings

⟨. . .⟩ As a RESULT of well-known phonetic processes, the forms of declension and conjugation do not remain the same, but undergo changes. The changes consist chiefly in a shortening of the forms.

The question arises: do only the endings become shortened, or do the stems as well? Are only the endings subject to change, or the stems too?

In the view of most investigators, one can speak only of a history of endings, but not of stems. This view is based on the assumption that once stems had been shaped and formed in a certain way, they exist somehow, like fossils, outside of man, and remain independent of our thought processes.

Thus, if we assume that proto-Indo-European had stems ending in the vowels –a, –i, –u, then we must posit them in all languages continuing the original proto-Indo-European language despite the various changes which these underwent in the course of time, despite the fact that some of them have not preserved the slightest trace of –a, –i, –u nor, for that matter, of any ending. Thus, although the proto-Indo-European *varka–s*[1] is represented by the modern Russian *volk*, the primary root *varka–*, or at least *volka–*, is still assumed to be present in *volk*. It is as if we were faced with a grey-haired man whom, despite appearances, we still think of as dark-haired, because we know that his hair used to be dark. And what would we perceive if we met this man for the first time and had no idea that he used to be dark-haired? We would still insist that he is dark or blond or a redhead but never that he is grey.

Similarly, we can see no clear connection between one or another isolated Slavic noun and a vocalic stem in *–a, –u* etc., but we continue to treat it as if it were a vocalic stem and not knowing the details, assume that the given noun contains an *–a, –i, –u, –ia* or other kind of stem.

We see a bald man before us, but we do not regard him as bald because in his youth he had a splendid head of hair, and we still believe him to be thick-haired and handsome.

At a point in man's embryological development, he had a small tail which later shortened and disappeared, leaving only an unnoticeable rudiment. In line with the view that the Slavic and other Indo-European languages still contain *–a, –i, –u* stems, every man should then be described as having a tail, a small one to be sure, but still a tail.

American farmers have bred a new, hornless breed of cow from the usual horned breed; but to the followers of the *–a, –i, –u* stem-theory, the heads of these cows are still graced with long horns.

Somewhere on earth a mountain has appeared where there had been none, and somewhere else a mountain has disappeared; in a third place, the sea has given way to dry land, and in a fourth, dry land has yielded to the sea. To the eye of a follower of the theory of the immutable *–a, –i, –u* stems, there stand as before, a plateau, a mountain, the sea, and dry land.

What would we say about biologists and geologists if they proceeded in a similar fashion? And yet this is precisely the sort of logic pursued by the champions of the incontrovertible *–a, –i, –u* stem-theory.

What is the *raison d'être* of this stubborn stem-theory? What prevents its champions from reexamining its worn-out and illusory truth and from embracing an evolutionary point of view, which has prevailed as the only valid one in the biological and social sciences?

To answer this question we shall turn for a moment from linguistics to psychology.

The founders of comparative grammar took Sanskrit as the basis for their study of all Indo-European languages. Even at the birth of this discipline, which was not so long ago, its practitioners did not attempt to explain the structure of the Indo-European languages, but were intent only to compare them with Sanskrit, looking at their development through Sanskrit glasses and imposing upon them Sanskrit categories. They found the *–a, –i, –u* stems in Sanskrit itself (although even here they are not retained intact), and what is more important, in Indic grammatical literature. And since these stems existed in Sanskrit, it was concluded they must exist in all other Indo-European languages. The followers of the early comparativists made this theory their own, and it is well known how strongly people feel about what they learn at the beginning of their study. Were is not for teachers who cannot distinguish sounds from letters, there would not be that profusion of grammarians (among whom some enjoy fame and respect) who confuse sounds and letters in the most simplistic manner, for whom the Russian *šč* is a simple consonant, *ja* is a soft vowel, ъ and ь semivowels, and so on, to give but a few examples.

If it were not for the inspiration of the Indic grammarians, if the comparative grammar of the Indo-European languages had instead begun with Latin, Greek, or the Slavic languages, and if Greeks, Romans, or Slavs, and not the ancient Indians, had been the authors of illustrious treatises on the morphology of language, then all those ardent champions of the *–a, –i, –u* stems in all Indo-European languages would have probably failed to see them not only in their own languages, but even in Sanskrit and proto-Indo-European. Such is the power of suggestion and habit. As someone once said, the strongest drive behind human activity is laziness. And laziness is, no doubt, the main reason why scholars cling to the theory of the *–a, –i, –u* stems in all Indo-European languages⟨. . .⟩.

I propose that each subject be first of all treated in terms of its own properties without imposing upon it alien categories. A feeling for language, and especially for its psychological aspect, must serve as an objective criterion for the scientific investigation of the facts of language. I submit that "feeling for language" is not just a clever formula or a will o' the wisp, but a real and objective phenomenon of language.

Even a foreigner, or rather, a speaker of a foreign language, can discover and acquire a feeling for a given language if he studies it thoroughly, if he masters its facts with insight and perspicacity and, above all, if he is free of all the prejudices which we acquire by tradition.

If we approach language in this way, it appears that the stems or themes are not merely fictions in the hazy atmosphere of the proto-language, not merely echoes of a golden age of language frozen in their immobility, but living parts of declined and conjugated words. They are a necessary component of inflection so long as the latter is not replaced by a different word-structure consisting of morphologically indivisible wholes, which happens when declined and conjugated words cede their place to an "analytical" form of language development.

Since it is generally agreed that stems, like other morphological parts of the word, become petrified in the secondary or "analytical" languages, why not admit that they could similarly develop and change in the primary languages, in which we recognize the development and regeneration of roots, suffixes, and endings?

Furthermore, if the theory of fixed and petrified stems concedes that certain "consonantal" noun stems were replaced by vocalic stems, that and –*i* and –*u* stems were replaced by –*a* stems, and moreover that the stems admitted phonetic diversity (e.g., the distinction of strong, middle, and weak stems in Sanskrit), then why rule out the possibility that the end of a stem could have been reduced and its final vowels –*a*, –*i*, and –*u* dropped?

In the light of the forgoing remarks we would have to conclude that stems or themes, like everything else in language, are subject to constant change. These changes are either (1) purely phonetic or (2) due to analogy. Because of these changes, the once extant stems in –*a*, –*i*, –*u* and the like (which were not fully retained even in Sanskrit) lost their final vowel in Slavic and other Indo-European languages and changed into shorter, consonantal stems. The phonetic reflexes of the old endings now serve in Slavic, as in the other primary Indo-European languages, as simple endings expressing different case relations.

This reduction of stems in favor of endings must have begun in proto-Indo-European in those instances where the final vowel of the stem coalesced with the initial vowel of an ending into one long vowel. Thus, for example, one can hardly detect a vocalic –*a* stem in abl. sg. masc.-neut. in –*ād* or –*āt* (Sanskrit –*āt*, Lat. –*ōd*, Lith. –*o*, Slavic –*a*), or in other cases that were similarly formed. The proto-language itself showed in such instances a reduction of the stem in favor of the endings yielding a shorter stem form (which included only the last consonant).

The historical development of declined nominal stems from proto-Indo-European to the present as represented, for example, by the Slavic languages, can be reconstructed approximately as follows:

The posited oldest proto-Indo-European period contained two groups of stems:

I. Stems ending in vowels and diphthongs.

II. Stems ending in consonants.

The first group was more numerical both in terms of the words belonging to it and in the variety of thematic types.

The principal types included:

1. Stems in final –*ā* (long *a*) (fem. and in part masc.).

2. Stems in final –*ă* (short *a*) or –*e* | –*o* (masc. and neut.).

3. Stems in final –*u* or –*u* | –*eu* | –*ou* (of all three genders, but preponderantly masc.).

4. Stems in final –*i* or –*i* | –*ei* | –*oi* (also of all three genders, but preponderantly fem.).

Types 3 and 4 were transitional to the second principal group of stems ending in a consonant.

The final vowels of the first and second type were preceded either by a "hard," nonpalatalized consonant, or by *j* (alone or clustering with a preceding consonant). This distinction is of great importance for the development of proto-Slavic from proto-Indo-European, since the final vowel split into two vowels, depending on the quality of the preceding consonant.

The second principal group of proto-Indo-European declensional stems was represented by only one subgroup, comprising substantives of all three genders, but only a few isolated forms belonging to this type were retained in the transition to the individual Indo-European languages, especially proto-Slavic, namely: stems ending in –*ū* | *ŭv* (fem.), –*er* | –*r* (–*ter* | –*ter*) (fem.), –*men* | *mn* (masc. and neut.), and –*as* (–*es* | –*os*) (neut.).

The transition from proto-Indo-European to proto-Slavic was marked by two phonetic processes which are reflected in the declension. One was the influence of the consonant *j* on the following vowel. Under the influence of *j*, the first and second declensional types of the first principal group split into two subtypes, (A) and (B) exhibiting the following vocalic endings:

in subtype A:		in subtype B:
o	....	*e*
ŭ (ъ)	....	*i* (ь)
y (ы)	....	*ę* (ѧ)
ē (ѣ)	....	*ī*

The phonetic process was the loss of all consonants at the end of syllables and the appearance of open syllables at the end of all words. The endings, too, lost their final consonants. But the loss of final consonants did not eliminate the need to express case relations by means of endings, which came now to be expressed by the vowels of the former stems, whereas the new stems terminated in a consonant. Thus, there came about a *general reduction of the stems in favor of the endings*. The endings at that time consisted either of a part of the former stem, or of a part of the former stem combined with the phonetic continuation of the old ending.

The two phonetic processes brought about morphological changes only in the first principal group of declensional types, that is, in the group going back to the proto-Indo-European vocalic stems (*–a, –u, –i. . .*). The result of the first process was a rearranged distribution of the first and second subtypes of the first group, while the second process affected the morphological character of all four subtypes of the first group.

In the second (consonantal stems) group the word-final consonants disappeared without entailing morphological consequences.

The declension of proto-Slavic and its more or less faithful continuation in Old Church Slavonic presents the following main types:

I. The first group includes six subtypes instead of the previous four.

1a. continues proto-Indo-European type 1 with a final "hard" consonant. Its characteristic endings are: nom. sg. *–a*, abl.-gen. sg. *–ȳ* (Ⱐ); all newly formed endings begin either with back vowels (*a, o, ŭ, ū, ȳ, ǫ*), or with front vowels (*e, ĭ, ē*).

2a. continues proto-Indo-European type 2 with a final "hard" consonant. Its characteristic endings are: acc.-nom. sg. masc. *–u* (Ⱐ), acc.-nom. sg. neut. *–o*, abl.-gen. sg. *–a*; as in type 1a, its endings begin with either a back or a front vowel.

1b. continues proto-Indo-European type 1 with the final stem consonant *j*. Its endings are: nom. sg. *–a*, rarely, *–ī* (И), abl.-gen. sg. *–ę* (Ѧ); the endings begin with the back vowels (*a, ǫ, u*), or the front vowels (*ī, ĭ, e, ę*). The front vowels of certain endings developed from back vowels under the influence of a preceding *j*.

2b. continues proto-Indo-European type 2 with the stem final consonant *j*. Its endings are: acc.-nom. sg. masc. *–i* (И), acc.-

nom. sg. neut. –*e*, abl.-gen. sg. –*a*; as in type 1b, they begin with either a back or front vowel.

3. continues proto-Indo European type 3. Its endings are: nom. sg. –*ŭ* (Ъ), abl.-gen. sg. –*ū* (◊y), dat. sg. –*ov–i* (◊ВИ), nom. pl. –*ov–e* (◊ВЕ); in general all newly formed endings begin with back vowels (*ŭ, ū, o, y*).

4. continues proto-Indo-European type 4. Its endings are: nom. eg. *ĭ* (6), abl.-gen. sg. –*ī*; they all begin with a front vowel.

Proto-Slavic type 3 contains only masculine nouns, and type 4 masculine and feminine nouns. Types 1a and 1b have mostly feminine nouns and a small number of masculine nouns. Types 2a and 2b remain, as before, masculine and neuter.

Even in proto-Slavic the nom. sg. forms had become associated with particular genders: *a* with feminine, *ŭ* (Ъ) with masculine, and *o* or *e* with neuter.

II. The second, consonantal group of proto-Indo-European stems relinquished many individual types. Proto-Slavic retained the following types:

$$–ȳ \ || \ \breve{u}v– \ (– Ъ_{\mathsf{I}} || \ – ЪB –), \text{fem.}$$
$$–tĭ \ || \ –ter– \ (–ТИ \ || \ –ТЕР \ –), \text{fem.}$$
$$–mȳ– \ || \ –men– \ (–МЪІ \ || \ –МЕИ \ ), \text{masc.}$$
$$–me– \ || \ –men– \ (– МѦ \ || \ –МЕИ \ ), \text{neut.}$$
$$–o \ || \ –es– \ (– ◊ || \ –ЕС–), \text{neut.}$$

All these types share the ending –*e* of the abl.-gen. sg.

The old morphological relationships were retained in this group with minor modifications.

If we now compare the two major proto-Slavic groups I and II with the corresponding proto-Indo-European groups, we obtain the following features characteristic of both groups.

Group I:	Group II:
Nom. sg. = stem + ending	Nom. sg. ⟨ stem (shorter than the stem)

The ending of the abl.-gen. sg. is phonetically the continuation of either a diphthong or a long vowel; morphologically it consists of a part of the old stem plus the old ending.	The ending of the abl.-gen. sg. is phonetically the continuation of the short vowel *e* (*es*); morphologically it is the old ending itself.

The distinctive features between proto-Indo-European and proto-Slavic are:

In group I	In group II
there occurred a morphological reduction of stems in favor of endings.	there occurred only phonetic reduction of whole case forms, while the morphological boundaries between the stems and endings remained the same.

This period witnessed the development of one generalized type of ending: *every Common Slavic ending had to contain at least one vowel,* and had to begin with that vowel.

Thereafter we can distinguish three periods in the development of Slavic declensional types:

1) The period of morphological distinctions, discussed above. These distinctions are reflected in Old Church Slavonic monuments and, to some extent, in the oldest monuments of other Slavic languages.

2) The period of redistribution of declensional types according to genders, characterizing almost all contemporary Slavic languages.

3) The period of decline of declensional stems, reached conspicuously in Bulgarian.

The transition from the first Common Slavic period to the second was furthered principally by the loss of the final vowels ŭ (ъ) and ĭ (ь).

This phonetic process introduced, on the one hand, forms with a *zero* ending and established on the other hand, the phonetic identity of the stem with the nominative case in many substantives of the first group.

The phonetic process, furthermore, prevented the preservation of the old morphological distinctions of declensional types, causing their regrouping and redistribution. One of the principal results of this process was establishment of a connection of particular endings (including the zero ending) with distinctions of gender.

Various semasiological and lexical features now took precedence over purely morphological ones. Thus there was a gradual shift from a purely morphological to a semasiological and lexical distribution of the declensional types.

Along with the new declensional types based on semasiological and lexical distinctions, there continue to exist residues of the old morphological distinctions. In this context it should be noted that:

1) Some old types merged. Original group II, continuing the proto-Indo-European consonantal stems, was absorbed by group I. In general, the original first and second subtypes of group I predominate over the other subtypes. Subtype 3 merged with 2a, subtype 4 with 1b.

2) The original, purely morphological differences were utilized for new semasiological purposes. It is enough to mention the distribution of the endings –*a* and –*u* (*y*) in the abl-gen. sg. in Russian, Polish, and other Slavic languages. These endings come from types 2 and 3, but are now used to convey different meanings. Similar distinctions are attached to the various endings of the nom. pl. which differentiate between the personal and nonpersonal, animate and inanimate genders, and so on.

3) In addition, there evolved purely morphological distinctions, but along different principles than in the old declensional types. Thus, for example, several Slavic languages distinguish declensions with final "hard" and "soft" consonants, with stems ending in consonants which are modified according to meaning or case (according to psychological association) and stems ending in consonants which are not so modified. In some stems the vowel preceding the final consonant or consonant cluster remains the same in all forms ⟨of the declension⟩ without undergoing psychologically determined changes, and in others the final vowel is subject to change (e.g., Polish *ród – rodu,* Czech *bůh – boha,* Slovenian *bug – bogá,* Ukrainian *nič – nočy*). In languages with short and long vowels the stems display quantitative alternation: some stems retain the same vowel in all forms, while in other stems there appears a short or long vowel depending on the declensional form.

In all Slavic languages the stems may alternate as a result of the split of the old vowels *ŭ* (*ъ*) and *ĭ* (*ь*) into zero and full vowels; one and the same stem may appear with or without the vowel (e.g., Russian *son– ‖ sn–a, pen' ‖ pn–ja. . . . ,* Polish *pień ‖ pń–a. . .*). Finally, in languages with a morphologically determined stress, there are stems with a fixed stress, as opposed to stems with a mobile stress.

The development of stems reached its extreme point with the full merger of declensional types, the fusion of stems and endings into a single morphological unit, the appearance of one general "case" (*casus generalis*) and, where the need to retain the inflection remained, the replacement of all endings by syntactically separable suffixes and case determinants, i.e., "prepositions." This stage of development is tantamount to the complete disappearance of the category of declensional stems in the old sense and the appearance of a new kind of stems. These new stems combine not with endings, but with prefixes which are at first syntactically separable (in free combination) and later on syntactically inseparable from the stems (bound combinations and the germ of new declensional forms based on new principles).

Among the Slavic languages, Bulgarian has almost reached the stage outlined above. In that language the only distinctions preserved are those of the singular and the plural and the continuation of the old vocative case with a special ending, i.e., the case which in proto-Indo-European had only a bare stem without any formal marker, i.e., without an ending.

The transition from a "synthetic" or centralized to an "analytic" or decentralized morphological structure has been accelerated to a significant degree by the mixture of ethnically different tribes.

N O T E S

_____

1. I wish to remind the reader that this article was written in 1870, at a time of the absolute dominance of the theory of three original vowels, *a, i, u,* which lay at the basis of Schleicher's *Compendium.*

X I

Linguistics of the Nineteenth Century

THIS ⟨THE 19TH⟩ CENTURY has seen science make increasingly rapid progress and achieve greater successes than ever before. Not the least among the various sciences is linguistics (glottology, glottics), which has come to be organized as an independent discipline in Europe only in this century.

When we speak of 19th century linguistics, we refer exclusively to the European-American world, i.e., to the world which has already gone beyond the 19th century. The Chinese, Japanese, and Moslem nations, let alone the nations which have not participated in the intellectual life of this world, have not yet made the transition from the 19th to the 20th century. Thus it is only in the European-American sphere that an inventive and progressive generation has created a genuine linguistic science, and a new form of understanding and studying human speech in all its variety and complexity.

The beginnings of today's impressive science of linguistics are noticeable in the 18th century, and even earlier. These were at first only narrow, shallow currents of knowledge, but as they broadened and deepened, they merged into a vast ocean of knowledge. ⟨. . .⟩

What then were these currents, these initial impulses, which gradually led to modern 20th century linguistics?

The main current was the uninterrupted philological tradition of Greek and Latin language and literature, to which was later added the philological study of the ancient Hebrew and Arabic languages that had become accessible to European scholars, as well as Indic philology, including Sanskrit and the theories of the Hindu grammarians, which Europeans came to know in the latter half of the 18th century.

In European schools they taught Latin, and sometimes Greek, besides the national languages. The need to speak and write correctly forced people to consider the characteristics of different languages. Outside the schools, foreign languages were also studied, and all this gave rise to the production of textbooks, practical grammars, and dictionaries. These purely practical considerations were soon combined with scientific interests, with an intellectual quest for a deeper understanding of linguistic problems: attempts were made to define the peculiarities of one or more languages, to juxtapose and compare various languages by compiling dictionaries and in works containing logical speculations. Attempts were made to classify individual languages and groups of languages.

There appeared philosophical or rational (logical) grammars (in France as early as the second half of the 17th century); studies on the origin of language (Herder's work in the second half of the 18th century); attempts at physiological investigations of pronunciation, including even machines to reproduce some sounds of human speech (Kempelen, Kratzenstein); similar experiments continued in the second half of the 18th century.

Leibniz, the famous philosopher and mathematician, who lived at the turn of the 18th century, pointed out the analogy between the study of linguistics and the natural sciences and the importance of studying living languages above all; it took a long time (until the second half of the 19th century) for this approach to become the motto of linguists, yet by no means of all. At the beginning of the 17th century European missionaries had begun to write down words in the languages of other parts of the world, and to describe the grammatical properties of these languages. The monarchs of multilingual states also took an interest in these questions.

Contemporary linguistics, linguistics of the 19th century, which has developed from and continues philology, is inspired by a more modern outlook.

The following factors contributed to its final development and character:

a) The ideas of Leibniz had opened up wide horizons to students of languages.

b) Acquaintance with the Hindu grammarians brought about an increasing awareness of phonetic differences and the ability to analyze and break up words into their constitutent parts.

c) The method of observation and of experimentation practiced in the natural sciences found practical application in linguistics.

d) The philosophical ideas of W. Humboldt and the application of the psychology of Herbart and others to the study of linguistic concepts imparted to linguistics a genuinely scientific character, based on a psychological approach to language.

e) Darwinism, and the theory of evolution in general, which gained popularity in the last century, had a positive influence on the views of linguists concerning the life of language. In this connection it should be noted that linguistics adopted these principles earlier and more boldly than the natural sciences.

The part of linguistics which is called "comparative grammar" is an offspring of the 19th century. For its method it is indebted to the Hindu grammarians, from whom they ⟨the linguists⟩ learned to analyze language and to break up words into constituent elements that provided, in turn, the impetus to compare words of various languages in "comparative dictionaries."

Franz Bopp's modest work on the system of conjugation of Sanskrit in comparison with several other Indo-European languages published in 1816 must be viewed as the beginning of so-called comparative grammar of the Indo-European (Indo-Germanic, Aryo-European) languages. Bopp convincingly proved the genetic relationship of these languages; and this led to the creation by Bopp himself and his contemporaries, especially Pott, of comparative grammar in general and, subsequently, to the improvement of this branch of science which has gone through two basic stages. A synthesis of the views characterizing these two stages can be found in the comparative grammars of Schleicher (published between 1868 and 1870) and Brugmann and Delbrück (published more recently).

In the beginning investigators slavishly repeated certain mistakes of the Hindu grammarians, but they began to discard them rather early; comparative phonetics is now free of these mistakes, while morphology is still in need of some serious corrections. European and American linguists still find it hard to free themselves of some residues of medieval scholasticism and the antiquated tenets of classical philology. Its tradition is very old, and the force of habit much stronger.

Alongside comparative grammar, there began to develop a "historical" grammar, which drew its material from literary records which it arranged according to the uninterrupted and gradual development of language. The true creator of historical grammar in the field of the Germanic languages was Jacob Grimm (1819).

A separate trend in the field of linguistics is, finally, represented by the so-called philosophy of language or philosophy of speech, whose most illustrious representative in the first half of the 19th century was Wilhelm von Humboldt. This philosophy of language was dominated at first by a metaphysical orientation which gradually changed into a psychological one. The credit for this change is due to Steinthal and to the journal *Zeitschrift für Völkerpsychologie und Sprachwissenschaft* (1860–1878) founded by Steinthal and Lazarus. So-called philosophy of language profited further from the various generalizations and conclusions contained in the works of Whitney, Paul, Romanes, Sayce, Bréal, Potebnja, Appel, and others.

In outlook, contemporary linguistics is becoming more and more psychological. The latest work by Wundt[1] shows best of all the importance which some of the foremost philosophical psychologists attribute to linguistic studies.

Around 1880 psychological data began to be utilized quite consciously to explain changes in linguistic forms (e.g., by Scherer, Leskien, Sayce, Bréal, Havet, Brugmann, Osthoff). A contemporary linguist who does not know how to apply consciously the notions of association and of relation of concepts falls below the standards of his science.

In the history of 19th century linguistics one can observe a gradual but more and more decisive emancipation from the influence of preconceptions and unfounded opinions which either were inherited from older times or originated in the 19th century itself.

To a considerable degree linguistics freed itself of the influence of philology and the dominance of the letter over the sound. It began strictly to distinguish spoken discourse from the written text. Instead of the notion of the arbitrary changes of letters which had been held by philologists, it first introduced the concept of transition from sound to sound and, subsequently, the concept of alternation.[2]

It replaced the naive explanation of linguistic changes in terms of euphony by an explanation of these changes in terms of the tendency to economize linguistic behavior in three areas: in phonation or sound-formation, in audition or listening, and perception in general, and finally in cerebration or in linguistic thought.

As I have already noted above, it also freed itself of some false theories of the Hindu grammarians.

The old aristocratic attitude which was inspired by admiration for the erudition of philology and which considered worthy of investigation only noble, literary languages conferred with divine or regal power had to cede to the ever growing democratization of linguistic thought. Today there is no language that would be considered unworthy of study.

The renowned thesis about "the organism of language" (Becker) was subjected to devastating criticism by Steinthal in his work, *Grammatik Logik, und Psychologie* (Berlin, 1857).

August Schleicher had likewise held that linguistics is a natural science, and believed accordingly that language is a single, whole organism. This theory was bound to collapse under a trifling objection: it was noticed that no language can exist without man. Moreover, language as a physical phenomenon does not exist at all, and the basis of the individual continuity of language is exclusively psychological.

The genetic classification of languages, i.e., the classification based on historical affinity, was at first presented in the form of a genealogical tree (Schleicher, Curtius, and others), and later in the form of concentric waves (Schuchardt, I. Schmidt). But neither the first nor the second theory can withstand criticism, for on the one hand they are based on the supposition that language exists independently of man, and on the other hand, they fail to take into account the complexity of linguistic facts.

In the genetic classification of languages, linguistics has rid itself of the notion that Sanskrit constituted the proto-language of the Indo-Europeans, or that Old Church Slavonic was the proto-language of the Slavs; it came to be understood that the proto-languages of these families and peoples could not be preserved owing to changes in various directions.

In short, the characteristic feature of the development of 19th century linguistics was the empancipation from the authority of sorcerers and soothsayers of all kinds and the liberation from preconceptions which might even have appeared well intended and scholarly at first sight.

Linguistics adopted the principle of gradual development, or evolution; new attention was paid to the relative chronology of changes and to the chronological sequence of linguistic processes; separate strata were now distinguished in language, i.e., linguistic phenomena were viewed in their historical perspective and not on a single temporal plane, as was done by the Hindu grammarians. Evolutionism compelled consideration of the laws of genetic succession and adaptation or accommodation; at the same time a scientific explanation of the so-called rules and exceptions became possible.

Embryonic phenomena, archaisms of various kinds, the interaction of various factors, particularly the historical tradition and physiological-psychological causes peculiar to a given period of linguistic development—all these are new concepts and they characterize linguistics of the second half of the 19th century.

The rigorous and skillful inquiry into the historical sequence of processes as well as the derivation of later branches from an assumed common source makes it possible to reconstruct the former state of the language, and to predict its future development.

Today we know that in language, as in other phenomena of life, change, continuous motion (*pánta rhei*) are uninterrupted, and the influence of constant factors which are infinitesimal at any given moment may bring about radical alternations.

The notion that there is a connection between linguistic characteristics and the world-view and disposition of people speaking particular languages has gained acceptance, while the generalizations drawn from particular changes indicate that there are certain steady directions of change and mutual dependence, ⟨a notion⟩ reminiscent of functional dependence in higher mathematics.

The methodology of linguistics increasingly resembles that of the exact sciences: there is more and more refined analysis and more abstraction. A quantitative mode of thinking finds ever larger application. We can characterize languages on the basis of statistical counts; we can apply the notion of infinitesimal quantities, infinitesimal distinctions, embryonic differences, limits (boundaries) of development in a certain direction, etc. The explanation of linguistic phenomena also warrants the application of mechanical concepts as, for example, the use and distribution of psychological energy; we can define the conditions of stability and fluctuation, that is, the variability of certain linguistic formations.

An index of the growth of scientific thought in the 20th century is the ever increasing connection between the various sciences and, consequently, the connection between linguistics and other sciences which are close to it for one or another reason. To be sure, there is greater specialization in the problems of research, but at the same time there is a tendency toward constant synthesis, generalization, and the establishment of common viewpoints. The conviction of the necessity of a common scientific mode of thinking underlying the different sciences affirms itself more than ever, and goes hand in hand with the rejection of any kind of sorcery, uncritical thinking, and reverence for authority that is exempt from criticism, in short, with the banishment from science of all residues of an antiquated mental attitude. The methods of science must differ in their particulars, but the foundations of thought are common and identical.

Let us now look at the internal divisions of linguistics in the 19th century and at the various aspects and topics of its research.

Along with the investigation of the languages of peoples and nations at various stages of their development, the language (speech) of the individual has become a subject of careful study. This exploration of individual speech, which is characterized by uninterrupted development, i.e., by development in the true sense of the word, has a direct bearing on general linguistics, whereas the study of tribal and national languages with their peculiar traditions and history is of concern primarily to historical linguistics. The study of individual life, in contradistinction to social or phylogenetic life, is connected with the embryology and pathology of language. In embryology we investigate the formation and development of children's speech, and in pathology the language of dysphasics, i.e., of people who are linguistically underdeveloped.

The quest for a thorough exploration of the phylogeny of language has led inevitably to the study of the languages of peoples who have probably remained on the lowest level of mental development, as well as to the investigation of the speech of those animals, particularly apes, who are closest to man. In accordance with anthropological and biological facts, one has to agree that the prehuman or even the formed human being could enter the road of linguistic development only after he rose on two feet.

The problem of the origin of language is also of interest to anthropologists and sociologists (cf., for example, the hypotheses of the sociologist Gumplovič).

The question has been raised whether human language has one

or many origins, whether it was formed at one time and in one place or at various times and in various places; this is a genuine scientific question ⟨. . .⟩.

The 19th century has also made significant advances in the study of linguistic material. Thus it was discovered that Celtic, Armenian, Albanian, and the ancient languages of Asia Minor belong to the Indo-European linguistic group. Extremely valuable material came to light through the study of the records of the oldest representatives of this group: Zend and Old Persian in the Iranian family; Oscan, Umbrian, and Vulgar Latin in the Italic-Romance family; Gothic and other ancient Germanic languages in the Germanic family; Old Irish in the Celtic family; Old Prussian in the Baltic or Aistian (Lithuanian-Latvian) family; Old Church Slavonic in the Slavic family, etc.

The discovery and study of various languages including extinct languages which have been preserved only in written records have likewise contributed to the broadening of the linguistic horizon. It is enough to mention the deciphering of Accadian and Sumerian, the study of Etruscan and Basque, the exact description of many Caucasian, Finno-Ugric, Uralo-Altaic, American Indian, African, Australian, Polynesian, Eastern Siberian, and other languages.

In many cases it was possible to determine the genetic relationship or kinship of the newly discovered languages and of those already known. Thus, for example, the texts of the Accadian and Sumerian languages (in the area of ancient Chaldea) which were deciphered in the second half of the 19th century allow us to state that these languages are ancient representatives of the Uralo-Altaic or "Turanian" group, but with a different morphological structure. According to Professor V. Tomsen of the University of Copenhagen the language of the ancient Etruscans might also possibly belong to this group.

Information about exotic languages that are still alive has been furnished to linguistic science either by individual scholar-travelers, or by joint undertakings, by scientific expeditions. We owe considerably more to the work of individual investigators than to those collective efforts.

The democratization of linguistics, which has come to recognize the equality of popular dialects with literary languages, has in the 19th century led to the creation of a new branch of linguistics called dialectology, or the science of dialects. The results of dialect studies are of utmost importance not only for linguistics, but also for ethnology and the history of peoples and nations. One consequence of these studies has been to apply the term "language" only to literary languages, and to designate living linguistic communities by such terms as "linguistic territory," "linguistic area," or "dialect group."

Along with dialectology there also developed epigraphy, or the science of inscriptions, which makes it possible to determine the characteristics not only of ancient, extinct dialects, but also of contemporary dialects, and which serves thereby as an ancillary discipline of dialectology. The science of inscriptions in the broad sense of the word also includes the study of the writing of dys-alphabetics, i.e., people who have not fully mastered a given orthography. Thus the use of written records helps us to arrive at dialectological conclusions.

In all these branches of linguistics (in the investigation of individual languages, of whole linguistic territories of various peoples, of national dialects and of literary languages, of live speech and of written documents, etc.), attention is being paid to the various aspects of language, constituting the following divisions of general and of particular (specific) grammar:

Phonetics (phonology), the science of sound-representations or of pronunciation, which is subdivided into anthropophonetics (physiology of human speech) and psycho-phonetics;

Morphology, the science of the structure of words (morphology in the proper sense), and the science of the structure of sentences (syntax);

Lexicology, the science of the word in general;

Semasiology (semantics), the science of the meaning of words, i.e., the combination of linguistic and extralinguistic representations;

Etymology, the study of the composition of words and their meaningful parts from the point of view of their historical origin.

A great many successful and lucky discoveries were made in all these branches of our science in the 19th century. To this day however lexicology has remained isolated. Anthropophonetics has developed most of all, since it has attracted the attention not only of linguists, but also of psysicists, physiologists, and others.

Anthropophonetics, also called the physiology of human speech, is a separate branch of science which deals with the investigation of the conditions of pronunciation and of the phonational-auditory production of language. Anthropophonetics also includes phenomena which lie outside of language and which consist exclusively of the combination of representations, i.e., which have a purely psychological basis. Anthropophonetics employs physical-physiological methods: it devises experiments and utilizes physical apparatus (the phonograph, the glossograph, and other specialized equipment). There has even been invented a synthetic device which imitates the human voice. This talking machine (*Sprechmaschine*), constructed by Faber in 1830, was, unfortunately, lost to true science.

Anthropophonetics is a part of general phonetics, whose second part is psycho-phonetics and historical phonetics, which already belong entirely to psychological linguistics proper.

Among the 19th century discoveries in the field of phonetics special mention is due to the results of accentual investigations, especially in the field of Slavic and of Lithuanian, and of the Indo-European languages in general (Vuk Karadžić, Daničić, Valjavec, Masing, Škrabec, Rešetar, Kurschat, Baranovskij, Jaunis, Leskien, Werner, Wheeler, de Saussure, Fortunatov, Šaxmatov, Meillet, Hirt, and many others).

In addition to phonetics there is the morphology of the word, which in the last three decades of the 19th century has become a strict science, especially in application to the Indo-European languages; in some respects it is perhaps a more strict science than morphology in the biological sciences.

In the last years a solid foundation was also given to the science of the meaning of the words, or of the relation between linguistic and extralinguistic concepts, i.e., to the science called semasiology or semantics (thanks to the works of Bréal and others).

In the area of etymology, which studies the composition of words and their meaningful parts from the point of view of their historical origin within the limits of one or more languages, the 19th century can boast of many extremely fortunate and successful findings which shed light on the development of human concepts in the most diverse areas of thought and life.

The 19th century laid the scientific foundations for the classification and the systematization of languages; the influence of certain languages upon others began to be carefully investigated; and attention was turned to the problem of the formation of mixed languages (Schuchardt, Petriceicu-Hasdeu).

The utilization of linguistic data in the field of other sciences (mythology, history of legal concepts, ethnology, etc.) produced more or less worthwhile results. Special mention should be made of the attempts to reproduce a picture of primitive culture by means of linguistic reconstruction (Kuhn, Pictet, Schrader).

Modern linguistics has found least application in the realm of pedagogy, in the study of languages in the schools, although it is clear that the methods of practical instruction of languages have been considerably improved during the 19th century.

The second half of the 19th century has also witnessed attempts to create universal, international artificial languages. The first attempt at the creation of such a language, but of a philosophical character, dates back to the 17th century (the *Mercury* language by the Englishman Wilkins, which was published in 1665). Leibniz also worked on the creation of an international philosophic language. In the 19th century efforts in this direction were made by the Frenchman Letellier (*La Langue universelle,* 1856) and by the Spaniard Sotos Ochando (1858). We can further cite the *Chabé* language created by the engineer Maldant, the *Spokil* language by Dr. Nicholas, and the *Ars signorum* by a certain Dalgarno. None of these philosophical languages could claim to be generally used. This problem could only be solved by artificial languages in the full sense of the word, which were the creation of the 19th century. Among the many attempts in this direction (for example, the *Catholic* language [*Langue Catholique*] by Liptay or the *Lingua internacional* by J. Lott) only three attracted the attention of wide circles of society and scholars. The first was the most popular—*Volapük* by Schleier, the pastor of Baden; the second was the *Espero* or *Esperanto* by Dr. Zamenhof of Warsaw; Leon Bollack in Paris recently invented the *blue language (la langue bleue).*

Side by side with these developments in linguistics which made full use of human reason and of sober minds, there were throughout the 19th century, just as before, dreamers talking in their sleep, people of unbridled fantasy, who, impressed by accidental sound similarities, derived *Gepidi* from *kiep* ⟨"fool"⟩ and *Thuringians* from *durni* ⟨"fools"⟩. The "learned" works of such "scholars" are of interest primarily to psychiatrists or to humorists.

Furthermore, in linguistics, just as in statistics, history, anthropology, etc., the real state of affairs has more than once been distorted and falsified. This was done unconsciously or half consciously because of greed and patriotic sensitivity, or quite consciously when knowledge was bargained away and "convictions" prostituted.

Nineteenth-century linguistics, like other sciences, largely increased the various channels of diffusion of its knowledge. The enormous growth of scientific literature, the variety of special works, brochures, publications, journals etc., significantly aided speculation about language and the investigation of linguistic problems.

The works and scientific studies were either of a general, synthetic or of a specialized, monographic character. On the one hand we have complete grammars of some languages, and on the other only parts of grammars, such as phonetics, syntax, etc. Along with these we have "comparative grammars" of larger or smaller scope, classifications and systems of languages, philosophic-linguistic synthetic works, etc. Finally there are books devoted to the bibliography of linguistics, works and studies on the history of this science, etc.

Scholarly journals have appeared, dealing with linguistic facts from both pedagogical and nonpedagogical viewpoints. These were either of a purely linguistic character or they dealt with linguistics in relation to other sciences. Among the specialized linguistic journals we can distinguish three main types: journals of general linguistics, journals of anthropology and phonetics, and journals devoted to the study of separate linguistic families. In the journals of mixed content, linguistics was combined with philology (classical, Oriental, Romance, Germanic, Slavic, etc.) or with ethnography and anthropology, etc. Linguistics also received attention in general scientific and popular science journals. Much valuable and important linguistic data can be found in physical, physiological, medical, pedagogical, philosophical, psychological, anthropological, ethnographic, and historical journals.

Among the great quantity of linguistic publications special attention is due to the publication of ancient texts (for example,

248

the *Rigveda* published by Max Müller) and of dialectological texts, as well as excellent lexicographical works, i.e., dictionaries impressive for size as well as for thoroughness and soundness of composition: the Sanskrit dictionary of Böhtlingk and Roth (published by the Academy of Sciences in Petersburg); the German dictionary of the brothers Grimm; the French dictionary of Littré; the new editions of Ducange's memorable dictionary (of the 17th century). The following works were initiated and planned on a large scale: the enormous dictionary of the Swedish language; the dictionary of Turkic dialects by V. Radlov (published by the Academy of Sciences in Petersburg); the *Rigveda* dictionary of Grassmann; the Polish dictionary of Linde; the Czech dictionaries of Jungmann and Kott; the Serbo-Croation dictionary (begun under the editorship of Daničić); the Russian dictionary ("of the Living Great Russian Language") of V. Dal'; the dictionary of the Russian language published by the Second Section (of Russian language and literature) of the Academy of Sciences in Petersburg, at first under the editorship of J. Grot, and then of A. Šaxmatov and many others.

Linguistic chairs at universities and in other institutions of higher learning were not created until the 19th century. It is true, they were connected to a large degree with instrutcion in literature and philology in general (for example chairs of Classical Philology, Romance, Germanic, Slavic, various Oriental languages, Russian language and literature, Polish language and literature, etc.), but along with these there also are exclusively linguistic chairs (for example, of the comparative grammar of the Indo-European languages, Sanskrit and comparative grammar, comparative linguistics, general linguistics, comparative grammar of the Slavic languages, the comparative grammar of the Urgo-Finnic languages, etc.). Today such chairs exist under different names in different European countries, in America, in Japan, in the Russian universities since 1823, and for the last few years at the University of Cracow as well.[3]

Academies of science and scientific societies in various countries devote part of their works and funds to linguistic research; they publish various works and journals, organize scientific expeditions, give stipends to specialists, etc.

Only in elementary schools and particularly in high schools has linguistics until now been treated as a stepchild. But in all fairness one must note that the Scandinavian countries (Denmark, Sweden, and Norway), Finland, Switzerland, and North America are exceptions in this respect. In these countries language teachers try as much as possible to utilize the results of linguistic research.

Nineteenth-century linguistics was first organized as a separate science in Germany. The Germans were ahead in both the number of scholars and in the quantity of scientific attainments; at any rate, Germany remained the center of intellectual ferment in the field of linguistics. But other nations and countries soon emerged in several fields, perhaps even surpassing the Germans. Linguistics developed quite rapidly among the English and Americans (Sayce, Whitney, Wheeler), among the French and Swiss, (Benloew, Bréal, Darmsteter, Bonaparte, Vinson, de Saussure, Meillet, Rousselot), in the Scandinavian countries (Rask, Lundell, Verner, Tomsen, Möller, Torbörnssen, Broch, Lidén, Pedersen, . . .). Several branches of linguistics were also developed independently in other states and countries, reflecting the general trend of international linguistics and the needs of their particular society; e.g., in Italy (Biondelli, Ascoli), in Russia (Potebnja, Fortunatov, Korš, V. Miller, Brandt, Il'inskij, Kruševskij, Bogorodickij, Sobolevskij, Šaxmatov, . . .), in Holland (Uhlenbeck, . . .), among the Czechs and Slovaks (Dobrovský, Šafařik, Gebauer, Zubatý, . . .), in Hungary (Hunfalvy, Budencz, Genecz, Munkacsi, Szinnyei, . . .).

Anthropophonetic studies dealing with the pronunciation of the sounds of human speech attained the highest development among the English and Scandinavians (Danes, Swedes, Norwegians) and among the French, although the Germans, too, have obtained some noteworthy results in this field. In dialect research in their own states and countries, particular credit is due the Italians, French, Scandinavians, Czechs, Serbs and Croats, Bulgarians, Slovenians, Russians, and Poles. Comparative grammar of the Indo-European languages was greatly advanced by the French (and Swiss), the Dutch, the Danes, and the Germans. The most remarkable successes in the study of new, previously unknown languages have been achieved in North America (the languages of the ancient indigenous peoples), in Russia (Caucasian, Siberian, and other languages), and in Hungary (languages related to Hungarian).

The philosophy of language and the quest for generalizations in the field of linguistics made rapid advance not only among the Germans, but also among the English and Americans, the French and the Scandinavians and, to some extent, among the Roumanians.

But even in smaller countries and among smaller nations various linguistic problems have received original and successful treatment as, for example, among the Finns (Castrén, Ahlquist, Lönnrot, Donner, Setälä, Viklund, Mikkola, who studied not only Finnish and the Ugro-Finnic languages but also the languages of other nations); in Roumania (Petriceicu-Hasdeu), Portugal, Belgium (Bang), Greece, Bulgaria (Miletič, Matov); among the Serbs, Croats, and Slovenians (Miklosich, Daničić, Budmani, Jagić, Škrabec, Oblak); Estonians (Wiedemann, Veske), Latvians (Bielenstein), Lithuanians (Kurschat, Bishop Antanas Baranauskas, the priest and professor Kazimir Jaunis); and the Lusatians (Ernest Muka). In all these countries we find works which are not only of local significance but which also belong to international science. One may assume that even Japan, which has recently joined the international intellectual community, will soon come forth with original contributions in the field of linguistics.

The various directions of linguistic thought have also exerted a greater or lesser influence upon the Polish scientific community. This influence, coming almost exclusively from the West, has either evoked passive adoption of a ready made foreign, or rather alien science, or has also provided an impulse for speculation and original research. Scholars adopting this science (which has in the meantime provoked a strong opposition against "heretical novelties from abroad") worked either in the specialized area of Polish linguistics (particulary in the area of the history of the language and dialectology), or made their own contribution to the international and universal science.

In the very near future, i.e., in the 20th century, linguistics will have to face and solve the following problems:

1. It will have to rid itself once and for all of the scholastic views inherited from the original grammatical attempts of the Greeks and Romans and also of some later ideas which were slavishly adopted from the Hindu or Arabic and Jewish grammarians. Consequently, modern linguistic terminology will have to be changed fundamentally not only in form, but also in its essence, with regard to its concepts.

2. It will have to implement Leibniz's idea, and following the example of natural science, start always and everywhere with the

study of living languages which are accessible to observation, proceeding only afterwards to the study of languages which are reflected in the written documents of antiquity.

3. Wherever possible, it will have to apply the experimental method. This can be best accomplished in anthropophonetics, which must broaden the range of its observations to include on the one hand sounds emitted by animals and on the other hand languages with peculiarities of pronunciation which until now have remained incomprehensible for us. Broadened in this way, anthropophonetics will in fact become a general science, based on a real foundation.

4. In this connection the signs of the alphabet will have to be replaced by signs of a transcription based on the analysis and identification of the sounds of various languages.

5. It will be necessary to apply quantitative, mathematical methods in linguistics more often in order to bring it closer to the exact sciences.

6. Linguistics will also become a more exact science depending on the degree of the refinement of the qualitative method in psychology, the science on which it rests.

7. The study of linguistic facts will have to become strictly objective; it will have to comprise statements of actual facts of a given period and in a given linguistic area without imposing alien categories on them.

8. The first and cardinal requirement of objective research must be the recognition of the psychological and social character of human speech.

9. The concept of "sound laws" must be once and for all discarded from linguistics and replaced by its psychological equivalent.

10. Languages under study must be subjected to a multifarious analysis of their elements from every possible viewpoint.

11. The concepts of development and evolution must become the basis of linguistic thinking. This will lead *eo ipso* to the eradication of the anthropocentric prejudice that isolates man from other living beings, and also to liberation from the megalomania which is based on the conviction that "our" kind of languages represents the peak of morphological development among the languages of the world.

12. The concept of evolution must allow for the existence of constant fluctuation and variation in the structure of a language

(in the area of complex linguistic forms, words, expressions and sentences, the transition from centralization to decentralization, and vice versa).

13. Lexicology, or the science of words, as a separate branch of grammar will be the creation of the 20th century.

14. It is possible that new genetic relations will be discovered between languages and groups of languages, and even the very concept of the nature of interlingual relations may undergo fundamental change. Completely new horizons will open up. The attempts hitherto made in the 19th century to compare genetically the Semitic and Indo-European languages or the Ugro-Finnic and Indo-European languages were doomed to failure because of the lack of sufficient proof. Perhaps the 20th century will be more successful in this respect. A true and excellent discovery in this area is the proof adduced for the genetic relationship of a group of Semitic languages with Caucasian (Georgian-Mingrelian) languages (this discovery was made by Professor Marr at St. Petersburg).

15. Linguistic generalizations will gain greater breadth and will bring linguistics ever closer to other sciences: psychology, anthropology, sociology, and biology.

16. Etymological and semasiological studies will exert a tremendous influence on psychology and will provide it with completely new data for conclusions and generalizations.

17. Along with the two well-established contemporary modes of knowledge, i.e., the intuitive-artistic and analytic-scientific, there will be a third, linguistic one.

But linguistics will be in a position to prove its usefulness in the very near future only if it will rid itself of its ties with philology and ⟨the study of the⟩ history of literature. Above all, university chairs of linguistics must become autonomous, and combine rather with departments of sociology and natural science than with those of philology. The preparation for all this must begin in elementary schools and high schools, in which the application of linguistic knowledge is bound to occupy a serious place. But to achieve this it will be necessary to disabuse onself of the notion that the science of language begins with "dead" languages and that instruction in foreign languages must proceed through translation, without recourse to the observational method. In schools, grammatical terminology must be made uniform, and the "native" language, or any other acquired in a similar way, must constitute the basis for the mastery of grammatical concepts. The pedagogical utilization of linguistic material will consist in providing the students with an insight into the unconscious processes of language. To achieve all this the schools will have to free themselves of the reign of obscurantism, which prevents the light of true science from penetrating into the minds of students.

NOTES

1. *Völkerpsychologie. Eine Untersuchung der Entwicklungsgesetze von Sprache, Mythus und Sitte* von Wilhelm Wundt, vol. I, *Die Sprache,* Leipzig. 1900, XV + 627 pp., X + 644 pp. Cf. also: *Grundfragen der Sprachforschung mit Rücksicht auf W. Wundts Sprachpsychologie* erörtert von B. Delbrück, Strassburg, 1901, VII + 180 pp.

2. Cf. my *Próba teorji alternacij fonetycznych,* Cracow, 1894.

3. At the present time the chair of comparative linguistics and Sanskrit at Cracow University is held by Jan Rozwadowski, a completely independent scholar and the best Polish expert on the Indo-European languages in all their diversity.

XII

Toward a Critique of Artificial World Languages

. . . BRUGMANN is mistaken when he maintains that "French, like every living language, has a homeland."[1]

A collective "language" does not have a "homeland" in the sense that Brugmann has in mind. Individual language may indeed have a "homeland" in the mind of its bearer, that is, the speaker of the language. And if several languages coexist in the same mind, then they have a common "homeland," without persecuting and dislodging each other. At that, it is not at all necessary that a given language belong to the so-called living ones. Latin, Greek, Hebrew, Sanskrit, etc. have a homeland insofar as they exist as different languages in the minds of individuals.

In the same sense there is a "homeland" for the "artificial world language which has no firm base, but is only a bold independent undertaking of certain individuals" (p. 25).

Any "language" can be learned by a normal human being. Individual languages are by no means something innate. Only the most general preconditions of language are transmitted through heredity; while among specific ethnic characteristics only minimal differences, only minute distinctive tendencies are inherited. A child born as a Chinese or Hottentot can easily become a German in the linguistic sense if it is from the beginning raised in a German milieu, and vice versa. Linguistic ancestors are thus something entirely different from biological ones. The identification of origin with linguistic affiliation, or even with the pressure of a linguistic system, rests on a lamentable confusion of concepts which is illogical, as well as unjust (*unmoralisch*). . . .

. . . 13. Does man exist for language or language for man? *Language*

255

is neither a self-contained organism nor an untouchable fetish; it is a tool and an activity. Man not only has the right, but also the social duty to improve his tools in accordance with their purpose, and even to replace the existing tools with better ones.

Since language is inseparable from man and constantly accompanies him, man must master it more completely and subject it to greater conscious control than other areas of his psychological activity.

Even the most ardent opponents of artificial languages will admit that even if we disregard the case of artificial world languages we still do restrict and, with premeditation, change the "natural course" of language through "artificial" and conscious interference. Thus, any instruction in a language, whether this language be "native" or "foreign," is an offense against the "natural development of language." When we correct "mistakes" and "slips of the pen," we sin against the principle of naturalness. All linguistic purism, all persecution of linguistic "aliens," as well as all kinds of orthographic reform, are artificial devices restricting the natural course of things. Many new expressions and scientific and technical terms *(termini technici)* arise only "artificially," thanks to conscious interference.

14. "Well, all right," it will be argued, "let us grant that in all such cases there is artificial encroachment upon the natural course of language, but all this is quite different from inventing a special language for, after all, a language cannot be invented."

This seemingly sound objection is, unfortunately, refuted by the way some languages are actually invented. Such inventions are made either "unconsciously" (or we should say semiconsciously) as a result of "spontaneous tendencies," or they are made consciously, intentionally, "artificially." The first category includes "artificial" border languages ("mixed" languages), which make possible communication between speakers of different languages (for example, between Russians and Chinese, between Englishmen and Chinese), as well as secret languages and the argots of students, street urchins, tramps, etc., which are found in various countries and at various times. The second category includes the more or less "scientifically" constructed, "artificial" languages which are designed to function as auxiliary world languages. What is realized only partially and without planning in the languages of the first category is carried out on a significantly broader scale and with utmost consistency in the languages of the second category.

N O T E S

---

1. K. Brugmann and A. Leskien, *Zur Kritik der künstlichen Weltsprachen,* Strassburg, 1907, p. 25. The page numbers refer to that edition.

XIII

The Classification of Languages

... I AM NOT speaking here of genealogical classification, that is, of the attempts at a scientific and hypothetical reconstruction of the historical divergences and interaction of "cognate" languages, but of the so-called morphological classification of all languages, without regard to their actual kinship.

Nonetheless, I cannot help saying a few words about genealogical classification as well.

I give, of course, decided preference to the so-called wave theory over the "tree theory," although I must confess that even the "wave theory" leaves me with the impression that it approaches language apart from man, as something made up of wood or water, or suspended in the air. One salient fact is generally ignored in this approach, namely, that languages do not exist by themselves, but only in individuals who possess, along with other knowledge, the knowledge of one or more languages, which embody a specific type (or types) of linguistic thought. Linguistic intercourse consists in the fact that the members of a given speech community (*Genossenschaft*) communicate with each other by means of their speech organs and corresponding acoustic impressions[1] which are associated with and evoke the linguistic concepts present in the mind of the speakers. This being the case, we can only conclude that the currently accepted "wave theory" pays insufficient attention to the following irrefutable phenomena:

1) The uninterrupted *interpenetration and mixture of linguistic thought* of various, including individual, languages. This mixture is, on the one hand, a consequence of linguistic intercourse in general and, on the other hand, of the fact that the human brain is capable of combining linguistic thought of more than one

language, or more simply speaking, of mastering more than one language. Multilingual thinking exerts an influence in various directions;

2) Changes of habitat, the consequence of nomadic life, which bring about a dislocation of the so-called languages or, to be more precise, of the speakers of these languages. . . .

NOTES

1. In written language we are concerned on the one hand with manual activity which is implemented in the physical world, and on the other hand with optical impressions.

XIV

Phonetic Laws

DESPITE AN EXTENSIVE LITERATURE, the question of so-called phonetic laws is still insufficiently elucidated and not exhausted. The reason for this lies in the confusion of certain concepts whose precise formulation must be the first task of linguistic theory.

It would be presumptuous on my part to maintain that my modest remarks can bring us nearer the solution of this problem; nevertheless, I think that they will not be without some interest.

I am presenting here my views on the method of solving this problem. In essence, I am not proposing anything new. Everything written here has been stated and elaborated before by others. If I raise this question again, it is perhaps only out of pedantry. I always insist on the necessity of pursuing an object of research to the very end, putting its results in precise formulas in conformity with the facts, using technical terms with the utmost care and consistency as dictated by these facts, and devising symbols for the elements of speech activity established in the course of linguistic analysis.

An adequate formulation of the concept of phonetic law requires that we place this concept within the proper framework. One must take into account man's experience in the various spheres of life, man's relation to the various areas of nature as a whole, and the importance of a general world-view.

⟨. . .⟩ We shall try to present clearly the linguistic processes which connect the psychological system that carries linguistic representations with other psychological systems. Assuming that linguistic phenomena and processes are manifestations of *social intercourse among individuals,* we must consider the four "worlds" which make up the object of theoretical inquiry:

1) *the psychological world of the individual,* the basis for the existence of invariant and lasting linguistic ideas;

2) *the biological and physiological* world of a given organism, the first centrifugal transmitter of linguistic representations from one individual to another;

3) *the external, physical world,* the second transmitter;

2^b) *again the biological and physiological* world of the members of the speech community, now the centripetal transmitter of linguistic representations from one individual to another;

1^b) *the psychological* world, etc.;

4) the transmission of linguistically expressed ideas from one individual to another by means of the human organism and the external world is a linguistic process that takes place in the *social world,* but presupposes man's faculty of speech (PT. 41–42).[1]

All this refers both to articulatory-auditory language and to the graphic-visual language of people who know more or less how to read and write. I shall leave aside the graphic-visual aspect and dwell here only on the articulatory-auditory aspect of language, with which the notion of "phonetic law" is closely connected.

All linguistic communication, including the transmission of the articulatory-auditory properties of a language, can be seen as a complex process of transition from one phase of development to another.

The articulatory-auditory representations that exist potentially in the psychological system of an individual are converted into *physiological energy* when they are implemented with the help of the speech organs, that is, when they are discharged by the *organism* which sets the speech organs into motion. *The operation of the speech organs* in turn converts the physiological energy into physical energy, which involves not only acoustic phenomena but also phenomena of a mechanical order (such as thermal, electrical, or metabolic phenomena). The acoustic vibrations in the physical world which evoke *auditory impressions* affect the receptive powers of other organisms and produce corresponding types of physiological energy that are converted into perceptive energy of the psychological system. The acoustic impressions activate *sensory nerves* which transmit these impressions to the cerebral center. The *apperception* of the received impressions takes place in this system. Thanks to apperception, each representation is potentially and actively *associated* with and enriched by other existing representations (PT. 43).

In view of the above, we may distinguish two types of phonetics: an *anthropological phonetics* (an anthropophonic or even zoophonic phonetics), which is a phonetics of articulation and hearing (and which is an ethnic and national property), and an *etymological phonetics,* which is associated with morphological and semasiological representations (and which is relevant for history, ethnography, etc.) (PT. 4–5, 34, 40–41).

Only articulatory-auditory representations are transmitted in the process of social communication. The transmission is of an acoustic nature and is effectuated through the physiological (biological) and physical worlds. Everything that goes beyond articulatory-auditory representations, everything that is related to morphology and semasiology, or even to morphological and semasiological phonetics, must occur and renew itself in each individual ⟨PT. 42⟩.

As I have said, there exists only *individual language,* which is the sum total of articulatory-auditory representations that are associated with linguistic and extralinguistic concepts. The articulatory-auditory representations manifest themselves in phonetic phenomena which, being transient by nature, mere fleeting moments of social intercourse, can in no way be considered to have any real existence. That is why languages are neither phonetic nor acoustic in their nature.

Since phonetic language does not exist, it follows that neither are there sounds of language. And what does not exist, what is of only a transient nature, what is but a sign, so to speak, of that which does exist, can neither change nor develop. Thus *there is no phonetic development of sounds or of words composed of sounds.*

In individuals endowed with speech there is only development of:

1) general linguistic representations, in particular articulatory-auditory ones, and

2) functions of the speech organs, of the faculty of phonation and audition.

Thus, one may speak about "phonetic laws" only with respect to acoustics, but not phonetics (PT. 5–6).

It is impossible to point to those connections and causal relations of speech sounds that would qualify as genuine "laws." Instead of "phonetic laws" we should speak of:

1) *psychological laws* concerning the human mind, that is, laws of psychological states and change, and

2) *laws of the ways* through which social communication comes about, the laws of the manifestation of linguistic representations by means of organic and physical media.

We must assume that in the course of many generations, witnessing the various changes that go under the name of "phonetic laws," there was an infinite number of moments in which each transition depended both on the *conditions of individual linguistic thought* and on the *conditions of social interaction,* including interaction of each individual with himself. These moments made themselves felt (1) in the psychological system of the individual (both in isolation and collectively), (2) in the manifestations of the articulatory-auditory ideas, and (3) in the process of perceiving speech through the auditory organ, that is, during hearing (PT. 7, 9–10).

Thus, we have to deal with (1) *psychological* "laws" (of association, perception and apperception, emotion, etc.); (2) *physiological* laws (reflex motions, mechanical responses of the organism); and (3) *physical* laws (of acoustics, mechanics, optics, etc.).

The interplay of various factors which is subject to the law of *regularity* (conformity to rules, *Gesetzmässigkeit*) has, in other words, a psychological, psycho-physiological, physical-physiological, mechanical, and acoustic basis, as well as a psychological-receptive one which depends on the individual's psychological state and the socio-linguistic conditions of communication.

The historical results of the causally related phenomena which are used to transmit linguistic representations and are based on habits of articulation and perception are governed by *uniformity* and *regularity* (PT. 46).

Socially conditioned linguistic behavior is thus a highly complex process consisting of more specific processes. Each of these processes is based on an infinitely large number of possibilities which vary under certain conditions. These possibilities include:

1) individual and collective-individual psychological systems;

2) individual and collective-individual organisms;

3) the physical world; and

4) the social world, or the representations formed as a result of social solidarity.

In speaking of *individuals,* we must separate the *anthropological* aspect pertinent to all living *organisms* from the *social* aspect concerning human *individuals,* who possess the faculty of speech and are members of specific speech communities. We must also pay attention to factors of *heredity* and *adaptation* to the physical and social world; adaptation begins at the embryonic stage of the individual.

Heredity is determined both biologically (anatomically and physiologically) and psychologically. In dealing with "phonetic laws," it is important to note the effect of heredity on the structure of the speech organs (primarily their histological structure), on the ability in particular to speak a given language, and on the articulatory and auditory abilities and tendencies of a given individual (PT. 34).

We must, furthermore, take into consideration (1) the different psychological states of speakers; (2) their different linguistic abilities; (3) differences in the responsiveness to linguistic stimuli (which ranges from 0 to 1, i.e., to a maximum); (4) different articulatory and auditory dispositions; (5) differences in automatization of the organs of speech and hearing; (6) differences in adroitness in controlling the functions of the speech organs; (7) differences in morphologization and semasiologization of the articulatory-auditory representations; (8) differences in the instinct for self-preservation, which goes with the tendency toward economy of labor in all three areas of language: (a) in cerebration; (b) articulation (or manifestation of the linguistic representations); and (c) audition, perception, etc. It should be added that there is a difference between linguistic cerebration and the various systems of pronunciation and perception that are found within one and the same speech community (PT. 14–16, 20–21, 38–39).

There is also a difference between the psycho-linguistic system of people who can only speak, that is, communicate by means of articulatory-auditory representations, and the psycho-linguistic system of people who can also read and write, and thereby correct and regulate their pronunciation and auditory impressions on the basis of graphic and optic impressions. The psychological difference between these two categories of people also has a bearing upon phenomena of their ethnic or national language that pertain to the problem of "phonetic laws."

The anatomical and physiological differences between individuals belonging to the same speech community are connected with deviations in the articulatory-auditory development of a given language. These may depend on age, on individual idiosyncrasies, on organic defects, including paralysis and deafness (e.g., the various kinds of aphasia and, in particular, dysphonia) ⟨. . .⟩ (PT. 34–36).

The auditory impressions of our speech activity may, in turn, depend on the channel of transmission, especially on the atmospheric conditions of a given locale (the seashore, mountains, village, city, etc.) and their changes (fog, humidity, etc.). So far, such a dependence can only be postulated, for no one has, as yet, shown that it exists.

The receptive side of linguistic intercourse is, furthermore, affected by visual impressions. Visually perceived articulations (for example, lip movements) leave a stronger and more permanent impression than invisible articulations produced inside the vocal apparatus. In the latter case, the speaker relies on his muscular sensitivity for control and regulation of the auditory impressions, whereas the hearer imitates potentially the articulatory activities of the speaker (PT. 29).

The individual peculiarities exerting an influence on the articulatory-auditory development of a language are, as we have seen above, either of a collective-individual character (i.e., ethnic or national), or individual in the proper sense of the word.

Linguistic intercourse between *normal* members of a speech community, that is people who do not suffer from speech defects, activates the collective-individual characteristics of their psychological system; the mobilization of these traits takes place both in the speaker and, by means of perception, apperception and association, in the hearer.

Other individual peculiarities affecting the articulatory and auditory qualities of verbal intercourse retain their individual character, even though they are interpersonal. One such psychological and organic peculiarity is the manner of speaking which is determined by the social status of the speaker, his environment, way of life, diet, etc. (PT. 37).

In the final analysis, however, it is difficult to draw a sharp line between individual-collective and purely individual peculiarities. We might say that the occurrence of individual peculiarities ranges from I (restricted to one individual) to Σ (shared by all members of a speech community).

As happens in other fields of social life, language in general and its articulatory-auditory aspects in particular is affected by the drive to imitate, by the herd instinct, which is a social factor of a lower order.

We have noted above (p. 262) the various ways for the transmission of the articulatory and auditory features which lie at the foundation of any language regardless of its fullness and diversity. One kind of energy passes into energy of another kind: the central, psychological energy of performance passes into physiological energy of performance; the latter is transformed into external, physical energy; this again, into physiological energy of reception which is converted, finally, into the central, psychological energy of reception. During these various conversions certain changes inevitably occur, as a result of the discrepancy between the intention, or original impulse, and its implementation. The psychological arrangement of elements on the side of performance, that is, at the starting point of the cycle of conversions, may differ from its arrangement on the side of perception, at the end of the cycle of conversions. The action of the above-mentioned forces may account for the discrepancy between the psychological value of the phonemes and their realization (PT. 12–13, 38).

Furthermore, the ways to be transversed by the articulatory and auditory elements may be so complex that some of them become weak and disappear without a trace. In such cases the movements of the speech organs may reach the physical world without reaching the receptive organ, the ear. But then, hearing varies in different people, what one person cannot hear, another will hear quite well.

We must note an extremely important fact: the *facultativeness* in the manifestation and duration of the articulatory elements. An articulatory element may be activated in the psychological system, with the corresponding innervation of the muscles, without yielding the articulatory work itself. These facts have a singular bearing on the social-ethnic and national language (PT. 21, 23–24, 39).

The facultativeness in mobilizing the articulatory-auditory elements is closely connected with the degree of their *morphologization* and *semasiologization*. Phonemes whose elements are weakly morphologized and semasiologized tend to disappear when language is transmitted from one individual to another. Conversely, phonemes whose elements are more strongly morphologized and semasiologized, though superficially they may seem to be identical, have a greater social value and remain stable for a long time.

The degree of morphologization and semasiologization depends on (1) the *psychological prominence* or *psychological stress* (accent), a special case of which is the psychophonetic stress, *sensu stricto,* and on (2) the occurrence of *syntactic junctures* between syntagms (between words and expressions) and *morphological junctures* between morphemes. It is clear that the psychological accent and degree of morphologization of the phonetic elements of morphemes are stronger when the morphological formants are *monomorphic,* and weaker when they are *polymorphic* (as is the case in most Indo-European languages) (PT. 16, 20–21).

The above-stated dependence of the stability of articulatory-auditory representations on their morphological and semasiological functions, or on their degree of morphologization and semasiologization, also has a bearing on the so-called phenomena of analogy and folk etymology, or *morphological assimilation* and *semasiological attraction.* The ability of morphology and semasiology to resist purely phonetic change, that is, *prohibitive analogy,* requires no further explanation (PT. 20–23, 39).

The various psychological, morphologized, and semasiologized units of collective-individual language function either as indivisible units or as complexes of different parts forming a scale that includes: *syntagms,* as components of the sentence, *morphemes,* as components of the syntagm, and *phonemes,* as components of the morpheme. However, requirements of scientific analysis, which is obliged to do justice to the realities, do not allow us to stop with the phonemes. The phonemes consist of ultimate psychological (articulatory and auditory) elements which cannot be decomposed into smaller elements. From the point of view of linguistic production, or pronunciation, these ultimate elements are the *kinemes,* whereas from the point of view of audition or perception, they are the *acousmemes.* I consider these terms indispensable for the greater precision of the abstract concepts of our science (PT. 10–12, 22–23).

I must emphasize the importance of errors in hearing (*lapsus auris*), when one word is mistaken for another, as a factor of change at any given moment of linguistic intercourse and in the history of language as a social phenomenon. Experimental methods can help to define the types and directions of these errors which depend on physical conditions, on the sense of hearing of individuals, and on the degree of morphologization and semasiologization of the mobilized articulatory and auditory representations.

Mistakes in hearing are sporadic or permanent in any speech community whose members possess a greater or lesser command of their native language. Among the errors in hearing we must count those mistakes, or rather inaccuracies of "comprehension," that occur when speakers of one language are confronted with the new and incomprehensible articulatory and auditory elements of another language. Such errors can be viewed as a kind of collective-individual auditory (acoustic) Daltonism and as a distinctive anthropological and ethnic trait (PT. 17–22).

In the process of linguistic intercourse, of which I have spoken above, we also encounter the so-called confusion of tongues, that is, the influence of speakers on each other in the realm of linguistic concepts in general and of psychophonetic representations in particular, and in the area of automatized (articulatory and auditory) habits. Along with the influence of speakers on each other, there also is the influence of each speaker upon himself. In the articulatory-auditory domain we find thus the following types of mixing of languages that are related to the problem of "phonetic laws":

a) in the brain of each *individual* there is constant interaction of linguistic and extralinguistic concepts. Moreover, each speaker has at his disposal several individual "languages," which differ from each other articulatorily and auditorily and which are endowed with different social values: an everyday language, an official language, a language of church sermons, a language of university lectures, etc. The use of these languages may vary according to age, mental state, time of day, season, and recollection of former and newly acquired linguistic habits;

b) interaction of people belonging to the *same milieu*: members of a family, profession, etc.;

c) interaction of people belonging to different *ethnic* and *national groups,* to which they owe their heterolinguistic and heteronational concepts and habits;

d) interaction of generations. The basic tendencies in children's language, which accumulate over generations, may bring about historical changes in the language of the entire ethnic group;

e) the influence of people suffering from speech defects, from various kinds of aphasia and other deviations from normal speech upon their environment; and

268

f) the influence, finally, of "inert" and organic nature upon hearing.

Uniformity and purity of language are then fictions based on prejudice. Language did not emerge, like Minerva from the head of Jupiter, all at once, but was formed and is constantly being formed in each speaker through the fusion and interaction of multiple and diverse automatized concepts and habits (PT. 25–26, 29–34, 35–36, 36–37, 37–38, 41.

Thus it should be apparent that the articulatory and auditory representations of each individual—his muscular sensitivity (sensitivity of the muscular apparatus), his acoustic impressions, etc.—are in a state of constant fluctuation, qualitative variation, and quantitative change.

The fluctuations and variations are most apparent when individual languages are being compared. For example, the degree of morphologization and semasiologization of the articulatory and auditory elements differs in various speakers, though at first glance it seems to be identical in all of them. Even if we were to assume the lack of such difference, we would soon enough become aware of the existence of "accidental" variations in the speech of different speakers.

There are, furthermore, fluctuations in the processes accompanying linguistic intercourse, namely in the psycho-physical behavior of man's organism and in the physical world. Given the constant changes in the make-up of any speech community, we must admit *a priori* the existence of fluctuation in that fiction which is known as the "average" ethnic or national language.

The transmission of language from one individual to another, constantly involves a rearrangement of linguistic concepts ($A \geqslant A_1 \geqslant A_2 \geqslant A_3 \ldots \geqslant A_n$).

The history of language in general, and of its articulatory and auditory representations in particular, is a history of continuous change; something is constantly being born and something constantly disappears.

Nevertheless, and in spite of all the flucuations and variations, we must note the presence of "conservatism." The saying "something is constantly changing" should, consequently, be supplemented with "and something is constantly being preserved, something remains stable."

The articulatory and auditory representations of the contemporary variant of a given "average" language form, on the one hand, the same combinations as in the past, in the various stages of historical succession and, on the other hand, they yield new combinations which vary to a large extent according to:

1) the articulatory-auditory composition of the phonemes, that is, the combinations of the *kinemes* and *acousmemes* of the phonemes;

2) the stability of the articulatory base; and

3) the degree of morphologization and semasiologization (PT. 13–15, 38–39, 16–17, 20–23).

The whole set of *representations,* and particularly of the articulatory and auditory representations, the *receptive* and *productive* habits are *bound* and *interconnected with each other*, and are transmitted through linguistic intercourse from one person to another, from one generation to another, from one ethnic group to another, and from nation to nation. Through all the fluctuations and deviations the linguistic facts and their causal relations exhibit remarkable uniformity and regularity and constant coincidence (PT. 43–47).

Uniformity and regularity characterize both the stability of the combinations of the articulatory and auditory elements and their fluctuations and changes. They apply to:

1) alternations within one language (phenomena of a monolingual character);

2) correspondences, or relations of morphologized articulatory and auditory elements among several languages (phenomena of a multilingual character);

3) variations and differences, both microscopic and macroscopic;

4) coincidence of certain special conditions and of the interrelation of peculiarities of phonetic systems; and

5) the general character of historical-phonetic differences and the general direction of articulatory-auditory changes. In one way or another, the *psychological* processes accompanying the mobilization and manifestation of phonemes together with social processes bring about historical changes in the average ethnic language.

The uniformity and regularity which is observed in the narrow sphere of individual cerebration and in linguistic intercourse must not, however, be viewed as a relationship which can be embraced by an exact formula of "phonetic law"; it is rather a statistical constant of coincidence under certain conditions of socio-linguistic intercourse (PT. 46–48, 5, 7–9).

From an epistemological point of view, the results of observation and theoretical thought depend, on the one hand, on the observed object, and, on the other, on the mind of the observer, who formulates the results of his findings and judgments.

In like manner, the formulation of "phonetic laws" is different for the individual and the collective-individual types of thought and understanding (PT. 44–45).

Our thought is influenced by graphic and visual representations which are associated with phonetic and acoustic representations. Even the simplest elements of writing are the result of a deeper analysis of complex linguistic representations. But the application of this analysis to the choice of our graphic symbols (graphemes), stops with the phonemes which are, from the point of view of simultaniety, heterogeneous combinations of more basic articulatory and auditory activities of a certain type. The decomposition of phonemes into these elements is only partially reflected in writing. This peculiar relationship between writing and pronunciation and auditory perception has left its mark on the interpretation of "phonetic laws." It is the *suggestive power of our writing* that has led and is leading linguists to their customary doctrines of "phonetic laws."

The *confusion* of letters with sounds, of *graphemes* (representations of letters) with *phonemes* (representations of sounds), is responsible for:

1) conclusions about the difference and identity of sounds based on the difference or identity of letters;

2) the transfer of the notion of homogeneity and indivisibility from graphemes to phonemes. The proper analysis of the phoneme should lead us, on the contrary, to conclude that it is an objectively complex concept, a composite of irreducible elements, of the most simple real representations which are psychologically no longer divisible. On the articulatory side, they are representations of different activities (which are, in my opinion, incorrectly called "articulations"); and on the auditory side, they are representations of acoustic differences, resulting from the uniformity of representation of the vocal activities. I shall call the representations of the vocal articulatory activities *kinemes* and the representations of the

acoustic, psychologically indivisible differences, *acousmemes*. The unity of *kinemes* and *acousmemes* constitutes a *phoneme*. Phonemes are not like separate notes, but are like chords composed of several elements.

The totality of phonemes, kinemes and acousmemes found in any linguistic cerebration constitutes the systems of phonetic notions which are objectively present in men's "souls" (PT. 6–7, 52, 10–12).

The articulatory aspect is, moreover, usually confused with the auditory aspect, the emission of sound with perception, the representations of muscular sensations (the sensations of performed activities) with the acoustic and perceptive sensations. "Sounds" are called "labial," "dental," "palatal," etc.

It must be said that this confusion of ideas is characteristic of many scholars; only a few make the effort of thinking clearly and precisely.

Many scholars, who are either undemanding or incapable of critical thinking, confuse law, that is, functional interdependence, with statistical statements of facts or with plain coincidence. Others posit logical, methodological, and epistemological axioms, set up conditions *sine qua non* for each scientific proposition, and formulate subjective laws for any theoretical idea in place of objective laws that account for the relationships of observable facts. Almost all "phonetic laws" formulated by Kruszewski (PT. 52–53) belong to the latter category.

As happens in other fields of theoretical thought, the part of linguistics which contemplates the nature of "phonetic laws" breeds two kinds of theoreticians: those who are capable of dealing only with the concepts of elementary mathematics, such as the mathematical forms of discontinuity, integers, sums, intervals, finite states, and those who are capable of conceptualizing continuity in higher mathematical terms of differential and integral calculus.

Many linguists fail to understand that *causal relationships* can be subsumed under the *idea of law* precisely because there exist *imperceptible microscopic fluctuations and changes*. Between the starting and ending point of historical change (such as the transition from an original *k* to *č*, or *ei* to *i*), there is no relationship that could be interpreted as a law of evolution. On the contrary, the path of evolution taken by a series of generations presents an infinite number of discrete points, such that *each successive stage depends directly on the conditions of individual linguistic thought and on the conditions of social intercourse.* These points appear either in the individual or collective-individual psychological systems, or in the manifestation of articulatory and auditory representations (through the speech organs in the process of phonation or when the perceptive organ, the ear, receives the corresponding impressions).

Thus we must *exclude* from the domain of phonetic laws: (1) all the historical interrelations of the articulatory and auditory representations which can be stated in terms of precisely defined *alternations* of a given linguistic system (for example, in the linguistic system of Polish); (2) all the *phonetic correspondences of heteronomous linguistic cerebrations* (for example, the various correspondences in the linguistic cerebration of Slavic, Romance, Indo-European, and other languages); (3) the various *errors in pronunciation (lapsus linguae)* and *in hearing (lapsus auris)* (when we mistakenly hear one word instead of another); and (4) all easily observed cases of *substitution* of separate *phonemes*, etc. All *changes* which fall under the concept of "phonetic law" *occur unnoticeably,* like the changes in the mental states of a man or in the development of an organism (PT. 7–8, 33–34).

The confusion of the *individual language* with the *common language* is one of the greatest obstacles to the proper understanding of linguistic relationships and in particular of the problem of "phonetic laws." This confusion gave birth to Mr. Schuchardt's theory, according to which the "frequency of repetition of a word" determines its change and shortening. If it were only a matter of the constant repetition of a word by one speaker, the consequence of this purely mechanical effort and ensuing fatigue would, indeed, conform to the proposed theory. But this kind of repetition is peculiar to all members of a speech community, so that each individual, on his own part, pronounces the same word, if not for hours on end, at certain intervals (PT. 26–27, 40).

In the history of scientific and pseudoscientific linguistics the problem of phonetic laws has given rise to the following theories and interpretations:

1) According to those for whom language is an organism similar to the organisms of animals and plants, that is, an organism existing apart from man, all phonetic laws without exception are

"laws of nature" (*Naturgesetze*). This "theory" is a dogma, an article of faith, without practical consequences. Despite its vacuousness, it has for some time enjoyed popularity and is even now unconsciously at the basis of conclusions concerning individual linguistic behavior and linguistic thought in general. At any rate, the claims that language is born and dies independently of people, that the development, growth, and the history of a language are mutually exclusive, that there are no mixed languages, that words do not exist, etc., are closely connected with this viewpoint (PT. 49).

2) Another theory, which is the antithesis and complement of the first theory, sees language only as caprice, chaos, anarchy, and derides any attempt to discover in it relationships, causation, and to formulate scientific laws (PT. 44–45).

3) The appearance of the Neogrammarians (*Junggrammatiker*) and their followers should be seen as a protest against the theory which treated language as an organism apart from man. The Neogrammarians placed language again on a solid basis, regarding it as a function of man's organism. They explained the interdependence of phonemes or "sounds" of language and the "transitions" of sounds into other sounds in connection with the changes taking place in the speech organs. Unfortunately, the mind of many proponents of this theory is befuddled by that confusion of ideas which we spoke of earlier. Such is the confusion of the idea of individual language with that of average language or, in other words, the *fiction of the continuity of a linguistic base* in time and in space, and of the temporal continuity of one and the same pronunciation. For these scholars there is always an individual personifying all mankind or some ethnic group or a nation, who speaks continuously, never closing his mouth; this phonetic *perpetuum mobile* speaks, futhermore, so artfully that he constantly, without sleep and without rest, utters simultaneously all sounds or phonemes. The proponents of this theory, which confuses individual evolution with the history of an ethnic group (with polygenetic evolution), admit, it is true, the existence of gradual changes of phonetic representations (*Erinnerungsbilder, Lautbilder*), but they treat these changes as if they were taking place in a colossal brain of a single man or, at least, of an ethnic group (as far as the anatomical and physiological side of language is concerned) or in a monolithic psychological system of all mankind or, at least, of an

ethnic group (as far as the psychological side of language is concerned).

It would be unjust to assume that the proponents of this doctrine do not realize that changes in the so-called ethnic or national language cannot occur without the aid of social intercourse. In dealing with the question of "phonetic laws," they nevertheless choose to close their eyes to this outstanding fact. The carrier of linguistic variations is for them some imaginary being, representing all mankind, and the respective linguistic facts are investigated without any reference to the social interaction of people (PT. 49–50).

The Neogrammarians preach the dogma of the "unexceptional character of phonetic laws." If this is not to be an empty phrase, it can mean only that there is a *certain uniformity of phonetic correspondences* in the area of monolingualism and multilingualism, of correspondences that are conditioned historically by provenience from a common source or rather from common sources (PT. 8–9).

4) The Neogrammarian lack of respect for the fact that the general and abstract concept of an ethnic and national language is dissolved in the multitude of individuals, in the actually existing world of speakers and hearers who communicate through the intermediacy of the external world, has evoked opposition and brought forth a critique of their views. Most decisive and vigorous was the critique launched by Schuchardt.

This far-reaching critique and total rejection of the Neogrammarian dogma have, on the other hand, led to the view that linguistic, and in particular phonetic, changes are the result of more or less conscious *imitation,* that is, simply the result of *fashion* and the *mixture* of languages (PT. 50–51).

According to this view, which is now quite widespread and which arose in reaction to the rigid conception of the "unexceptional character of phonetic laws," each phonetic change has its own author, its own initiator (sex, age, and social position are irrelevant, though prominant personalities are supposed to play an important role), whom other people imitate, like sheep or geese. I suggest that we have to do here with a misunderstanding that will be overcome when the concept of *collective individuality,* which I am proposing, is generally accepted. Certainly any change, in nature or in social life, must have some starting point, must originate in some individual "soul," but this does not exclude the *simul-*

taneous beginning of a certain tendency, of a certain trend in different places and in different minds. This simultaneity should not be interpreted in a strictly mathematical sense. The difference of a second or even of several days (which cannot be pinned down *a posteriori*) is, from a historical point of view, still a case of simultaneity. In any event, I definitely *reject the opinion* that ascribes *to one man* the introduction of a linguistic innovation in the entire development of a language of a given ethnic group (PT. 24–25, 39).

There is no doubt that the consciousness and will of a people may exert a certain influence on changes of language. The same must be said of the role of literacy, education, etc. (PT. 27–28, 41–42). But if these were decisive, there would have to be noticeable, *macroscopic* differences in pronunciation. And, as I have already pointed out, any conditioned combination falling under the concept of "law" belongs to the field of imperceptible, *microscopic* differences.

The same applies to all kinds of mixing of languages and to borrowings that cause changes in pronunciation. As far as they carry the mark of macroscopic differences, they must be excluded from the concept of "phonetic laws," and if the concept of "phonetic laws" is to hold, the specific changes must be viewed as being microscopic and imperceptible (PT. 25–26, 30–34, 51).

After all that has been said, my opinion on this question should be clear. I shall complete it with a few remarks.

The "unexceptional character" of all phonetic correspondences and generalizations which go under the pretentious name "phonetic laws" can be compared with such "laws" as apply to meteorological generalizations or to various kinds of statistical generalization; in fact, they are only statements of what occurs on the surface of phenomena. Genuine "laws," the laws of causality, are *hidden in the depth,* in the intricate combination of the most diverse elements. "Laws" do exist, but not where they are being sought (PT. 9).

Of course, in any field, scientific thought, if it is not to be self-defeating, must start from the premise that nothing happens without a "cause," nothing happens outside a successive chain of causal connections and independently of condtions. The lack of exceptions is merely a corollary of logical thinking. We do not reject causality, leaving it to the nihilists and anarchists of science to do so.

We recognize *necessity, lack of exceptions,* and *absolute condi-*

tioning; we recognize *regularity* and the *necessity of absolutely
identical changes and the absence of absolutely identical changes
under absolutely identical conditions.* But at the same time we
must remember that the object of our observations, language,
presents extremely complex conditions, a multitude of the most
diverse combinations, and a variety of factors that operate in individuals as well as in the process of social interaction, including the
interaction of the individual with himself. We must also remember
that absolute identity of conditions is an extremely rare case (PT.
9–10, 45–46).

In the light of all this, it is even more amazing that we so often
encounter agreement between phonetic facts and their determining factors. And it is this very agreement that gives the impression
of a "law" and which has given birth to the fiction of "phonetic
laws."

N O T E S

1. ⟨This article is a translation of the French summary (pp. 57–82, in the
Sov. edition erroneously pp. 37–82) following the Polish article "O prawach
gtosowych."⟩ The abbreviation PT and the page numbers refer to the Polish
text.

X V

The Difference between Phonetics
and Psychophonetics

BRANCHES OF DIFFERENT SCIENCES often use the same name; thus "morphology" is used to designate both a branch of biology and a branch of glottology (linguistics). In linguistics itself the term "phonetics" is employed in two different senses that may cause a confusion of concepts: on the one hand, it refers to the "phonetics" or "phonology" of an individual or collective language or to "comparative phonetics" of several languages and, on the other hand to anthropophonetics, i.e., experimental, instrumental, or general phonetics, for which special chairs have even been set up at some universities.

Like so-called "experimental psychology," experimental phonetics is actually a natural science; neither of them deals with truly psychological or linguistic processes, but they examine only those psysiological and other phenomena that underlie and make possible the psychological and linguistic processes.

General or experimental phonetics includes: description of the speech apparatus (pronunciation, phonation); description of the auditory apparatus; description of the cerebral apparatus, the instrument of the linguistic thought processes; description of the medium (air) or natural channel of linguistic communication. The data of anthropophonetics or experimental phonetics are the phenomena which affect our senses in the process of social-linguistic intercourse and which are associated with mental concepts.

All sciences operate with representations and concepts. The

world provides data for thought only insofar as these are reworked into representations and concepts and become a part of man's psychological activity.

Sciences are divided into (1) those which do not conspicuously deal with the reflection of phenomena and their impressions and which include such outstanding products of the human mind as mathematics, logic, and gnoseology, or the theory of knowledge, and (2) those which deal with phenomena that are reflected in the human mind. The latter sciences study: (a) either the psychological surrogates of what is assumed to occur outside ourselves, that is, in nature, including our own body; and (b) what is assumed to occur only in us, that is, the psychological processes in the broadest sense, including individual psychology, social psychology, sociology, etc. However, inasmuch as interpersonal communication is impossible without the mediacy of physical means acting upon our senses, psychology itself must at each step take into account physical and physiological phenomena.

Like Janus, therefore, the life of man (and animal) presents a double face: one turned to the external world, to nature, and the other to the world of the mind, to the person. Halfway between the natural sciences and the so-called humanistic (or we should say animalistic) sciences stand such sciences as biology, anthropology, psychology, sociology, ethnology, and glottology (or linguistics). Some of them deal primarily with the natural element, others with the animalistic element.

The functions, processes, and impressions which, in the field of linguistics, refer to the external world and are transient, constitute the subject matter of the natural sciences, whereas insofar as they are constant and fixed concepts of the mind, they are the subject matter of linguistics proper.

The terms "sounding," "sound," "resonance," etc., designate the transient representations of linguistic thought and, therefore, belong to ⟨natural⟩ science; but insofar as they are representations of linguistic thought based on individual and individual-collective mental processes, they should be replaced by ⟨proper linguistic⟩ terms, such as:

phoneme, the psychological equivalent of physical "sound," the actual and reproducible phonetic unit of linguistic thought. The phoneme consists, in turn, of constituent elements of which we are not aware during linguistic intercourse but which can be obtained by analysis; they are:

the *kineme,* the articulatory, phonational element of linguistic thought;

the *acousmeme,* the simplest psychological element of audition or acoustic perception; and

the *kinakeme,* the complex representative of both the articulatory (phonational) and auditory elements.

This is the way things stand in psychologically oriented linguistic acoustics. In the graphic-visual sphere, in psychologically interpreted linguistic optics, we need similar terms, such as *grapheme,* etc., instead of such terms as "letter" and others, in order to designate the rendering of graphemes and their elements that are a part of socio-linguistic behavior.

The mechanical-acoustic and mechanical-optic phenomena that serve to render linguistic thought present neither continuity nor identity, but solely infinite change and diversity. They owe their identity only to the articulatory-auditory and graphic-visual representations that are ingrained in the human mind, although the representations themselves are, by no means, petrified or fixed; they are mobile, variable and accompanied by countless nuances.

The articulatory-auditory and graphic-visual representations exist in linguistic thought only insofar as they are *semasiologized* and *morphologized.*

The foregoing remarks lead us to conclude that we must distinguish two separate sciences: (1) a natural science, *phonetics* (phonology) or anthropophonetics, closely related to mechanics (dynamics, kinetics) and physics (acoustics, optics), and (2) *psychophonetics,* which is a "humanistic" science closely related to psychology and sociology. Of course, these two sciences are not altogether separated but rather overlap. As a linguistic science psychophonetics studies only that which exists in the form of articulatory-auditory representations.

But even psychophonetics, or phonetics which is related to the collective-individual (i.e., tribal, or national) forms of linguistic thought, must take into account the results of experimental anthropophonetics or natural phonetics, which enable us to discern that which is residually semasiologized (and morphologized) and that which contains the germ of future distinctions among articulatory-acoustic elements and their eventual semasiologizations.

An example of residual distinctions is the difference between the two *j*'s, i.e., between *j* continuing the proto-Indo-European *i̯*, and the *j* which stems historically from proto-Slavic *di̯* (*dj*), a difference that Belić established, in my presence, for the Slavic dialects of Istria.

An example of phenomena that point to future distinctions is the historical transition from the distinction of the velars *k, g, x* depending on the following palatal or nonpalatal vowels into an autonomous distinction independent of the phonetic sequence: *k, g, x*, and *k', g', x',* ⟩ *č, ž, š*.

Just as it is necessary to distinguish phonetics and psychophonetics, sounds and phonemes, etc., so one must keep apart letters and sounds, graphemes and phonemes. There is no direct relationship between the optical impressions of letters and the acoustic impressions of sounds; there exist only associations of written-visual representations with articulatory-acoustic representations, of graphemes with phonemes, and vice versa.

Two types of confusion must then be guarded against: (a) that of letters with sounds, graphemes with phonemes (and their respective constituent elements), and (b) that of phonetic-auditory phenomena with their fixed psychological counterparts. For example, in Polish there is no psychological distinction between the phoneme rendered by the grapheme *y* and the phoneme rendered by the grapheme *i*. Instead of two apparently different phonemes *y* and *i*, Polish has only one–i_m (*i mutabile*).

All psychophonetic and psychographic representations, insofar as they exist in linguistic thinking, are semasiologized and morphologized. Acoustic or optic impressions may exist outside the sphere of semasiologization and morphologization, but they are not a part of linguistic thinking.

With respect to their morphological role, individual phonemes may:

form a part of the syntagm, i.e., of the word as a morphological element of the sentence; e.g., Polish *o, a, u, i_m*;

or constitute a morpheme within a word; e.g., *a* in *vod–a, śan–a, bik–a, gad–a*; *u* in *stoł–u, ojc–u, pis–u–je*. . . ; *o* in *śan–o, žon–o*. . . ; *e* in *pol–e, stol–e, ńeś–e*. . . ; i_m in *vod–i_m, m'ez–i_m, ńić–i_m, stoj–i_m, vol–i_m*. . . ; *b* in *lič–b–a, šej–b–a*. . . ; *n* in *trud–n–, lič–n–, da–n–*. . . ; *t* in *b'i–t–, dar–t–, bi–t–*. . . ;

or enter into the structure of a morpheme as its main semasiologized and morphologized component; e.g., Polish $o \parallel a$ in *mog-* $\parallel$ *mag-, noś–i–* $\parallel$ *naš–, vol–i–* $\parallel$ *val–.* . . .

The morphological structure of words must be distinguished from their articulatory-acoustic structure, as evidenced, for example, by the existence of rhymes.

Semasiologization and morphologization contribute to preservation of phonological distinctions acquired in the history of a national language.

The morphologization of articulatory-acoustic differences may show different tendencies at different periods of the history of a given linguistic community. For example, in Polish the connection between the various endings of the declension and the final consonants of the stem was once different from what it is now: *sto–l–e* | *król–u, muř–e* | *kuř–u, pań–e* | *koń–u.* . . ; *śćań–e, ręc–e* | *putsi*$_m$*–ń–i, m'eʒ–i, šij–i.* In the past the chief distinction was between palatal and nonpalatal consonants; at present it is between consonants which change psychophonetically in the declension vs. consonants which remain unchanged.

Morphologization affects only certain articulatory-auditory distinctions and different ones in different languages; for example, intonation, length (i.e., length or shortness, *quantitas temporalis*), accent, palatalization or nonpalatalization, the degree of opening of the oral cavity ($o \parallel u, a \parallel \mathring{a}, e \parallel e^i$), the place of articulation ($e \parallel a$), voicing or voicelessness. . . . Semasiologization, on the other hand, affects all articulatory-auditory distinctions: *to* $\parallel$ *po, kot* $\parallel$ *pot, do* $\parallel$ *no, tom* $\parallel$ *dom, kos* $\parallel$ *kąs, sam* $\parallel$ *tam, car* $\parallel$ *čar.* . . .

Semantic differences allow for a different morphological analysis of homonyms: *dam–Ø* "of ladies" ($Ø$ = zero) | *da–m* "I give". . . .

The degree of morphologization affects the varying historical susceptibility of the phonemes of a national language to articulatory-auditory change; for example:

$-m \rangle -n$ when the morphologization of $-m$ is weak, but
$-m \rangle -m$ when the morphologization of $-m$ is strong;
$-t \rangle (-t)$ (facultative t) when the morphologization of $-t$ is weak, but
$-t \rangle -t$ when the morphologization of $-t$ is strong.

The relationship between the individual, psychological and the collective, social element may vary in different phonemes: in some of them there is a preponderance of the individual and changeable, of physiology and phonation (in the phonemes $t. . . , s. . . , x. . .$), and in others a preponderance of the collective and general, of acoustics and audition (in the phonemes of nasal resonance, in l, $r. . .$, in the vowels).

The assumptions of "sound laws" operating "without exceptions," of gradual, purely physiological change in a definite direction, and of gradual "transition" of some phonetic nuances into others (n_1, n_2, n_3, n_4, . . . n_n) are not confirmed by the actual facts of language and are in contradiction with its socio-psychological character. ⟨. . .⟩ The first of these assumptions is confirmed neither by scientific phonetics nor by historical psychophonetics. "Sound-laws" would be possible only if we ignored the existence of individuals, collectivity, social life, linguistic intercourse—in brief, the impact of sociology on linguistic behavior.

The physiological-mechanical production of phonemes and their combinations yields various kinds of temporary and transitory *adaptation*, whereas psychophonetics involves psychological *habits* (for example, the habit of narrowing vowels before nasal consonants).

Psychophonetic differences and identities exert an influence upon the *morphological types*. For example, in the Bohinj-Posavian dialects of Slovenia, the merger of l and v into a single phoneme w yields the declension: *gwawa, gwale, gwali; mrtw, mrtli* instead of the older *głava, głave, głavi; mrtv, mrtvi.* Compare also the Polish *kakауo* "cocoa" | *v kakale.*

XVI

The Influence of Language on World-View and Mood

. . . 20. In the first lecture I spoke about the dependence of world-view and mood on language in the proper sense of the word, that is, on articulatory-auditory language. For in addition to language in this sense, there is, as a result of civilization, a graphic-visual aspect of language, that is, writing, literacy.

Writing, too, can exert an influence on world-view, on the capabilities and mood of the writer and reader, which is similar to that of the various forms of auditory language.

Let us consider first the differences in the mental processes of the literate person as opposed to those of the illiterate person.

Literacy weakens the memory of acoustically received and transmitted phenomena. A literate person is not capable of storing in his memory (on the basis of hearing alone) such great folk epics as the Russian *byliny* (even if we should agree with Rožneckij that they are Slavic reworkings of Scandinavian sagas) or the Serbian heroic songs. The memory of a literate person regresses and can no longer do without the aid of reading and writing.

The objectivization of linguistic representations, of what is thought and spoken by means of language, differs likewise in the literate and illiterate person. For example, when I, as a literate person, want to imagine something that can be expressed through language, I visualize, as it were, written words and phrases. I can no longer remember how I imagined the same thing in my childhood before I had learned to read and write. (Most likely I made no effort in this direction at all.) In this context we should also notice that aural hallucinations are far less frequent than visual hallucinations.

21. As for other questions concerning the relation of writing to world-view and mood, we must first distinguish two forms of writing:

1) writing that bears a more or less close relationship to the phonetic-acoustic side of language;

2) writing that bears a relationship to the extralinguistic concepts of the external world.

The second form of writing (e.g., ideograms, Egyptian hieroglyphics, Chinese writing) evidently influences the human mind differently than the alphabetic writings which were and are now dominant among most nations.

Ideographic writing can actually be read in any language, while our customary writing system mobilizes the phonetic-acoustic side of our particular linguistic thinking.

22. The simplest elements of a written language do not correspond at all to the simplest elements of sound language. As a rule, the simplest elements of writing are *graphemes,* that is, representations of letters or syllables, while the corresponding *phonemes,* that is, the representations of sounds, can be decomposed into more elementary phonetic and acoustic, psychologically determined elements. A letter, or sometimes a complex of letters, is itself indivisible, but represents the phonetic-acoustic aspect of language in such a way that it is associated with the phonetic-acoustic elements of a particular phonema and the phoneme as a whole.

The orthography of our written languages is based on two main principles: (1) phonemography and, (2) morphemography.

Phonemography is the one-sided, strictly phonetic way of writing, in which the division of the sentence into syntagms or syntactic elements and of the word into morphemes or morphological elements is not taken into consideration. Conversely, morphemography focuses on psychological affinity, on the associations of the sentence with other sentences and of the word with other words.

The grammatically regulated (normalized) method of writing in Sanskrit is a classic example of one-sided phonemography. But along with the phonemographic method of writing, or *Samhita,* we find in the texts of the *Rigveda* a parallel word-by-word commentary (*Pada*) which separates the individual words of the sentence (and the components of compounds) in approximately the European way. This method makes use of syntagmography, as opposed to morphemography in the narrow sense, which is based on the segmentation of words into etymologically different morphemes. The last method is alien to Sanskrit orthography which has no spellings such as German *schreibt* (with *b,* as in *schreiben*), *gestrebt* (with *b* as in *streben*), *ragt* (with *g,* as in *ragen*), *Tod* (with *d,* as in *Todes*), *Sieb* (with *b,* as in *Siebe*), alongside *Stock* (with *ck,* as *Stockes*), *Lump* (with *p,* as *Lumpes*), *steckt* (with *ck,* as in *stecken*), or Polish *sad* (with *d,* as in *sadu*), *rog* (with *g,* as in *rogu*), *grob* (with *b,* as in *grobu*), alongside *kot* (with *t,* as in *kota*), *rok* (with *k,* as in *roku*), *chłop* (with *p,* as in *chłopa*). Spelling within the ⟨Sanskrit⟩ word is based thoroughly on phonemography.

Phonemography is also the principle of Old Church Slavonic spelling, though here it is not applied consistently.

23. One-sided phonemographic writing reflects the tendency of our thinking toward monism and the selection of a single principle, while morphemography in combination with phonemography favors a *dualism* or even a *pluralism* of principles.

Pluralism of orthographic principles is found primarily in the writing systems of those people whose orthography (spelling) was created in ancient times on the basis of the orthography of a foreign language, and when the phonetic-acoustic aspect of the given language was still subject to serious gradual change.

Pluralism of orthographic principles characterizes, for example, French orthography, but a more typical case is written English. Side by side with phonemography, and to a somewhat lesser degree, morphemography, English spelling has some elements of syntagmography, and makes constant reference to the language's past, to Old English, and to the languages that influenced English. Just as a country may issue special documents to aliens living in it temporarily, in order to set them apart from the natives and immigrants, the Englishman marks the words which appear to him as borrowings by a special spelling. This is why he distinguishes the letters *k* and *c* and the different pronunciations of the sequences *gi, ge,* etc. The discrimination of real, or supposed, borrowings by a special spelling is practiced in the orthographies of other languages as well (e.g., in French, German, Czech, and Polish), but nowhere is it applied with such consistency as in English.

When we read an English written (or printed) text, we associate the visual with extralinguistic concepts, i.e., representations of meaning, so that vision and hearing operate simultaneously. The extralinguistic representations are in part directly related to the visual ones without the intermediacy of pronunciation although in part, they depend on this intermediacy. In this respect, English orthography recalls to a certain extent ideographic and hieroglyphic systems of writing.

24. All writing systems exhibit, in addition, some elements of *ideography*. Here we refer primarily to punctuation marks, blanks between words, divisions into chapters, variations in the size and thickness of letters, etc.; but that form of ideography which is characteristic of English, namely the direct association of visual representations of words with extralinguistic concepts without the intermediacy of hearing, is evidently rare.

Differences in writing are in all probability connected with differences of world-view. But how this connection actually comes about I could not attempt to explain.

I shall venture to remark only that, for example, the English system of writing forces thought to move simultaneously in various directions, enhancing the activity of the mind. Impressions connected with both hearing and vision (and their corresponding associations) are aroused simultaneously.

25. The influence of orthography on world-view and mood also depends on whether it renders the speech-sounds clearly and accurately or leaves certain things incompletely expressed and to the reader's conjecture.

Thus, in the Semitic systems of writing, only the consonants were originally indicated; the supplementation of vowels, that is, of the various syllable-forming elements of speech, was more or less left to the reader. This method is sometimes applied in the printing of European textbooks (for example, in Poland), in which letters are used to represent consonants, and dots vowels. It is left to the wit of the student to supply the missing letters.

Most orthographies do not mark stress (accent), which characterizes the spoken word in any language, or the singing quality that is carried by various types of intonation, or quantity (length or shortness) of vowels; in other words, all those quantitative elements of human speech that accompany the activity of the vocal cords. In order to pronounce correctly a written word of German, French, English, Danish, Russian, Serbo-Croatian, Slovenian, Lithuanian,

Latvian, or some other language, one must first understand the word. To the speaker of a given language this presents no special problem, but for the foreigner this is a difficult task.

Not all peoples are as considerate of outsiders as the Magyars, Czechs, or Slovaks, who designate vowel length employed by their language by special diacritical marks; and since stress in these languages is always bound to the first syllable, the foreigner confronted with a Hungarian, Czech, or Slovak text can generally pronounce the words correctly.

The Poles are rather fortunate in that their language completely ignores the quantitative differences mentioned above. And since stress plays no morphological role in the pronunciation of individual Polish words (that is, it does not serve to separate morphemes but pertains entirely to the field of sentence phonetics (*Satzphonetik*), where it serves to separate syntagms of more than one syllable within the sentence by stressing the penultimate syllable of these syntagms), the Poles can afford, without any orthographic effort, to be altruistic with respect to people speaking other languages.

Systems of writing in which important elements of pronunciation are left to the reader's acumen probably have a positive influence on his ingenuity and ability to solve problems and crossword puzzles.

26. The history of the people accounts for a great deal in the writing systems of French, English, Swedish, Danish, and other languages that does not occur in the respective spoken languages. The French spelling *est* reflects the original Latin pronunciation; although the French word lost its consonants, the old spelling was preserved thanks to the written tradition and the influence of sentence phonetics (*liaison*). All the above-mentioned languages present two norms (*die doppelten Sprachen*): one of pronunciation, and the other of spelling, with numerous examples similar to the French one.

In the history of a given collective language, some phonemes may, furthermore, disappear, that is, not be reproduced by succeeding generations or survive only facultatively. In the latter case they may continue to exist as morphologized phonetic-acoustic representations, but they vary in their acoustic implementation: in careful speech they are pronounced and heard, but in rapid speech they are too weak to reach the periphery of the speech apparatus and to appear in the physical world of the speaker and listener.

Such facultativeness is of interest in the case of languages whose orthography makes use of the historical principle even when they are chiefly based on the principles of morphemography and phonemography (or contemporary pronunciation). For example, when the Polish words, written *jabłko, szedł, rzekł, garnka, ziarnko* are pronounced *japko, šet, žek, garka, žarko,* or in a higher style, *japłko, šetł, garnka, žarnko,* the speakers are primarily aware of the morphological connection of these forms with the forms *jabłek, szła, rzekła, garnek, ziarnek,* but the spelling as well as the careful, solemn pronunciation continue the earlier state of the Polish collective language. . . .

28. In systems of writing which combine the principle of phonemography with elements of morphemography, the parallelism or lack of parallelism between the chain of sounds and the chain of printed symbols, between the sequences of graphemes and the sequences of phonemes, generally exerts an influence upon the mode of thinking.

Thus, for example, in Russian phonemography, certain properties of the consonants are graphically rendered not by graphemes which usually stand for consonants but by the symbols for vowels that follow them or by the substitutes for vowels. In the Russian letter combinations *ba/bja, tu/tju, sè/se, p″/p′, l″/l′, ly/li,* etc., the symbols for the consonants are identical, but the symbols for the vowels differ; in pronunciation the reverse is the case: the consonants differ (*l″/l′, p″/p′,* etc.), but the following vowels (excluding the zero vowel) are identical.

This lack of parallelism leads to a confusion of concepts, to a confusion of letters with sounds, of graphemes with phonemes, so that one speaks ⟨misleadingly⟩ of the "soft" vowels *ja, ju, je, ji* and the "hard" vowels *a, u, e, u.*

A similar confusion affects the phonemography of Ukrainian, White Russian, and Bulgarian, as well as of Polish, Slovak, and Czech, which use the Latin alphabet.

Complete parallelism of the written and the pronounced word is found in the Serbian and Croatian orthographies, no matter whether they use the Cyrillic (Russian) or Latin alphabets.

A lack of graphic-phonetic parallelism, similar to that in the Russian system of writing, is found in French, Italian, and in general in the modern Romance languages (as well as in English and earlier in German). Cf. the pronunciation of the graphic sequences *ca co cu ga go gu* vs. *ce ci* . . . , *ge gi* . . .

French: *que, qui, gue, gui* . . . , *ça ço çu* . . . *ja jo* . . . ;

Italian: *che chi* . . . *ghe ghi* . . . *cia cio ciu* . . . *gia gio giu.* . . .

The confusion of letters with sounds is paralleled in other areas of human thought (compare, for example, the confusion of religious denomination with nationality, citizenship, or personal qualities). . . .

XVII

Facultative Sounds of Language

1. The Rezian dialects (spoken in the communities of Resia ⟨Rezija⟩ and Ucce in the district of Moggio near Udine in northeast Italy), which I investigated first in 1873 and several times thereafter, are, in my opinion, a separate dialect group, as are the dialects of certain other language areas (especially Slovenian and Serbo-Croatian). The following ⟨Rezian⟩ phenomena, among others, attracted my attention:

At various times I perceived as different the seemingly identical (linguistically speaking) final consonant –*t* of the words and word groups: *pôt* "way," *svît* "world," *lît* "year," on the one hand, and *pêt* "five," *dœvat* "nine," *dœsat* "ten," *šejst* "six," ..., *pêt lît* "five years," *dœvat lît* "nine years," *dœsat lît* "ten years," *šejst lît* "six years" ..., on the other hand. Sometimes I heard the –*t* in all these words, but more often only in *pôt, lît,* ..., but not in *pêt, dœvat,* ... i.e., *pê, dœva, dœsa, šejs* ..., *pê lît,* and, less often, in none of these words; i.e., not only *pê* ..., but also *pô, lî,* ... *pe li.* ...

What we are dealing with here is obviously not only the different perception of words ending in –*t* but of all words with a final consonant. (Cf. my "Versuch einer Phonetik der resianischen Dialekte," *Opyt fonetiki rez'janskix govorov* [Warsaw-Petersburg-Leipzig, 1875], §§ 89–103).

2. In the Serbo-Croatian dialect of southern Italy (the communities of Acquaviva, Colle-Croci, San Felice Savo, and Montemitro in the district of Molise of Campobasso province), I discovered a similar phenomenon affecting the final vowels. Thus, for example, the word *udovica* "widow" is sometimes pronounced *udovica,* but more frequently *udovic.* This is evidently connected with the fact that in the Slavic dialect of Molise the importance of

291

the desinential endings as syntactic morphemes has sharply declined under the influence of the neighboring Albanian and Italian dialects and especially the Italian literary language, which is used in schools, business, government, the church, military service, cultural affairs, and literature. We see here one of the final stages in the weakening of the morphologization of endings, a manifestation of the tendency to eliminate inflection.

3. Upon a cursory examination one might regard this as a contradiction of the laws of logic: what seems to be psychologically identical sometimes appears externally as a positive unit and sometimes as a zero. This logical and gnoseological puzzle can be solved if one approaches the question from a psychological viewpoint and bears in mind the fact that in one's own language, i.e., in actual individual linguistic thought, we do not encounter strictly *phonetic* or phonetic-acoustic phenomena, but psychologically live *psychophonetic phenomena*, images, and psychological-social processes. In linguistic thought there are no sounds; there are only *representations (concepts) of sounds*. But in linguistic intercourse (i.e., in collective linguistic behavior), there are not only linguistic concepts in the individual soul or brain, but the speaker also informs the hearer, by physical means, that he has mobilized at a given moment some of his linguistic concepts, while the hearer receives the impressions and sensations thereby formed. Not everything that is either consciously or semi-consciously dormant in linguistic thought manifests itself every time.

4. Let us consider, for example, the case cited at the beginning of this article: the pronunciation or nonpronunciation of consonants at the end of a word in the Rezian dialect (§ 1). What factors are here to be considered operating and operative?

First, there is the general psychophonetic tendency to an ever greater weakening of consonants at the end of a word, a tendency which gradually must lead to the total psychological loss of these consonants (more precisely, to their not being reestablished in the minds of a given generation).

Second, there are various degrees of morphologization and semasiologization, various degrees of psychological stress (psychological accent) of individual morphologized and semasiologized phonemes.

Third, there are differences of tempo and style of speech. On the one hand, though more rarely, there is a greater or lesser degree of

292

solemnity and carefulness; on the other hand, in everyday life there is a greater or lesser degree of carelessness. With increasing carelessness in pronunciation, there is a decline in the ability to resist weakening and change. A well-known example is the pronunciation or nonpronunciation of the French *e muet.*

5. The above-mentioned tendencies toward the weakening and ultimate disappearance of final consonants in the speech of a community is only a special case of the general tendency toward abbreviation, simplification, and relaxation of effort which is present in individual and collective linguistic behavior.

Just as two seemingly identical pieces of iron, glass, or sealing wax behave differently, depending on whether they do or do not possess magnetic or electric energy, so, too, the relative ability of seemingly identical phonemes to withstand quantitative or even qualitative change depends on the degree of their semasiologization and morphologization.

In the Rezian (cf. § 1) indeclinables *pêt* "five," *dœvat* "nine," the $-t$ is only the final consonant of a single word used in the "general case" (*casus generalis, casus unicus*), and it plays no special morphological or inflectional role; an understanding of the word in connection with other words hardly requires that its existence be signaled aloud in the communicative process, i.e., that the word be pronounced or perceived as either *pêt* or *pê*. Conversely, *pôt* "way" and *lît* "year" represent only one case among several others: *pôta, pôtu, pôton* . . . , *lœto, lœton, lîta, lîtan.* . . . The final stem consonant $-t$ plays here a highly important morphological role as a morphological link or boundary between two morphemes, and we are constantly reminded of its role. Thus, while the psychological *pêt* is rendered physically as an audible *pê*, with *pêt* being used only in high, solemn speech, the final $-t$ in *pôt, lît,* resists elimination even in the physically weakened or reduced pronunciation of everyday linguistic intercourse. If, however, carelessness in pronunciation prevails, the psychophonetic tendency toward eventual weakening of the final consonant can cancel out even strong morphologization, so that even *pôt, lît,* etc., whose final $-t$ is present in the speaker's mind, are rendered by the shortened sound forms *pô, lî.* . . .

6. The same applies to all cases of weakening of psychophonetic energy, of lessening of psychological stress, of the decrease in the semasiologization and morphologization of speech elements that

takes place with the passage of time in the history of all collective languages without exception. There is a continuous "struggle" between two opposing tendencies: between a progressive drive toward simplification, ease, and elimination of superfluous activities, and a conservative, therapeutic force striving, also physically, to underscore indispensable psychophonetic elements. If one takes his speech activity seriously, accurately, and responsibly and wishes to express and to project into the external world everything that is mobilized in the mind, then the conservative principle prevails. But if one treats his own speech less rigorously, the mobilization of the sound image, or the linguistic representation of the less essential elements of language in the mind will not be strong enough to reach the world of the senses or to become perceptible and to signal its presence. Then only the intention remains, without its psychological realization. When carelessness of speech is increased, i.e., when speech energy is reduced, the tendency toward a psychophonetic weakening of the categories that correspond to the acoustic elements prevails, so that they all remain, regardless of the degree of their semasiologized or morphologized prominence, in a state of psychological mobilization without affecting the world of external perception.

7. There are, of course, individuals who speak very carefully and clearly and whose pronunciation counteracts the weakenings and changes in the language of the community. But such individuals are the exception. Most people speak slovenly. An unaccustomed listener or participant in a conversation "does not get the full message," is not in a position to understand it, and asks that it be repeated; upon repetition, the intended psychological sound-representation is, as a rule, rendered with precision.

But even individuals who are extremely slovenly in their speech usually write far more accurately, conveying their linguistic concepts and representations more precisely in the sphere of optics than in that of acoustics. Writing thus exerts a conservative effect on speech habits. It often happens that children learning to read conceive their natural speech as faulty and unsuitable, and instead of *speaking*, begin, in fact, to *read*. Their speaking is guided by their reading.

8. The weakening and disappearance of phonemes and other psychophonetic elements which are not sufficiently semasiologized and morphologized is counteracted by practice in the solemn and

high style of speech which is used in schools, offices, on the stage, on the podium, at official meetings, at public gatherings, etc.

9. The revival or restoration of psychophonetic elements that have seemingly disappeared and can no longer be reproduced in the national language can be effected through communication with representatives of other dialects in which a certain phoneme is still psychologically present and externally manifested.

10. An inhibiting influence on the course of change and a stimulus toward the revival of disappearing elements is, in the case of literate and educated speakers, exerted by the familiarity of these speakers with the earlier stages of the development of the given linguistic forms (material): knowledge of Latin among the French and Italians; knowledge of standard literary French (or of standard Italian or standard Spanish) by those who speak the modern and recent French patois.

11. The use of slovenly speech in everyday life is, nevertheless, far more common than the use of clear and solemn speech; and because of its high frequency, it ultimately prevails. The accretion of the phenomena of slovenly speech in the course of many generations, i.e., the nonpronunciation of weakly equipped phonemes, brings about their extinction. A phoneme approaching extinction conveys to the representatives of one or another generation such weak acoustic impressions of its psychological stress that these no longer suffice to mobilize their psychological attention, i.e., to awaken the old sound image in the mind of the next generation.

The phoneme looses the energy necessary for its existence, and there occurs a historical transition of a certain positive quantity into a historical-phonetic zero.

What was acoustically and physically facultative for an earlier generation ceases to exist even psychologically for a later generation.

12. This is, for example, how we should think of the transition of the final consonants inherited from the Latin linguistic state to a zero in Italian, French, and in all other Romance dialects, i.e., a reduction of consonants characteristic of the later phase of the Italo-Romance linguistic material. . . .

XVIII

Problems of Linguistic Affinity

---

1. The comparison of languages, the determination of their similarities and differences, their comparative characterization and classification can be studied from three points of view:

1) *Historical affinity,* actual affinity of languages as a result of transmission and borrowing between generations by way of tradition, i.e., in a direct line of historical succession, or through communication, both articulatory-auditory and graphic-visual, among speakers of different languages (among peoples of different origin) This viewpoint involves questions of linguistic kinship, linguistic families, "genealogical trees" (*Stammbäume*), "proto-languages" (*Ursprachen*), primary languages (*Grundsprachen*), and secondary ones. But it is also concerned with the question of the "polygenesis" of each language, with the fact that each language is the result of fusion and interaction of various languages.

2) *Affinity,* based on the *communality* and *similarity* of *features in languages* that are in *geographic contiguity* and share the same substratum.

3) *Similarities and differences common to all mankind,* dependent neither on genealogy (historical kinship) nor on spatial contiguity (geography).

The first type of comparison makes reference to a substratum which is mainly historical; the second, to a substratum which is mainly geographical, and the third, to a substratum which is physiological-psychological. But in all three types the explanation of facts requires simultaneous reference to history and geography, physiology and psychology, and even to physics and mechanics.

2. Here, as in other branches of linguistics, we are faced with the deep-rooted habit of personifying and spiritualizing language, that

is, with the habit of treating languages as if they were individual beings, "living organisms," independent of their speakers. It is this habit which accounts for both the theory of the "genealogical tree" of related languages (*Stammbaumtheorie*) and the "wave theory (*Wellentheorie*). According to the first theory language is a living being, animal or vegetable (as Schleicher says, "Sprachen, wie alle Naturorganismen"), whereas according to the second theory (*Wellentheorie*), first advanced by Johann Schmidt, waves spread out from individual centers with tendencies toward a particular kind of change emanating from neighbors. Language is accordingly divorced from man and is viewed as a flowing, liquid substance, something like water or a poison gas.

The concept of isoglosses, which is connected with the wave theory, has in fact, however, a solid foundation and must figure in any sober approach that treats language as an anthropological phenomenon involving the subject, or man as a speaking being.

I have already criticized the one-sidedness of the genealogical tree and wave theories in my Petersburg doctoral dissertation, *Očerk fonetiki rez'janskix govorov,* and I have emphasized the importance of linguistic fusion for any comparative characterization and classification of languages in my various later works (for example, in "On the Mixed Character of all Languages") and lectures at scientific congresses. At the same time I was able to refer to the concurring views of such outstanding scholars as Hugo Schuchardt and G. I. Ascoli.

3. The disintegration and fusion of languages can and must be considered with relation to the history of interacting *human communities.*

Even individual languages are to be treated as products of fusion, inasmuch as each individual language is the result of interaction of the existing individual languages.

Even within one and the same family the formation of individual languages allows for great variations. Given a free range of development along a certain line, these variations may increase to such an extent that children of the same parents, brought up under the same roof, will eventually begin to speak different dialects, if not entirely different languages.

Individual peculiarities of the articulatory-auditory apparatus, and the system of associations that underlies the formation of morphological types, account for the tendency to substitute some of the articulatory processes and their concomitant auditory impressions (for example, the substitution of *u* for *ł*, velar and uvular *r* for apical *r*), and to replace complex morphological types with simpler ones (for example, *płaka* instead of *placze,* from *płakać*). Environmental influence and standards of grammatical correctness tend to suppress these deviations from the prevailing norms of a given speech community. But the embryonic deviations do not disappear without trace: as long as the descendants reiterate the incipient (individual or hereditary) tendencies of their ancestors, and as long as the same process recurs over successive generations, the gradually accruing tendencies may become strong enough to resist the pressure of the existing linguistic norm and to affect its structure by way of "neologisms" which the given and following speech communities will consider correct and obligatory.

In general, however, the individual and embryonic deviations from the social norm decrease in the process of linguistic intercourse within a given social environment; the individual languages are drawn closer together and are eventually unified.

4. We are familiar with *mixed* languages, that is, languages that everyone (both linguists and the ordinary speakers of the language) recognize as being mixed.

One such typical mixed language is the Russian-Chinese language of Kjaxta and Majmačina on the Siberian-Chinese border, or the "Kjaxta dialect of the Russian language." Its lexicon, its inventory of words, is almost exclusively Russian, but its structure, its morphology bear a clear imprint of Chinese.

In the same way there arose English-Chinese, Portuguese-Chinese, and other dialects. The study of these dialects was primarily advanced by Hugo Schuchardt, who also directed his attention to the mixed Creole containing Romance material.

A Romance base was also assumed by G. I. Ascoli when he tried to explain the strikingly common properties of the linguistic area that he called *Zona Ladina* (the area of Friuli in the provinces of Udine and Gorica, the Ladins in Tyrol, and the Grisons in Switzerland). According to G. I. Ascoli, to whom we are indebted for the hypothesis of linguistic fusion, various parts of this territory that is now occupied by the Friulians, Ladins, and Grisons was at one time settled by foreign tribes which assimilated Latin, or Romance linguistic material into their native idioms. The problem of the *Zona Ladina* is closely connected with the problem of the diffusion of the Franco-Gallic dialects.

English and Roumanian are similarly considered to be "mixed" languages. The former absorbed Germanic, Romance, and some Celtic elements, and the latter, Romance and Slavic elements.

5. The historical emergence of Latvian was due to the fusion of the Aistian or Baltic language (which is now represented by Lithuanian, but which at one time also included Old Prussian) with a Finnic, or rather Finno-Ugric language. As the famous Latvian-German investigator, Pastor Bielenstein, was able to show on the basis of historical documents the Finnic tribe of the Courlanders gradually lost its linguistic identity during the thirteenth century when it came into contact with an Indo-European population, the presumed ancestors of the present-day Lithuanians.

6. We could observe with our own eyes the formation of mixed German-Slavic dialects on a Slovenian base in the former southwestern part of Austria (now in Yugoslavia and partly in Italy, which occupied a large part of purely Slavic territory after World War I). The Germans from Tyrol and Bavaria who had settled various parts of Krajna and Gorica were concentrated mostly in Kočevje (Gotschee) around Novo Mesto, in Ribnica (Reifniz) in Lower Krajna (Dolenjsko), in several scattered villages of Upper Krajna (Gorenjsko), and in the province of Gorica. Here and there we still encounter the name *Nemški Rovt* (*Deutschreuth*). Upon my visit to these places in 1872 and 1873, I came right at at transitional period: old people spoke German with each other, but they understood Slovenian; middle-aged people spoke mainly Slovenian with each other, but German with the older generation; young people and children generally understood German, but spoke Slovenian with each other as well as with their parents and grandparents. When heard at some distance so that separate words could not be distinguished, this Slovenian speech of theirs sounded just like German. From an articulatory-auditory viewpoint it was nothing but a precise replica of German phonetics and psychophonetics. But even the morphology, word-formation, syntax, and other areas of linguistic thought were based on the German linguistic system of previous generations. The pulpit, school, military service in Slovenian regiments of the Austrian army, as well as the constant contact with other Slovenians had eventually exerted an influence

on this *German-Slovenian* dialect, cleansing it, as it were, of its German substratum, and Slavicizing it. What happened to this dialect is similar to what happens in the language of children, whose embryonic individual deviations are exposed to the pressures of the normal language of the family and nation to which I have alluded above. I suppose that the present-day Slovenian spoken in these formerly German areas no longer gives the impression of a German dialect and no longer contains enough elements to qualify it as German in a linguistic analysis.

Let us suppose, however, that in the period of transition, that is, at the time of my visit at the beginning of the second half of the past century, a significant part of the speakers of this unique Slovenian dialect which had to be qualified as mixed German-Slovenian, had to emigrate and settle either on an uninhabited island or in foreign, non-Slavic surroundings (let us say, in Romance, Germanic, Finnic, or Altaic areas) without abandoning their peculiar dialect for a number of generations. Each unprejudiced investigator would then have the right, and duty, to acknowledge the existence of a particular Slavic linguistic community along with the other Slavic linguistic communities. We may recall the descendants of the Serbo-Croats from Dalmatia and neighboring districts and the descendants of the Albanians who, after the death of Skanderbeg in the fifteenth century, fled from Turkish persecution to the Campobasso Province in Southern Italy, and who have to this day retained even the articulatory-auditory nuances of their native languages. In the same way the descendants of our hypothetical German-Slovenian emigrants from the Krajna and Gorica could have retained for generations the peculiarities of their dialect of the middle of the nineteenth century caught at a stage of transition.

Some Slovenian and Serbo-Croatian dialects of Istria, Gorica, and Krajna bear distinct traces of the Roumanian language of colonists who were assimilated by the neighboring Slavs, but whose survival in the modern language could not be explained without recourse to this hypothesis, a hypothesis which is, furthermore, supported by the presence of Roumanian speakers, the so-called Ciribiri, in Istria, near Mt. Učka (Montemaggiore). (I am not sure, by the way, whether the inhabitants of this place still speak a Roumanian dialect.)

7. As a typical example of how a given language may adopt the

traits of a totally different language (including its articulatory and auditory features), I can cite the situation of the valley of Rezija with its neighboring Ucce (Wolf) Valley, which have been the subject of my investigations. This territory has only a few settlements (Bilja or San Giorgio, Ravanca or Sul Prato, Niva, Korito, Stolbica or Stolvizza, Osojane and Ucce) with a population (in 1873) of about 3250 persons. The differences between the Slavic dialects spoken here were, nevertheless, so great, that here and there they divided entire linguistic territories, and could serve as the basis for drawing isoglosses. For example, one Rezian dialect had at the time the difference between *g* and *h* (*x*) (*ga, góra, gnat, grébit* . . ., *xódi* or *húdi, xüd* or *hüd* . . .), another between γ and *x* (*γa, γóra, γnat, γrábit* . . ., *xódi, xüd* . . .), a third fused both into *h* (*ha, hóra, hnat, hrábit* . . ., *hódi, hüd* . . .), and a fourth had a zero phoneme in place of both (*a, óra, nat, rábit* . . ., *odi, üd*. . .). In some Rezian dialects *l* was retained at the end of a syllable (*dal, bil, sul* . . .), in others it was replaced by *ṷ* (*daṷ, biṷ, suṷ*. . .). In some dialects *j* is retained at the beginning of a syllable (*ja, jáma, jásno, jœzœrü* . . .), in others this *j* is absent (*a, áma, ásno, œzœrü*. . .). This diversity permits the separation of these dialects to roughly the same degree as that of Slovak and Czech, or of Kashubian and Polish.

The Rezian people must, in effect, be viewed as speakers of one language as opposed to the neighboring Slavs (i.e., the various Slovenians, the Slavs of Ter who derive their name from the river Ter [Torre], the inhabitants of Nadiško [Natisone] also known as Šempeter [San Pietro al Natisone, or San Pietro degli Slavi], the Serbo-Croats, etc.), inasmuch as their language had a common foreign substratum of a Finno-Ugric type which exhibited synharmonism, i.e., assimilation of vowels in dependent, secondary syllables to the vowels of dominating syllables. The Rezians were furthermore bound into one linguistic-national unit by a foreign, non-Slavic superstratum.

Thus, the multidialectal Rezian "language" is derived from a number of "protolanguages": from many Slavic dialects, from some unknown Finno-Ugric or Uralo-Altaic ("Turanian") language. It includes, in addition, recent heterogeneous elements which the Rezians borrowed from their Slavic, Romance, and Germanic neighbors, as well as from inhabitants of more distant places (Italy, former Austria, Hungary, Germany, Poland, and Russia, including Siberia, and all of the Balkan peninsula), with which the Rezians came into contact when they were forced to travel in search of work and a living. ·

8. The accumulation of similar deposits and layers on a given linguistic base can be stated or assumed to have existed in a number of places.

Contemporary speakers of Polish in the vicinity of Białystok, Bielsk, and Sokółka do not have nasal vowels in their speech, having replaced them by combinations of oral vowels with nasal consonants of a varying position: e.g., *domp, demba, kempa, skompy, penta, p'onty, mondry, mendžec, monce, šv'eńće, mońći, p'eńć, reŋka, šeŋga, roŋk, ośoŋga* . . . , as well as *monš, donži, m'enso, menža, v'enži, genśi.* . . . This inherited articulatory-acoustic peculiarity must be explained by the fact that the ancestors of these speakers of Polish were Byelorussians or other non-Poles who, at some point, at a period of transition, where they were subject to linguistic Polonization, were unable to pronounce nasal vowels, splitting them into two successive phonemes: a purely oral vowel and an occlusive consonant of different localization in the oral cavity, but involving the lowering of the soft palate with concomitant nasal resonance.

In the Balkan peninsula, in Macedonia and near Lake Ohrid there are likewise Bulgaro-Macedonian dialects which preserve the nasal resonance in morphemes corresponding to the morphemes which contained nasal vowels in Old Church Slavonic and in proto-Slavic: *jenzik, srenšta* or *sreńka, bendem,* etc. This is not at all some kind of "archaism," but on the contrary is a consequence of the fact that the Slavicized former speakers of a foreign language were unable to precisely render the Slavic pronunciation; they split the perceived single nasal vowels into two successive articulations. The same kind of substitution is encountered in the vicinity of Gorica which had a Slovenian base: *srenča, venč* or *vanč, sa kompat,* etc.

I shall take this opportunity to remark that the views of Prince Trubetzkoy on the proto-Slavic and Slavic nasal vowels, recently stated in the journal *Slavia*[1], are, in my opinion, mistaken.

9. Since linguistic fusion and the emergence of mixed languages is a recurrent and necessary aspect of language and of all individual and social interaction, we are entitled, and even obliged, to state

that *a considerable foreign admixture also pervades Polish and the other northwest Slavic languages.*

For it is hard to imagine that having preserved a complex system of inflection and productive morphological forms, a language could simply renounce such a useful ancillary device as mobile stress, i.e., stress which is not bound to a particular syllable of the word or syntagm or which does not have a syntactic function but rather a morphologized stress which characterizes some morphemes in the word in contradistinction to other ones. Such a loss of the morphological stress could have come about only when the speakers of a certain language in which the formants (i.e., the suffixes, endings, and prefixes) but not the stress were strongly morphologized, acquired a new language. The speakers of this new language could not cope with the morphological mobility of stress, and they eliminated it. Such a linguistically Slavicized people could have been any of the Finno-Ugric tribes whose morphological system is suffixal-inflectional but which lacks a morphologized stress and intonation. And since the Finnic languages do not distinguish three series of apical spirants (*s, z, c, ȝ̂; š, ž, č, ǯ; ś ź, ć, ʒ́*), using at most only two, I venture to ascribe the so-called phenomenon of *mazurzenie* (i.e., the fusion of *š ž č ǯ* with *s z c ȝ*, which is found in most Polish dialects) to the Polonization and linguistic Slavicization of a Finnic tribe that had at one time occupied the same territory as the Slavic ancestors of the Poles. Research in other fields also seems to suggest that the Polish tribe originated with the merger of Slavs and Finns, just as the above-mentioned Latvians emerged through the Lithuanianization of the Finnish tribes of Courland and Livonia.

10. It is also most plausible that various languages of Europe were subjected to the influence of the Celts who spread throughout Europe and in Asia Minor, of the Iranians, Scythians, and Sarmatians, and of the Iberians (cf. the lack of distinction of *b* and *v* and the confusion of *f* and *x* which, by the way, are also found in some Slovenian dialects).

Professor N. J. Marr has recently advanced the popular *japhetic theory* which ascribes enormous influence to a certain tribe of "Japhetites" who were related to the Semites and widely spread "in prehistoric times"; their contemporary representatives are allegedly various tribes and nationalities of the Caucasus who were either direct descendants or speakers of other languages that had mixed with the "Japhetites" but preserved most elements of their own languages.

A representative of the second type might be Armenian. One must not forget that Armenian lacks the distinction of grammatical genders which is so characteristic of the Indo-European languages.

Some Armenian features are found in German; first of all, the so-called *Lautverschiebung*, that is, the special development of occlusive consonantal phonemes. Some plausibility cannot be denied the hypothesis that Armenian and Germanic are the result of the mixture of a common foreign substratum with various elements of Indo-European.

11. The above remarks lead us to conclude that there can be no question of a unilateral branching out from some homogeneous *Ursprache,* as if from a single tree trunk, of several parts that, in turn, undergo disintegration and splitting. It is clear that there is a continuous and steady process of disintegration, but there is also continuous mixing, fusing, integration, amalgamation, and reduction of diversity.

In the field of biology each four-legged, four-armed, or two-legged individual has 2^{10} or 1024 ancestors for the 10 generations preceding him. In the field of tribal or collective linguistic genealogy, the situation is of more modest scope and, in any case, quite different. For example, when we think of the collective Polish language we may imagine a long chain of predecessors scattered in the East, West, North, and South and reaching back to older and more recent times. In addition to direct transmission along a straight line of historical succession, there are also lateral influences and forces, influences through direct contact and influences from a distance, articulatory and acoustic communication, as well as communication through graphic and visual signs.

In any case, even in the sphere of linguistic kinship we must posit the existence of n, i.e., of many ancestors.

12. A special kind of linguistic problem is the occurrence of common traits and peculiarities in languages of different nations that are in geographic proximity.

Thus, for example, we can discern a certain unity among the languages of the Scandinavian peninsula and the adjacent countries occupied by the Germans and Finns.

Special features unify the various languages of the Balkan peninsula: the postpositive article (which also exists in the Scandinavian languages), the absence of the infinitive, which is also characteristic of modern Greek whose distant ancestor, Classical Greek, had in this respect (in its various dialects) a veritable *embarras de richesse*. And thus it is from one extreme to another!

Geographic proximity also accounts for the common traits of the Caucasian languages. It is clear that the communality of features which is related to geographic proximity, is also due to linguistic "fusion" that follows the line of least resistance: the more difficult gives way to the easier, and the simpler wins over the more complex.

13. All aspects of language, linguistic thought, its expression and the produced auditory impressions are, of course, deeply affected by the linguistic changes that occur in time. There are changes in the articulatory-auditory aspect of language (that are matched in the optical field by changes in the graphic-visual representations, whether expressions or impressions) and in its very structure—in the morphology of the word (in morphology proper) and of the sentence (in syntax).

As living and growing beings are characterized and classified according to age and periods of transition, so tribal and national languages can be characterized and classified according to the various stages in the history of their structure, and according to their complex and heterogeneous elements and interrelations of their simplest component parts.

For example, among the Indo-European languages (which have absorbed other languages) we can distinguish old and new languages, "primary" (that is, relatively primary) and "secondary" languages, languages of various periods, epochs, and stages which carry and transmit approximately the same, that is, identically named sets of linguistic concepts. Italo-Romance (Latin and the related Italic dialects) which was itself a product of fusion and mixture with old Italic languages (at first with Etruscan, and then with Volscan and Celtic), has in the course of time expanded far beyond its original Italic homeland giving rise, by way of separation and fusion with other languages, to a number of medieval Romance languages, which have in turn produced, as a result of uninterrupted, gradual change, a multitude of modern Romance dialects (Italian, Ladin, Gallo-Italic, Provençal, French, Walloon, Spanish, Catalan, Galician, Portuguese, Roumanian, etc.).

Similarly there are old and more recent Germanic languages and Slavic languages of different age and structure; there are old Indic (Vedic and Sanskrit) and old Iranian (Avestan or "Zend" and Old Persian languages, and more recent ones (Prakrit, Pali, Phalavi) in addition to the great variety of modern Indic and Iranian dialects.

In a comparative approach all these languages can be grouped and classified chronologically. For example, Latin and the other old Italic dialects can be grouped with old Indic and old Iranian, setting them off from the (1) later Romance languages and Prakrit dialects, and (2) still later stages of the modern Romance, Indic, and Iranian dialects.

14. In attempting a comparative characterization and classification of the agglutinative Uralo-Altaic, or Turco-Altaic languages, we are compelled to notice the existing contradiction in their word-structure and sentence-structure: the semantically dominating morpheme, the root, occupies the initial, principal position in the word, whereas the other word- and syntagm-forming (inflectional) morphemes are attached and phonetically assimilated to it; in the sentence, on the other hand, the formally dominating syntagm, the subject of the main sentence, occupies the end of the utterance, or phrase, whereas the other syntagms or members of the sentence, which are formally dependent on it, as well as the adverbial, determinative and complementary clauses, precede it.

15. Some forty years ago, shortly after the discovery of the Sumerian rock carvings (which were discovered in connection with Akkadian), I worked out for myself a general, though probably very superficial, idea of the structure of this language, which was assigned by some people hypothetically to the "Turanian" group of languages. Comparing the ancient structure of that language with that of its later linguistic stages, I came to the conclusion that in the course of time (of over a millennium) this structure was subjected to a series of radical changes. The once strongly morphologized suffixal-inflectional structure became gradually weakened and could no longer render its morphological functions. Consequently, more expressive, prefixal elements were called into play. Their role kept increasing, while the role of the suffixes continued to grow weaker, until they disappeared altogether. But the continuous increase of prefixation led at the end to the same result that had previously been the fate of suffixation. The purely suffixal

structure changed into a structure with weakened suffixes and with auxiliary prefixal markers; this in turn, changed into purely prefixal structure which, after some time, became weakened and replaced by a suffixal structure. The suffixal structure then changed into a mixed one, then into a prefixal; this became, in turn, mixed, and then again suffixal, and so on, *da capo al fine*. The result ⟨of linguistic change⟩ is thus constant oscillation, vibration, and external evolution which is reminiscent of the ebb and flow of the tides.

This "hypothesis" which I have formulated for myself, for my own personal use, I have called *evolutiones linguarum terrestrium*. But who knows whether some kind of misunderstanding and confusion of concepts does not lurk in this expression?

NOTES

1. N.S. Trubetzkoy, "On the Reflexes of Common Slavic *ę* in Czech," (in Russian) *Slavia,* vol. VI, 1927/28, pp. 662–84 (Sov. ed.).

XIX

A Survey of the Slavic Linguistic World with

Relation to Other Indo-European Languages

⟨. . .⟩ THE SLAVIC LANGUAGES and dialects are related to other Indo-European (or Indo-Germanic) languages. Relationship here means only that all Indo-European languages are peculiar modifications of the same primordial linguistic material, reshaped and further developed by each Indo-European people. The present and past Indo-European languages and dialects are only separate descendants of a single, common proto-language which in the course of time evolved in various directions.

At the stage of the proto-language there already existed minute, at first individual, and then dialectical peculiarities that formed the basis of subsequent differentiation. The increase of these minute dialectal differences led in the end to the formation of separate dialect groups.

There is no reason, however, to assume that this differentiation followed an uninterrupted, ever more disparate development. The centrifugal process was at all times paralleled by a centripetal development. The latter led to ethnic leveling and assimilation by way of borrowing and mixing. However, many transitional dialects, which served as connecting links between various groups, have disappeared, whereas the languages or dialect groups which clearly differed from each other have survived. Of all the clearly differentiated and mutually interacting Indo-European language groups, the following have been preserved until now:

—major groups with a large number of speakers: Indic, Iranian, Romance, Germanic, and Slavic;

—minor groups with a small number of speakers: Armenian, Greek, Albanian, Celtic, and Baltic (i.e., Letto-Lithuanian).

From the geographic or topographic point of view, the Indic (or Indo-Aryan) and Iranian peoples are found almost exclusively in Asia; Armenians and Greeks, in Asia and Europe; the Celtic and Baltic peoples and the Albanians, almost exclusively in Europe (though some Celts have emigrated to America). The Romance and Germanic peoples are found primarily in Europe and America, but they are also scattered in other parts of the world.

The Slavs occupy a compact area in Europe and in northern Asia; recently they have formed colonies in America as well. They comprise the following distinct dialect groups:

In the East Slavic linguistic area are the Russians; i.e., Slavs who speak the various Russian dialects. The Russian dialect group is divided into two large subgroups: a northern or *Great Russian-Byelorussian,* and a southern or *Ukrainian.*

In the northwest, the Russian linguistic area borders immediately on the Polish (and Baltic) ⟨linguistic⟩ area, and in the southwest it is separated by the Roumanians from the *Bulgarian* linguistic area in the Balkan peninsula.

Northwest of the Bulgarians are the various *Serbo-Croatian* dialects.

Beyond them there is a mixed dialectal area, occupied by various Slavic tribes which go under the general name of *Slovenes.*

The South Slavic linguistic area extends to the north of Italy; some remnants of older Serbian and Bulgarian colonies continue to exist in southern Italy.

The Slovenes occupy the extreme portion of the South Slavic linguistic area, which is separated from the Northwest Slavic area by the Hungarians and Germans.

The southeastern part of the Northwest area is occupied by *Slovaks,* who border in the east on the Ukrainians, better known in these localities as Ruthenians or Rusnaks. The Slovaks are separated from the Polish linguistic area by the Carpathian Mountains.

West of the Slovaks are the people most closely related to them, the *Czechs.* The latter make up the Slavic population of Moravia, Bohemia, and of the small port of Silesia which is not occupied by Poles.

North of the Czechs, but separated from them by a broad belt of German inhabitants, are the *Sorbians* or *Lusatian Wends,* who form a Slavic island in Saxony and Brandenburg and who are divided into Upper and Lower Sorbians.

Some Slavic tribes, designated by the general name *Polabians,* were located earlier north of the Lusatian Wends. Assimilated by their immediate German neighbors and conquerors, they completely lost their ethnic identity. The *Kashubians,* who occupy the shores of the Baltic Sea near the mouth of the Vistula, may be viewed as a remnant of one of the Polabian tribes. The language of the Kashubians is at present very similar to that of their immediate Slavic neighbors, the Poles, and their dialect is usually treated as a dialect of Polish.

Finally, there are the *Poles,* the most numerous of the Northwestern Slavs in spite of the heavy losses which they suffered in the ethnic struggle with the Germans.

In most cases it is easy to determine the dialect boundaries between the above-mentioned Slavic peoples. Thus, there are no transitional dialects between the Poles and the Russians, the Serbs and the Bulgarians, the Poles and the Slovaks, the Poles and the Czechs, or even between the Great Russians and the Ukrainians.

The topographic boundaries between the various Slavic peoples can in most cases be drawn quite easily, but sometimes, as in the case of the Poles, this is not so simple. Eastward the Poles do not form a compact mass even within the borders of their own Polish kingdom, overlapping in the north with the Lithuanians and in the south with the Byelorussians and Ukrainians. But the Polish population reaches far east of this line. For in addition to the compact Polish settlements in certain parts of the Grodno and Vilno provinces, Poles are also scattered in the area occupied by the compact Russian population in the east.

At any rate we can state that generally the Slavs do not form compact linguistic areas. The linguistic area occupied by the Poles, Byelorussians, and Ukrainians also has a strong admixture of Jews who speak a variety of a German dialect, and must be grouped ethno-linguistically with the Germans.

We may now ask the question: how did the differentiation and designation of these various linguistic groups come about? Was the distinction between the Slavs and other Indo-European peoples, and between the Slavs themselves, established scientifically? Were the linguistic traits of the Slavs established first, and of the separate

Slavic groups later? This was patently not the case. The designation of a people and its difference from other peoples, as well as the difference between languages, were mostly established intuitively, on the basis of overall impressions. Originally no one appealed to scientific linguistic criteria in separating the Slavs from the Balts or the Poles from the Czechs. These questions were broached only later when scholars began to define linguistic differences and to work on the classification of languages.

This work was not at first confined to a simple scientific justification of generally accepted distinctions; it aimed at the discovery of new groupings and the establishment of the various degrees of relationship between the members of a given language family.

Until now, however, efforts in this direction have yielded insignificant results. The ⟨scientifically⟩ established distinctions have mostly been too negligible to serve as a basis for the genetic classification of languages. Under close scrutiny all the genealogical schemes, which have absorbed so much energy, appear to be inadequate.

Thus, for example, the Slavic languages form a separate language family within the Indo-European linguistic group. The question of whether this family is in some particularly close relation to another family of the same linguistic area remains at best uncertain. The classification of the Slavic languages themselves is not much clearer. The genealogical schemes suggested until now remain, at any rate, less scientific than the commonly accepted division of the individual Slavic languages or, rather, the individual Slavic dialect groups.

What is, however, quite clear is that there never existed an Italo-Celtic, Italo-Greek, or Germano-Balto-Slavic proto-language, just as there never existed a Southeast, Northwest, or South Slavic proto-language. The Slavs are ethnically no closer to the Germans than are the Greeks to the Romance peoples, and the Russians no closer to the Bulgarians than to the Poles. The posited proto-languages are fictions which never existed in reality.

The scholars have, furthermore, sought in vain to provide a genetic classification that would reconstruct the actual course of linguistic development. This, unfortunately, cannot be achieved with the means available to contemporary science. The solution of this problem is a matter for the future. But what is indisputable is that such a reconstruction cannot be based on the notion of a genealogical tree. The genealogy of languages is not as simple as the personal genealogy of the nobility. It is too complex, too confused.

The attempted genealogies of related languages lend themselves to the following objections.

Even *a priori* it is clear that the branching of languages is not as simple as is usually assumed (proto-language A splits into daughter languages B and C, and each of them again splits into several daughter languages—for example B into D, E and F and C into G, H, etc.). The actual situation is quite different. For at two distant points of a continuous linguistic area the same tendencies may arise quite independently, yielding similar, though genetically unrelated, results. Several variant dialects, B, C, D, etc., may, furthermore, develop in the same originally single linguistic area A. Later on, however, a part of C may develop, under certain conditions, into a vernacular differing not only from B and D, but also from the rest of C to a larger extent than the latter differs from B and D. No one will deny that the difference between Russian and the Russo-Chinese dialect of Kjaxta[1] is greater than the difference between Russian and other Slavic languages. The difference between High German and Yiddish, a Judeo-German language which is related to High German, is greater than that between High German and the other German dialects or even the Germanic languages. Thus, it is impossible to ignore the enormous role of ethnic mixing, on the one hand, and of emigration and other forms of ethnic separation, on the other.

This being the case, we must abandon the supposedly precise genetic classification of languages and be content with a precise characterization of separate languages and language families including the periods of transition from older to more recent stages.

What is important, however, is to identify characteristic traits that are of general significance, that pervade the phonetic and morphological structure of language, and not disparate facts of a secondary nature or details which are mere surrogates of the general features.

Unfortunately, very little has so far been done in this area. Preliminary investigations do not yet permit us to form an idea of the general patterning of languages and to establish those features which occur in some languages but not in others.

Every language presents two sides: a phonetic and a psychological one. Every utterance can thus be dismembered and analyzed from a double viewpoint. A purely phonetic analysis yields ultimate, indivisible, linguistic units: the sounds of the language. An analysis from a psychological viewpoint deals, on the other hand, with the relationship of the psychological content of language with the psychological equivalent of sounds, i.e., with the sound images. We shall not dwell longer upon the question of what is psychological in the strict sense, leaving its solution to philosophers and physiologists. But what is a proper linguistic problem is the means by which the phonetic aspect of language is linked with its psychological content. Insofar as we deal with linguistic form, we can speak of morphology, or the study of forms in the broad sense of the word (including syntax); insofar as we study the psychological content, we can speak of semasiology, or the science of meaning.

The most useful characterization of languages would be in terms of their common morphological and semasiological features. The current state of our science hardly permits such a characterization of the Indo-European languages or of the Slavic languages either. Such a characterization is, at any rate, far more difficult than a characterization of phonetic features and of their historical development.

The latter type of characterization of individual languages opens to us several different approaches.

First, the state of a phonetic system can be characterized descriptively and statically. This characterization is in terms of phonetic statics. It includes a description of those organs of speech (e.g., the larynx, nasal cavity, tongue) which participate in the production of the sounds of a given language.

Second, we may investigate phonetic dynamics, i.e., the causes and conditions under which sounds emerge at any given moment, under what conditions they are pronounced more or less energetically, when they play an active role and when a passive one, and so forth. The accumulation of a long series of such dynamic moments permits us to deal with a third kind of phonetic characterization of languages: namely, the characterization of the historical process of phonetic evolution. This approach attempts to establish two actually given periods in the development of a language, and to determine the direction of change of the various categories of sounds and of the sound system as a whole. This, then, is a characterization of language in terms of its development, of the paths taken by the sound system of a language in its transition from an earlier to a later stage.

I shall not dwell at greater length on the application of these principles to the characterization of the Slavic languages as opposed to other Indo-European languages or the various Slavic dialects. But in order to show approximately how such a characterization might look, I will adduce the following example.

In the transition from the proto-Indo-European (proto-Indo-Germanic) to the proto-Slavic period, there occurred a general forward movement of the speech organs, from the larynx toward the tip of the tongue. It involved, among others, the loss of aspirates, the forward shift of the two original series of the so-called "guttural" consonants, etc. The orignal aspirates became simple voiced consonants and coalesced with the corresponding old ones. Thus, one of the phonetic distinctions connected with the activity of the larynx was lost. The two series of velars, which are usually referred to as "gutturals," shifted forward, so that the entire back series became fronted and the old series of fronted gutturals changed into the consonants *s, z* or similar dental consonants. If we were to turn to the history of the Slavic languages of a later period, we could detect a continuing development along the same lines.

Although such a development is not exclusive to the Slavic languages, it nevertheless proceeded in these languages most consistently and in a peculiar fashion.

Such general conclusions concerning the phonetic development of individual groups of languages are by no means negligible, and have an import not only for linguistics but also for anthropology.

The transition period from proto-Indo-European to proto-Slavic was marked, in addition, by the change of all closed syllables into open ones, that was generally caused by the elimination of consonants at the end of syllables. This was also accompanied by a loss of certain consonantal elements that were replaced by zero. Conversely, the transition from proto-Slavic to the modern Slavic languages was characterized in the first place by the loss of some vocalic elements and in the second place by the loss of some consonantal elements.

The above examples for the characterization of languages are taken from the history of their phonetic development, whereas a static characterization of the phonetic system would point out, for example, the relatively large role of the larynx in the production of sounds in Serbo-Croatian, its minor role in Russian, and its minimal role in Polish and Czech. The role of the nasal cavity is, at the same time, somewhat greater in Polish than in the other Slavic languages.

The strong influence of stress on the character of Russian vowels in contrast to its passive role in Polish and in Czech is an example of a characterization pertaining to the field of phonetic dynamics.

In addition, one must consider the various chronological layers, or strata, of phonetic processes. If some strata are shared by two or several related dialect groups, then one can unhesitatingly acknowledge the close genetic relationship of these dialect groups as opposed to other dialects. Thus, for example, there can be no doubt that Ukrainian and Byelorussian belong to the same Common Russian dialect group in contradistinction to all other Slavic dialect groups. Thus, only the Russian group (which includes Great Russian, Byelorussian, and Ukrainian) has the disyllabic sequences –*oro*, –*olo* in such words as *boroda, golova*, which are in the other Slavic languages matched by monosyllabic sequences: *brada, glava; broda, głova*, or *borda*, etc. This trait, like other typically Common Russian traits, shows that the entire Russian dialect group was for a certain period of time subject to a common development which differed from that of the other Slavic dialects.

So far we have been primarily concerned with those phenomena of Slavic linguistic development that were of a natural and spontaneous character. Side by side with these, there were developments of an artificial or, more precisely, cultural character that led to the formation of the Slavic literary languages.

The road to them has always been through writing. Every written language, even if it be insignificant, can be viewed as a source of the entire cultural-linguistic life ⟨of a nation⟩. There are a good number of more or less significant written languages among the Slavs. Each Slavic people which considers itself independent has developed a written language of its own. Not all of these written languages have become literary languages in the broad sense of the word; for example, one can hardly speak of the existence of a Kashubian literature. Other minor Slavic literatures include Lusatian-Wendish (Upper and Lower Lusatian), Slovak, Bulgarian, Slovenian, and Ukrainian. In no way can they be considered on a par with the great literatures of the Serbs, Croats, Czechs, Poles, and especially Russians (Great Russians). The internal importance, range of ideas, sphere of influence, depth and breadth, and geographic spread of these respective literatures are incommensurable.

Every written language can, in addition, become a common language, a language of communication for all the members of a speech community, or for all those who identify themselves with a given nation, so that it becomes a model, an ideal norm, for all more or less educated people.

Depending on circumstances, this language may penetrate into the various spheres of social life. It may become the language of the school, church, and so forth, transcending, finally, the national boundaries to become a language of international communication, a world language.

So far no Slavic written language has risen to the level of an international language that would encompass at least all the Slavs. What the future will bring we cannot tell. It is known, however, that the Latin written language, which at one time was dominant in almost all of Europe, is steadily losing both in sphere of influence and in importance. It is also known that French, which is so widespread today, did not emerge until the ninth century, that New High German is of recent origin, and that the third world language, English, is fairly young. Will some world language also emerge among the Slavs in a few centuries? Who can tell? It is possible but not inevitable. Each language is entitled to be used for this purpose, but whether it has the strength required for it is another matter. "Every tongue shall glorify the Lord," wrote the Apostle Paul (*Romans*, XIV, 11). And if every tongue is eligible for communication between man and God, then it is so much the more eligible for communication among people.

It cannot be denied that there is no common Slavic written language and no common Slavic literature. There is only a Russian, Polish, Czech, Serbian, or Slovenian written language. For that matter there is no common Germanic, but only an English, German, Dutch, Swedish, Norwegian, or Danish written language. Nor is there any common Romance written language, but only French, Italian, Spanish, Portuguese, and Roumanian. Latin was once the literary representative of the Romance linguistic world, but neither the Germans nor the Slavs developed such a literary vehicle.

I will not go into the external description of the Slavic written languages (for example, into the question of their alphabets and religious affiliation) or into the question of their internal classification and their use outside of literature (e.g., in the schools, church, administration, and government). I shall only touch upon a linguistic question which is of a major interest to any Slavist—the question of *Old Church Slavonic.* Its ethnic origin remains even now a matter of dispute. Most likely it originated in the Balkan peninsula, for among the living Slavic languages it comes closest to Bulgarian. At first this language was used by the Slavs for missionary purposes, for the translation of the Scriptures and other ecclesiastical literature. At a more recent date it was used in the Orthodox Slavic countries (in Russia, Serbia, and Bulgaria) in a form that was markedly changed under the influence of local dialects, and in secular literature as well. It exerted a significant influence on the Russian literary language. The study of this ancient church language is also very important for a correct understanding of the structure of the other Slavic languages. However, one must not overrate its importance; one must never forget that the study of modern languages, which are still alive and accessible to observation, is far more instructive and variegated than the study of a language which has ceased to exist and which is accessible only through its writing. This statement may seem strange to some people, but the naturalist will grasp its meaning immediately: he knows that firm results in paleontology can be attained only if a solid foundation is first laid in the fields of zoology and botany.

I see, gentlemen, that I have not met the demands of my task with the resources at my disposal. I wanted to give you a survey of the Slavic languages, but you have received only a very approximate picture of this linguistic world. Not everyone has the gift of saying a great deal in a few words. Alas, I am not so fortunate. Perhaps I shall succeed in the future in acquainting you more closely with the Slavic languages and their history and in presenting a general picture of the Slavic dialects.

Thus we shall obtain the factual material which should enable us to draw conclusions of a general linguistic character and to establish general laws of language in all its variety. Bulgarian will afford us an example of transition from the so-called "synthetic" to the so-called "analytic" state of language. We shall see how dialectal differentiation proceeds differently in various areas. We shall find the almost unique linguistic phenomena of minimal dialectal diversity in the immense Great Russian linguistic area, as well as profound dialectal diversity in the tiny Slovenian area—a diversity due to a number of historical, geographical, and other causes. The mutual borrowings among Slavs, and those from other peoples, will confront us with cultural-historical problems. The Russo-Chinese dialect of Kjaxta, in which the Russian linguistic material has been adapted to Chinese content, will provide us with an example of a mixed language resulting from contact of neighboring peoples. Finally, we shall tackle the question of the effect of social contradictions upon the distribution of languages.

The Slavic linguistic world is extensive enough to allow us to study all those general linguistic questions which I have raised, as well as those which I have not raised.

We shall, besides, not forget that the Slavic languages do not form a closed linguistic group but that they must, on the contrary, always be studied in relation to other, cognate and noncognate, languages. ⟨. . .⟩

NOTES

1. Kjaxta is a town in Russia south of Lake Baikal and on the border with Outer Mongolia. In the eighteenth and most of the nineteenth century (before the opening of the Suez Canal) it was an important center for trade with China. Therefore there were many speakers of both Russian and Chinese living in the city, and a local dialect (*Kjaxtinskij*), based on Russian but containing many elements of Chinese, developed ⟨cf. note 39, p. 77⟩.

X X

Comparative Grammar of the Slavic Languages

3. The constantly used term "language" has a vague meaning when applied to everyday speech in all its variety. Thus, for example, the term "Russian language" refers to the entire complex of Russian dialects (e.g., Olonec, Rjazan', or even the various Ukrainian dialects). The term "language," however, must of necessity designate a finite, definite whole. Consequently, the term "Russian language" cannot apply to the speech of all speakers of Russian, as the latter presents an almost infinite variety. It is correct to speak of the "Russian language" only with respect to its literary language, a language which has been normalized and subjected to certain rules. The most suitable and objective term to be used with respect to any living speech community would be "linguistic area" or "linguistic territory." Thus we could speak of a Russian linguistic area, Slavic linguistic area, etc. (pp. 8–10).*

. . . Since "grammar," in the strict sense, deals only with one language, it would be appropriate to replace the term "comparative grammar" with the terms "comparative survey" or "comparative study" of a certain group of languages or language areas.

6. Comparative surveys, and comparison in general, of linguistic phenomena can be of three types:

I) Linguistic processes can be examined without regard to linguistic kinship, in order to establish the degree of similarity or difference between the structures of two languages. For example, Slavic forms exhibit side by side a *k* or a *č* in the root: *peku – pečeš*. This alternation is a clear case of coexistence which was determined by historical facts: the presence of *k* in *peku* was brought about by conditions favoring its retention, whereas *č* appeared at a certain moment under conditions which caused the "softening" (palatalization or centering of the tongue position) of *k*. Three stages can be singled out in this process:

... 1) There is a *k* which is independent of conditions, and a *k* which is palatalized under certain conditions.

2) *k* and palatalized (softened) *k'* exist side-by-side.

3) *k* and *č* (from the earlier *k'*) exist side-by-side.

A similar coexistence of *k* and *č* can be found in almost all languages: in Romance, Germanic, Indic, Semitic, Finnic, etc. From this one may conclude that the alternation of *k* and *č* under certain conditions is a universal linguistic phenomenon.

II) Two or more linguistic areas may be compared without regard to their historical origin, if they show similar linguistic phenomena as a result of their territorial proximity. Thus, for example, Armenian, one of the Indo-European languages, can be compared with other Caucasian languages with which it shares phonetic and other peculiarities as a result of geographic contiguity. We observe a similar phenomenon on the Baltic shores: here too, some fundamental linguistic similarities between genetically unrelated languages, such as Latvian (an Aistian or "Baltic" language) and Estonian (a Finnic language) can be explained only by the geographic proximity of the peoples speaking these languages and who (judging from historical data) came into mutual contact and lived together as far back as the 13th century. As a result of this mixing, Latvian acquired several features peculiar to Estonian: stress on the first syllable (instead of a mobile stress), the distinction of long and short syllables (*quantitas*). The role of geographic proximity on languages of diverse origin is also apparent in the Balkan peninsula where, along with the descendants of ancient Greeks, we find Albanians (a tribe belonging to a separate Indo-European branch), Slavs, and Roumanians (of Romance origin). Bulgarian, Roumanian and Albanian show, for example, the same use of the postpositional article. The similarity of linguistic phenomena enables us to give a comparative survey of such linguistic areas.

The cultural influence of the literature of a representative of one or another linguistic area can also serve as a basis of comparative surveys. Good examples of this type are the Romance and other West European languages which underwent the influence of Latin literature, or the languages of the Russian area which experienced the impact of Church Slavonic.

III) Finally, there is the comparative study of linguistic areas which are assumed to stem from a common historical source and which can, therefore, be viewed as variants of one originally common state that has subsequently broken up into the very same variants that are being compared. This kind of comparison constitutes so-called comparative grammar in the strict sense of the word (§§ 14–19).

26. "Comparative grammar" or the comparative survey of a definite group of languages consists of the following main parts:

1) Phonetics, or the study of phonetic representations.

2) Morphology, in the broad sense, or the study of the concepts of a given language. Morphology encompasses two parts: (a) the study of concepts pertaining to the structure of words and phrases (morphology in the narrow sense of the word); and (b) the study of concepts pertaining to the structure of sentences, their parts and combinations (syntax).

3) Lexicology, or the study of words as parts of speech and of the various categories of words, such as the grammatical genders and verbal aspects.

Phonetics. 27.

1) Because of their common morphological origin we can compare identical morphemes occurring in different words of the same language, as for example, the radical *pt–* in ⟨Russian⟩ *pt–ic–a* and *pt–aš–k–a.*

2) Because of their assumed etymological or historical relationship, we can compare morphemes occurring in different languages, as, for example, the Russian *boloto,* the South Slavic *blato,* and the Polish *błoto.*

3) We can compare phonemes on the basis of their pronunciation. Take, for example, the representation of *č*: the Polish *cz* ⟨*č*⟩ is pronounced differently than the Russian *č*; in Russian it is mediopalatal, whereas in Polish it is apical. In "comparative grammars" such comparisons have almost no place; their main attention is focused on the kinship of phonemes that form a part of genetically related morphemes.

To shorten this exposition we should ⟨only add that we shall⟩ not compare individual sounds, but the various elements of sounds, their phonic components. Take, for example, the sound *b,* which combines the representations of several specific articulatory activities: labial closure, nasal closure, vibration of the vocal chords, etc. We can, in turn, consider the representations of the labial activity which characterize the pronunciation of this phoneme. In our comparative approach to phonetic problems we shall ask: does this activity of the lips occur in other languages? And if not, how does it differ? Etc. (pp. 94–96).

N O T E S

---

* ⟨Page numbers refer to the Russian original.⟩

XXI

An Outline of the History
of the Polish Language

CHAPTER 11

AN OUTLINE OF THE HISTORY OF THE
ARTICULATORY-AUDITORY SYSTEM OF POLISH

⟨. . .⟩ §13. This is a history of the phonemes (or sound-representations) and their smallest components, i.e., their psychologically indivisible articulatory-auditory elements on the one hand, and the various combinations of phonemes on the other.

But are we justified in comparing in a historical framework the differences and similarities between phonemes and their components apart from the morphemes, or morphological elements, of which they are a part? Can we speak of an identical history of the Polish phonemes associated with the letters or graphemes *c, e, s, d,* etc., just because all the phonemes associated with each letter are identical from an art.-aud. ⟨articulatory-auditory⟩ viewpoint, and because they can be reduced to the same art.-aud. representation?

We cannot.

In the present linguistic system, the phoneme *c* has a different historical origin and different variants in the morphemes *świec–, płac–, piec–, tłuc–, rzec, noc–, moc, móc, strzec* . . . , *ręc–, rzec– (rzek–a, rzec–e), owc–, kupc–, lic–, plac–, tac–a, cegła, cesarz, car.*

Despite its art.-aud. identity, the Polish phoneme *e* has a different history in the morphemes *wiezie, wiedzie, bierze, plecie, miedza*

. . . , *wiedza, świeci* . . . , *wieś, len, cześć* . . . , *sen, mech, łeb, krew*
. . . , *pełny, bełtać* . . . , *ser, sierota, zabierać* . . . , *cera, telegraf,* etc.

The phoneme *s* (or *ś*) of *sad, syn, siedem* . . . is historically connected with the proto-IE phoneme *s;* the very same phoneme *s* of *słoma, pros–* (prosić), *pros–* (prosię), *sto, osiem, dziesięć, wieś* . . . is historically related to the IE phoneme k_1 (fronted *k*), whereas the phoneme *ś* of *pleść, kłaść* . . . alternates with (i.e., is a variant of) *t, d* and developed historically from *t, d.* The phoneme *s,* furthermore, is a part of many loan-words, or rather, of assimilated morphemes.

The phoneme *d* of *dać, dom, wiadomo* . . . has its origin in a nonaspirated IE *d;* whereas the *d* of *dym, wdowa, broda, rudy* . . . goes back to an aspirated *dh;* in addition, the phoneme *d* occurs in many assimilated words.

Thus we can see than an art.-aud. history of a language must consider the phonemes and their components not as art.-aud. elements independently of meaning, but as art.-aud. elements endowed with semasiologized and morphologized functions.

§14. One could shorten and simplify the exposition by presenting the history, not of the whole, psychologically complex phonemes, but of the psychologically indivisible components, i.e., of the simplest articulatory and auditory elements making up the phonemes. I shall explain this with examples.

In the consonantal phoneme which is associated in Polish with the grapheme *s,* we can single out the following ultimate, indivisible elements: (1) the art.-aud. element which is connected with the action of the tip or front part of the tongue (the art. element) and the acoustic effect corresponding to this position (the acoustic element); (2) the art.-aud. element of constriction (the art. element) which produces the effect of hissing or friction (the aud. element); (3) the art.-aud. element of the separation of the vocal cords (the art. element) which produces the expulsion of air without acoustic vibration (the aud. element); and (4) the art.-aud. element resulting from the activities of raising and pressing the soft palate toward the lower and rear opening of the nasal cavities, activities which prevent the production of an acoustic or auditory resonance in the nasal cavities.

The phoneme corresponding to the grapheme *ą* includes the following constituent elements: (1) the art. element of contracting and rounding the lips, combined with the activity of the back section of the tongue. Together they modify the passive position of the oral cavity to produce : (2) an aud. element of resonance due to this very modification of the oral cavity; (3) an art.-aud. element consisting of the contraction of the vocal cords (the art. element), producing a corresponding acoustic vibration (the aud. element); and (4) the non-participation of the soft palate, i.e., its lax position (the art. element) which allows the expelled air to pass through the nasal cavity and produce a nasal resonance (the aud. element).

Each psychologically indivisible articulatory element we shall call a *kineme,* and each psychologically indivisible acoustic element, an *acousmeme,* whereas the acoustic result corresponding to the articulatory activity we shall call a *kinakeme.* This is the indivisible and twofold art.-acoustic element, which, Janus-like, has one face turned toward the physiological and motor activities of the speech organs, and the other toward the sphere of acoustics, i.e., the sphere of vibrating air and auditory impressions produced by these vibrations.

The above terms may at first glance seem strange and will undoubtedly startle the reader, and I only use them with reluctance. But I cannot avoid using them, since any newly formulated scientific concept requires its own verbal symbol.

§15. In order to give a historical outline of the art.-aud. aspect of the Polish linguistic system, whose direct predecessors include Slavic and proto-Slavic, and the more remote predecessors, IE and proto-IE, we must first of all establish the art.-aud. make-up of proto-IE and then show how its elements developed in the course of time, by either remaining more or less the same as in their initial period, or by changing their form, i.e., by changing the place or manner of articulation, by splitting into two or more variants, or by disappearing altogether.

§16. The juxtaposition and comparison of the various IE languages which constitute the branches of a once common language enables us to infer that original IE contained three categories of phonemes which differed in syllabicity, the configuration of the oral cavity and the articulatory-acoustic activities of the speech organs. These categories were:

1) pure *consonants,* i.e., phonemes which are incapable of forming syllables and are, from an articulatory viewpoint, occlusive, with the oral cavity being completely or partially closed. The corresponding auditory element results from the specific manner of

closure of the lips or the tongue (the graphic symbols of these phonemes are *p, b, t, d, k, g* . . . , *s*. . .);

2) pure *vowels*, i.e., syllabic and open sounds which are produced when the movements of the lips and some part of the tongue modify the oral cavity, making it into a resonator for the vibrating air expelled from the lungs: *a, o, e, u, i*. . . ;

3) *semiopen* sounds, or phonemes, which are intermediate between consonants and vowels with regard to both syllabicity, the behavior of the lips and tongue, and the shape of the oral cavity. These include the phonemes which are represented by the graphic symbols *r, l* ("liquids"), *m, n* (nasals), *u, i* (the semi-vowels $\underset{\sim}{u}, \underset{\sim}{i}$ or *w, j*). All these phonemes may function both as non-syllabics (consonants) or as syllabics (sonants).

§17. The proto-IE consonants may be assumed to have had the following distinctions:

1) five kinakemes differing as to their position in the oral cavity, namely: (1) labial (*p, b, ph, bh*); (2) dental-alveolar (*t, d, th, dh, s*); and three kinds of retracted ("back-lingual") consonants (*k, g, kh, gh*): (3) fronted (palatal), (4) medial, and (5) back ("deep-back" velar);

a sixth medial (mide-tongue) position can be assumed for the nonsyllabic *i*;

2) the distinction between a kinakeme of friction (*s*) and that of occlusion followed by an explosive release (*t, d,* and the other consonants);

3) two distinctions in the articulation of the occlusive consonants: (1) one between the kinakeme of voicing (*b, d, g_1, g_2, g_3*) and voicelessness (*p, t, k_1, k_2, k_3*), and (2) another between aspiration (*ph, th, kh* . . . , *bh, dh, gh* . . .) and lack of aspiration (*p, t, k* . . . , *b, d, g* . . .);

4) In their consonantal, or nonsyllabic function, the half-open phonemes *m, n* were distinguished through the kinakeme of a lowered soft palate with the corresponding acousmeme of nasal resonance, as opposed to the kinakeme of a raised soft palate with the corresponding acousmeme of the lack of nasal resonance characteristic of the other consonants;

5) Proto-IE contained only one autonomous, independent, separate phoneme of friction, the asyllabic (voiceless) *s*. Its voiced counterpart *z* could have occurred only before a voiced consonant (e.g., *zb, zd, zg*). The other spirants, the labial *v* (*w*) and the palatal *j*

were only a special case of the nonsyllabic function of the vowels
u and *i*.

6) Proto-IE lacked consonantal diphthongs (affricates) of the
type which are represented in Polish spelling by the graphemes or
groups of graphemes *c, dz, cz, dż, ć, dź*; in Polish these arose historically from back or front phonemes which became centralized
or "softened" under the influence of the adjacent palatal phonemes *i, e . . . , j. . . .*

7) Proto-IE also lacked the palatal consonants *ć, dź, ś, ż, ń . . . ,*
p', m', w' . . . , k', g', ch', which are found in modern Polish. Palatal
j was the vowel *i* in its nonsyllabic function, and not an independent consonant.

The proto-IE vowels, or open syllabic phonemes are assumed to
have carried:

1) the distinction between simple vowels (*a, o, e, u, i*) and vocalic
diphthongs (*au, ai, ou, oi, eu, ei . . .*);

2) the distinction between short (*a, o, e, u, i . . .*) and long
vowels (*ā, ō, ē, ū, ī*);

3) three different positions of narrowing of the oral cavity:
labial, combined with a back articulation (*o, u*), back (*a, ə*), and
palatal (*e, i*);

4) two degrees of narrowing: medium and extreme, pertaining
to the labial vowels (*o, u*), and the palatal (*e, i*), and back vowels
(*a – ə* [narrow *a*]);

5) supplementary back narrowing of the labial vowels (*o, u*) and
the absence of labial narrowing of the palatal vowels (in other
words, the absence of the kind of phonemes known to modern
German and French, where they are rendered by the graphic symbols *ö, ü, eu* and *eu, u* respectively).

6) the absence of nasal vowels.

The sonants or syllabic "liquids" (*r, l*) and nasals (*n, m*) may be
assumed to have been distinguished by:

1) palatal narrowing (the "soft" syllabic *r', l', n', m'*) and its
absence ("hard" syllabic *r, l, n, m*);

2) by shortness (short syllabic *r, l, n, m* of both the "soft" and
"hard" varieties) and length (also of both types).

§18. According to established custom, the simplest art.-aud. elements which receive graphic representation are not the kinemes,
acousmemes, or kinakemes, but the phonemes. In adhering to this
custom, we posit for proto-IE the following system of phonemes,

i.e., of semasiologized and morphologized units which are independent of the influence of their environment, which constitute the point of departure for the history of the Polish phonetic system:

Nonsyllabic Consonants				Syllabic Vowels			Syllabic or nonsyllabic Sonants		
p ph b bh	[v]	[m]		short	[u] o	[m]	v(w)	u,	m
t th d dh s	[l]	[n]		long	[u] o	[m]		u,	m
	[r]			short	[l]	[n]	l		n
					[r]		r		
				long	[l]	[n]	l		n
					[r]		r		
k_1 k_1h g_1 g_1h				short ə	a				
k_2 k_2h g_2 g_2h				long	a				
k_3 k_3h g_3 g_3h				short	[i] e		j | i		
	[j]			long	[i] e		i		

The short and long sonants *l, r, n, m* can be divided into those without (*l°, r°, n°, m°*) and those with a palatal kinakeme (*l^i, r^i, n^i, m^i*).

From the standpoint of the proto-IE system, as well as from a historical viewpoint, we must posit, along with the individual phonemes, the following dipthongs and combinations:

au	*ou*	*eu*	*ai*	*oi*	*ei*
ar	*or*	*er*	*al*	*ol*	*el*
an	*on*	*en*	*am*	*om*	*em*

These were pronounced with a different intonation, that is, showing different nuances and yielding historically different results. Thus it can be assumed that the syllabic and nonsyllabic phonemes had, in addition to quantity, a changeable accent, i.e., different degrees of stress and intonation.

The history of an art.-aud. system includes, finally, the history of the structure of syllables and whole words, as well as the history of the relation between the art.-aud. structure of morphemes and the division of words into syllables, i.e., the difference between *tautosyllabism* (when the final phonemes of a given morpheme are a part of the same syllable) and *heterosyllabism* (when the final syllabic phoneme of a given morpheme marks the end of the syllable and the consonant or consonantal cluster following the vowel marks the beginning of the next syllable).

§19. Let us consider now from a historical viewpoint what happened to the art.-aud. elements (*kinemes, acousmemes, kinakemes*) of proto-IE when they passed into proto-Slavic and the subsequent Polish linguistic system.

First it should be noted that some semasiologized and morphologized art.-aud. elements (kinemes, acousmemes, kinakemes) making up the phonemes may disappear from the system of subsequent generations. This may occur when the environment and position in the word group cause the disappearance of the phonemes containing these elements, or when entire words or morphemes containing the phonemes and their elements disappear.

If, however, the minimal art.-aud. elements do not disappear, but are, on the contrary, reproduced together with the phonemes that contain them, we are faced either with straightforward linguistic conservatism, or with transformation and a new arrangement of the elements.

§20. The following art.-aud. distinctions have been preserved without change from proto-IE to the present:

1) There is not a single case of change of nonsyllabics or consonants into syllabics or vowels, or conversely, of vowels into consonants. This is true not only of the first two clearly differentiated categories of phonemes, namely the pure consonants and vowels (*to, wozu, wóz, piek–, widzi, ducha*. . .), but also of the third category, the so-called sonants (which may function both as nonsyllabics and syllabics). If any of these transitional phonemes was nonsyllabic (consonantal) in proto-IE, it remained nonsyllabic also at a later period (*ma–t–ka, nos, dymu, syna, raz, łoże*. . .). If they were syllabic, however, they could have maintained their syllabic function or lose it, as is the case of the Polish phonemes *l, ł, r, rz, n, m*. . . . In Polish the syllabic function is performed either by a full vowel that has replaced the entire sonorant phoneme (cf. the nasal vowels in *piąć, na–pię–cie, czą–ć, żąć*. . .), or by the syllabic element of the original sonant which is otherwise preserved in the adjacent consonant (*kark, targ, smark, mrug–a, pierści–eń, na–parst–ek, wilk, pełn–y, długi*).

§21. 2) If we turn to the consonantal and sonant phonemes in prevocalic position, we observe that they preserved the distinction between the kineme of a lowered soft palate (with a corresponding acousmeme of nasal resonance) and the kinakeme of a raised soft palate (with the corresponding acousmeme of the lack of nasal resonance). The kineme of a lowered soft palate has been preserved in morphemes which in Indo-European had a consonantal, nonsyllabic *m* or *n* before a vowel of the same morpheme or in morpheme: e.g., *ma–t–k–a, morz–e, nos, nowy, mięs–o, nie. . .* ; *dom–, dym–, syn–, jun–. . . .* On the other hand, there is not a single morpheme in which the kineme of a raised soft palate was historically replaced by a lowered soft palate, or where nasal resonance replaced its absence. The IE phonemes of the type *b, p. . . , d, t. . . , g, k. . . , s. . . , r, l. . . , a, o, e, i, u. . .* have remained nonnasal until this day.

The nasality of the nonsyllabic *m, n* has been absorbed into the art.-aud. composition of the preceding vowel of the same syllable, giving rise to proto-Sl. nasal vowels. In such a manner, the IE syllabic nasal sonants have in most cases yielded a proto-Sl. nasal vowel *ę*. The nasal resonance disappeared only in those cases where the syllabic *m* was replaced in pre-Sl. by a short *u*, and in proto-Sl. by a short *y*. The reflexes of proto-Sl. nasal vowels are in Polish almost always nasal vowels or their substitutes, sequences of vowel plus nasal consonant: *wąs–, wącha, kąsa, gęś, męski, węch, mięso, grzęźnie, więzy . . . , wiązać, pląsa. . . , ząb–, dąb–, zęb–, dęb. . . , sąd, wątek. . . , męty, tędy. . . , sądzić, mącić. . . , sędzia, pięć. . . , piąty. . . , ręka rąk. . . , cięgi, ciągnąć. . . , spiąć, spięcie. . . , –cząć –częcie. . . .*

§22. 3) The so-called liquid phonemes which, like the nasals, could function in proto-IE as either nonsyllabics or syllabics, were even more resistant to historical change. As we have seen the nasality of the nasal phonemes could have been lost historically in some environments, whereas the phonemes *r* and *l* (which were either nonsyllabic or syllabic in the IE period), though they could mix with and replace each other, have been preserved to this day as a separate pair. We can thus formulate the stability of a "liquid" // "nonliquid" opposition: on the one hand there is *r* and *ł, l,* as in *ra, rok, ruch, ryba, rudy, rydz, rdza. . . , łamać, łuna, łoże, łysy, łeb. . . , leży, lice. . . , prosi, grodzi. . . , słoma, głowa. . . , lże. . . , lgnie, łży;* and on the other hand, all the other morphologized and semasiologized phonemes.

It should, however, be noted that in Polish the liquid phonemes have been subject to some constraints: in certain positions they depended on the following or preceding consonant, becoming either voiced (*rdza, łgać, łże, łży, lgnie, łba.* . .) or voiceless (*rtęć, łkać, lśni.* . . , *wiatr, zmysł, myśl.* . . , *jabłko.* . .).

But a similar dependence and weakening also affected the nasal consonants (*mgła, mgli, mknie, mchu, mści.* . . , *pasm, drachm, widm, piosnka, pieśń, waśń.* . .).

The phoneme *r* underwent palatalization ("softening") both in the proto-Sl. period when it became *ŕ* before *j* (*burza, morze, stwarza.* . .), and later, in the period of a separate Polish language, when it "softened" before the palatal vowels *i, e, ę* (*parzy, dworzec, rzeka, rzecze, rzęsa, rząd, grzebie, grzęda, brzeg, drzewo.* . . , *przy, trzy, krzywy, prze, trzeba, krzemień.* . .). This *ŕ* has, in turn, become *rz,* i.e., a consonant proper which was at first a diphthong (an "affricate"), and then a spirant.

The phoneme *l,* which was originally fronted or "hard" (*ł*), has in the pronunciation of most Poles become a nonsyllabic, bilabial vowel (*w* or nonsyllabic *u*).

§23. 4) Among the consonantal phonemes, the kinakeme of labiality was transmitted without change from IE to contemporary Polish. The labiality of the phonemes *p, ph, b, bh* has been preserved in proto-Sl. and Polish: *po, piana, ból, baśń, być.* This psychologically autonomous noise-producing action of the lips has also been preserved in the phonemes *v* (*w*) and *m* in their nonsyllabic, consonantal function: *wóz, widzi.* . . , *morze, masło, mięso.* . . .

Thus the consonants have preserved without change the difference, or we should rather say, opposition between the kinakeme of labiality and any lingual kinakeme. The history of Polish offers no instance of interchange between labial and lingual consonants. Such an interchange takes place, however, in the case of fricatives or spirants where *f* may be replaced by *ch, chw* or vice versa; but these are special cases which do not affect the general regularity of the historical continuity of linguistic material.

§24. 5) The kinakeme of fronting (*przedniojęzykowość*) which characterized some IE phonemes as components of morphemes, was also transmitted via proto-Sl. to contemporary Polish: *to, stoi, ty, dać, dom, widzi, dym, broda, wdowa.* . . . The number of fronted elements was, furthermore, increased in proto-Sl. when some back phonemes acquired a fronted point of articulation, either spontaneously, i.e., owing to the peculiar make-up of these phonemes, or combinatorily, i.e., owing to their phonetic environment (s, z instead of IE k_1, g_1, g_1h; cz, c, $ż$, dz instead of IE k_2, k_3, g_2, g_3; cf. §§28, 29). The series of fronted consonants (*przedniojęzykowość*) suffered only a minor loss when IE s changed under certain historical conditions to proto-Sl. x (*ch*).

§25. The following IE elements and distinctions of IE were preserved without change in proto-Sl. and in pre-Polish: 1) the nonpalatal ("hard") and palatal ("soft") varieties of syllabic r and l. The transition from proto-Sl. and pre-Polish to a separate Polish period was marked by the breakdown of the simultaneous combination of the consonantal r or l elements with the reduced (nonpalatal or palatal) vowel elements into two successive, nonsimultaneous elements, i.e., into a vowel and consonant or consonant and vowel; e.g., *garb, kark, smark*. . . , *mrug–a, mruk*. . . , *czatn–, żarn–, martw–, –parst–, wart–, śmier–ć, pierści–eń, wierc–i*. . . , *pierw–, wierzb–, wierzg–, pierzch–, wierzch–*. . . ; *wilk–, milk–, wilg–*. . . , *pełn–, bełt–, pełz–*. . . , *czołg–, czółn–, żółt–*. . . , *dłub–, dług–, tłust–*. . . .

§26. 2) The quantitative difference between short and long vowels and syllables. The IE short vowels (a, $ə$, o, e, u, i) are continued in proto-Sl. as short (o, e, y, i), and the IE (or pre-Sl.) long vowels (a, o, e, u, i) and diphthongs (au, ou, eu, ai, oi, ei. . . an, on, en. . . ar, or, er, al, ol, el. . .) are continued in proto-Sl. and Common Slavic as long vowels, or as half-open long sonants (a, e, y, i; u, e, i; $ǫ$, $ę$, and syllabic long r and l with a palatal or nonpalatal vocalic element).

The transition from proto-Sl. and Cm. Sl. to later stages was characterized by the merger of the original long and short vowels. Differences in accent and intonation brought about the shortening of original long vowels, whereas the loss of the short y and i caused the lengthening of certain short vowels.

Pre-Polish may be assumed to have inherited from IE the distinction between originally short or shortened vowels and originally long or lengthened vowels. At a later period, and especially in contemporary Polish, the psychological ability to distinguish the temporal quantity of vowels is lost. Polish vowels are neither short nor long; they are quantitatively neutral.

The original distinction between long and short vowels is partially reflected in Polish as a qualitative distinction in the vocalic configuration of the oral cavity.

§27. 3) IE had a morphologically mobile accent, i.e., an accent which accompanied different syllables of the word and differentiated certain morphemes. This morphologized and semasiologized art.-aud. property was transmitted with some modifications to proto-Sl. and Cm. Sl., and, in one way or another, to the later stages of the separate Slavic languages. However, in Polish this property was suppressed and lost, leaving only some traces of its former existence. The Polish accent became fixed and relinquished its morphological role; now its function is purely syntactic, in that it serves to distinguish different words.

Such a transformation in the art.-aud. structure of the language could hardly have occurred without foreign influence. In this respect we must regard Polish as an ethnically mixed language. In Kashubian dialects and elsewhere in the Lekhitic linguistic community, we find phenomena of morphologized accentual mobility.

§28. In passing from IE and the oldest reconstructible stage of Polish to its subsequent stages, certain art.-aud. features underwent qualitative or quantitative change. Some elements of the linguistic system disappeared without a trace, and others were replaced. These shifts in the mutual relation of art.-aud. elements also changed their numerical ratio. While the number of elements of one category increased, the number of elements of another category decreased or disappeared completely. On the one hand, some elements disappeared in the neighborhood of other elements as, for example, certain consonants before other consonants (e.g., the simplification of IE *vr* into Slavic *r*), and at the end of words or syllables; on the other hand, certain distinctions between phonemes were lost.

In the transition from IE to proto-Sl. there disappeared:

1) the distinction between aspirated and unaspirated stops. On the basis of the Slavic languages alone, no one could have thought that the historical source of the phonemes *b* (in *ból*), *d* (in *dar, dom, siada*), *z* (in *ząb, zna*), going back to the IE unaspirated voiced stops *b*, *d*, *g*, differs from that of the phonemes *b*, *d*, *z* (in *by–ć, ba–śń, dym, wdowa, brod–a*. . . , *woz–u, zim–a, zorz–a*), going back to the IE aspirated stops *bh, dh, gh*.

2) the distinction between three series of IE velar stops k_1, g_1, g_1h; k_2, g_2, g_2h; k_3, g_3, g_3h. The first series moved into the class of fronted fricatives *s, z* (*słoma, słowo, sto, sroka, pros–*; for examples with *z*, cf. 1 above).

The ratio of the original semasiologized and morphologized phoneme *s* was, at the same time increased by *s* from k_1, whereas the change of g_1, g_1h to *z* gave rise to a new independent phoneme, the fronted voiced fricative *z*. The remaining two series k_2, g_2, g_2h and k_3, g_3, g_3h remained in the class of velars, but without any difference in position [localization], so that proto-Sl. has only one psychologically defined velar (*tylnojęzykowe*) position *k*, *g* (and only one *g*, because of the loss of distinction between aspirated and unaspirated consonants); e.g., the suffix –*k*–; *krzyw–*, *krew*, *ko–go*, *wilk–*. . . , *góra*, *śniegu*, *gawiedź*. . . , *gorzeć*, *goni*. . . .

3) the distinction between an IE narrow *a* (i.e., *ǝ*) and a short open *a*: *ǝ* merged with *a* which, in turn, merged with *o*; proto-Sl. short *o* thus continues all three IE phonemes (*stoi*. . . , *ostry*, *oś*, *sol–*. . . , *ośm–*, *owca*. . .).

4) The kinakeme of labiality of long *u* and short *u* was lost (delabialization); these vowels were replaced by proto-Sl. long *y* and short *y* (*dym*, *być*, *syn*, *wymię*; *krew*, *mech*, *sen*, *łeb*. . .).

The labiality of long *o* was likewise lost, merging with a long *a*, whose ratio increased: (*dać*, *dar*, *dwa*, *nagi*. . .).

The ratio of short *o* increased, however, at the expense of short *a*, which had merged with it. (Examples under 3).

5) The IE vocalic diphthongs became long vowels (§26).

Thanks to all these changes, which marked the transition from IE to proto-Sl., the latter acquired new phonemes and series of phonemes; among others:

1) more fronted consonants; more positions and combinations of fronted consonants;

2) more spirants (*z*, *ż*. . . , *ch*. . .);

3) a series of palatal [*średniejęzykowe*] consonants which appeared as a result of the palatalization [*ześredniojęzykowienie*] of back consonants in a palatal environment (*cz*, *z*, *sz*; *c*, *dz*) or as a result of the merger of fronted and labial consonants with *j* (*tj*, *dj*, *sj*, *zj*; *pj*, *bj*, *vj*, *mj*, *rj*, *lj*, *nj*);

5) consonantal diphthongs *cz*, *c*, *dz*, *dż*. . . ;

6) the vowel *y* (long and short);

7) nasal vowels (§26).

§29. Some of these art.-aud. innovations were the result of combinatory, i.e., environmental influence which split an originally single phoneme into two or more phonemes. These include:

1) the appearance in some environments of proto-Sl. *x* (*ch*)

from IE *s*, which in other environments remained unchanged (e.g., *such, duch–, mech, wierzch, pych–a, chory.* . . , the locative plural ending *–ch.* . . , side by side with *s* in *such–, syn, bos–, nos–, sad–.* . .).

2) the split of velar consonants into velars and palatal spirants or consonantal diphthongs: *k* vs. *cz* (*piek– -piecze, rok - roczy, wilk - wilczyca.* . . , *mog– - moż, śnieg– - snież, bog– - boż–.* . . , *such– - susz, strach– - strasz, much– - musz.* . .).

3) the split of the combinations of dental and labial consonants with the vowel *i* (*ti, di, si, zi, ni, ri, li, pi, bi, mi, vi*) into the same combinations in syllabic position (i.e., before consonants and in word final position) and into palatal consonants before *t', d'* (mod. Polish *c, dz*), *sz, ż, n', r', l', pl', bl', ml', vl',* or *p', b', m', v'* before a vowel (e.g., mod. Polish *płaći - płac, chodzi - chodz–, nosi - nosz–, wozi–, woż, gani - gań–, tworzy - tworz–, chwali - chwal–, topi - top'–, lub'i - lub'–, tłum'i - tłum'–, łow'i - łow'–.* . .).

The proto-Sl. phoneme *t'* (from *tj*) also developed from the group *kt* (*kt, gt*) before *i* (mod. Polish: *piec, noc, tłuc, wlec* . . . *lec, moc, móc, strzec.* . .).

4) in the pre-Sl. combinations *jo, ju*, later *jo, jy*, the vowels became fronted under the influence of the preceding palatal *j*, yielding the combinations *je, ji* . . . (*morze, pole.* . . , *kraj, koń, mąż, płacz.* . .). The ratio of the vowels *e, i* was thus increased at the expense of *o, y*.

§30. Passing from IE to proto-Sl., certain phonemes and series of phonemes merged, whereas others, previously autonomous, split into two or more phonemes. But here we must distinguish merger and splitting of phonemes in immediate contact with other phonemes from the same kind of processes which take place in the psychologically existing phonetic system of a language.

The following mergers took place in immediate contact:

—combinations of consonants with *j* (i.e., *kj, gj, chj,* . . . *tj, dj, nj, lj, rj,* . . . *sj, zj.* . .) (§28);

—one-syllable combinations of vowels with nasal consonants which changed into nasal vowels (§26).

The following splits took place under the same conditions:

—palatal velar consonants changed into consonantal diphthongs (*k' - cz, c; g' - dz*) (§28);

—labial consonants, palatalized through merger with the consonant *j*, changed into the groups *pl', bl', ml', vl'* (§29).

§31. The following phonemes merged in the phonetic system:

—aspirated with nonaspirated (§28);

—velar stops of the series k_1, g_1 with the fronted spirants s, z (§28);

—the vowel a with the vowel o;

—the combinations jy (ju), jo with ji, je;

—vocalic diphthongs with long vowels.

The following phonemes and phonemic series split in the phonetic system:

—the consonant s into s and ch (§29);

—the velar consonants (resulting from the merger of k_2, g_2, g_2h with k_3, g_3, g_3h) into velar k, g and fronted consonants cz, $\dot{z}$, which later became c, dz (§29);

—the diphthong oi into long e and long i.

§32. Considering all the above-mentioned changes which marked the transition from IE to proto-Sl., we may represent the art.-aud. system of proto-Sl. by the following table of phonemes and historically indivisible groups or combinations of phonemes:

1) p	b	m		v			
t	d	n	s	z		r	l
k	g		x				
				j			
pl'	bl'	ml'		vl'			
t'	d'	ń					
					c	dz	r'	l'
			sz	ż	cz		

2) short y long y long u short i long i

long a short o short e long e long $ą$ long $ę$

3) syllabic sonants r^o r' l^o l'

4) Pre-Sl. or, er, ol, el (= proto-Sl. and C. Sl. long r^o, long r', long l^o, long l').

NOTE: x had approximately the same value as Polish ch. The nasal vowels $ę$ $ą$ were probably long.

This presumed phonetic system of proto-Sl. and Common Slavic represents, from the viewpoint of Slavic comparative phonetics and Polish historical phonetics, a hypothetical cross section of the art.-aud. representations which had formed over a certain period of time.

§33. We may now examine the subsequent fate of the individual components of this system and of the system as a whole as it evolved into an autonomous Polish linguistic system.

Certain of the art.-aud. components and distinctions of proto-Sl. have remained the same up to the present, whereas others have undergone either qualitative or quantitative changes. In examining the invariance and changes, we shall first consider those that were shared by all branches of the Slavic linguistic world, by all "Slavic languages," second, those which Polish shared with some other Slavic languages, and third, those which are characteristic only of Polish in contradistinction to the other Slavic languages.

Before analyzing the common and individual Slavic changes, let us first single out those elements, groups, and series of elements which underwent neither common nor separate change. To some extent we will have to repeat what was said above (§§20—24) about the preservation of the IE elements and distinctions in the present state of the ⟨Polish⟩ language.

Thus, in the evolution of proto-Sl. and Common Slavic to later stages, including Polish, the following elements remained unaltered:

—labiality of the consonants *p, b, v, m;*

—frontedness of the consonants *t, d, s, z, c, sz, ż, cz, r, l, n;*

—backness of the consonants *k, g, x (ch)* (insofar as these did not become palatalized ("soft");

—palatality of the consonant *j;*

—occlusive articulation of the consonants *p, t, k, b, d, g, m, n;*

—the specific oral articulation of *s, z, c, r, l, j;*

—closure of the nasal cavity and the nonnasal acoustic character of all proto-Sl. nonnasal consonants and vowels, and openness of the nasal cavity and the nasal acoustic character of the nasal consonants *m, n.*

By contrast, there is not a single vowel that has not changed in some way or other.

§34. Among the common changes and invariance of the proto-Sl. state in its later phases, including Polish, we may list:

—the gradual change of the consonants going back to the original groups *sj, zj,* which finally became *sz, ż (noszę, wożę);*

—the gradual change of palatalized ("softened") consonants going back to *k, g, ch,* which first became *sz, ż, cz* and then *c, dz;*

—the disappearance of the autonomous, psychologically distinct vowel *y,* which may be regarded as the last step of a pre-Sl. process. Originally the long *u* had become delabialized into a back vowel *y,* which was psychologically distinct from other vowels; this stage of development is still reflected in OCS records. Later, however, this vowel lost its independent status and either merged completely with the reflex of the vowel *i,* or became only a variant of that vowel, which varied according to the preceding consonants.

§35. Another change shared by the entire Slavic world was the general phonetic shortening and weakening of words, which was realized in two ways:

1) the original proto-Sl. long vowels *a, i, e, y, u, ǫ, ę* became shortened (this stage is reflected in the oldest OCS records);

2) the short vowels *y* (from IE *u*) and *i* disappeared or became phonetic zeroes under certain conditions, particularly in word final position.

The latter historical-phonetic process had the following consequences:

1) the shortening of a large number of words by one or more syllables;

2) the appearance of new closed syllables, i.e., syllables ending with a consonant;

3) the appearance of new consonantal groups;

4) the creation of new conditions of phonetic accommodation (phonetic adaptation) between adjacent words, i.e., at the juncture of the end of a word and the beginning of a following word;

5) the appearance of new syllabic "liquid" sonants *r, l* and nasal sonants *n, m* (which are alien to Polish, but which are found in Czech and in some other Slavic languages), or of voiceless, non-syllabic "liquid" and nasal consonants, such as are found in the Polish *wiatr, jabłko, myśl, piosnka, pieśń, pasm.* . . ;

6) lengthening and "compensatory" strengthening of vowels in syllables preceding those syllables in which the short vowels *y* and *i* became phonetic zeroes, e.g., *bóg, wóz.* . . , *śnięg, chléb.* . . , *sen, pies, wieś.* . . from older **bogy, *vozy.* . . (with short *y*), **snegy, *chleby.* . . (with long *e* and short *y*), **syny* (with the first *y* long and the second short), **visi, *pisy* (with short *i* and *y*).

§36. Among the changes, as well as manifestations of conservatism which Polish shares with some, but not all Slavic languages are:

—the reflexes of the consonant clusters *kv, gv* in combination with front vowels among the Northwestern Slavs (including the Poles) (*kwiat, kwilić* . . . *gwiazda.* . .). The Southern and Eastern Slavs have replaced these groups by *cv, zv;*

—a similar territorial division corresponds to the treatment of

338

the proto-Sl. consonant groups *dl* (*dł, dl*), *tl* (*tł, tl*). The North-western Slavs (including the Poles) have retained these groups without change (*mydło. . . , padła. . . , plotła. . .*), whereas the other Slavs simplified them to *l* (*ł, l*);

—the proto-Sl. nasal vowels which have been preserved, albeit with some modifications, only in Polish, were also used by those Slavs whose speech provided the basis for the OSC graphic-visual language or literature, i.e., by the early Bulgarian and Macedonian Slavs who occupied the Eastern part of the Balkan peninsula. Only the OCS literary documents reflect the proto-Sl. stage in which the *ǫ* (continuing the pre-Sl. group *on*) and the *ę* (continuing the pre-Sl. group *en* or the syllabic sonant *n*) were differentiated. Among the other Slavs, including the linguistic descendants of the early Bulgarians and Macedonians, we find only traces of nasality in the reflexes of the proto-Sl. nasal vowels. In Polish the two nasal vowels have merged; *ę* and *ą* continue both proto-Sl. *ę* and *ǫ*. But if these vowels are preceded within the same morpheme by a consonant, the consonant itself provides a clue to the historical origin of the nasal vowel. If the preceding consonant is nonpalatal in modern Polish, and was also hard in the past, the nasal vowel in question stems historically from a proto-Sl. *ǫ* (e.g., *tępy, będzie, bądź, tędy, stąd, sąd, sędzia; ząb, zęby, ręka, rąk, męka, mąka, wązki, zwęzić, gęba, gąbka. . .*). If, on the other hand, the consonant is palatal or can be traced back historically to a palatalized or "softened" consonant, the nasal vowel in question goes back to a proto-Sl. *ę* (*pięć, piąty, więzić, wiązać, mięso, miąższ, cięży, ciąża, dzięcioł, dziąsło, sięgać, siąkać, ziębi, ziąb, lęka się, zląkł się . . . , część, cząstka, żęty, żąć, rzędy, rząd, przędzie, prząść. . .*). Of course, after the consonant *j* it is impossible to determine the origin of the nasal vowel, since *j* as a nonsyllabic *i* has ever since IE been an autonomous palatal consonant not subject to palatalization; in proto-Sl. it could be followed by either *ę* or *ą* (*jęczeć, jąkać się. . .*). (The word *język* has its own particular history);

—the proto-Sl. palatal phonemes *t'* (from *tj* and *kt*) and *d'* had the same development in Polish as in Slovak (*tracę, świeca. . . , chodzę, miedza. . .*), whereas Czech has *c* from *tj*, like Polish and Slovak, but *z*, not *dz* from *dj*;

—Polish shares only with the Lusatian languages its treatment of the pre-Sl. tautosyllabic groups *or, er, ol, el* (*broda, grodu, proch, krowa, prosię, droga, sroka, mrowie. . . , przodu, drzewo, brzeg, źrebię. . . , głowa, kłos, płochy, błoto, tłok, dłóto, słoma, złoto, młot. . . , mleko, plon. . . , człon, żłób. . .*). The other Slavic languages have different reflexes of these diphthongs.

§37. For Cm. Sl., as opposed to IE, we have established two types of palatalization ("softening") of consonants: (1) two successive palatalizations of velar consonants caused by adjacent palatal phonemes; (2) palatalization of dentals and labials which have merged with a following *j* (nonsyllabic *i*) (§§28–30). Later, North Slavic, including Polish, acquired a new series of palatal consonants as a result of the palatalization of dental and labial consonants before front vowels and front syllabic sonants: *t', d', s', z', r', l', n', p', b', v', m'*. In some of these consonants, the palatal element was subsequently strengthened; consequently the palatals *t', d', s', z'* became *ć, dź, ś, ż* with a prominent element of friction; *r'* became *rz*; and the phonemes *p', b', v', m'* yielded the diphthongs *p'j, b'j, v'j, m'j* with a characteristic fricative *j* (e.g., *ci, ciało, ciężar, ciemny, ćma, cierń. . . , dziw, dzieci, dzierżeć. . . , siła, siano, siodło. . . , zima, zięć, ziarno. . . , darzy, brzytwa, rzec, rzeka, rzadki . . . , lizać, lewy, lęk, len. . . , ni, niesie, dzień. . . , pisze, piechota, piasek, pięć, pies, pierwszy. . . , bić, bierze, biały. . . , widzi, wieś, wierci, wilk. . . , miły, mięso, milknąć. . .*).

Of all Slavic languages, Polish and the Northwestern Slavic languages in general, have felt most strongly the influence of consonants upon the quality of vowels and sonants. Of paramount importance here is not only the distinction between palatal ("soft") and nonpalatal ("hard") consonants, but also that between fronted (dental) and nonfronted (nondental) consonants. It is sufficient to point out the difference in such words as *grzebać, trzepać, piekę, niech, ulegać, niemy, mleko, pierwszy, wierzch, cierpnąć. . . , w lecie, w lesie, w mieście, na czele, wiedzie, niesie, plenić, twierdza, smierć pierścień. . .*, but *lato, las, miasto, czoło, wiodę, niosę, plon, twardy, martwy, naparstek. . .*; also *wilk, wilgoć, milknąć. . .*, but *pełny, żółty, tłusty, długi. . . .*

*The Historical Phonetic Changes Which
Took Place in the Period, or rather, in the
Various Periods of a Separate Polish Language*

§38. In addition to the changes touched upon in §§34–36, we shall now reiterate or state for the first time, the following historical-phonetic processes:

1) the proto-Sl. fronted (palatalized or "softened") consonants *t', d'* (from *tj, jt, dj*) became *c, dz* (§36);

2) the pre-Sl. groups *or, er, ol, el* (in proto-Sl., long syllabic sonants (§36)) underwent metathesis with the restoration of the pre-Sl. shortness of their vowels: *ro* (*ró*) (*broda, gród*), *rze, rzo, rzó, re, ro, ró*) (*brzeg, trzewia, przodu, przód, trzoda, trzód, średni, żrebię, środa, śród*), *ło* (*łó*) (*głowa, głów, błoto, słoma, młot, głód...*), *le* (*lo*) (*mleko, plon...*) (§37);

3) like all other Slavic languages, Polish underwent a general temporal shortening of words, and in particular the elimination in many cases of the short *y* (from pre-Sl. *u*) and *i*, and shortening of words through the loss of whole syllables, with all the far-reaching consequences which this development had for the general phonetic character of the language. Where the short vowels *y, i* were not eliminated, they changed historically to *e*: *sen, mech, łeb..., pies, dzień, len...* (§35);

4) in connection with the last change, Polish acquired a whole series of *phonetic zeroes* of vocalic origin, whereas the phonetic zeroes of proto-Sl. were mostly of IE consonantal origin (§28). In the course of the shift of the art.-aud. representations from proto-Sl. to Polish, and in the independent history of Polish, there also was, of course, a loss of some inherited consonants, so that there also appeared a phonetic zero of consonantal origin. As for the vowels which became phonetic zeroes in Polish, it should be noted that in addition to the articulatory-auditory weak and short *y, i* (which disappeared primarily in word final position, but also within the word), other vowels (which were either short in proto-Sl. such as *o, e...*, or long, such as *a, y, i...*) could likewise disappear if they were weakly morphologized and semasiologized. Thus, for example, the infinitive desinence *–ć* is historically derived from *ci* (with a long proto-Sl. *i*) and has a phonetic zero in place of the vowel *i*;

5) the secondarily lengthened vowels *a, o, e* (§§26, 35) were narrowed, creating a new historical category of narrow (*pochylone*) vowels: *á* (medial between *a* and *o*, with a tendency toward *o* or *a*), *ó* (medial between *o* and *u*, with a tendency toward *u*), and *é* (medial between *e* and *i*, with a tendency toward *i* or *e*). The distinction between *á* and *a, ó* and *u, é* and *i* was eventually lost;

6) a specifically Polish historical-phonetic phenomenon is the change in certain consonantal groups and combinations of *ś ż, ć,*

dź, ść, ždź. . . into *j: wiejski, wejrzy, ojca, ogrójca, Zamojski* (cf. *Zamość*), *Ujejski* (cf. *Ujazd*). . . ;

7) a phenomenon which is also known in other languages, but which is, historically speaking, a particularly Polish phonetic development, is the change of the vowel *i* (from proto-Sl. long *i* and *y*) into *e* before a following *r: sierota, ser, Serock, Zgierz, ubiera, umiera, rozpiera*. . . but *rozcina, zaczyna, zżyma*. . . ; also *ćwierć, śmierć, pierwej, wierzch, wierzba* from older *ćwirć, śmirć, pirwej, wirzch, wirzba*. . . ;

8) in the transition from IE to proto-Sl., the syllabic nasal sonants *n, m* (which were distinguished as palatal and nonpalatal and as short and long) disappeared, yielding a nasal vowel *ę* or a pre-Sl. short *u* and a Slavic short *y* (§21). The syllabic "liquid" sonants *r, l* (which had the same distinctions as the sonants *m, n*) were replaced by various combinations of vowels with the consonants *r (r, rz)* and *l (ł, l): ar, ru, ir* (later *er: er, erz*); *il, eł, oł, łu*. . . (§37). The original syllabic "liquid" sonants *r, l* thus contributed to an increase both of corresponding nonsyllabic consonants, and of syllabic vowels. We have here to do with one of the cases illustrating the historical loss of intermediate, transitional categories in favor of opposite, clearly defined categories.

A similar breakdown of the proto-Sl. syllabic sonants *r, l* into combinations of vowels and consonants is found in the Northwest and East Slavic territories, as opposed to those of the Southwest (beginning with Czech and especially with Slovak), which have, to a minor or lesser extent and in one way or another, preserved the original syllabic sonants.

Table of Autonomous Independent Phonemes of the Polish Linguistic System

§39. This table cannot be considered absolutely precise and exhaustive, for it is by its very nature in flux and variable, depending upon dialectal influences and the usage of individual speakers of Polish.

§40. If we compare the table of the Polish phonemes with that of the proto-Sl. phonemes, we arrive at the following conclusions:

1) the phoneme *f*, which was lacking in IE and in proto-Sl., appeared in the Polish system mostly as an art.-aud. component of morphemes borrowed from other languages; in addition, it is char-

1) p   b   m   f   w
   t   d   n   s   z   c   dz   ł
             sz   ż   cz   dż   [rz]   r
   k   g   ch   j
   p'   b'   m'   f'   w'
   (t')   (d')   ń   ś   ź   ć   dź   l
   k'   g'   ch'

2)   u   o   ą̊
              a   ą (nasal *a*, conventionally written *an*)
        i   e   ę

NOTES: 1. The phonemes associated with the graphic combination *rz* are from an acoustic-auditory viewpoint *ž* or *š;* only a relatively small part of the Polish linguistic territory has a separate phoneme *rz*, which is a kind of consonantal diphthong, i.e., a combination of a weak *r* with *ž* or *š⟨ř⟩*.

2. The digraph *ch* in this table stands for either *ch* or *h* of the conventional Polish orthography.

3. *i* is a symbol for the conventional Polish *y* (*być, ty, syn*) or *i* when not followed by a letter denoting another vowel (*bić, ci, siny . . .*).

4. I have used the letter *a* to denote both the representation of the vowel *ą* (nasal *o*) and the combination *an*.

acteristic of some onomatopoeic words. Only in rare cases is it the historical continuation of phonemes and phonemic combinations in morphemes or in morphemic groups which are of IE and proto-Sl. origin (e.g., *ufać. . .*);

2) the nasal phoneme *ą* occurs only in words and morphemes which are of foreign origin: *ansa, awans, kwadrans, kontredans, rewansz, blamanże.* Compare also *Francja, bankiet, lampa, trampolina, gangrena. . .* vs. *ponsowy, bronz, bonza, koncha. . . , pensum, pensja, sensat. . .* ;

3) in the phonemic table of proto-Sl. it was already possible, without further reservations, to group *m, n* with the consonantal phonemes, for, unlike IE, proto-Sl. lacked syllabic nasal sonants proper. The phonemes *r, l*, however, had to be listed under both the consonantal and the vocalic phonemes. In Polish the phonemes *r* and *l* (*l, ł*) have definitively switched to the series of nonsyllabic consonants. The once palatal ("soft") *r* has likewise dropped out (in acoustic-auditory terms) of the class of semi-vowels capable of performing a syllabic function; it became either a purely nonsyllabic consonant *rz*, or it underwent further reduction to *r* when

the elements *ž* or *š* were, in some cases, lost (*środa, żrebak, źródło*...).
The hard *ł*, on the other hand, has lost its dental consonantal character in the speech of most Poles, who pronounce it as a bilabial,
nonsyllabic vowel *u* (§22).

§41. 4) In the table of proto-Sl. phonemes (§32), the phonemes
c, dz, sz, ż, cz are listed as palatal ("soft"), for according to their
historical origin they really contained a palatal element; their
Polish reflexes have lost this palatal element and have become nonpalatal ("hard");

5) the proto-Sl. palatals *t', d'* have been replaced in the same
positions in historically related morphemes by the Polish nonpalatal phonemes *c, dz* (§§36, 38); the palatal *r'*, which had greatly
increased in frequency owing to the palatalization of dental and
labial consonants before front vowels, gave way at a much later
period to the phoneme *rz* (§37);

6) owing to this very palatalization of dental and labial consonants before front vowels and to the further development of
these palatal consonants, Polish acquired a new category of palatals,
ś, ź, ć, dź, which did not exist in proto-Sl. The series *p', b', m', f', w'*
belongs, in fact, to the same category and is partially matched (in
a far smaller number of cases) by the proto-Sl. series *pl', bl', ml', vl'*.
The latter were actually groups of two consonants, but we treat
them as indivisible units on the basis of comparison with other
phonemes: in proto-Sl. they were variants of *pi, bi, mi, vi*, and
their subsequent Slavic correspondences (e.g., the older *pj, bj, mj,
vj* or younger ⟨Pol.⟩ *p', b', m', w'*) are single phonemes. These indivisible units can, of course, in turn be broken down into psychologically no longer divisible elements such as kinemes, acousmemes, and kinakemes (§51);

§42. 7) The proto-Sl. phonemic system did not tolerate the palatal ("soft") consonants *k', g', ch'*, inasmuch as the back phonemes
k, g, ch, which became palatalized in their transition from pre-Sl.
to proto-Sl. had changed into *cz, ż, sz* or *c, dz, sz*, whereas they did
not undergo palatalization in the groups *ky, gy, chy* (where *y* was
long or short). The new vocalic phonemes of a palatal character,
which arose when long *y* merged psychologically with the historical
reflex of long *i* (thus ceasing to be a separate phoneme), and when
short *y* (which merged psychologically with the reflex of short *i*) became *e* (if it did not become a phonetic zero), failed to exert a palatalizing ("softening") effect upon the labial and dental consonants.

344

By compensation, the velar consonants, which are in general more susceptible to palatalization, in turn underwent the effect of palatalization. Thus there appeared in place of the original proto-Sl. combinations *ky, gy* (with long *y*) the groups *k'i, g'i,* and in place of the combinations *ky, gy* (in which the short *y* is preserved), the groups *k'e, g'e.*

The velar spirant *ch,* which involves acoustically not only backlingual but also glottal activity, did not undergo this new palatalization, and remained a hard consonant. Thus, although we have forms such as *kisiel, kipi, boki, ręki. . . , ginie, gil, stogi, nogi. . . , kierz, kieł, bokiem. . . , giez, rogiem,* we also have such forms as *chytry, chybi, duchy, strzechy. . . , duchem, piachem. . . .* Only iterative and durative verbs formed with the suffix *–iv–a (–ywa)* exhibit a soft *ch;* thus we have not only forms such as *przepłókiwać, odskakiwać, pobrzękiwać, usługiwać, obełgiwać. . . ,* but also *rozdmuchiwać, rozmachiwać.* This is obviously not the result of a historical-phonetic process, but rather the effect of a strong morphological assimilation, or "analogy," inasmuch as the forms *rozdmuchywać, rozmachywać* are likewise possible. In this respect Polish differs, for example, from Great Russian which, along with the soft *k', g',* also has a "soft" *ch.* Before *ę,* which continues proto-Sl. *ą,* the non-palatal ("hard") *k, g* have been preserved: *kępa, kędy, kęs. . . , gęś, gęgać. . . , rękę, nogę. . . ,* though dialectally we also have *k', g': kiempa. . . , gięś. . . .*

The number of cases containing "soft" *k', g'* has considerably increased since they appear in many words of foreign origin, or in adopted words: *kierat, rakieta, kimono. . . , gienjusz, gieografja, gigant. . . .* One should also keep in mind cases of onomatopoeia, such as *chichotać. . . .*

In Kashubian-speaking territory, this third phase of palatalization produced a new set of velar consonants which became palatal. In Kashubian we have not only examples of the oldest proto-Sl. layer to which we owe *cz, ż, sz (piecze, ręczyć, rączka. . . , może, dłużyć, nóżka. . . , straszyć, dusza. . .)* and the subsequent proto-Sl. layer to which we owe *c, dz (ręce, wielcy, lice, owca. . . , nodze, drodzy. . .* §34), but also examples of the youngest—no longer proto-Sl., but rather Kashubian stratum with its *ć, dź* (such as *ćiwać, ciede, taći, dzinie, drodźi* instead of *kiwać, kiedy, taki, ginie, drogi. . .*).

At any rate, velar consonants with a palatal element *k', g', dz'* are a new phenomenon in Polish which was unknown in proto-Sl.

§43. As a result of the later historical-phonetic processes which marked the transition from proto-Sl. and Common Slavic to pre-Polish, and subsequently to an autonomous Polish language with all its historical varieties, the Polish-speaking community acquired the following phonemes and series of phonemes which were alien to proto-Sl.:

1) the consonants *ć, dź, ś, ź*;
2) the consonant *rz*;
3) the consonants *p', b', m', w'*;
4) the consonants *k', g', ch'*;
5) the vowel *i*, continuing proto-Sl. *i*;
6) the vowel *e*, continuing short *y* (from pre-Sl. short *u*) and exerting no palatal effect (except when combined with the velar consonants *ky, gy,* §42);
7) new short vowels (later neutral, neither long nor short): *i (i, y), u, a, e, ą, ę*;
8) new long vowels formed through compensatory lengthening (later likewise neutral) *o, e, i, u, a*;
9) narrowed vowels: *á ó é*;
10) the vowels *ą* (from *ę*), *ę* (from *ą*), and nasal *a*.

In addition, we have in contemporary Polish some sounds which are not psychologically independent phonemes, but speech-sounds which are due to the impossibility of implementing the phonetic (articulatory) intention:

1) weakened consonants at the end of words and of syllables: *–p, –t, –k; –b, –d, –g; –p', –b', –m', –f,' –w', –f, –s, –sz, –ch, –ś, –w, –z, –ż, (–ż, –rz), –ź, –c, –cz, –ć; –dz, –dż, –dź*;
2) voiceless *–r, –ł, –l, –m, –n, –ń* (§35).

The Strengthening of Consonantism and the Weakening of Vocalism

§44. In the history of Polish, as in the history of many other languages, we can observe an ever greater strengthening of consonantism at the expense of vocalism. This phenomenon expresses itself, among other ways, in the ever greater importance of the palatal element, as well as in the ever growing influence of the consonantal distinctions upon the quality of vowels (e.g., the strong influence of dental consonants as opposed to ⟨the minor influence of⟩ other consonants, §37).

In comparison with the less remote pre-Sl. past, Polish displays a great increase and intensification of palatal activity, whereas in comparison with the more distant past, it displays an increase of dental (front-lingual) activities.

Although the "hard" labial and dental consonants in Polish underwent palatalization (or "softening") under the influence of following palatal vowels (§37), this seeming increase of the influence of vowels upon consonants has gradually turned in favor of the consonants, which have acquired the distinction between non-palatals and palatals which was originally peculiar to the vowels. The two vocalic phonemes of proto-Sl., long y and i, merged into one i which was variable and dependent on the preceding consonant. The corresponding short vowels merged with e, if they did not disappear and become phonetic zeroes (§35). But their original psychological distinction is to this day reflected in the different preceding consonants, e.g., *być* but *bić*, *chłopek* but *chłopiec*, *dech* but *dzień, ten* but *ciemno*. . . . A similar differentiation of consonants dating back to proto-Sl. and having its origin in a pre-Sl. and IE difference in the following vowels applies only to the original IE velar consonants; cf. on the one hand, *ky, gy, chy* (with proto-Sl. *ch* continuing IE s, and long or short y continuing u) and, on the other hand, *czi, żi, szi* (with short or long i); e.g., Polish *kipi, ginie, chytry*. . . , *kieł, giez*. . . ; *czysty, żywy*. . . , *cześć*. . . . Further, proto-Sl. *ka, ga* (with a going back to IE long a or o) vs. *cza, ża* (with a going back to IE long e); e.g., Polish *każe, kara*. . . , *gani, gasi, gad*. . . , but *czas, czar*. . . , *żar, żal, żaden*.

Proto-Sl. short e, the long e, $ę$, $ą$, and the syllabic sonant r with a palatal element have split, either under the influence of the following dental consonant or from other causes; thus short e split into e and o, long e into e and a, $ę$ into $ę$ and $ą$, $ą$ into $ą$ and $ę$. But whether these vowels were in proto-Sl. o or a, and short or long e, can be deduced only from the preceding consonants; e.g., *wozi, nosi, płot, wyboru*. . . , *wada, maść, dar, tak, sadło, swat, łazi, raz*. . . , but *wiozę, niosę, plotę, biorę*. . . , *wiadomo, miasto, dziad, ciało, siadło, świat, lazł, rzadki*. The same can be said about nasal vowels (§36).

Another phonemonon pointing to the strengthening of consonantism and weakening of vocalism is the stabilization of the Polish accent and the loss of the psychological distinction of quantity, i.e., the length and shortness of vowels (§27).

In line with the same historical tendency is the decrease of laryngeal activities in favor of activities and distinctions made within the oral cavity (§§28, 31, 27, 18).

Historical Changes in the
Structure of Syllables and Words

§45. The transition from IE and pre-Sl. to proto-Sl. and Common Slavic was marked by a tendency to eliminate narrowed or closed syllables. This general historical-phonetic process consisted of the following specific changes:

1) the elimination of consonants at the end of words and syllables. In other words, tautosyllabic syllables comprising vowels and consonants are continued by syllables ending in vowels; e.g., *slovo* from *slovos, to* from *tod.* . . (§28);

2) the change of vocalic diphthongs into homogeneous long vowels (§26);

3) the change of combinations of vowels with nasal consonants *on, om, en, em* into nasal vowels *ǫ, ę* (§21);

4) the change of the pre-Sl. combination of vowels with "liquid" sonants *or, er, ol, el* into presumed syllabic long *r, l,* which later yielded different combinations in various Slavic languages; in Polish *ro, re, ło, le* (§36).

In the transition from Common Slavic to Polish, there appeared a great variety of closed or narrowed syllables, due mostly to the loss of syllables containing a short *y* or *i*.

The Importance of Semasiologization and Morphologization
for the Distinction of Phonemes and for the Preservation
of their Distinctions

§46. If the distinctions between phonemes or, to be more precise, between the art.-aud. elements (kinemes, acousmemes, and kinakemes) which make up the phonemes did not play a part in distinguishing morphemes (the morphological-semasiological elements which are associated either with a particular meaning, that is, with a group of extralinguistic concepts, or with a particular form such as case, person, etc., in connection, of course, with some suffixes or desinences, including zero suffixes or desinences), or, in other words, if the distinctions between phonemes were not semasiologized and morphologized, they would not be so persistently preserved and would have gradually been lost in the transmission from one generation to another.

In contemporary Polish, as inescapably in all languages, all phonemic distinctions must be semanticized (semasiologized). In *mama,* as opposed to *baba,* the semanticized distinction is that of a lowered soft palate with the acousmeme of nasal resonance vs. the kineme of a raised soft palate (that prevents the passage of air to the nasal cavities) with the acousmeme of the absence of nasal resonance. In *kosa* as opposed to *koza,* the distinction is that of a kinakeme of the activity of the vocal cords. In *tom* and *tam, kora* and *kura, bok* and *byk,* there is a semanticized distinction of vocalic arrangements of the oral cavity with corresponding differences in their resonance.

The morphologization of certain art.-aud. distinctions is, on the other hand, only a transitory phenomenon in the history of languages. It is usually brought about by some historical-phonetic split of one phoneme into two or more phonemes. These new varieties of an original single phoneme acquire the value of psychophonetic alternants which become associated with different forms. In Polish, for example, such psychophonetic alternants or correlatives consist of the distinction between nonpalatal consonants and those which are, or were historically palatal; e.g., *ryba, kopa, słoma, sowa, sofa, robota, woda, osa, koza, rana, siła, kora, ręka, noga, mucha.* . . , but *rybie, kopie, słomie, sowie, sofie, robocie, wodzie, osie, kozie, ranie, sile, korze, ręce, nodze, musze.* . . ; *ręka, suka, paka, noga, mucha.* . . , but *rączka, suczka, paczka, nóżka, muszka.* Vocalic differences are similarly morphologized: *głowa, broda, robota, noga, ręka, wstęga.* . . but *główka, bródka, robótka, nóżka* . . . , *rączka, wstążka.* . . .

Morphologization supports phonemic distinctions more firmly than semanticization, but it operates only as long as there is a clear morphological division of words and a clear-cut distinction between various types of declension, conjugation, etc.

Alternants or Phonemic Alternations Going Back to Different Stages of the History of the Language

§47. The following alternants of Polish go back to IE:

1) alternants based on the distinction of tautosyllabism (membership in the same syllable) and heterosyllabism (membership in

two syllables). The following specific categories are involved:

a) combinations of simple vowels with simple consonants; e.g., *nieb–o* beside *niebi–os–a, nie–bi–es–ki.* . . , *wymię* beside *wymienia* . . . , *cielę* beside *cielęci–a.* . . ;

b) combinations of two vowels: the tautosyllabic or diphthong-ized *ou* with the heterosyllabic *o–u* or *o–v*; eg., *ku–ć* beside *kow–al.* . . ;

c) the tautosyllabic *or, ol, er, el.* . . with heterosyllabic *o–r, o–l, e–r, e–l*; e.g., *pró–ć, kłóć, brze–mię, mle–ć.* . . vs. *porz–e, kol–e, bierz–e, bior–ę, miel–e*;

2) alternations based on the split of the IE vowel *e* into *e* and *o* (short or long): of *ei* into *ei* and *oi*, of *eu* into *eu* and *ou*, of *en* into *en* and *on*, of *er* into *er* and *or*, and *el* into *el* and *ol*; e.g., *wiezie, wiozę* beside *wozi; siedzi, siada* beside *sad, sadzi; widzieć* beside *wiedzieć wiadomo; lęk* beside *łęk; sięk* beside *sączyć; krzątać* beside *kręcić; wrzeciono* beside *wrota; wlecze* beside *zawłoka.* . . ;

3) alternations due to the weakening and loss of vowels in un-accented syllables, i.e., alternations of a historical-phonetic zero with the vowels *e* and *o* plus sonant: zero vs. *e* and *o; i* vs. *ei, oi; u* vs. *eu, ou*, syllabic *u; m* vs. *en, on, em, om*; syllabic *r* vs. *er, or*; syllabic *l* vs. *el, ol*. Examples: *jes–t* beside *s–ą, dech* beside *duch; sechł, schnie* beside *such–; wierci, wartki* beside *wrzeciono, wrota; dłubać* beside *dłóto.* . . .

§48. To the continuation of alternations which were formed in proto-Sl. but had their beginning in IE, we owe:

1) *ży, czy, szy* beside *ż, cz, sz; li, ni* beside *l, ń; rzy* beside *rz* (e.g., *trwoży, toczy, straszy, pali, rani, tworzy.* . . beside *trwożę, toczę, straszę, palę, ranię, tworzę.* . .);

2) *p'i, b'i, m'i, w'i,* beside *p' b' m' w'* (e.g., *topi, robi, tłumi, łowi.* . . beside *topię, robię, tłumię, łowię.* . .);

3) *śi, źi* beside *sz, ż; ći, dźi* beside *c, dz* (e.g., *nosi, gasi, wozi, grozi* . . . *noszę, gaszę, wożę, grożę.* . . ; *świeci, traci, chodzi, kadzi.* . . *świecę, tracę, chodzę, kadzę.* . .).

Alternations of proto-Sl. origin, i.e., those brought about pho-netically and art.-aud.–ly in the proto-Sl. period or in a transitional period from IE to proto-Sl.;

1) *g, k* beside *ż, cz* (e.g., *naga, ręka, mogę, piekę.* . . beside *obnażyć, ręczyć, może, piecze.* . .);

g, k beside *dz, c* (e.g., *noga, ręka, druga, wielka.* . . beside *nodze, ręce, drudzy, wielcy.* . .);

c, dz beside *cz, ż* (e.g., *chłopiec, owca, lice, ksiądz, drudzy* beside *chłopcze, owieczka, liczko, księże, drużyna. . .*);

2) *z* beside *s* (e.g., *mazać* beside *masło, wiozę* beside *wiosło. . .*);

3) *w* beside historical-phonetic *zero* (e.g., *warzyć, wóz, włóczyć. . .* vs. *obarzanek, obóz, obłok. . .*);

4) consonants alternating with phonetic zero at the end of words and syllables (e.g., *niebiosa* beside *niebo, cielesny* beside *ciało. . .* §45).

§49. The following alternations are due to tradition, but their phonetic causes go back to Old Polish:

1) *ś, ż, ć, dż, ść, żdż* beside *j* (§38);

2) reflexes of "hard" consonants beside "soft" consonants (e.g., *chłopy, schody* beside *chłopi, schodzi. . .* ; *tęgi* beside *ciężki, wożę* beside *wiozę, wieś* beside *wioska, twór* beside *tworzy, dworek* beside *dworzec* §44);

3) *k', g'* beside *k, g* (e.g., *bok, boku, stóg, stogu, ręka, rąk, noga, nóg. . .* beside *boki, bokiem, stogi, stogiem, ręki, nogi. . .* §42);

4) *o* beside *u* (*ó*), *ę* beside *ą* (e.g., *rodu, mrozu, głogu; bobu, noża. . .* beside *ród, mróz, głóg, bób, nóz. . .* ; *woda, koza, ozdoba* beside *wód, kóz, ozdób. . .* , *wódka, kózka, ozdóbka. . .* ; *męża, dębu. . .* beside *mąż, dąb. . .* ; *część, gęś. . .* beside *cząstka, gąska. . .* §38);

5) *e* beside *phonetic zero* (e.g., *sen, mech, zamek, dech. . .* beside *snu, mchu, zamku, tchu. . .* ; *pies, chłopiec, goniec, wieś, szedł. . .* beside *psa, chłopca, gońca, wsi, szła. . .* §55);

6) *consonant* beside *phonetic zero* (e.g., *szedł* beside *szła, cztery* vs. *cz(t)woro, cześć* vs. *cz(ś)ci; ciskac* vs. *cis(k)nąć, pisk* vs. *pis(k)nąć. . .* §55);

7) *e* beside *o, e* beside *a, er* beside *ar*: *wiezie, bierze, plecie. . .* beside *wiozę, biorę, plotę. . . ; leci, w lesie, w mieście, strzeli, wierzy, ścienny. . .* vs. *lata, las, miasto, strzał wiara, ściana. . .* ; *twierdza, cierń, pierścień. . .* vs. *twardy, tarnina, naparstek. . .* §37).

Traditional alternations, i.e., alternations due to traditional conditions but whose phonetic, art.-aud. conditions are still in effect today: *d* beside *t, b* beside *p. . .* ; e.g., *dech* beside *tchu, łba* beside *łeb, łepek; z* beside *ź, s* beside *ś: zły* beside *źle. . . ; sumienie, sfora, smutek. . .* beside *śmierć, śmietana, śmiecie, ślub. . .* ; *cz* beside *ć: czworo, czwarty, cztery* beside *ćwierć.*

§50. Finally, there is the most recent layer of alternations, which are alive and determined by present-day conditions:

1) the difference in energy and autonomy of the phonemes when the intended articulation is fully realized, on the one hand, and weakly or not at all realized on the other; e.g., *słup, ryk*. . . beside *słupa, ryku*. . . ; *głód, rydz, wóz*. . . beside *głodu, rydza, wozu*. . . §43); *wiatr, myśl, pieśń, pasm, drachm*. . . beside *wiatru, myśli, pieśni, pasma, drachmy*. . . §§22, 35); *drop, paw, drób*. . . vs. *dropia, pawia, drobiu*. . . ;

2) the difference in quantity when a phonetic zero or a facultative syllable (i.e., a possible but not obligatory one) alternates with a full syllable; as a unit of thought, as a phoneme, it retains its identity ⟨?⟩; e.g., *niósł, padł, rzekł* . . . beside *niosła, padła, rzekła*. . . , *jabłko* beside *jabłek*. . . , §55.

These two kinds of alternations are of a quantitative character, since they imply a difference of intensity, or quantity. Other alternations are of a qualitative character; they are as follows:

3) alternations in the activity of the vocal cords with the corresponding acoustic effects: *w gaju* beside *w kraju, z żyta* beside *z czego, pod bokiem* beside *pod pasem, nad bramą* beside *nad podłogą*. . . ;

głodu, głodny, głodzić beside *głód, męża* beside *mąż, prosić* beside *prośba*. . . ;

wiatru beside *wiatr, Piotrek* beside *Piotrka, mech* beside *mchu, pasmo* beside *pasm*. . . ;

ryk beside *ryk wód, jest* beside *jezdem, dwuch* beside *we dwucheśmy byli, rzekł* beside *rzegem, niech* beside *niech no przyjdzie*. . . ;

4) alternations based on palatal activity: *kostka* beside *kość, pasę* beside *paść, niosła* beside *nieśli*. . . ;

pies beside *psa, kupiec* beside *kupca, krawiec* beside *krawca*. . . ;

dropia, drobiu, gołębia, pawia, karmi, Radomia beside *drop, drób, gołąb, paw, karm, Radom*. . . ;

5) alternations based on activities of the front part of the tongue: *s, z* || *sz, ż* || *ś, ź*;

z domu, z masła, z ogrodu beside *z tańca, z kaszy* beside *z dżumy, z żyta* beside *z czego, z szafy* beside *zziąbł, z ziemi, z dziury* beside *z sił, z ciebie, z cicha*. . . ;

6) alternations of the nasal element of the nasal "vowels" (§§21, 51).

The Reflection of Dialectal Differences
in the Pronunciation of Common ⟨Standard⟩ Polish

§51. Nowadays it is assumed that the Common Polish language, which unifies the entire nation in a single community and is reflected in its literary language, had its beginnings in Wielkopolska and was later influenced by other regions of the Polish linguistic territory. Of course, even today the dialectal variation which is observed in different parts of this territory, or more precisely community, leaves its imprint on the external form, i.e., on the art.-aud. perception of the Common Polish language and its literary language which, in turn, modifies and lends variety to its corresponding art.-aud. representations.

Three possibilities should be mentioned:

1) the same phoneme is "pronounced" in different ways;

2) dialectally colored speech presents differences and phonetic nuances which are not found in the larger part of the Polish linguistic territory;

3) dialectal pronunciation presents fewer differences and nuances than the Common language.

The different regional pronunciations affect the following phonemes and phonemic series:

a) the "hard" or "normal" pronunciation of the consonant *ł* (i.e., with dental occlusion and lowering of the ridges of the tongue) is found among only a minority of Poles; in rare cases the consonant is pronounced as *l* (like the German or Czech *l*). More often, and in the speech of most Poles, it is pronounced as a nonsyllabic vowel, either with a velar narrowing and a place of articulation close to the vowel *a*, or with a labial narrowing which is close to a bilabial *w*, that is a nonsyllabic *u*;

b) the "soft" *l* varies territorially in degree of "softness" (palatality), ranging from a nonmedial *l* to an *l* which resembles the French *l* "mouillé" with very strong palatality;

c) the series of palatal-dental consonants *ś, ź, ć, dź* is territorially graduated from an almost pure dental pronunciation with the addition of palatality (as, for example, in the "model" pronunciation of the Russian consonants s', z') through pure palatals *ś, ź, ć, dź*, to consonants which merge acoustically with *sz, ż, cz, dż*. Among the Kashubians the latter consonants have merged with the dental consonants *s, z, c, dz*;

d) as one moves northwards, the palatal element of the consonants *p', b', m', f', w'* becomes intensified, developing into a separate phonetic art.-aud. unit which leads to a split of these phonemes into consonantal diphthongs *p'j, b'j, m'j, f'j, w'j*. The *j* acquires a definite degree of friction such as *ź* or *ś*, and like *n'* after *m'*. This change of the labio-palatal phonemes into the groups *pś, bź, wź, mń* and into the simple phonemes *ś, ź, ń* is a characteristic dialectal feature of the northern part of the Polish speaking territory;

e) in the pronunciation of some Poles, a velar *n* appears when a nasal vowel is followed by a velar stop (*męka, mąk, gęgać, drągal.* . .) and in place of the dental consonant *n* followed by a velar stop (*panienka, wanienka, wianka, piastunka.* . .). Some Poles pronounce the velar *n* only in the first of the above cases, while others (e.g., in Lithuania) employ only the dental consonant. In the mixed Polish-Byelorussian territory, vowel plus consonant *n* is used instead of a nasal vowel, even in the case when the latter is followed by the spirants *s, z, sz, ż, ś, ź, ch, w*; thus *mięso, wąs, kąsa, więzy, wiązać, ciężko, męża, zdąży, gęsi, gąsior, więzi, wącha, wąwóz.* . . are here pronounced *mienso, wons, konsa, wienzy, wionzać, cienszko, menza, zdonzy, gensi, gonsior, wienzi, woncha, wonwóz.* . . . This phenomenon is of great importance for the ethnic history of these regions;

f) the pronunciation of the "soft" *k', g', ch'* varies regionally.

§52. Art.-aud. differences and nuances alien to most Polish-speaking areas and not admitted in the contemporary literary language:

a) The vast majority of Poles do not employ any vocalic narrowing intermediate between a narrow vowel *u* and a narrow *o*, pronouncing the vowel which is graphically rendered by the letters *u* and *ó* in the same way. In some parts of the Polish-speaking area, primarily in the Southwest, *ó* is pronounced as a narrow *o*, i.e., an intermediate vowel between *u* and *o*. Such words as *mur* and *mór*, *buk (Bug)* and *bóg, gul* and *gól, stuł* and *stół*, clearly differ here in their pronunciation. Similarly, there are some areas which distinguish three degrees of the front vowels *i, é, e* and other areas that have an *á* "pochylone" or a narrow labialized *a*, intermediary between *o* and *a*.

b) The phoneme which is graphically represented by *rz* is not, in contemporary pronunciation, distiguished from *ż* and *sz* (e.g., *morze = może, rzeka = żeka, drzewo = dżewo, trzy = tszy, prze =*

psze, krzak = *kszak*. . .). However, in certain regions (e.g., in Silesia) this phoneme is pronounced with a prominent *r*-like vibration differing from both *ż* and *sz*. These regions thus have two additional consonantal diphthongs *rż* (*rzeka, drzewo*. . .) and *rsz* (*trzy, prze, krzak*. . .).

c) Although the great majority of Poles do not employ an autonomous voiced *h* as opposed to voiceless *ch,* in some regions (especially in those which are adjacent to Byelorussian, Ukrainian, and Czech or Slovak areas) there is such a phoneme, which is clearly distinct from *ch*.

d) In the pronunciation of some Poles speaking the common language, there is a greater number of nasal vowels. In addition to the nasal vowels *o* (*ǫ*) and *e* (*ę*), these Poles also use the nasal vowel *a* (*ą*). Such a nasal vowel *a* appears otherwise in the speech of all Poles who employ such words as *ansa, pasjans, kwadrans*. . . (§40; cf. however §51, 1e).

3) Dialectal influence is responsible for the decrease of phonetic (art.-aud.) nuances in the case of the above-mentioned distinction (§34) of the two *i*'s, two *e*'s, and two *ę*'s when they are preceded by palatal (*ni, pi, ci*. . . *nie, pie, cie*. . . *nię, pię, cię*. . .) as opposed to nonpalatal consonants (*ny, py, cy, ty*. . . , *ne, pe, ce, te*. . . , *nę, pę, cę, tę*. . .). But in the Southeastern part of the Polish-speaking territory there is not the slightest difference between these vowels. Here the words *syn, ryba, ty, być, łysy*. . . (*s'in, r'iba, t'i, b'ić, l'is'i*. . .), have exactly the same *i* as the words *siny, ci, bić, lisy*. . . (*śin'i, ći, b'ić, l'is'i*. . .).

XXII

Isoglosses in the Slavic Linguistic World

THESE ISOGLOSSES can be established from various points of view.

I. A purely descriptive treatment considers the contemporary state of the Slavic languages without regard to their history. For example, from an articulatory-acoustic standpoint we can draw areal boundaries marking the different pronunciations of the phonemes g (g, γ, h) and x (x, h, $\emptyset$); separating the different pronunciations of l and t (t, l, u, w, l); singling out the areas which lack a medio-velar (palatal) r: separating areas that do or do not distinguish voiced and voiceless consonants; areas with three series of prevalar spirants ⟨sic!⟩: $s\ z\ c\ ʒ$, $š\ ž\ č\ ǯ$ and $ś\ ź\ ć\ ʒ́$ as opposed to areas with two series, i.e., either $s\ z\ c\ ʒ$ and $š\ ž\ č\ ǯ$ or $s\ z\ c\ ʒ$ and $ś\ ź\ ć\ ʒ́$; distinguishing areas with a predominance of vowels over consonants, or vice versa.

II. Isoglosses from the written, visual standpoint; the use of different alphabets.

III. Isoglosses of dialect areas in contradistinction to isoglosses of national or literary languages.

IV. Isoglosses from the standpoint of different changes in originally common, proto-Slavic linguistic material:

Areas with dl, dn, vs. areas with l, n.

Among some Slavs the reflexes of the chronologically first palatalization of the three velars (k, g, x) are distinct from the reflexes of the second palatalization of the three velars, while among other Slavs the reflexes of the palatalizations of k and g differ, but those of x are identical.

In general the articulatory-acoustic processes connected with the so-called palatalizations and depalatalizations require the establishment of many isoglosses going in various directions.

Among some Slavs the reflexes of *nj, lj,* and *rj* are kept distinct from the reflexes of *n, l, r* that at one time preceded the palatal (fronted) syllabic vowels *i* and *e* etc., while among other Slavs they are not distinguished. The same applies to the combinations of the labial consonants *p, b, m, f, v* with *j* and the originally soft (syllabic) sonants. Finally, there is the difference between the reflexes of the consonants: *tj, dj, sj, zj* and *tV*ⁱ, *dV*ⁱ, *sV*ⁱ, *zV*ⁱ.

The reflexes of pre-Slavic *tj* and *dj,* or the proto-Slavic *t* and *d* yield the most diverse isoglosses.

Further, there are the various isoglosses marking the distinction or fusion of the proto-Slavic vowels *y* (ЪІ) and *i* (И), *ў* (Ъ) and *ĭ* (Ь), *ě* (Ѣ) and *e* (Ɛ).

Special isoglossses mark the different reflexes of the proto-Slavic nasal vowels *ę* (Ѧ) and *o* (Ѫ).

The isoglosses reflecting the diverse reflexes of proto-Slavic *ȳ* and *ī, ў* (Ъ) and *ĭ* (Ь) are, in turn, connected with the isoglosses distinguishing the reflexes of the combinations of the velar consonants *k g x* with the vowels *ȳ* (ЪІ) and *ў* (Ъ).

Various Slavic linguistic areas can be distinguished by isoglosses which pertain to the influence of consonants on vowels and which concern, in particular, the influence of dental consonants upon the development of depalatalization in vowels and sonants; or the distinction between the features of dentality and that of velarity and labiality.

Isoglosses that represent a boundary between Slavic areas with initial *je–, ju–* and areas with an initial *o–, u–.*

We obtain numerous isoglosses if we consider the diverse reflexes of the pre-Slavic and proto-Slavic *liquid sonants ṛ; ṛⁱ, ḷ, ḷⁱ,* and especially the pre- and proto-Slavic *or, er, ol, el,* occurring both between consonants and in initial position (i.e., the groups called [following Miklosich] *tort, tert, tolt, telt, ort, ert, olt, elt*).

We may obtain special isoglosses by focusing on the diverse Slavic processes of secondary lengthening of vowels, or of the so-called "compensatory lengthening" (*productio suppletoria, Ersatz-dehnung*), which resulted mainly from the loss of the vowels *ў* (Ъ) and *ĭ* (Ь) and on the reflexes of alternation of vowels with "zero."

By means of isoglosses we can show the boundaries of Slavic areas which do or do not possess the distinction of proto-Indo-European and proto-Slavic intonations, the psychological distinction of length (*quantitas temporalis*) of vowels and syllables, distinctions of accent or of stress (*ictus*) which concern the accentuation of certain morphemes of the word (the morphological use of stress), or of certain syllables of the word (the syntactic use of stress).

V. The Slavic linguistic world also yields a number of distinct areas from a morphological standpoint. Special isoglosses define the borders of areas that have retained the original types of word-structure, and of their combinations, or which have formed new ones. In some territories suffixes predominate, and in others prefixes and prepositions. Along with a prevailing centralized ("synthetic") structure, we encounter manifestation of a decentralized ("analytic") structure; along with syntagms that have coalesced into a single unit, we find special morpheme-syntagms expressing certain formal concepts; there exist both pre- and postpositional determinants of gender ("articles"); there is the loss of inflectional declension and its replacement by agglutination; diversity of grammatical gender (physiological, biological, and sociological genders); the continuation of one or another morphological type of declension, conjugation, and word formation; the preservation of three numbers (singular, plural, and dual) and the disappearance of the dual; diverse relations of declension types (nominal and pronominal declension, adjectival and numeral declension, etc.). In the system of the verb, a difference in the retention of the *verbi finiti* not only in the forms of the present tense, but also in the forms of the preterite (aorist, imperfect); formal similarity of the future and the present tenses vs. the formation of the future tense by means of various auxiliary verbs; the retention of a special form of the infinitive or its disappearance and replacement by a *substantivum verbale*; the differentiation or identification of the supine and the infinitive.

Thus, the map of the Slavic linguistic world presents also from a morphological standpoint a network of various isoglosses.

VI. Finally, it is desirable to draw isoglosses distinguishing Slavic areas that have been subject to various foreign influences (tribal, religious, or national) and those which have been formed either through oral-aural contact or through graphic-visual impressions. We can distinguish the Slavic East, which has been subject primarily to Graeco-Byzantine influence, and the Slavic West, which fell under the power of Rome and its Romano-Germanic successors. In addition, one must take into account the influence of some Slavs upon others (the role of Church Slavic, Czech, Polish, etc.), as well as the influence of Germanic (German, English, Scandinavian), Romance (French, Italian, Roumanian), of Finno-Ugric (Hungarian, Finnic), Turko-Tartar and others.

APPENDICES

1. Sources of Translated Texts

I. Nekotorye obščie zamečanija o jazykovedenii i jazyke, *ŽMNP*, 1871; Soviet ed. I, pp. 47–77.

II. Programma čtenij po obščemu kursu jazykovedenija v primenenii k arioevropejskim jazykam voobšče, a k slavjanskim v osobennosti, *Otčety komandirovannogo* . . . *IKU* III, 1877, 3, pp. 272–84; Soviet ed. (excerpts) I, pp. 78–87.

III. Podrobnaja progamma lekcij . . . v 1876–1877 uč. godu, *IKU*, 1877; ed. I, pp. 88–107.

IV. Podrobnaja programma lekcij . . . v 1877–1878 uč. godu, *IKU*, 1879; Soviet ed. (excerpts) I, pp. 108–17.

V. Z patologii i embriologii języka, *PF*, 1885–1886; Soviet ed. (introduction and conclusions only) I, pp. 142–45.

VI. O zadaniach językoznawstwa, *PF*, 1889; Soviet ed. I, pp. 203–21.

VII. *Versuch einer Theorie phonetischer Alternationen; ein Kapitel aus der Psychophonetik*, 1895; Soviet ed.; I, pp. 265–347.

VIII. (Obščie položenija), S. A. Vengerov, *Kritiko-biografičeskij slovar' russkix pisatelej i učënyx*, 1897, pp. 33–35 Soviet ed. I, pp. 348–50.

IX. O smešannom xaraktere vsex jazykov, *ŽMNP*, 1901; Soviet ed. I, pp. 362–72.

X. Zametka ob izmenjaemosti osnov sklonenija, v osobennosti že ob ix sokraščenii v pol'zu okončanij, *RFV*, 1902; Soviet ed. II, pp. 19–29.

XI. Językoznawstwo czyli lingwistyka w wieku XIX, *Szkice językoznawcze*, 1904, pp. 1–23; Soviet ed. II, pp. 3–18.

XII. Zur Kritik der künstlichen Weltsprachen, *Annalen der Naturphilosophie*, 1907; Soviet ed. (excerpts) II, pp. 139–40.

XIII. Die Klassifikation der Sprachen, *IF*, 1910; Soviet ed. (only introduction) II, pp. 187–88.

XIV. Les Lois phonétiques, *RS*, 1910 (French summary of "O prawach głosowych"); Soviet ed. II, pp. 189–208.

XV. Różnica między fonetyką a psychofonetyką, *STWarsz*, 1927; Soviet ed. II, pp. 325–30.

XVI. Einfluss der Sprache auf Weltanschauung und Stimmung, *PF*, 1929; Soviet ed. (excerpt) II, pp. 331–36.

XVII. Fakultative Sprachlaute, *Donum natalicium J. Schrijnen,* 1929; Soviet ed. II, pp. 337–41.

XVIII. Zagadnienia pokrewieństwa językowego, *BPTJ,* 1930; Soviet ed. II, pp. 342–52.

XIX. Übersicht der slavischen Sprachenwelt im Zusammenhange mit den andern arioeuropäischen (indogermanischen) Sprachen, *Antrittsvorlesung . . . ,* 1884; Soviet ed. I, pp. 127–38.

XX. *Sravnitel'naja grammatika slavjanskix jazykov v svjazi s drugimi indoevropejskimi jazykami,* 1902; Soviet ed. (excerpts from lithograph), II, pp. 30–32.

XXI. *Zarys historii języka polskiego,* 1964 (excerpt, ch. II, pp. 22–76); Soviet ed. (only introduction and conclusion) II, pp. 294–310.

XXII. Izoglosy w świecie językowym słowiańskim, *Sbornik praci . . .* 1932; Soviet ed. II, pp. 353–55.

2. *Editorial Deletions*

A. in Soviet edition

III. p. 92, 93, 95, 97, 98, 99, 100, 102, 103, 104, 105, 107, 108	bibliography	Sov. ed I, p. 88, 89, 91, 92, 93, 94, 95, 96, 97, 98, 99, 100, 101, 103
IV. p. 114, 115, 116, 117, 118, 119, 120	bibliography and portions of text which repeat Ch. III.	Sov. ed. I, p. 108, 109, 110, 111, 114, 115, 116, 117
V. p. 124	§§ 9–103 article	Sov. ed. I, p. 145
IX. p. 216	introductory remarks	Sov. ed. I, p. 362
XII. p. 255	most of article	Sov. ed. II, p. 139, 140
XIII. p. 258, 259	most of article	Sov. ed. II, p. 187, 188
XVI. p. 284	most of article	Sov. ed. II, p. 331, 336
XVII. p. 295	end of last paragraph	Sov. ed. II, p. 341
XX. p. 319, 320	most of article	Sov. ed. II, p. 30, 31

B. in English text

I. p. 69	last 2 para.	Sov. ed. I, p. 77
p. 75	5 words	Sov. ed. I, p. 66
p. 76	1 sentence	Sov. ed. I, p. 69
IV. p. 117	para. 13, 15	Sov. ed. I, pp.111–14
VII. p. 166, 168, 173, 180, 181, 186(4), 204, 209, 211	formulas and equations	*Versuch*, pp. 31–35, 38–40, 48–49, 60, 61, 69–70, 71–72, 102, 108, 111–21
p. 195	examples	*Versuch*, pp. 84–85
X. p. 227	5 para. (Intro.)	Sov. ed. II, pp. 19–20
p. 229	2 sentences	Sov. ed. II, p. 22
XI. p. 237	1 sentence	Sov. ed. II, p. 3
XIV. p. 260	10 para.	Sov. ed. II, pp. 189–91

p. 265	1 sentence	Sov. ed. II, p. 196
XV. p. 283	1 sentence	Sov. ed. II, p. 329
XIX. p. 318	6 § (Intro. and conclusion	Sov. ed. I, pp. 127–28, 138

For further discrepancies between the Soviet and English editions, see *Sources of Translated Texts,* pp. 363.

3. Glossary of Polish and Russian Words

A. Polish*

ansa, animosity
arkusz, sheet of paper
awans, promotion
baba (pej.), woman
badać, study
bankiet, banquet
baśń, fable, tale
bełtać, stir
biały, white
bić, beat
blamanż, blanc mange
błahy, trivial
błazen, buffoon
błogi, blissful
błoto, mud; swamp
boczyć (się), look askance
bok, side
bonza, bonze (Buddhist monk)
bosy, barefoot
bób, bean
bóg, god
ból, pain
bór, pine grove
bóść, bodę, gore
brać, biorę, take
brama, gate
broda, beard
bronz, bronze
bródka (dim.), beard
brud, dirt

brudzić, soil
brzeg, bank, shore
brzytwa, razor
buk, beech
burza, storm
być, jestem (pres.), będę (fut.), be
byk, bull
car, czar
cegła, brick
cera, complexion
cesarz, emperor
chichotać, giggle
chleb, bread
chłop, peasant
chłopiec, boy
chodzić, walk
chory, sick
chód, walk
chwalić, praise
chybić, miss
chytry, cunning
ciało, body
ciąć, tnę, cut
ciągnąć, pull
ciąża, pregnancy
cichy, quiet
ciec, ciekę, drip.
cielesny, corporal
cielę, calf
ciemny, dark

* For the relation of Polish spelling to pronunciation see p. 375.

cierń, thorn
cierpnąć, be numb
cięgi (pl.), beating
ciężar, load
ciężki, heavy
ciężyć (or *ciążyć*), weigh upon
ciskać, hurl; pinch
cisnąć (pf., see *ciskać*)
cnota, virtue
czar, spell
czas, time
–cząć (see *zacząć*)
cząstka, particle
czcić, czczę, worship
cześć, czci, honor
część, part
człon, member
czołgać (się), crawl
czoło, forehead
czółno, boat
cztery, four
cztę (arch., 1 sg.), read
czwarty, fourth
czworo (collective), four
czynić, do
czysty, clean
czytać, read
ćma, moth
ćwierć, quarter
dać, give
dar, gift
darzyć, present with
dąb, oak
dążyć, strive
dech, tchu, breath
dłóto, whittle, chisel
dłubać, burrow
długi, long
dłużyć, lengthen
dno, bottom
dogodzić, accede
dom, house
donica, pot
dowcip, wit
drachma, drachma
drągal, beanpole
droga, road

drop, dropia, bustard
drób, drobiu, poultry
drugi, second
drużyna, team
drzeć, tear
drzewo, tree, wood
duch, spirit
dusza, soul
dwa, two
dworek, farmhouse
dworzec, railway station
dychać, pant
dym, smoke
dynia, pumpkin, squash
dziad, old man, beggar
dziąsło, gum
dziecko, dzieci (pl.), child
dziedziniec, courtyard
dzień, dnia, day
dzierżyć, hold
dziesięć, ten
dzięcioł, woodpecker
dziura, hole
dziw, wonder
dźwięczeć, sound
dźwięk, sound
dżuma, plague
gad, reptile
gaj, grove
gangrena, gangrene
ganić, blame
garb, hump
gardzić, scorn
garnek, pot
gasić, extinguish
gawiedź, rabble
gąbka, sponge
gąsior, gander
gąska (dim.), goose
geniusz (B.d.C.: *gieniusz*), genius
geografia (B.d.C.: *gieografja*),
    geography
gęba, mouth
gęgać, cackle
gęś, goose
giąć, gnę, bend
giez, gza, horsefly

gigant, giant
gil, bullfinch
ginąć, perish
głodny, hungry
głodzić, starve
głowa, head
głód, hunger
głóg, hawthorn
główka (dim.), head
głuchnąć, grow deaf
głuchy, deaf
gnić, rot
gnieść, gniotę, squeeze
gnoić, dung, fertilize
gołąb, gołębia, dove
goniec, courier
gonić, chase
gorzeć, blaze
gość, guest
gościniec, highway
góra, mountain
grodzić, fence (in)
grosz, a copper coin
grozić, threaten
grób, grave
gród, citadel, castle
grzebać, scrape
grzęda, perch
grzęznąć, sink
gula, lump, bruise
gwiazda, star
hańba, infamy
hardy, haughty
herb, coat of arms
hrabia, count
iść, idę, go, walk
jabłko, apple
jąkać się, stutter
jęczeć, groan
język, tongue
kadzić, cense
kalosz, overshoe, galosh
kara, punishment
kark, back of neck
karm, food
karmić, feed
kasa, cash-box

kasza, porridge
kat, hangman
kazać, order
kąsać, bite
kędy, whither
kępa, clump
kęs, bite
kiedy, when
kieł, fang, tusk
kierat, treadmill
kierz, bush
kimono, kimono
kipieć, boil
kisiel, (kind of) jelly
kiwać, wag
kląć, klnę, swear
klucha (pej.), noodle
kluski, noodles
kłaść, kładę, lay
kłos, ear (of grain)
kłuć (kłóć), kłuję, pierce
kmin, caraway seed
koń, horse
koncha, conch
koniec, end
kontredans, contredanse
kopa, stack
kora, bark
kos, blackbird
kosa, scythe
kostka, ankle, knuckle
kość, bone
kot, cat
kowal, blacksmith
koza, goat
kózka (dim.), goat
kpić, ridicule
kraj, country
krawiec, tailor
krew, krwi, blood
kręcie (się), turning
krowa, cow
król, king
krynica, spring, source
krzak, bush
krzątać się, be busy
krzemień, flint

krzywda, wrong, harm
krzywy, crooked
ksiądz, priest
książę, prince
kto, kogo (gen.), who
kuć, kuję, forge
kupiec, merchant
kura, chicken
kurz, dust
kwadrans, quarter hour
kwiat, flower
kwilić, whimper
lampa, lamp
las, forest
lato, summer
lec, legnę, lie down
lecieć, fly
len, lnu, flax
lewy, left (side)
leźć, lezę, creep up, crawl
leżeć, lie
lęk, fear
lękać się, dread
lgnąć, stick
lice, face
liczba, number
liczko (dim.), face
liczny, numerous
lis, fox
lizać, lick
lśnić (się), glisten
lubić, like
lżyć, insult
łamać, break
łazić, crawl; ramble
łączyć, join
łeb, łba, (animal's) head
łęk, bow
łgać, łżę, lie (tell lies)
łkać, sob
łowić, catch
łoże (fig.), bed
łóżko, bed
łuna, glow
łup, loot
łupić, rob
łysy, bald

łza, tear
macierz (arch.), mother
mama, mama
martwy, dead
masło, butter
maść, ointment
mateczka (dim.), mother
matka, mother
mazać, anoint
mącić, disturb
mądry, wise
mąka, flour
mąż, husband
mech, mchu, moss
mędrzec, wise man
męka, torture
męski, masculine
męty, dregs
mglić (się), grow foggy
mgła, fog
mgnąć (arch.), twinkle
miasto, city
miąższ, pulp
miednica, basin
miedza, (field) boundary
mieść, miotę, sweep
mięso, meat
migać, wink
milczeć, be silent
milknąć, become silent
miły, dear
mknąć, flit
mleć, mielę, grind
mleko, milk
młot, hammer
mnożyć, multiply
moc, power
moczyć, soak
morze, sea
móc, mogę, be able to
mór, plague
mówić, speak
mrowie, swarm
mróz, frost
mrugać, blink, wink
mruk, grouch
mścić (się), mszczę, take revenge

mucha, fly
mur, wall
muszka (dim.), fly
mydło, soap
myśl, thought
nabór, selection
nagi, nude
naginać, bend down
naparstek, thimble
napięcie, tension
naród, nation
nasz, our
nić, thread
nie, not, no
niebo, sky
niech (particle), let
niemy, mute
nieść, niosę, carry (on foot)
noc, night
noga, leg
nos, nose
nosić, carry (on foot)
nowy, new
nóż, knife
nóżka (dim.), leg
obarzanek, cracknel
obełgiwać, insult
obłok, cloud
obnażyć, denude
obowiązek, duty
obóz, camp
oddech, breath
oddychać, breathe
odpocząć, rest
odpoczynek, rest
odskakiwać, jump away
ogród, garden
ogrójec, the Garden of Olives
ojciec, ojca, father
osa, wasp
osiągać, reach
osiem, eight
ostry, sharp
oś, axis, axle
owca, sheep
owieczka (dim.), sheep
ozdoba, ornament

ozdóbka (dim.), trinket
ósmy, eighth
paczka, package
paka, crate
palić, burn
pan, gentleman
panienka (dim.), young lady
parzyć, burn
pas, belt
pasmo, band
paść, padnę, fall
paść, pasę, tend (cattle)
paw, pawia, peacock
pełny, full
pełzać, crawl
pensja, pension
pensum, homework
pęta, fetters
piach (augm.), sand
piana, foam
piasek, sand
piastunka, foster mother
piąć (się), pnę, climb
piąty, fifth
pić, drink
piec, piekę, bake
piechota, infantry
pierścień, ring
pierwszy, first
pierzchać, flee
pies, psa, dog
pieśń, song
pięć, five
piosnka (dim.), song
Piotr, Peter
pisać, write
pisk, squeak
pisnąć, squeak
plac, plaza
pląsać, dance
plenić (się), multiply
pleść, plotę, braid
plon, crop
płaca, payment
płacić, pay
płacz, crying
płochy, timid

płot, fence
po, through, after
pobrzękiwać, tinkle
początek, beginning
poczet, list; train
poczynać, begin
podłoga, floor
poić (B.d.C.: *pojić*), water (animals)
pojmować, conceive of
pokój, room
pole, field
położyć, lay
pomóc, pomogę, help
ponsowy, scarlet
poseł, messenger
postać, figure
posyłać, send
powrót, return
pożerać, devour
proch, dust, powder
prosić, request
prosię, (young) pig
prośba, request
pruć, pruję (B.d.C.: *próć*), undo, rip
prząść, przędę, spin
przeć, prę, push
przepłókiwać, rinse
przód, front
przy, at
ptak, bird
pustynia, desert
pycha, haughtiness
rad, glad
rakieta, rocket
rana, wound
ranić, wound
raz, (one) time; blow (in pl.)
rączka (dim.), hand
rdza, rust
rewanż (B.d.C.: *rewansz*), return match
ręczyć, guarantee
ręka, hand
robić, do, make
robota, work
robótka (dim.), work
rodzić, bear (a child)

rok, year
rozbierać, undress
rozcinać, cut
rozczyniać, dissolve
rozdmuchiwać, fan
rozmachiwać, swing
rozpierać, expand
ród, family; descent
róg, horn
rtęć, mercury
ruch, motion
rudy, (brownish) red
ryba, fish
rydz, saffron cap (mushroom)
ryk, roar
rzadki, rare
rząd, government
rzec, rzeknę, say
rzeka, river
rzezać, cut
rzęsa, eyelash
rżnąć, cut
sad, orchard
sadło, fat
sadzać, plant
sączyć, leak
sąd, judgment, court
sądzić, judge
schnąć (p. tense [arch.] *sechł*), dry up
schody (pl.), stairs
schodzić, go down
sen, snu, sleep, dream
sensat (arch.), dour person
ser, cheese
sędzia, judge
sfora, pack (of hounds)
siadać, sit down
siadło (arch.), settlement
siano, hay
siarka, sulfur
siąkać, blow one's nose
siec, siekę, cut
siedem, seven
siedzieć, sit
siejba, sowing
sierota, orphan
sięgać, reach out

sięknąć (siąknąć), trickle
silny, strong
siła, force
siny (adj.), (dark) blue
siodło, saddle
skąpy, stingy
skracać, shorten
skutek, result
słać, ślę, send
słoma, straw
słowo, word
słońce, sun
słup, post
smark, snot
smutek, sadness
sofa, couch
sowa, owl
sól, salt
spać, sleep
spiąć, zepnę, fasten
spięcie, clasp
spoczywać, rest
sroka, magpie
stać, stoję, stand
stąd (adv.), from here
sto, (one) hundred
stóg, haystack
stół, table
strach, fear
straszyć, terrify
strata, loss
stroić, build
struga, stream
strzał, shot
strzec, strzegę, guard
strzelić, shoot
stuła, (priest's) stole
stwarzać, create
suchy, dry
suczka (dim.), bitch
suka, bitch
sumienie, conscience
suszyć, dry
swat, matchmaker
syn, son
szafa, wardrobe
szlachta, gentry

ściana, wall
ścienny (adj., see *ściana*)
ślub, marriage
śmiecie, garbage
śmierć, death
śmietana, sour cream
śnieg, snow
śnieżny, snowy
średni (adj.), middle
środa, Wednesday
świat, world
świeca, candle
świecić, shine
święcie (adv.), saintly
szedł, szli (p. tense of *iść*)
szyja, throat
taca, tray
tak (adv.), yes, thus
taki, such
tam, there
taniec, dance
targ, market
tchnąć, breathe
telegraf, telegraph
ten, (pl.) *ci, te*, this
tędy, this way
tęgi, stout
tępy, dull
tkać, weave
tłok, piston
tłuc, tłukę, pound
tłumić, suppress
tłusty, fat
toczyć, roll
tok, course
tom, volume
topić, melt, drown
tracić, lose
trampolina, trampoline
trudny, difficult
trudzić, fatigue
trwoga, fright
trwożyć, frighten
trzeba, it is necessary
trzepać, dust
trzewia (pl.), viscera
trzoda, herd, flock

trzy, three
twardy, hard, stiff
twierdzić, affirm
tworzyć, produce
twór, creature
ty, you (sg.)
tykać, touch
ubierać, dress
ubiór, dress
ulegać, yield
umierać (impf. of *umrzeć*)
umrzeć, die
usługiwać, serve
wada, defect
wanienka (dim.), small tub
warstwa, layer
wart (adj.), worth
wartki, quick
warzyć, brew
wasz, your
waśń, strife
wąchać, sniff
wąs, whisker
wąski (B.d.C.: *wązki*), narrow
wątek, weft, thread
wątpić, doubt
wąwóz, ravine
wdowa, widow
wejrzeć, look in
węch, scent
wiadomo, it is known
wianek, wreathe
wiara, faith
wiatr, wind
wiązać, bind
widmo, specter
widzieć, see
wiedza, knowledge, science
wiejski, rural
wielki, great
wiercić (B.d.C.: *wiercieć*), drill
wierzba, willow
wierzch, top
wierzgać, kick out
wierzyć, believe
wieś, *wsi*, village
wieść, *wiodę*, lead

wieźć, *wiozę*, transport
więzić, imprison
więzy, fetters
wilczyca, she-wolf
wilgnąć, become moist
wilgoć, humidity
wilk, wolf
wioska (dim.), village
wiosło, oar
wlec, *wlokę*, drag
Włoch, Italian
włóczyć, drag
włos, hair
woda, water
wodzić, lead
wola, will
wolić, prefer
wozić, transport
wódka, vodka
wóz, wagon, car
wracać (imp., see *wrócić*)
wrota (pl.), gate(s)
wrócić, return
wróżka, fortuneteller
wróżyć, forebode
wrzeciono, spindle
wstążka, ribbon
wstęga, band
wstyd, shame
wstydzić się, be ashamed
wybór, choice
wycierać (imp., see *wytrzeć*)
wycinać, cut out
wymię, *wymienia*, udder
wyprać, wash (clothes)
wyprzeć, push out
wytrzeć, wipe off
wywód, conclusion
wyżynać, mow; cut out
zabierać, take away
zacny, decent
zacząć, *zacznę*, begin
zaczynać (imp., see *zacząć*)
zamek, castle
zawłoka, vagabond
ząb, tooth
zbierać, collect

zbiór, collection

zdążyć, be on time

ziarnko (dim.), seed

ziarno, seed, grain

ziąb, chill

ziemia, land

ziębić, chill

zięć, son-in-law

zima, winter

zlęknąć się, become afraid

złoto, gold

zmysł, sense

znać, know

zorza, dawn

zwęzić, narrow

zziębnąć, chill

zżymać, wring

źrebak, colt

źrebię, foal

źródło, source

żaden, none

żal, regret

żar, heat

żarno, grindstone

żąć (1) żnę, reap

(2) żmę, wring

żelazo, iron

żłób, crib

żółty, yellow

żona, wife

żyto, rye

Following is a list of letters and diagraphs which are peculiar to Polish with their corresponding phonetic equivalents:

ę, ą = ę, ǫ; before stops and affricates they are pronounced as sequences of vowel and homorganic nasal consonant (em, es, eń), before spirants as nasal vowels, and before l, w as e, o; at the end of a word ę is pronounced as e.

ó = u

ś, ź, ć, ń = "soft" (mellow) palatals; before vowels they are spelled si, zi, ci, ni.

h = x; dialectally and in high style h

ł = w (bilabial)

w = v (labiodental)

y = i after hard consonants

ż = ž

ch = x

ki, gi, chi = k', g', x' before vowels.

pi, bi, fi, vi, mi = p' (or pj) etc., before vowels.

dz, dż = ʒ, ǯ

dź = ʒ́; spelled dzi before front vowels.

sz, rz, cz = "hard" (strident) palatals š, ž, č.

2. Russian

bába (pej.), woman

bal, dance

beréč, beregú, take care

béreg, shore

berémja (dial.), load

blistát', shine

bog, god

bogátyj, rich

bolóto, swamp

borodá, beard

brat, brother

brat', berú, take

brěg, (Ch.Sl., see béreg)

brémja, burden

brosát', throw

búdka, booth

bytié, existence

car', czar

čast', part

čeredá (dial.), turn

črědá, (Ch.Sl., see čeredá)

čúždyj, alien

čužój, strange, foreign

dolbit', chisel

drémljuščij, dozing

dremúčij (les), dense (forest)

èíot, this

glavá, chief, head

glávnyj, main

gnuť, bend

god, year

golová, head

golovnój, (adj.) head

gorjáščij, burning

gorjúčij, inflammable

górod, city

gorožánin, townsman

gospód', the Lord

gospodín, Mr.

gosudár', sovereign

grabëž, robbery

grad (Ch.Sl. See *górod*)

graždanin, citizen

gresti, grebú, row

iskáť, seek

iždivénie, support

izostríť, whet

javlénie, appearance

kipjáščij, boiling

kipúčij, seething

klevetáť, slander

koljúčij, thorny

kolóť, prick

kon', horse

konéc, end

koróľ, king

koroléva, queen

kóška, cat

kusáť, bite

lgan'ë, lie

ljubíť, love

marúda (dial.), dawdler

mat, checkmate

mať, mother

mel, chalk

meľ, shoal

mërtvyj, dead

mérzkij, repulsive

mërznuť, freeze

mjatéž, riot

mladój (Cm.Sl. See *molodój*)

mlěko (Cm.Sl. See *molokó*)

molodój, young

molokó, milk

mraz', riffraff

múxa, fly

načálo, beginning

napërstok, thimble

nébo, sky

nëbo, palate

nesti, nesú, carry

nezabvénnyj, unforgettable

nórov, whim

nosíť, carry

nráv, temper

óblako, cloud

odëža (dial.), clothes

odéžda, clothes

ograždáť, protect

osveščáť, light up

osvjaščënnyj, sanctified

ožidáť, expect

padéž, (grammatical) case

padëž, epizootic

paxúčij, odorous

peč, pekú, bake

péred, before

peredók, (carriage) front

perst, finger

pisánie, writing

pisk, squeak

pišča, food

piščáť, squeak

pitáť, feed

pláksa, crybaby

plavúčij, floating

plen, captivity

*pl
eníť,* captivate

plesti, pletú, braid

plyvúščij, floating

počténnyj, honorable

počtënnyj, honored

polón (obs., see *plen*)

poloníť (see *pleníť*)

pomóč, pomogú, help

porosënok, shoat

pórox, powder

poslánie, message

prax, ashes (of the dead)

prěd (See *péred*)

prédok, ancestor
prekraščát', cease
preosvjaščénnyj, Reverend
prevraščát', convert
próčit', intend
prosvéčivat', shine through
prosveščénie, enlightenment
ptíca, bird
pustít', leave, let
rab, slave
rábskij, servile
rávnyj, equal
rázum, reason (mind)
robét', be timid
róbkij, timid
rodít', bear (child)
rost, growth
róvnyj, level, even
rožát', bear
roždát' (see *rodít'*)
roždestvó, Christmas
rózysk, search
rýba, fish
sbor, collection
seredína, middle
sládkij, sweet
smerdét', stink
smértnyj, mortal
smrad, stench
sobáka, dog
sobór, cathedral, synod
sólod, malt
soveršénnyj, perfect
soveršënnyj, completed
sovratít', pervert
sredá, Wednesday
steréč', steregú, guard
stojáčij, standing
storoná, side
straná, country
stróit', build
súka, bitch
svád'ba, marriage
svátat', arrange a marriage
svečá, candle

svetít', shine
svistét', whistle
syn, son
teč', tekú, flow
tolóč', tolkú, pound
ubeždát', persuade
umertvít', mortify
véred (dial.), boil (sore)
vertét', spin, turn
vestí, vedú, lead
veztí, vezú, carry (by vehicle)
visjáčij (adj.), hanging
visjáščij (part.), hanging
vlačít' (obs.), drag
vleč', vlekú, involve
vljublënnyj, in love
volóč', drag
vonjájuščij, stinking
vonjúčij, putrid
voróčat', spin, turn
vórot, collar
vorotít', turn
voz, cart
voždelénnyj, longed for
vozdvíženie, Elevation of the Cross
vozít', carry (by vehicle)
voznesénie, Ascension
vran'ë, lies
vraščát', turn, rotate
vratá (Cm.Sl.), portal
vraždá, enmity
vredít', harm
vvedénie, introduction
xodít', walk
xoždénie, walking
zaklánie, slaughter
zakón, law
zapodózrit', suspect
ždat', wait
žit'ë-byt'ë, life
žitié, (Saint's) Life
žran'ë, gluttony
zvučát', sound
zvuk, sound

BIBLIOGRAPHY

Abbreviations of Sources

BPTJ	Biuletyn Polskiego towarzystwa językoznawczego, Cracow.
ĖS	Ėnciklopedičeskij Slovar, ed. by Brokgauz and Ėfron, St. Petersburg.
FZ	Filologičeskie zapiski, Voronež.
IF	Indogermanische Forschungen, Strassburg.
IKU	Izvestija i učenye zapiski imp. Kazanskogo universiteta, Kazan'.
IOLJa	Izvestija Otdelenija literatury i jazyka, Moscow.
IORJaS	Izvestija Otdelenija russkogo jazyka i slovesnosti, St. Petersburg.
JA	Archiv für slavische Philologie, Berlin.
JP	Język polski, Cracow.
KSB	Beiträge zur vergleichenden Sprachforschung, Berlin.
NĖS	Novyj ėnciklopedičeskij slovar', ed. by Brokgauz and Ėfron, St. Petersburg (from 1914– Prague).
PF	Prace filologiczne, Warsaw.
PrzFil	Przegląd filozoficzny, Warsaw.
PrzKr	Przegląd krytyczny, Cracow.
RĖ	Russkaja ėnciklopedija, ed. by S. D. Andrianov, St. Petersburg.
RFV	Russkij filologičeskij vestnik, Warsaw.
RS	Rocznik slawistyczny, Cracow.
RWF	Rozprawy Wydziału Filologicznego (Polskiej) Akademii Umiejętności w Krakowie, Cracow.
SAU	Sprawozdania z posiedzeń (Polskiej) Akademji Umiejętności w Krakowie.
STWarsz	Sprawozdania z posiedzeń Towarzystwa Naukowego Warszawskiego, Warsaw, Cracow.
UčZapJU	Učenye zapiski Jur'evskogo universiteta, Dorpat.
VJ	Voprosy jazykoznanija, Moscow.
WE	Wielka powszechna encyklopedia ilustrowana, Warsaw.
ZKU	Zapiski kazanskogo universiteta, Kazan'.
ZMNP	Žurnal Ministerstva narodnogo prosveščenija, St. Petersburg.

Selected Bibliography of
Baudouin de Courtenay's Linguistic Works*

A. General linguistics

Einige Beobachtungen an Kindern, *KSB*, 6 (1868), 215–22.

Nekotorye obščie zamečanija o jazykovedenii i jazyke, *ŽMNP*, 153 (February 1871), 279–316.

Rev.: H. B. Rumpelt, *Das natürliche System der Sprachlaute und sein Verhältnis zu den wichtigsten Kultursprachen, mit besonderer Rücksicht auf deutsche Grammatik und Orthographie*, *ŽMNP*, 158 (November 1871), 158–63.

Otčety komandirovannogo Ministerstvom narodnogo prosveščenija za granicu s naučnoj cel'ju. J.A.B. de K. o zanjatijax po jazykovedeniju v tečenie 1872 i 1873 gg., *IKU* (1876–1877), 45–80; 122–206; 270–90; 291–99. Separate edition, Kazan'-Warsaw-St. Petersburg (1877).

Podrobnaja programma lekcij v 1876–77 uč. godu, *IKU* (1877), 309–24; (1878), 61–133. Separate edition Kazan'-Warsaw (1878), 93 pp.

Podrobnaja programma lekcij v 1877–78 uč. godu, *IKU*, 2 (1879), 353–82; 6 (1879), 445–92; 6 (1880), 370–480; (1881), 481–608. Separate edition, Kazan'-Warsaw (1881), II + 320 + XV pp.

Rev.: N. Kruševskij, *K voprosu o gune; Issledovanie v oblasti staroslavjanskogo vokalizma*, *ZKU*, 3 (1881), 18–20.

Rev.: A. Aleksandrov, *Detskaja reč'*, *IKU* (1883), 234–35.

Rev.: N. Kruševskij, *Očerk nauki o jazyke*, *IKU*, 2 (1883), 233–34.

Rev.: F. Techmer, *Naturwissenschaftliche Analyse und Synthese der hörbaren Sprache*, *ŽMNP* (October 1884).

Z patologii i embriologii języka, *PF*, 1 (1885–86), 14–58, 318–44. Separate edition, Warsaw (1886), 72 pp.

O zadaniach językoznawstwa, *PF*, 3, 1 (1889), 92–115. Reprinted in *Szkice języko-znawcze* (1904).

---

* This bibliography is based on the one by St. Szober in *PF*, 15, 1 (1930), XXIV–LIV, and on the one given in the Sov. edition, vol. 2, 378–81.

O ogólnych przyczynach zmian językowych, *PF*, 3, 2 (1890), 447–88.

Sprawozdanie z części I pracy: "Próba teorii alternacji fonetycznych," *SAU* (April 1893), 213.

Vermenschlichung der Sprache, Hamburg (1893), 27 pp. (Sammlung gemeinverständlicher wissenchaftlichen Vorträge, ed. by Virchow-Holtzendorf, Neue Folge, Achte Serie, Heft 173).

Einiges über Palatalisierung (Palatalisation) und Entpalatalisierung (Dispalatalisation), *IF*, 4 (1894), 45–52.

Próba teorii alternacji fonetycznych; część I, Ogólna *RWF*, 20 (1894), 219–364.

Versuch einer Theorie phonetischer Alternationen. Ein Kapitel aus der Psychophonetik, Strassburg–Cracow (1895), 130 pp. (Longer version of preceding).

Svoeobraznaja èksperimental'naja popytka po antropofonike. Rev. of A. Kamskij, *Opyt ob"jasnenija zvukovyx izmenenij reči izmeneniem raboty organov, IORJaS*, 3 (1898), 933–37.

Fonema, fonemat, *WE*, 22 (1899), 787–88.

Fonologia, *WE*, 22 (1899), 791–98.

Fonologia (fonetyka) arioeuropejska, *WE*, 22 (1899), 798–802.

Fonologia (fonetyka) polska, *WE*, 22 (1899), 811–19.

Fonologia (fonetyka) słowiańska, *WE*, 22 (1899), 802–11.

O pewnym stałym kierunku zmian językowych w związku z antropologią, *Kosmos*, Lwów, 4–5 (1899), 155–73.

Lingvističeskie zametki. 1. O svjazi grammatičeskogo roda s mirosozercaniem i nastrojeniem ljudej, govorjaščix jazykami, različajuščimi rod; 2. Neskol'ko obščelingvističeskix vyvodov iz rassmotrenija materialov dlja južnoslavjanskoj dialektologii, *ŽMNP*, 331 (October 1900), 367–74.

Gramatyka porównawcza, *WE*, 26 (1901), 615–18.

Gramatyk, Gramatyka, *WE*, 26 (1901), 609–15.

Językoznawstwo czyli lingwistyka w wieku XIX, *Prawda*, Warsaw, 1 (1901), 1–23. Slightly expanded version in *Szkice Językoznawcze* (1904).

O smešannom xaraktere vsex jazykov, *ŽMNP*, 337 (September 1901), 12–24.

Zametka ob izmenjaemosti osnov sklonenija v osobennosti že o ix sokraščenii v pol'zu okončanij, *Sbornik statej posvaščennyx . . . F. F. Fortunatovu*, (*RFV*, 48, 1902), 234–48.

Język i języki, *WE*, 33 (1903), 266–78.

Językoznawstwo, *WE*, 33 (1903), 278–96.

Lingvističeskie zametki i aforizmy. Po povodu novejšix trudov V. A. Bogorodickogo, *ŽMNP*, 346 (1903), 279–334; 347 (1903), 1–37.

O psychicznych podstawach zjawisk językowych, *PrzFil*, 6 (1903), 153–71.

Jazyk i jazyki, *ÈS*, 41 (1904), 529–48.

Jazykoznanie, *ÈS*, 41 (1904), 517–27.

Szkice językoznawcze, Warsaw, 1 (1904), VII + 464 + 7 pp.

Zur Kritik der künstlichen Weltsprachen (Veranlasst durch die gleichnamige Broschüre von K. Brugmann und A. Leskien), *Annalen der Naturphilosophie*, Leipzig, 6 (1907), 385–433.

O języku pomocniczym międzynarodowym, *Krytyka*, Cracow, 10–12 (1908), 243–49; 375–83; 461–72.

O związku wyobrażeń fonetycznych z wyobrażeniami morfologicznymi i semazjologicznymi, *STWarsz*, 1, fasc. 4–5 (1908), 9–28.

Zur Frage über die "Weichheit" und "Härte" der Sprachlaute im allgemeinen und im slavischen Sprachgebiete insbesondere, *Zbornik u slavu Vatroslava Jagića*, Berlin (1908), 583–90.

Zarys historii językoznawstwa czyli lingwistyki (glottologi), *Poradnik dla samouków*, Warsaw, Seria III, 2, fasc. 2 (1909), 35–302.

Zur "Sonanten"-Frage, *IF*, 25 (1909), 77–85.

Die Klassifikation der Sprachen, *IF*, Anzeiger, 26 (1910), 51–58.

O "prawach głosowych," *RS*, 3 (1910), 1–57 (French summary, "Les Lois phonétiques," 57–82).

Sbornik zadač po "Vvedeniju v jazykovedenie," po preimuščestvu primenitel'no k russkomu jazyku, St. Petersburg (1912), 96 pp.

Žargon, *RÉ*, 8 (1914), 40.

Zaimstvovanija (v jazyke), *RÈ*, 8 (1914), 159–60.

Vvedenie v jazykovedenie, St. Petersburg (1917), 233 pp.

O relativnosti v oboru jazykovém, *Atheneum, Vědecký sborník. Řidi Vilém Mathesius a Emanuel Ráde*, Prague, 5, II (1922), 80–87.

Względność w dziedzinie świata językowego, *Przegląd Warszawski*, Warsaw, 3, fasc. 17 (1923), 178–91.

Ilościowość w myśleniu językowym, *Symbolae Grammaticae in honorem Joannis Rozwadowski*, Cracow, 1 (1927), 3–18.

Różnica między fonetyką a psychofonetyką, *STWarsz*, 19 (1927), 3–9.

Einfluss der Sprache auf Weltanschauung und Stimmung, *PF*, 14 (1929), 184–255.

Fakultative Sprachlaute, *Donum natalicium J. Schrijnen*, Nijmegen-Utrecht, (1929), 38–43.

Zagadnienia pokrewieństwa językowego, *BPTJ*, 2 (1930), 104–16.

B. Comparative Slavic

Rev.: Neskol'ko slov po povodu 'Obščeslavjanskoj azbuki'. *'Obščeslavjanskaja azbuka s priloženiem obrazcov slavjanskix narečij. Sostavil A. Gil'ferding*, ŽMNP, 155 (May 1871), 149–95.

Rev.: V. Jagić, *Das Leben der Wurzel dê in den slavischen Sprachen*, ŽMNP, 176 (November 1874), 188–93.

Rev.: L. Malinowski, *Beiträge zur slavischen Dialektologie*, KSB, 8 (1874), 199–209.

Rev.: A. A. Krynskij: *O nosovyx zvukax v slavjanskix jazykax*, KSB, 8 (1874), 174–96.

O tak nazyvajemoj "evfoničeskoj vstavke soglasnogo *n* v slavjanskix jazykax," *FZ*, 1 (1877), 1–37.

Rev.: L. Malinowski, *Beiträge zur slavischen Dialektologie*, ŽMNP, 193 (October 1877), 233–51.

Rev.: A. Kočubinskij, *K voprosu o vzaimnyx otnošenijax slavjanskix narečij*, ZKU, 1 (1879), 1–45.

Rev.: *Neskol'ko slov o kul'ture pervobytnyx i drevnix slavjan, A. Budiloviča,*

Pervobytnye slavjane v ix jazyke, byte i ponjatjax po dannym leksikal'nym, RFV, 2 (1879), 165–206.

Nekotorye otdely "sravnitel'noj grammatiki" slavjanskix jazykov, RFV, 5 (1881), 265–344.

Note glottologiche intorno alle lingue slave e questioni di morfologia e fonologia ario-europea, *Atti del IV Congresso Internazionale degli Orientalisti,* Florence, II (1881), 3–21.

Rev.: L. Léger, *Esquisse sommaire de la mythologie slave,* ŽMNP, 220 (March 1882), 144–46.

Übersicht der slavischen Sprachenwelt in Zusammenhange mit den andern arioeuropäischen (indogermanischen) Sprachen. *Antrittsvorlesung gehalten an der Universität Dorpat am 6/18 September 1883,* Leipzig (1884), 21 pp.

Dva voprosa iz učenija o "smjagčenii" ili palatalizacii zvukov v slavjanskix jazykax, UčZapJu, 2 (1893), 1–20.

Sravnitel'naja grammatika slavjanskix jazykov v svjazi s drugimi indoevropejskimi jazykami (1901–1902 akad. god), compiled by A. Šilov, St. Petersburg (1902), 245 pp. (Lithograph).

Polskij jazyk v sravnenii s russkim i drevne-cerkovno-slavjanskim, St. Petersburg (1912), VII + 118 + II pp.

Różnorakie etymologie, JP, 4 (1919), 112–15; 129–31.

Dwie grupy wyrazów z utajonym rdzeniem (pierwiastkiem, radix) $ei \parallel oi$ 'ire'. Z dziedziny etymologii domniemanych, *Zbornik filoloških i lingvističnih studija A. Beliću povodom 25 godišnjice njegova naučnog rada posvećuju njegovi prijateli i učenici,* Belgrade (1922), 225–28.

Kilka zestawień etymologicznych (1. Różnorodność rdzeni, związanych z wyobrażeniem 'bycia', 'stawania się', 'istniena'. 2. Zmieszanie rdzeni $z\mathring{l}d \parallel z\bar{\imath}d$ 'lepić, tworzyć, budować' i $da\text{-}d \parallel da\text{-}s$. 3. Pol. $z \parallel s(\check{s})$ prasł. $s\underset{.}{z}$. 4. *uście = ujście, ście = jście*), STWarsz, 11–18 (1927).

Izoglosy w świecie językowym słowiańskim, *Sbornik prací I. Sjezdu slovanských filologů v Praze 1929,* Přednášky, Prague, I (1932), 448–50.

C. Non-Slavic Languages

Rev.: A. Ludwig, *Der Infinitiv in Veda mit einer Systematik des litauischen und slavischen Verbs,* ŽMNP, 161 (May 1872), 142–48.

Rev.: Fr. Müller, *Indogermanisch und Semitisch. Ein Beitrag zur Würdigung dieser beiden Sprachstämme,* ŽMNP, 161 (June 1872), 283–91.

Rev.: J. Karłowicz, *O języku litewskim,* PrzKr, 8 (1876), and *Wisła,* 2–3 (1904), 184–92.

Rev.: J. Jolly, *Geschichte des Infinitivs im Indogermanischen,* ŽMNP, 184 (April 1876), 364–78.

Neskol'ko slov o sravnitel'noj grammatike indoevropejskix jazykov, ŽMNP, 213 (December 1881), 269–321.

Iz lekcij po latinskoj fonetike, FZ, (1884–1892). Separate, Voronež (1893), 463 + XXXV pp.

Rev.: A. Bielenstein, *Die Grenzen des lettischen Volksstammes und der lettischen Sprache in der Gegenwart und im 13. Jahrhundert,* Wochenschrift für ausländische Völkerkunde, Stuttgart, 19 (1893).

Urindogermanische Alternanz e || o, *IF*, 4 (1894), 53–57.

Kwestia alfabetu litewskiego w państwie rosyjskim i jej rozwiązanie, Cracow (1904), 44 pp.

Zametki na poljax sočinenija V. V. Radlova (W. Radloff, *Einleitende Gedanken zur Darstellung der Morphologie der Türksprachen,* 1906), *Živaja Starina,* St. Petersburg, 2–3 (1909), 191–206.

Germanskie jazyki, *Ènciklopedičeskij slovar' A. i I. Granat* . . . , St. Petersburg, vol. 14 (1912), 346–61.

Grečeskij jazyk, *Ènciklopedičeskij slovar' A. i I. Granat* . . . , St. Petersburg, vol. 17 (1913), 57–68.

Kel'tskie jazyki, *Ènciklopedičeskij slovar' A. i I. Granat* . . . , St. Petersburg, vol. 24 (1914), appendix, 1–8.

D. West Slavic Languages

1. Polish

Einige Fälle der Wirkung der Analogie in der polnischen Deklination, *KSB*, 6 (1868), 19–88.

Hinneigung zu *e* im Polnischen, *KSB*, 6 (1868), 212–15.

Übergang der tonlosen Konsonanten in die ihnen entsprechenden tönenden in der historischen Entwicklung der polnischen Sprache, *KSB*, 6 (1868), 197–204.

Übergang des *i* in *u* im Polnischen, *KSB*, 6 (1868), 256–57.

Wechsel des *s* (*š, ś*) mit *ch* in der polnischen Sprache, *KSB*, 6 (1868), 221–22.

Wortformen und selbst Sätze, welche in der polnischen Sprache zu Stämmen herabgesunken sind, *KSB*, 6 (1868), 204–10.

Zetacismus in den Denkmälern und Mundarten der polnischen Sprache, *KSB*, 6 (1868), 220.

Zur Geschichte der polnischen Zahlwörter, *KSB*, 6 (1868), 247.

O drevnepol'skom jazyke do XIV-go stoletija, Leipzig (1870), VIII + 99 + 84 + IV pp.

Rev.: A. Semenovitsch, *Über die vermeintliche Quantität der Vokale im Altpolnischen, KSB,* 8 (1874), 212–26.

Rev.: I. Kopernicki, *Spostrzeżenia nad właściwościami językowymi w mowie górali Beskidowych, PrzKr,* 9 (1876).

Rev.: J. Rabbinowicz, *Grammatik der polnischen Sprache verglichen mit der deutschen und hebräischen, PrzKr,* 9 (1876).

Rev.: H. Suchecki, *Modlitwy Wacława, zabytek mowy staropolskiej, odkryty przez Al. hr. Przeździeckiego. Wiadomość o nich z rozbiorem filologicznym i lingwistycznym, IKU,* 1 (1877), 355–57.

Rev.: *Prace lingwistyczne K. Appela, Nowiny,* 238, 245 (1880).

Rev.: A. A. Kryński, *Z dziejów języka polskiego, FZ,* 2 (1880), 1–5.

Z fonetyki międzywyrazowej (aüssere *Sandhi-*) sanskrytu i języka polskiego, *SAU* (March 1894), 8–16.

Wskazówki dla zapisujących materiały gwarowe na obszarze językowym polskim, *Materiały i prace Komisii Językowej AU w Krakowie,* Cracow (1901), 115–39.

Rev.: A. Brückner, *Dzieje języka polskiego, RS,* 1 (1908), 90–121.

Charakterystyka psychologiczna języka polskiego, *Encyklopedia polska AU,* 2, 3, Język polski i jego historia. Część I, Cracow (1915), 154–226.

Rev.: Sigurd Agrell, *Przedrostki postaciowe czasowników polskich, in Handlingar angående Professuren i Slaviskae Språkvid Uppsala Universitet,* Uppsala (1920), 74 ff.

Zarys historii języka polskiego (Bibljoteka Składnicy pomocy szkolnych, 10), Warsaw (1922), 164 pp; scond edition, The Hague, Europe Printing (1964).

Ed. and supplement to: K. Drzewiecki, Teksty do nauki języka staropolskiego wieku XIV i XV. Wybór, objaśnienia i przypisy. Pod redakcją oraz ze słowniczkiem i innemi dodatkami . . . , Warsaw (1924), 183 pp.

Próby zestawień etymologicznych, *Studia Staropolskie, księga ku czci A. Brücknera,* Cracow (1927), 213–29.

Rdzenie (piewiastki, radices) czyli morfemy semantycznie centralne myślenia językowego polskiego: 1) *jest (jezd);* 2) *s (są);* 3) *bi (by);* 4) *będ* || *bęź, (bądź)* || *bǫd (bąd)* || *bǫź (bądź), PF,* 12 (1927), 1–17.

2. Kashubian

Rev.: P. Stremler, *Fonetika kašubskogo jazyka,* ŽMNP (August 1877), 307–13.

Kašubskij "jazyk," kašubskij narod i "kašubskij vopros," *ŽMNP,* 310 (April-May 1897), 306–57. Abstract in *SAU,* 2 (1897), 3–6.

Kurzes Resumé der "kašubischen Frage," *JA,* 26 (1904), 366–405.

3. Czech

Rev.: J. Jireček, *Nákres mluvnice staročeské, KSB,* 8 (1874), 226–34. Also in *ŽMNP,* 184 (March 1876), 212–19.

4. Polabian

Rev.: A. Schleicher, *Laut-und Formenlehre der polabischen Sprache,* ŽMNP, 168 (August 1873), 424–46.

E. East Slavic Languages

1. Russian

Rev.: J. Papłoński, *Praktyczne prawidła poprawnego pisania i czystego wymawiania po rusku, PrzKr,* 12 (1875).

Rev.: J. Paplonskij, *Praktičeskie pravila ruskogo pravopisanija i proiznošenija, FZ,* 5 (1876), 26–31.

Rev.: V. J. Xoroševskij, *Russkij bukvar' dlja pol'skix detej, ZKU,* 2 (1878), 295–301.

Rev.: *Glasnye bez udarenija v russkom jazyke* [a review of the dissertation of V. A. Bogorodickij], *IKU,* 4–6 (1881), 19–20.

Otryvki iz lekcij po fonetike i morfologii russkogo jazyka, *FZ,* 4–5 (1881), 1–32; 2–3 (1882), 33–88.

Ed.: V. I. Dal', Tolkovyj slovar' živogo velikorusskogo jazyka [3rd revised and enlarged ed.], St. Petersburg-Moscow (1903–1909).

Rev.: V. Černyšev, *Zakony i pravila russkogo proiznošenija. Zvuki. Formy. Udarenie. Opyt rukovodstva dlja učitelej, ćtecov i artistov, IORJaS,* 12, fasc. 2 (1907), 491–501.

[Preface to:] V. F. Traxtenberg, *Blatnaja muzyka,* St. Petersburg (1908).

Ob otnošenii russkogo pis'ma k russkomu jazyku, St. Petersburg (1912), 132 + V pp.

2. Byelorussian

Rev.: K. Appel, *O belorusskom narečii, FZ,* 5 (1880), 12–14.

3. Ukrainian

Kilka ogólników objektywnej i subjektywnej odrębności "Ukrainy" pod względem językowym, plemiennym, narodowym i państwowym, *Album Societatis Scientiarum Ševčenkianae Ucrainensium Leopoliensis ad sollemnia sua decennaliaguinta 1873–1923,* Lwów (1925), 1–19.

F. South Slavic Languages

1. Slovenian

Opyt fonetiki rez'janskix govorov, Warsaw-St. Petersburg (1875), XVI + 128 pp.

Rez'janskij katexizis kak priloženie k "Opytu fonetiki rez'janskix govorov," Warsaw-St. Petersburg (1875), 56 pp.

Rez'ja i Rez'jane, *Slavjanskij sbornik,* St. Petersburg, 3 (1876), 223–371.

Glottologičeskie (lingvističeskie) zametki. 1. Koe-čto po povodu rez'janskoj garmonii (sozvučija) glasnyx, *FZ,* 5 (1876), 1–16.

Samples of Friulian dialects in *Friul'skie slavjane I. I. Sreznevskogo i priloženija,* St. Petersburg (1878), Appendix to vol. 38 of *Izvestija Akademii nauk;* 57–60.

Rev.: *O narečii venecijanskix slovencev. Sočinenie A. Klodiča, FZ,* 5 (1880), 1–2.

Rev.: D. Terstjenjak, *Slovanščina v romanščini, FZ,* 2 (1880), 13–16.

Der Dialekt von Cirkno (Kirchheim), *JA,* 7 (1884), 386–404, 575–90.

Sprachproblem des Dialektes von Cirkno (Kirchheim), *JA,* 8 (1885), 103–19, 274–90, 432–62.

Rev.: K. Štrekelj, *Morphologie des Görzermittelkarstdialektes mit besonderer Berücksichtigung der Betonungsverhältnisse, JA,* 10 (1887), 603–15.

Il Catechismo resiano, St. Petersburg (1891), 28 pp.

O slovjanax v Italii, *Russkaja mysl'* (1892), 24–46.

Il Catechismo resiano con una prefazione del dott. Giuseppe Loschi, Udine, (1894), 113 pp.

Materialien zur südslavischen Dialektologie und Ethnographie. 1. Resianische Texte gesammelt in den Jh. 1872, 1873 und 1877. St. Petersburg (1895), XLVIII + 708 pp.

Materialien zur südslavischen Dialektologie und Ethnographie. 2. Sprachproben in den Mundarten der Slaven von Torre im Nordöstlichen Italien. St. Petersburg (1904), XXXII + 240 pp. (*SORJaS,* 78, 2).

Bibliography

Neskol'ko slučaev psixologičeski-morfologičeskogo upodoblenija ili uodno-obraženija v tersko-slavjanskix govorax severovostočnoj Italii, *IORJaS*, 10, 3 (1905), 266–83.
Latinsko-ital'jansko-slavjanskij pominal'nik XV-go i XVI-go stoletija sostav-lennyj v oblasti Terskih Slavjan, St. Petersburg (1906), 55 pp.
Materialien zur südslavischen Dialektologie und Ethnographie. 3. *Resianisches Sprachdenkmal "Christjanske uzhilo"*. St. Petersburg (1913), 138 pp. (*Za-piski istoriko-filologičeskogo fakul'teta imp. SPb. un-ta*, 114).

2. Serbo-Croatian

Rev.: St. Novakovič, *Fiziologija glasa i glasovi srpskoga jezika, KSB*, 8 (1874), 211.
Rev.: St. Novakovič, *Fizijologja glasa i glasovi srpskoga jezika, ŽMNP*, 176 (November 1874), 182–88.
Rev.: V. Jazić, *Podmladjena vokalizacija u hrvatskom jeziku, ZKU*, 3 (1877), 716–33.
Rev.: Ogled. *Rječnik hrvatskoga ili srpskoga jezika. Obradjuje Gj. Daničić, FZ*, 2 (1880), 9–13.
Texts in columns 299–322 of M. Rešetar's *Die serbokroatischen Kolonien Süd-italiens (Schriften der Balkankommission, Linguistische Abteilung,* 9), Vienna (1911).

G. Old Church Slavonic

Rev.: A. Leskien, *Handbuch der altbulgarischen (altkirchenslavischen) Sprache, ŽMNP*, 188 (November 1876), 152–64.
Zum altkirchenslavischen *oj6min б, IF*, 21 (1907), 196–97.

H. Portraits of Linguists

Jan Juszkiewicz, badacz, litewski, *Kraj*, 29–31, St. Petersburg (1886).
Zametki k nekrologu Nikolaja Vjačeslavoviča Kruševskogo, *RFV*, 20 (1888), 297–302.
Boduèn de Kurtenè (Baudouin de Courtenay), Ivan Aleksandrovič, *Kritiko-biografičeskij slovar' russkix pisatelej i učenyx*, ed. by S. A. Vengerov, St. Petersburg, 5 (1897), 18–45.
Aleksandr Ivanovič Aleksandrov, *Kritiko-biografičeskij slovar' russkix pisatelej i učenyx*, ed. by S. A. Vengerov, St. Petersburg, 1 (1889), 932–33.
Mikołaj Kruszewski, jego życie i prace naukowe, *PF*, 2, 3 (1888), 837–49; 3, 1 (1889), 116–75.
Dal' Vladimir Ivanovič, *ÈS*, 17 (1913), 529–32.
Mikkola József Juliusz, *WE*, 47–48 (1911), 64.
Brikner Aleksandr, *NÈS*, 8 (1912), 101–04.
Nering Vladislav, *ÈS*, 28 (1916), 42.
Mrozinskij Josif, *NÈS*, 27 (1916), 414.
Nič Kazimir, *ÈS*, 28 (1916), 657–58.

Selected Bibliography of Works
about Boudouin de Courtenay

Belinskaja, T. A., Učenie I. A. Boduèna de Kurtenè o foneme, *Autoreferat kand. diss.*, Tbilisi (1952).

Bezlaj, F., Baudouin de Courtenay, *Trinkov Zbornik*, Trst (1946), 109–18.

Bogorodickij, V., Kazanskij period professorskoj dejatel'nosti I. A. Boduèna de Kurtenè (1875–1883 g.), *PF*, 15, fasc. 2 (1931), 465–79.

——, Kazanskaja lingvističeskaja škola, *Trudy MIFLI*, 5, *Sbornik statej po jazykovedeniju*, Moscow, (1930), 265–94.

Čemodanov, N. S., Iz istorii sravnitel'no-istoričeskogo metoda v russkom jazykovedenii, *Sbornik statej po jazykoznaniju, Professoru Mosk. univ. akademiku V. V. Vinogradovu*, Moscow (1958), 312–29.

Čerepanov, M. V., Iz istorii kazanskoj lingvističeskoj školy (k 30–letiju so dnja smerti I. A. Boduèna de Kurtenè), *Voprosy teorii i metodiki izučenija russkogo jazyka*, Kazan' (1960), 130–47.

Černý, A., Za J. Baudouinem de Courtenay, *Slovanský Přehled*, 21 (1929), 641–59.

Doroszewski, W., Jan Baudouin de Courtenay na tle swej epoki i jako prekursor nowych prądów w językoznawstwie, *Nauka Polska*, Warsaw, 1 (1955), 47–58.

Grigor'ev, V. P., I. A. Boduèn de Kurtenè i interlingvistika, *I.A. Boduèn de Kurtenè (1845–1929)*, Moscow (1960), 53–66.

Guxman, M. M., Istoričeskie i metodologičeskie osnovy strukturalizma, *Osnovnye napravlenija strukturalizma*, Moscow (1964), 5–45.

Ivanov, V. V., I. A. Boduèn de Kurtenè i tipologija slavjanskix jazykov, *I. A. Boduèn de Kurtenè (1845–1929)*, Moscow (1960), 37–43.

Jakobson, R., Jan Baudouin de Courtenay, *Slavische Rundschau*, 10 (1929), 809–12.

——, Kazańska szkoła polskiej lingwistyki i jej miejsce w światowym rozwoju fonologii, *BPTJ*, 19 (1960), 3–34.

——, Znaczenie Kruszewskiego w rozwoju językoznawstwa ogólnego, in *Mikołaj Kruszewski, Wybór pism* (1967), X–XXV.

Karakulakov, V. V., Vopros ob istoričeskix izmenenijax morfologičeskoj struktury slova v trudax I. A. Boduèna de Kurtenè i predstavitelej Kazanskoj lingvističeskoj školy, *Uč. Zap. Stalinabadskogo gos. ped. in-ta,* 24 (1959), 85–96.

————, Obščelingvističeskie vzgljady I. A. Boduèna de Kurtenè i predstavitelej lingvističeskoj školy, *Uč. Zap. Stalinabadskogo gos. ped. in-ta,* 14 (1956), 69–86.

Kryński, A., Idee językoznawcze Jana Baudouina de Courtenay, *Sprawozdania z Posiedzeń Tow. Nauk. Warszawskiego,* Warsaw, 23 (1930), 1–18.

Leont'ev, A. A., Obščelingvističeskie vzgljady I. A. Boduèna de Kurtenè, *VJ,* 6 (1959), 115–24.

————, Obščelingvističeskie vzgljady I. A. Boduèna de Kurtenè, *Avtoreferat kand. diss.,* Moscow (1963).

————, Tvorčeskij put' i osnovnye čerty lingvističeskoj koncepcii I. A. Boduèna de Kurtenè, *I. A. Boduèn de Kurtenè* (1845–1929), Moscow (1960), 5–27.

Leška, O., Současnost díla Jana Baudouina de Courtenay, *Československá rusistika,* 10 (1965), pp. 193–96.

Meillet, A., [Necrology], *Revue des études slaves,* Paris, 10, 1/2 (1930), 174–75.

Nitsch, K., Jan Baudouin de Courtenay, *Polski słownik biograficzny,* Cracow, 1 (1935), 359–62; reprinted in Nitsch, K., *Ze wspomnień językoznawcy,* Cracow (1960), 182–93.

Porzeziński, W., Die allgemeine Sprachwissenschaft in Polen seit 1868, *BPTJ,* 1 (1927), 47–79.

Posvjanskaja, A. S., I. A. Boduèn de Kurtenè o pol'skom jazyke, *I. A. Boduèn de Kurtenè* (1845–1929), Moscow (1960), 44–52.

Požarnickaja, S. K., Metodika dialektologičeskix issledovanij I. A. Boduèna de Kurtenè, *Materialy i issledovanija po russkoj dialektologii, Novaja serija,* Moscow, 3 (1962), 165–75.

Schogt, H. G., Baudouin de Courtenay and Phonological Analysis, *La linguistique,* 2 (1966), 15–29.

Skalozub, L. G., Voprosy fonetiki russkogo jazyka v trudax I. A. Boduèna de Kurtenè, *Visnyk Kyjivs'koho universytetu,* 3 (1960), (*Serija filolohiji ta žurnalistyky,* vyp. 2), 165–75.

Ščerba, L. V., I. A. Boduèn de Kurtenè i ego značenie v nauke o jazyke (1845–1929), *Russkij jazyk v sovetskoj škole,* 6 (1929), p. 63–71; reprinted in his *Izbrannye raboty po russkomu jazyku,* Moscow (1957), 85–96.

————, I. A. Boduèn de Kurtenè (Nekrolog), *IORJaS,* 3, 1 (1930), 311–26.

————, I. A. Boduèn de Kurtenè i ego značenie v nauke o jazyke, *Russkij jazyk v škole,* 4 (1940), 83–90.

Štiber, Z. (Stieber), Teorija fonem I. A. Boduèna de Kurtenè v sovremennom jazykoznanii, *VJ,* 4 (1955), 89–93.

Tolstoj, N. I., O rabotax I. A. Boduèna de Kurtenè po slovenskomu jazyku, *I. A. Boduèn de Kurtenè* (1845–1929), Moscow (1960), 67–82.

Toporov, V. N., I. A. Boduèn de Kurtenè i razvitie fonologii, *I. A. Boduèn de Kurtenè* (1845–1929), Moscow (1960), 28–36.

Tymošenko, P. D., Jan Bouduen de Kurtene i ukrajins'ka mova, *Ukrajins'ka mova v školi,* 1 (1960), 30–35.

Ułaszyn, H., *Jan Baudouin de Courtenay, Charakterystyka ogólna uczonego i człowieka* (1845–1929), Poznań (1934), 43 pp.

Selected Bibliography of Works about Boudouin de Courtenay

————, W sprawie światopoglądu J. Baudouina de Courtenay, *Język polski*, 35 (1955), 233–35.

————, Kartka z historii językoznawstwa polskiego, *Poradnik językowy*, 6 (1956), 204–09.

Vasmer, M. J., Baudouin de Courtenay, *Indogermanisches Jahrbuch*, 16 (1932), 338–40.

————, Baudouin de Courtenay. Zum 100. Wiederkehr seines Geburtstages, *Zeitschrift für Phonetik und allgemeine Sprachwissenschaft*, 1 (1947), 71–77.

————, (Fasmer), Boduèn de Kurtenè, *Živaja starina*, St. Petersburg 2 (1906), 135–46.

Vinogradov, V. V., I. A. Boduèn de Kurtenè, in *Izbrannye trudy po obščemu jazykoznaniju*, 1 (1963), 6–20.

Weingart, M., Jan Baudouin de Courtenay, *Ročenka slovanského ústavu za rok 1929*, Prague (1930), 172–98.

Zemskaja, E. A., "Kazanskaja lingvističeskaja škola" prof. I. A. Boduèna de Kurtenè, *Russkij jazyk v škole*, 6 (1951), 61–73.

Zinder, L. R., Matusevič, M. I., K istorii učenija o foneme, *IOLJa*, 12, 1 (1953), 62–75.

I N D E X E S

Name Index

Ahlquist, August E. (1826–1889), Finnish Finno-Ugricist.

Ascoli, Graziadio I. (1829–1907), Italian Indo-Europeanist, Semiticist, Romance scholar; formulated "substratum" theory.

Appel, Karol J. (1857–1930), Polish general linguist, associated with B. d. C.

Bang-Kaup, Willy K. (1869–1934), Belgian philologist (Modern English) and Turkologist.

Baranauskas (Baranovskij), Bishop Antanas (1835–1902), Lithuanian grammarian and dialectologist.

Becker, Karl F. (1775–1849), German philologist and champion of "logical" approach to language.

Benfey, Theodor (1809–1881), German Orientalist, Indo-Europeanist, and historian of linguistics.

Benloew, Louis (1819–1901), French classicist and comparative linguist; author of *Aperçu général de la science comparative des langues*, 1872.

Bielenstein, August J. G. (1826–1907), Latvian pastor, linguist, and ethnographer.

Biondelli, Bernardino (1804–1886), Italian Romance linguist.

Bogorodickij, Vasilij A. (1857–1941), Russian linguist and phonetician; pupil of B. d. C. in Kazan' period.

Böhtlingk, Otto (1815–1904), German Sanskritist; co-author (with R. Roth) of seven-volume Sanskrit dictionary.

Bollack, Léon M. (b. 1859), French industrialist; inventor of *la langue bleue*.

Bonaparte, Lucien L., French linguist and ethnographer; Basque specialist.

Bopp, Franz (1791–1867), German Indo-Europeanist; founder (with Rask and Grimm) of the comparative method.

Brandt, Roman (1853–1902), Russian Slavic linguist, mostly comparativist.

Bréal, Michel (1832–1915), French linguist; pioneer in historical semantics.

Broch, Olaf (1867–1961), Norwegian Slavicist, phonetician and dialectologist.

Brugmann, Karl (1849–1919), German Indo-Europeanist, leading representative of the Neogrammarians.

Budenz, Joszef (1836–1892), Hungarian Finno-Ugricist.

Budmani, Petar (1835–1914), Croatian Slavicist, specialist in Serbo-Croatian.

Castrén, M. Alexander (1813–1852), Finnish Finno-Ugricist.

Čerepanov, S. I. (1810–1884), Russian

Kott, František S. (1825–1912), Czech lexicographer; editor of seven-volume *Česko-německý slovník* (1878 ·ff.).

Kratzenstein, Christian G. (1723–1795), phonetician and engineer.

Kruszewski, Mikołaj (1851–1887), Polish Indo-Europeanist and general linguist; most talented pupil of B. d. C. in the Kazan period.

Kuhn, F. F. Adalbert (1812–1881), German Indo-Europeanist; pioneer in "linguistic paleontology."

Kurschat, Friedrich (1806–1884), Lithuanian linguist.

Lazarus, Moritz (1824–1903), German philosopher and psychological linguist; collaborator of Steinthal.

Leibniz, Gottfried W. von (1646–1716), German philosopher, mathematician, historian, and linguist; champion of the study of modern languages and the creation of a universal language.

Leskien, August (1840–1916), German Slavicist; a founder of the Neogrammarian movement.

Letellier, Charles Louis Augustin, French schoolteacher; author of *Cours complet de langue universelle,* (1852–1853).

Liden, Evald (1862–1939), Swedish Indo-Europeanist.

Linde, Samuel B. (1771–1847), Polish lexicographer.

Liptay, Alberto (b. 1859), Chilean naval surgeon; author of "La lengua católica," 1890.

Littré, M. P. Émile (1801–1881), French physician, philosopher, and lexicographer.

Lönnrot, Elias (1802–1884), Finnish philologist; editor of literary version of the *Kalevala.*

Lott, Julius, Austrian artillery officer; author of *Grammatik der Mundolingue,* an artificial language (1890).

Lundell, Johan A. (1851–1940), Swedish phonetician and orthographical reformer.

Maldant, Eugène, French engineer; inventor of *Chabé Aban* ("Langue internationale").

Marr, Nikolaj Ja. (1864–1934), Georgian Caucasianist; inventor of the "Japhetic" theory of the origin of languages.

Masing, Leonhard (b. 1845), Russian Indo-Europeanist and Slavicist.

Matov, Dimitir A. (1864–1896), Bulgarian Slavicist.

Meillet, Antoine (1866–1936), French Indo-Europeanist and theoretical linguist.

Mikkola, Jooseppi J. (1866–1946), Finnish Slavicist; a pupil of Fortunatov.

Miklosich, Franz (1813–1891), Slovenian Slavicist, pioneer of comparative Slavic grammar.

Miletič, Ljubomir (1863–1920), Bulgarian Slavicist and dialectologist.

Miller, Vsevolod F. (1848–1913), Russian Orientalist and folklorist.

Møller, Herman (1850–1927), Danish Indo-Europeanist.

Moritz, Karl Philipp (1727–1793), German writer and prosodist.

Muka, Arnošt (1854–1932), Lusatian Slavicist.

Muller, Max (1823–1900), German Sanskritist and theoretical linguist; editor of the *Rigveda;* spent most of his career in England.

Munkácsi, Bernát (c. 1900), Hungarian folklorist and Finno-Ugricist.

Nekrasov, Nikolaj P. (1828–1908), Russian linguist and grammarian.

Nicolas, Adolphe C. A. M., French surgeon; author of "Spokil, langue internationale," Angers, 1900.

Oblak, Vatroslav (1864–1896), Sloven-

Oblak, Vatroslav—*Cont.*
ian Slavicist specializing primarily in South Slavic languages.

Osthoff, Hermann (1847–1909), German Indo-Europeanist; a leading Neogrammarian.

Paul, Hermann (1846–1921), German historical linguist and Germanist; renowned as theoretician of Neogrammarians.

Pedersen, Holger (1867–1953), Danish Indo-Europeanist.

Petriceicu-Hasdeu, Bogdan P. (1836–1907), Roumanian Indo-Europeanist and Romance scholar.

Pictet, Adolphe (1799–1875), French linguist, primarily Celtist, and founder of "linguistic paleontology."

Potebnja, Aleksandr A. (1835–1891), Russian linguist and folklorist; a follower of Humboldt.

Pott, August F. (1802–1887), German Indo-Europeanist, especially concerned with etymology.

Radlov (Radloff), Vasilij V. (1837–1918), Russian Turkologist associated with B. d. C.

Rask, Rasmus Ch.N. (1782–1832), Danish pioneer in comparative Indo-European.

Renan, J. Ernest (1823–1892), French man of letters, historian, and Semiticist.

Rešetar, Milan (1860–1942), Croatian Slavicist.

Romanes, George John (1848–1894), English naturalist and philosopher.

Roth, Rudolph (1821–1895), German Sanskritist.

Rousselot, Jean-Pierre (1846–1924), French priest and experimental phonetician.

Rożniecki, Stanisław, Polish folklorist; author of *Varaegske Minder i den russiske Heldedigtning*, Copenhagen, 1914.

Rozwadowski, Jan M. (1867–1935), Polish Indo-Europeanist, Slavicist, and theoretical linguist; colleague of B. d. C.

Šafařík, Pavel J. (1795–1861), Czech Slavicist and student of Slavic antiquities.

Šaxmatov, Aleksej A. (1864–1920), Russian philologist and linguist.

de Saussure, Ferdinand (1857–1913), Swiss Indo-Europeanist and theoretical linguist; author of *Cours de linguistique generale* (1916); a pioneer in structural linguistics.

Sayce, Archibald H. (1845–1933), English Assyriologist and Indo-Europeanist.

Scherer, Wilhelm (1841–1887), German Indo-Europeanist and literary historian.

Schleicher, August (1821–1868), German Indo-Europeanist and theoretical linguist; advocate of the "biological approach" to language.

Schleyer, Johann Martin (1831–1912), Swiss priest; inventor of *Volapük*, an artificial language.

Schmidt, Johannes (1843–1901), German Indo-Europeanist; advocate of the "wave" theory of language development.

Schrader, Otto (1855–1919), German Indo-Europeanist; pioneer in linguistic paleontology.

Schuchardt, Hugo (1842–1927), Austrian theoretical linguist and Romance scholar; critic of Neogrammarians.

Setälä, Emil N. (1864–1935), Finnish Finno-Ugricist.

Škrabec, Stanislav (1844–1918), Slovenian Slavicist.

Sławiński, F. F., Polish linguist of 19th century.

Sobolevskij, Aleksej I. (1856–1929), Russian historical linguist and dialectologist.

Sotos Ochando, Bonifacio (1785–1869), Spanish priest and philologist; author of *Gramática de la lengua universal.*

Sreznevskij, Ismail I. (1812–1880), Russian philologist and comparative Slavic linguist; advisor of B. d. C.'s dissertation.

Steinthal, Hermann (1823–1899), German philosopher-linguist; popularizer of Humboldt and founder of the school of ethnic psychology in linguistics.

Szinnyei, Joszef (b. 1857), Hungarian Finno-Ugricist; author of *Finno-Ugrische Sprachwissenschaft,* Leipzig, 1922.

Tomsen, Vilhelm L. P. (1842–1927), Danish Indo-Europeanist and Turkologist.

Torbjörnsson, Tore (1864–1936), Swedish Indo-Europeanist and Slavicist.

Trubeckoj, Nikolaj S. (1890–1938), Russian structural linguist and Slavicist; cofounder of the Prague School.

Uhlenbeck, Christianus (1866–1951), Dutch Indo-Europeanist.

Valjavec, Matija K. (1831–1897), Slovenian Slavicist.

Verner, Karl A. (1846–1896), Danish Indo-Europeanist; author of "Verner's law" of sound change in Indo-European.

Veske, Mixail P. (1843–1910), Estonian Finno-Ugricist.

Vinson, Julien (1842–1926), French orientalist.

Voigtmann, Christoph G., German historical linguist; author of *Das Gesetz der Polarität in der Sprache,* Göttingen, 1852.

Voss, Gerard J. (1577–1649), Dutch philologist.

Wheeler, Benjamin I. (1854–1927), American classicist.

Whitney, William D. (1827–1894), American Sanskritist and general linguist.

Wiedemann, Ferdinand J. (1805–1887), Estonian pastor, ethnographer, and Finno-Ugricist.

Wiklund, Karl B. (1868–1934), Swedish Finno-Ugricist.

Wilkins, Bishop John (1614–1672), English bishop; inventor of a philosophical language.

Wundt, Wilhelm (1832–1920), German philosopher, psychologist, and linguist.

Zamenhof, Ludwik (1859–1917), Polish occulist and inventor of Esperanto.

Zubatý, Josef (1855–1931), Czech Slavicist; follower of Neogrammarians.

Topical Index

Accent: accent and vowel harmony, 109; morphological, 303; psychological, 109, 265, 292 ff.

Acousmeme, 267, 271, 280, 325

Acoustics, (*See* Phonetics)

Alalia, 123

Alternants, (*See* Alternations)

Alternations: causes of, 186; classification of, 162 ff.; conflict of, 164 ff.; definitions of, 149; embryonic, 165, 174, 193 ff., 209; foreign, 166, 187 ff., 192; foreign monolingual, 163; historical layers of, 183, 349 ff.; in children's language, 208 ff.; innovations in, 181; layers of, 73, 349 ff.; living, 351; mixed (foreign-native), 161, 191; neophonetic, 194, 205; of alternations, 170 ff., 191; of correspondences, 187; of morphemes, 154; paleophonetic, 194, 204 ff.; paleopsychological, 204; petrified, 165; phonetic, 149 ff., 154, 270; psychophonetic, 181, 203, 205, 349; simple vs. complex, 170; traditional (inherited), 163, 185, 186, 201, 205, 211; vowel/zero alternations, 350 ff. (*See* also Correlations, Divergence(s))

Analogy (Morphological assimilation): 87, 103, 178, 190, 230, 345; "prohibitive," 173

Anthropophonetics, (*See* Phonetics; Divergence(s))

Anthropophonic alternations, (*See* Divergence(s))

Aphasia, 123, 264

Apperception, 58, 262

Articulatory-auditory elements, (*See* Representations)

Artificial (International, World) languages, 139, 142, 247 ff., 256, 315 ff.

Assimilation, 88

Automatization, 264

Categories (of linguistics and language), 73

Cerebration, 123, 135

Characterization, (*See* Classification of languages)

Children's language: 74, 122, 203, 215; alternations in, 208; development of, 208 ff.

Classification of languages (Characterization, Systematics): 60, 64, 118, 136, 304 ff., 312, 321; by internal form, 119; by similarities and differences, 136, 289; genetic, 64, 76, 108, 113, 136, 243 ff., 311; geographical, 117, 225; historical relationship, 225, 296; morphological, 64 ff., 77, 108, 120, 137, 258; morphological-semasiological, 313; morphological vs. genetic, 109; phonetic, 84, 312 ff.; principles of, 119; statistical, 242; structural, 224, 312